Tales from Bakloh

Recollections from the Newsletters
of the 4th Prince of Wales's Own Gurkha Rifles
Officers' Association 1947-2007

Compiled by M. J. Fuller

This book has been printed digitally and produced in a standard specification in order to ensure its continuing availability

Published by Antony Rowe Publishing Services in 2007
48-50 Birch Close
Eastbourne
BN23 6QT
England

© Fuller, 2007

All rights reserved. Unauthorised duplication contravenes applicable laws.

ISBN 9781905200610

Page make-up by MCS Publishing Services Ltd, Salisbury, Wiltshire
Printed and bound by CPI Antony Rowe, Eastbourne

Acknowledgements

Grateful thanks to Mike Ridge without whose patience, help and guidance this anthology would never have been published.

Thanks are also due to Ruth Needham of Tollingers, London with whom we negotiated permission to print the extract from "Bugles and a Tiger" originally published by Michael Joseph.

Dedication

To the deathless memory of all ranks who served from 1857 to the present day.

Contents

Acknowledgements   iii
Dedication   iii
Foreword   ix
Preface   xi

The Tiger of Bakloh	1
War's Shifting Kaleidoscope	6
Some Memories of Bakloh	11
Daughter of the Regiment	13
Recollections of 1/4 GR 1916–27	16
The Memorial Service at St Giles Church and Consecration of The Regimental Garden at Stoke Poges 7th June 1949	20
The Capture of Spin Baldak Fort—1/4 GR May 1919	24
Rifleman Ranbahadur Thapa 1/4 GR, Menin Gate Memorial	30
Khwab o Khayal	31
Joining the 4th—Pre-1930	36
The Frontier Scouts	39
Lionel Peter Collins—A Tribute	44
1935—A year in the Life of a Subaltern. Half a Century ago	47
My first Visit to Nepal	51
A Royal Shoot in Nepal	55
Kipling's India	60
Experiencing the Pyaulla	65
Lt Gen W. D. A. Lentaigne— A Tribute by Admiral Lord Louis Mountbatten	67
Young David	68
A Piper Remembers	71
My Biography of Nihility or How Hamish helped Britain to lose her Empire	74
Hugh Moule—A Tribute	77
POW on the Siam Burma Railway	80
Prisoners of War in Italy	86

Harold Bell Kingsley—A Tribute	89
Looking Back	94
Captain W. G. Walker—VC Citation	97
On Shikar in the Central Provinces	99
Jungle Jims	106
IMS Days—A Doctor Remembers	109
More IMS Days	113
Memories of India	119
Major-General Sir Arthur Mills CB, DSO **—A Tribute	122
From Here to There	126
It Happened in Budapest	134
Round the World in Eighty-Five Days	136
The Caribbean Cruise	141
Reminiscences of a 4th Gurkha Wife	145
Col R. A. N. Davidson MBE—A Tribute	150
The Regimental Centenary 1857–1957	152
The Battle of Sittang Bridge, Burma Feb 1942	158
A Nature Ramble in the Woods	161
The End of the Road—1st Bn Burma 1942	168
Trooping	181
Long Range Penetration Group Dec 1942—May 1943	186
Tuitum Saddle 22 Mar 1944	190
D Company Commander was also wounded	194
The Guiding Light: Libya 1942. A Night in a Minefield	197
2nd Bn Libya May/Jun 1942	280
Crossing of the Senio River—Dec 1944	205
Escape and Evasion in Italy 1943–45	211
Gurkha Officers in Captivity	216
NBG's Last Day	218
Ambush on the Frontier	222
1/4 GR in Kohat, Gardai and Wana 1945–47	224
1/4 GR in Amritsar Oct—Dec 1947	231
2/4 GR Escort Duties and Safe Passage for a Million Refugees	234
Chindits: 40 Column in Burma 1944	245
Irrawaddy Crossing 1945	251

The Mule that Got Away	256
The CO was again Wounded	260
Half a mile on a Good Day: 4/4 GR Battalion on the Mawchi Road	263
Forty Years On—Reflections of the 4th Gurkha Rifles in 1945	272
No Names No Pack Drill	292
Letter from America	294
Return to India and Bugles	297
John Masters—A Tribute	303
The Mandalay Lunch	306
Hamish Mackay—A Tribute	308
A Full Circle—Janet McCarraher Mackay Returns to Bakloh and Burma	309
The Re-raising of the 4th Battalion	312
I Remember, I Remember	316
Stoke Poges House	326
The Coronation of His Majesty The King of Nepal	330
The Valley of Nepal	337
Return to Burma	340
The Winds of Change 1947–49	348
Tales from the Malayan Woods	356
Waiting in the Jungle	361
Lieut-General Moti Sagar PVSM—A Tribute	363
Sweet Memories	369
Brigadier Raj Bir Chopra—A Tribute	380
Frankie Redl: A Shipwreck Party in Bakloh	381
The Reunion 1990	384
Soldiering at High Altitude	388
The Battle of Bilafond La—Sep 1987	394
Journey to India. Travelling in a Gurkha Family's Footsteps	404
Could this be Shangri-La?	409
The Haunted Shimla Road	418
HMS Gurkha	420
Full Circle	422

Foreword

General Sir Michael Rose K.C.B., C.B.E., D.S.O., Q.G.M., D.L.

It is a delight to be invited to write the foreword to 'Tales from Bakloh', – having already heard many of the stories over the years from my stepfather, John Masters, who has also contributed a number of pieces to this book. Tales from Bakloh is not only a fascinating account of a famous regiment written by those who served in it, but it is an important historical record. In an age of change and political correctness, when people are encouraged to ignore and even decry our great imperial past, this book gives a wonderful insight into the dedication, bravery and professionalism of the soldiers of the 4th Prince of Wales's Own Gurkha Rifles, – a regiment formed at the height of Britain's imperial power in 1875. They were typical of generations of people who, along with their families, gave their entire working lives to the service of the British Indian Empire, both in peace and war. The accounts of the dangers and difficulties that they together faced, are extremely moving. Nonetheless the book is filled with a sense of happiness and fun for they accepted hardship without complaint and found their rewards within the close bonds of friendship that existed within the regiment. They believed in duty and service not in individual rights. It was their sacrifices, and those of millions of others like them, that enabled Britain and the countries of the Indian sub-continent to become what they are today.

Throughout the many individual stories that make up 'The Tales from Bakloh' there runs a great sense of nostalgia – not just for the beautiful mountains and plains of India and its wonderful people – but also for a way of life that ended with Independence. The book is a true kaleidoscope of vivid memories that brings to mind all the colours, smells and clamorous noises of the subcontinent. Above all the book reminds the reader of the sturdy sense of loyalty, bravery and cheerfulness of the Gurkha soldier in battle during the past 150 years. Their allegiance to the British has never wavered in spite of high casualties, shortages of equipment, and often hopeless odds. In wars that stretched across the globe from the plains of Afghanistan, to the trenches of the Somme and the jungles of Burma, the soldiers of the 4th Prince of Wales's Own Gurkha Rifles have developed a reputation for steadiness that has always inspired others. So deep is the remaining bond of friendship that exists today between the Gurkha, Indian and British members of the regiment, a permanent memorial to the 4th Prince of Wales's Own Gurkha Rifles has now been established in India, – in the form of a hostel for orphaned Gurkha children.

In the 21st century, as the British Army once again becomes engaged in combat in Iraq and Afghanistan, it is fitting that we should remember the soldiers who fought on those same battlefields in the past. The political circumstances may have changed over the centuries, but the unique demands of the battlefield on an individual soldier have not done so. 'Tales from Bakloh' is a useful and timely reminder of the importance of the human element in war and the regimental system that sustains it.

Preface

The 4th or Extra Goorkha Regiment was raised at Pithoragarh, India a few miles from the western edge of Nepal on the 6th August 1857 by Lieutenant Donald Macintyre, who later won a VC in 1872.

The hill-station of BAKLOH, at the western end of the Himalayas, just below the slopes of Dalhousie, was established in 1864 as the home of the 4th Goorkha Regiment, as it was then known. The "eternal snows" of the high Himalayas can be seen to the north-east and the five rivers of the Punjab show up to the west. In 1886 the 2nd battalion was raised and the word Rifles incorporated into the title.

In World War 1, after many years of campaigning on the North West Fontier, China in 1900 and elsewhere, the 4th Gurkha Rifles fought in France and Flanders. They also participated in the fighting in Mesopotamia and Egypt, and became known as "*the most travelled regiment in the Indian Army*".

On 12th August 1924 they were honoured by the appointment of HRH The Prince of Wales as Colonel-In-Chief and by the grant of a Royal title, The 4th Prince of Wales's Own Gurkha Rifles.

In World War 2, the 3rd and 4th battalions were raised: the 1st, 3rd and 4th were heavily involved in Burma, whilst the 2nd fought in Libya and Italy.

On the 15th April 1947, the Officers' Association was formed by the then Colonel of the Regiment, Major General Sir Arthur Mills CB DSO [1] who edited the annual newsletters for many years, from which are drawn the recollections compiled in this book.

After Independence on the 15th August 1947 the regiment was handed over to the army of India to become the 4th Gorkha Rifles. Now, in 2006–7 the regiment has five front line battalions, each with a reputation Second to None.

IV

The Tiger of Bakloh

By John Masters
(Extract from Bugles and a Tiger)

My year with the depot did not pass without one exciting incident of the sort usually associated with India. A little after three o'clock in the afternoon of a cold and sunny February day in 1938, "Poppa" Donlea, who then shared a bungalow with me, came in and said that a grass-cutter had seen a leopard. We went out together to question the man. Oh, yes, he said, he'd seen a leopard, quite close. He pointed at Poppa's golden retriever and added, "About that size, it was." He had seen it first just below the squash-rackets court, and shouted at it. It had sneaked away through the long grass towards No 8 Bungalow, which was unoccupied.

Leopards are not uncommon in Bakloh, so we had no reason to doubt his story. I went up the lines to get a .303 service rifle and some beaters. Many men volunteered, and I selected five, including Naik Udiram and Lance-Naik Baliram. Turning back an eager mob of recruits, soldiers, small urchins, and the retriever, we set off to the squash court, where Poppa was waiting for us. He did not have a rifle, as we agreed it would be safer in this crowded cantonment to keep down the number of weapons in action. The hunt began.

We spread into line across the narrow, shallow valley leading down from the squash court to No 8 Bungalow, and moved slowly forward, throwing stones and beating the earth with sticks. Scrub and bushes dotted the valley floor, but Poppa and I moved along the right-hand slope, where it was clearer, and watched for the leopard to break cover ahead of the beaters.

We passed cautiously through the garden of No 8. The empty servants' huts belonging to it were just down the hill in a dense thicket below us, ten yards or less away, when we heard a sudden coughing roar. An incoherent scream followed, then shouts, and the ugly crackling of leaves and twigs in the thicket. I could not get down the bank direct to the but because it was so steep and overgrown. I ran forward and round and crept back into the thicket along a narrow, overhung path.

Nerves tensed, ears straining for the slightest sound in the scrub around me, rifle loaded, finger on the trigger, butt in my shoulder, I stepped steadily on, looking slowly right, left, up, down. On a flat ledge in front of the servants' huts I saw Lance-Naik Baliram, staggering about and muttering, "*Khayo!*" (It's bitten me).

I could see no damage to the right side of his face, which was towards me, but the corner of his mouth slowly dripped blood. I whispered urgently, "What's happened? Where's the leopard? Speak up man!". He swung blindly to face me, and the pit of my stomach turned over as the left side of his head came into view. A blow or bite had torn half of it away, so that it hung loosely outward, laying bare the inside of his head, the convolutions of the inner ear, and part of his brain. I saw no sign of the leopard, and Baliram could no longer speak. I shouted to Naik Udiram to come over from the other side of the valley and help, but no one came to me.

Silence hung heavy in the little clearing by the huts, and the bushes crowded in on me. Baliram looked through me with his dull eyes fixed on something miles away. The hanging flap of skin, muscle and bone swayed with his slow movements, and the blood dripped soundlessly out from the corners of his mouth.

I leaned my rifle against the wall of the hut. I was trembling but managed to take off my thin tweed coat and knot the sleeves over Baliram's head to hold his face in one piece. While my arms were above his head, tying the awkward sleeves together, a huge blur of black and gold stripes streaked across the extreme corner of my vision. I turned and saw that a tiger was charging out of the cleft between the back of the hut and the slope of the hill, nine or ten feet away. A coughing, grunting roar shattered the nerves in my head. I jerked back and to the right; a steel-tipped forearm whistled past my face and blew the hat off my head. Baliram moaned wordlessly.

Seeing the way now clear for escape, the tiger ran on down the path by which I had entered the thicket.

Udiram had never liked the look of that place. As the beaters advanced he had shouted to Baliram not to go into it but to throw stones from the shelter of the huts. Baliram had not heard, or did not heed. At the first roar Udiram looked across the valley, saw the tiger, saw it stand up and bite through Baliram's head, saw it creep into the narrow cleft between the hut and the slope. From then on he had been shouting desperately to warn me, but I had tensed my ears to some tiny animal noise, some leaf crackling, so that they had dismissed these loud human shouts as being irrelevant. I had heard nothing. So Udiram watched helplessly while I walked up to a cornered tiger and laid my rifle down within ten feet of it.

Action blew the uneasy, crawling fears out of me. Udiram and others came running. I left one man in charge of Baliram, sent another for the doctor, seized my rifle, and ran after the tiger. Behind No 8 Bungalow, Poppa and an Indian bystander were sharing an emaciated tree, which stood about 12 feet high and gave the impression that it could not support a cat, let alone a robustly built officer. Poppa sat further up the tree than the Indian, having won a sharp altercation with him as to who should go first. After charging me, the tiger had broken cover twenty yards from where they were and in full view of them. I believe a tiger can jump eighteen feet vertically, so they were not so safe as they thought.

The ground beyond No 8 sloped down steeply in broken cliffs and ledges, lightly scattered with pine trees and underbrush, to a bridle trail and then to a rifle range beyond that. On the right were two-storied apartment buildings occupied by married soldiers and their children. Men were firing on the range, women and children were talking and playing in the afternoon sun; and a considerable crowd had attached itself to the tail of our own small party. It was like stalking a tiger through Green Park on Whit Sunday.

I stepped rather more cautiously over the brow of the hill and saw the tiger at once, bounding down just above the trail. I dropped flat, cuddled the rifle into my cheek, and waited until he leaped onto the path. There his stripes stood out clearly against the even yellow background, and his pace became a steady trot. I was above and behind him, and fifty yards distant. As he settled into his stride I opened fire with three rapid shots, aiming at the tip of his nose. The first bullet broke his near hind leg high up, smashing into the great bone with such force that he spun across the trail as though he had been a cat kicked by a big boy. The second shot went through his off forepaw, and the third grazed his shoulders.

I jumped up and ran down the hill to get closer. As I ran, he dragged himself off the road into thin bushes below it. I came to the place, and the tiger roared, I backed off. I did not want to peer over the edge of the trail, where the ground fell steeply, at a wounded tiger that might only be a yard off. I moved along the trail for thirty yards and then went over the edge into thick thorn undergrowth. The invisible tiger watched me and accompanied each step with a sighing roar. I have never felt so anxious, keyed up, and angry, all at the same time.

I sat down with my back against a rock on the hillside and waited for my breathing to settle. I brought the rifle into my shoulder and tried to see the tiger. Steady, rasping groans came from the patch of thin scrub thirty yards away. I stared and stared, trying to pick out his form, but could see nothing. Yet a very large black and gold animal lay stretched out there. It was an extraordinary demonstration of the art of camouflage.

Suddenly a streak of gold caught my eye and, following along it, a patch of white which I hoped was his ruff. Aiming at that, I fired. The whole animal leaped into prominent focus as he started convulsively, and lay still.

By now the hill seethed with people. The men on the rifle range had stopped firing when they heard the hunt approach, and streamed up toward the scene of action. All over Bakloh crowds of Gurkhas dropped what they were doing and came running. The women and children, at first frightened, now poured out, chattering and squawking like so many jays.

I climbed up the path and edged along it, meaning to look over above the tiger and make sure he was dead. I got to the place and raised my head slowly, the rifle pushed forward and every nerve quivering with tense alertness. Something tickled my back. A hot breath blew on the hairs at the nape of my neck. I whipped round in a convulsion and all but shot Dallu.

His hand trembled on my back, his long moustaches quivered on my neck; his breath blew gustily down the collar of my shirt. He was carrying a twelve-bore shotgun loaded with Number 8 shot, which is very useful for snipe. He asked me eagerly where the leopard was. I told him to take his moustache away, brought him up to date with the facts, and again nerved myself to look over the edge of the trail. The tiger lay stretched out twelve feet below, dead. My last shot had gone in just above the left eye and out behind the right ear, killing him instantly.

I left Udiram to guard the body, particularly to see that the whiskers and claws were not taken for use as aphrodisiacs, and went off with Poppa to the hospital. The doctor was in the middle of the long and delicate operation. We waited for nearly two hours while he put forty stitches into Baliram's head.

My excitement slackened and at last failed altogether. Who had stricken Baliram so that he lay near death—the tiger, or I? Should I not have allowed the beaters to take arms with them? As soon as I thought it I knew it was impossible. There could be only one rifle in a hunt such as ours. Had I made him come against his will? No, he had volunteered. He had not listened to Udiram's warning, so it was his fault. But neither had I, and my head was in one piece.

The doctor came out, his face drawn with the long effort. He said there was not much hope, and nothing else that anyone could do. Subadar Dallu came, looked at me, and said curtly, "It's no one's fault, sahib. Come away."

Bakloh had gone crazy while we waited in the ether stillness of the hospital. Men ran about, laughed, danced in the road, and slapped me on the back. Women kissed my knees; children brought flowers. Two hundred soldiers slung the tiger on poles and brought it up to the mess, singing as they came. Machhindra, with a touch of grim humour, put it in the guest room and surrounded it with a circle of kerosene to keep off the ants. By midnight Poppa and I were again mad drunk with excitement. We sat in my room, and drank, and played my seven variations of "Tiger Rag" five times each on the portable gramophone. Gurkhas brought rum and growled hilariously in time with the rhythmic roars coming out of the gramophone.

Baliram had a good night and seemed to be recovering, but in the morning he died suddenly. Dallu said he was a good man, and a squad took him to the burning *ghat*.

The tiger was a young male, nine feet four inches between pegs, in perfect condition, with an empty stomach. No one knew what he had been doing in Bakloh, where no tigers had ever been heard of before, or where he was going. He became the Bakloh Tiger, and for the rest of my service, though I achieved rank and decoration, to the Gurkhas I was the Sahib who shot the Bakloh Tiger. They made a new song and sang it for me in Iran, Syria, Persia, India, Burma and on the seas between:

> *Urtis sale, February mahina,*
> *Bagh Maryo Masteri-sahib le.*
> In '38, in the month of February
> Masters-sahib killed the tiger.

War's Shifting Kaleidoscope

By Bill Tee

The cantonment hill station of Bakloh, in the foothills at the western end of the Himalayas, is about two thousand miles as the crow flies from the village of Pyu on the Sittang River in lower Burma. The link between these two small and distant villages that I am going to draw is separated in time from late 1940 to mid 45; five long years while Hitler's dreary war dragged on across three continents.

At the end of 1940 from the Royal Military College at Sandhurst I joined the Regimental Depot of the 4th Prince of Wales's Own Gurkha Rifles as a newly fledged one pipper in Bakloh.

Bakloh is a hill village clothed in pine trees; the eternal snows of the high Himalayas can be seen to the north east and the five rivers of the Punjab show up to the west far below in the mist shrouded plain. Bakloh was a quiet place, serene and calm dominated by my Gurkha Regiment's presence.

Many retired Gurkha soldiers lived there and the hill people native to these hills were well used to having Gurkhas among them. In the winter Bakloh was bitterly cold, but, for most of the year, it was mild and calm. The air coming off the high peaks is like wine. Bakloh is a splendid place to be and a healthy one.

Having settled into No 4 Bungalow overlooking the 1st Battalion's parade ground, I was allocated for weapon training to Naik (the equivalent of Corporal in the British Army) Purandhoj Gurung to learn about rifles and machine guns and other military weapons. He was a splendid teacher and I was his only pupil, our lack of common language was no bar as Purandhoj knew his weapons so well that his demonstrations were the best way of teaching and of being taught. In due course I was tested on various ranges and passed as a Marksman in all the weapons with which an infantry battalion was equipped in those days.

The 1st Battalion of my regiment moved off towards the war via Ambala in the Punjab in Central India in April 1941 and my mentor, Purandhoj, went with them — as I did. However, almost immediately, the powers that were posted me to help raise and train a new battalion for our Regiment I returned to Bakloh from Ambala within the month.

Purandhoj, with the 1st Battalion moved on to Secunderabad in the Deccan, 1000 miles away in southern India and I lost touch with him as an individual. In and around Secunderabad this Battalion trained for desert and amphibious warfare but, in the event, they moved by ship to Rangoon in Burma reaching there on the last day of January 1942.

Between then and the end of February this Battalion saw a lot of mixed action against the Japs as they advanced into Burma from the south east. Later on the Regimental Records Section in Bakloh learned that during a withdrawal over the Sittang River in Mokpalin at the head of the gulf of Martaban in lower Burma in March 1942, Purandhoj became separated from his platoon. He was left behind when the Battalion moved on to Pegu by train. Nothing further was heard from him and, in due course, he was posted "Missing; presumed KIA" (Killed in action). After an appropriate interval Purandhoj's death ceremony was performed in his village in West Nepal and his widow allocated a pension. After some long time she remarried.

The Japanese advance to the north along the road from Pegu to Meiktila and beyond continued. It continued until 1944 for over a thousand miles to the borders of India. My old Battalion fought through some of the bitterest battles of the war in and around Imphal sustaining savage casualties.

In late 1942, British Army intelligence in Burma found out that the Japs were holding a number of prisoners in Pegu prison; after some deliberation a decision was taken to ask the RAF to knock the walls of the prison down by bombing so as to give the prisoners held there a chance to escape into the countryside. Later on it became known that most of the prisoners escaped; that many had been recaptured, that some had been killed and that some remained at large in the countryside around Pegu; but no information about individuals came through. I did not know about Pegu Jail until much later.

The war went on.

Returning to my own story; back in Bakloh, the newly raised 4th Battalion's training went on apace. We left there in October 1941 on our way to an active service formation in South India. In fact we went through Ambala Railway Station where Purandhoj's Battalion, before their move to Secunderabad in the Deccan, lined the station and cheered us on.

We fetched up in Ahmednagar in Madras Province in Southern India. There we trained for desert warfare; for air landing operations; for amphibious operations; for mountain warfare; for war in the plains. Through 1942 into 1943 and on into 1944 we saw Bangalore, Secunderabad, the Nilgiri Hills (where I met my first wife, Liz) Madras, Pondicherry and Vizagapatam on the east coast, Cannonore and Mangalore on the west. We crossed and re-crossed and crossed again Madras and Mysore and Kerala, an area larger than Britain and, after interminable formation exercises under a succession of commanders, we finally took to training for jungle warfare. We were the best trained and least battle wise formation in the whole Army.

So 1942 and 1943 and part of 1944 passed into history and the war went on. Men came and went; officers were promoted and departed; new officers arrived; but I, with a few others, remained as the hard core of this new Battalion.

Towards the middle of 1944 we moved to Nasik not too far from Bombay. Nasik is one of the places where Indian rum is made; but, if you like to keep your health and sanity, take my, advice and avoid it like the plague. Its diabolical. It was here in Nasik that we had our motor transport taken away. To replace our lorries and carriers we were given twelve jeeps and forty five mules. We knew for sure that we would either fight in the mountains or in the jungle! No desert warfare for us! A little later we were told we were to fight the Japs in the jungle.

In October 1944 we were ordered to Burma 1000 miles away; to Imphal to be precise. With considerable awe we examined the battlefields where our 1st Battalion had fought and much else. From there we moved on and crossed the Chindwin River; another 300 miles. In December we moved to take Shwebo; 70 or 80 miles.

On 13th January the following year we crossed the mighty Irrawaddy at Thabeikkyin and later set out south for another hundred miles along the left bank of the river towards Mandalay. In March my Battalion captured Mandalay.

Then on again yet another 100 miles to Meiktila; by now it was April. But still on, urged by General Frank Messervy (an expert at urging speed!); and then to Toungoo yet another 100 miles further south. At Toungoo we turned east and fought up the Mawchi

Road—possibly the hardest fighting we experienced throughout our time in Burma; a very unpleasant affair often fought on a front of ten paces with precipitous hills rising on one side of the road and precipitous gorges falling away on the other.

In June 1945 we returned through Toungoo and resumed our advance south along the road towards Rangoon. By this time at the tender age of 25, I had been promoted and was commanding my Battalion.

One of the villages along this road was Pyu; the one that is about two thousand miles from Bakloh. On the Rangoon Road north of this village I was being driven in a jeep to a conference. It was a bright morning on a sunny day, warm without a cloud in the sky or a breath of wind; an unusual day for the time of year because the monsoon was about to break. The dirt road raised above the paddy fields ran on straight as an arrow into the hazy distance.

A lone Burman came into sight walking towards us. He was long haired, barefoot, dressed only in a loin cloth. He carried nothing. We had been warned extensively of Burman treachery and, when this man stepped into the middle of the road and raised his arm signalling us to stop, we were immediately alert with safety catches off ready for any tricks. My driver braked the jeep to a halt and the Burman came round to my side of it. He spoke Gurkhali, the language of the Gurkhas. A loose translation of what he said was "Good God, you're Tee Sahib!".

Yes, after our silent shock had worn off, slowly we came round to finding out that it was Naik Purandhoj Gurung! He had a story to tell.

When, in March 1942, he had been cut out from his platoon at Mokpalin he had followed on foot through the jungle and across the rice fields; but he was unlucky and was captured by the Japs and, with many others, he was put behind the high walls of Pegu Prison. When the walls were knocked down by the RAF he escaped. He spent the long years between 1942 and 1945 as the deaf and dumb son of a headman in a village north of Pegu.

Then in 1945, when the leading troops of Bill Slim's 14th Army, still being driven on relentlessly by Messervy, passed through his village on their way to Rangoon, Purandhoj had bidden his protector farewell and walked up the road to rejoin his Army. The first vehicle he met, the first person he met was my jeep and me.

Purandhoj had changed out of all recognition; our first dumbfounded reaction was disbelief. But he knew me; he knew Bakloh and he was recognised by others whom he met in our bivouac that evening. He drank rum with us and, having been totally teetotal during the long years since he had been separated from his platoon near Mokpalin, got soundly drunk in the process.

We sent Purandhoj back up the Lines of Communication all the two thousand miles to Bakloh.

He was fully paid for the years he was a prisoner and, later on, returned to his village in the hills of Nepal. The Hindu ceremony of rebirth is arcane and I do not pretend to understand it; nor do I know the situation in Hindu law that must have arisen between Purandhoj and his now remarried wife.

In the three score years and ten that I have lived I find this reunion on a lonely road in central Burma the most surprising coincidence that I have ever encountered. I can even now nearly half a century later recall the astonishment of being called by my name by a seeming Burman; a man whom I had last seen four years before, two thousand miles away. From the constantly shifting kaleidoscope of war that moment is etched indelibly on my mind; and always will be.

Some Memories of Bakloh

By Mrs D. I. McBurney

We regret that the dictates of space preclude publication of the full article. Ed.

My only right to offer these few slight memories of Bakloh and The Fourth is that I must be one of the oldest members of that happy circle of sixty years ago, when I lived there as a child.

In 1889 my father, Major Rundall, was appointed to the Regiment, thus fulfilling the wish of his heart. I remember arriving at Bakloh and thinking it the prettiest, gayest little place out of a fairy tale. The green woods, the medlar trees in their white blossom, the wild pink lilies and the gay little bungalows dotted about in their pretty gardens struck even a child's heart with delight.

My father's pride in his Regiment soon communicated itself to me, and my mother would point out the smartness of the orderlies who came with messages, saluted and swung round again so sharply, and marched off with their quick short stride—their little round pill-box caps set jauntily on one side, their dark green uniforms the last word in smartness. I was taught that it was the greatest honour to be the Daughter of the Regiment; for some time I was the only one, as the twelve other children in Bakloh were boys. Proud indeed was I to march round the Mess Square with the other children behind the pipers at the Mess At Homes.

I remember the first occasion I saw the Regiment depart on active service. We assembled on the 1st Battalion parade ground—a little group of wives and children waiting dry-eyed on a small hillock. The Band struck up "The Girl I left behind Me," my father swung me up for a last kiss, then kissed my mother, and off they marched, an inspiring sight and sound to the small beating heart of the little girl who watched them. The Colonel's lovely lady, Mrs Mercer, took my mother's arm as we walked back together. We held our heads high. Was not the best Regiment in India going forth to distinguish itself? At least so thought I ... (my mother remarked that the dust made one's eyes water).

Four months later my brother Lionel was born, in after years to join the 1st Gurkhas with the same pride that his father and Montie, our elder brother, had joined the 4th. Good was it for us in those happy days that we could not foresee that in 1914, twenty-four years after Lionel was born, both he and his brother would lie dead, killed on the same day before the trenches in France.

Soon after we came to Bakloh my mother set about collecting money to build a church there. This was eventually consecrated to the soldier saint, St Oswald, at my mother's especial request.

I remember that in one of the campaigns the son of a Subadar was killed in battle. My mother, after going to break the news to his family, told me of the calm courage with which his old mother had received the news and how she had rebuked the poor little wife for breaking down, saying that it was the highest honour to give one's life in the service of the Regiment.

It is good to know that pretty little Bakloh, with its gay gardens and medlar bloom, its lovely little church, and its pleasant Mess, is still there and, above all, that the Regiment of our hearts lives on with its high traditions.

Daughter of the Regiment

By Fiona MacKay McUrick

The year was 1945. We left behind a cold and dreary Edinburgh and sailed on the "Drottningholm" to Bombay. Our party consisted of my mother who had spent the greater part of her life in the East, my younger sister, her Burmese nanny and myself, newly graduated from St Leonard's School for Girls in St Andrews and hardly prepared for the incandescent kaleidoscope of India, confusingly coloured in saffron and magenta.

My father, who had returned to Bakloh at an earlier date, came down to meet us and accompanied us on the train to Pathankot, some two or so days' ride away. The train journey only added to my confusion—poverty and wealth, beggars tenaciously clinging to our carriage windows, and merchants incessantly calling their wares. Platforms crowded with people and cows, acrid spicy odours of marigolds and dust.

At Pathankot we transferred to a staff car for the journey to Bakloh and immediately the confusion was replaced by penitent prayers for self preservation, for the road was an agony of hairpin bends and steeply inclined stretches. As a family we were, with the exception of my father, appalling travellers. Motion other than our own sent screaming messages to our inner ears which responded unfailingly with waves of unremitting nausea. So it was, that our first view of Bakloh was with sweated brow, but inestimable joy for having survived.

The parade ground looked enormous. Was it really as large and were there crepe myrtles and jacaranda trees in bloom? Oddly I can no longer clearly recall the road to our bungalow, but know it passed my father's office, split the Mess from the tennis courts, barely connected with the church, elbowed the squash courts to the left and eventually passed our bungalow at the top of the hill from whence we had a wonderful view across the plains of the Punjab. Behind, the mountains rose to over 9,000 feet and touched the sky.

Here I was to live for two years. It was a time of political unrest of which I was barely aware. It was also a time of hurricane butties and pressure lamps primed and pumped to a hissing splendour; mosquito nets and punkahs; barefooted houseboys and self-effacing sweepers. Baths poured into tin tubs and emptied into tiny channels of concrete which subsequently watered the garden. Beef that came weekly and was sometimes alive with maggots.

My parents who had believed that a trip to India would be of infinite more value to me than "Highers" recognised that my ability and inclination were limited and set about to make the experience worthwhile. My mother, who was an incredible lady of great wisdom, wit and energy was determined to make it all an opportunity for growth. She organised activities and despatched me on journeys of joy.

She ran, and I assisted with a nursery school where the Lowis and Stannard children and my small sister learned their ABCs. She took her responsibilities seriously, coached me in Urdu and Gurkhali and toured me through the family lines and "weight stations" at the baby clinics. Together we turned out mountains of baby clothes and blankets for distribution. Recollections of many beautiful women, fresh from the hills of Nepal, with their fat black-haired babies and bare bottomed children are still vivid in my mind. Images of black cotton and silver jewellery, red beads and turquoise. Cheeks of soft peach stealing through pale walnut skin. Nose rings, earrings and laughing eyes.

We visited the hospital and maternity quarters frequently where the facilities were simple and immaculately clean. There she introduced me to Kunti, who is still the best midwife I have ever met. Quiet, reassuring and confident in her skills.

My mother entertained well. Visitors were always welcome and came frequently. She was an innovative hostess and must have filled many long and tedious evenings for those stranded in Bakloh.

We took prodigious walks and can remember on several occasions hiking back from Dalhousie, down the steep rocky slopes sparsely peppered with scarlet rhododendrons, both unexpected and beautiful. Once we went to Tara Ghar, which my father explained meant the House of Stars, and so it would have seemed isolated and lovely. Years later I saw a plebeian house of the same name in a Glasgow suburb and smiled to think of the owner's dreams.

There were sojourns in Dalhousie, a pleasant hill station busy with traffic and trees and monkeys and only reached by the inevitable snake-winding, nauseating road which would lay us low for a couple of days. Behind Dalhousie the mountain soared to 9,091 feet and was heavily wooded with deodars and sweet smelling, night-blooming lilies. Chamba glittered in the valley beyond.

Occasionally I would be taken to Lahore where we stayed at the Stiffles Hotel and were permitted to ride tongas, which I dearly loved. My father in the course of his duties took me to Delhi and Agra, up the hills to Rawalpindi and across the plains to Amritsar. He loved it all, knew the history and respected the people. Two days before he died this year in Scotland, he recounted to me the story of Akhbar the Great, his eyes dancing in a reverie of affectionate nostalgia.

Images of the Taj and the Red Fort across the river, Fatehpur Sikhri and gardens filled with cannas and zinnias are always lurking in my mind. At seventeen who could resist the great love of Shah Jehan and fantasise that life might be that remarkable again.

There were times of lesser glory when the rains came and I would sit at the bottom of the garden and marvel as the clouds rolled across the plains and climbed the mountains, spilling their benison of wetness until we would almost beg for them to stop. Ropes stretched out to bear the weight of airing clothes, and the rank smell of mildew would fill the houses.

I left Bakloh following the division of India. The plains were dotted with plumes of smoke and travelling to Delhi by convoy, we passed endless streams of refugees and a sea of devastation and death. Nobody believed in England when I told them: nobody seemed to care.

Presently I am living in America on the banks of the Mississippi river. Ten miles down the road there is a gentle rise of hills at Benton and stretched beyond, in their shimmering glory, lie the fields to Memphis. Every time I crest the hill, a flash of memory spreads the Punjab plains glittering ahead. Why are only oranges and lemons, turquoise and silver and laughter dancing in my head?

Recollections of 1/4 GR 1916–27

By the late Brig Ted Hughes
published as a tribute to his memory

I have been asked to give some account of regimental events and personal experiences as seen by a young 1st Battalion officer starting out nearly seventy years ago: I do so with a certain diffidence, conscious that my memory is both deficient and faulty, and accordingly asking for pardon and indeed correction if some of the facts are seen to be wrong.

When I joined the 1st Battalion in 1916 the road from rail head at Pathankot to Dalhousie was a bullock cart track used by the occasional motor but normally traversed by ekka or tonga—with halts for the night at dak bungalows at Dhar and Dunera; there was no wheeled access to Bakloh—one alighted at Dagoh and went up the hill on foot or on horseback or by coolie-carried dooly or dandy. Living conditions were primitive by modern standards—no electricity and no tapped water; water was carried by the bhisti and sanitation was the province of the mehta: despite the "deprivation" we all managed to live very cheerful lives.

In 1916 and indeed during all my time in regimental service, troops always paraded in two ranks and marched in fours. The Battalion consisted of four companies and an HQ (CO; 2/ic; Adjutant—on horseback; QM and Signal Section). There was no electrical signal equipment—communication was by heliograph in morse or by flag in semaphore. Although there was a maxim gun platoon there were no other automatic weapons until I think late 1917 when we received Lewis guns—one gun per platoon—mule carried.

Firstline transport was entirely by mules which carried for each Company their ammunition, entrenching tools and water; secondline transport was by mule-drawn AT cart and by camel—the Camel Corps being a vitally important branch of the transport corps. In those days there was no training centre as such, each Gurkha battalion was entirely self-contained in every respect—being responsible for its own recruiting and for the subsequent training of those recruits under the Adjutant.

The Battalion was extensively engaged in the Waziristan operations of 1917: our HQ and left-wing companies were halted at Nili Kutch opposite the Gwaleri Tangi where the Gumal river emerges onto the plains through a narrow rift in the mountains. A battalion of the Bombay Grenadiers had preceded us and having been ambushed in the Tangi, had been forced to retire leaving behind a number of wounded men: our HQ and left wing advanced through the Tangi next day and it was there that I saw my first battle casualties. A number of dead Grenadiers were propped up against big boulders having received the full Mahsud treatment—throats cut, eyes put out and their parts mutilated. It was a horrifying sight that I can never forget. What does Kipling say—"When you're wounded and left on Afghanistan's plains, And the women come out to cut up what remains, just roll to your rifle and blow out your brains, and go to your God like a soldier,"—very sound advice.

After considerable action in this campaign the battalion next saw service in the Third Afghan War when we led the capture of the Afghan fortress Spin Baldak on 27 May 1919: followed by the Waziristan Operations of 1921-2-3, when encamped at Sarwakai and Sararogha—later taking part in the Makin operations, the establishment of Camp Razmak and the Wana Column operations. The battalion was specially selected for and fully engaged in all these operations during which Theo Owens earned his MC. What is remarkable is how few battle casualties we suffered compared with a number of other units in the same force. We attributed the reason for this (and I think that we were right) to the fact that we were so very efficient in mountain warfare that the Mahsuds hesitated to take us on: on the other hand our low casualty rate in battle was more than made up for by our losses in sickness. The climate, the general conditions of service—rations, awful sanitation, flies, mosquito and other disease bearing insects all took their toll. Accordingly in 1923 1/4th GR returned to Bakloh grossly under-strength with more than three hundred recruits on the square waiting to be trained.

I often wonder whether present day junior officers in their early twenties still have the same views as I and my contemporaries used to have at that age: we certainly thought that all officers over forty years of age were senile and incapable of efficient regimental service: we also held to a general belief that there was no harm in killing a few people if thereby one could prevent more wholesale criminal killing and for that reason there was no shortage of support for General Dyer in April 1919.

This frontier activity was followed by a stay in Bakloh 1923-7 —a "peacetime" interlude but by no means an uneventful time for we were given plenty of internal security work to do. It was during these years that 1/4th GR acquired two most highly regarded commanding officers from other regiments, namely Colonel Bailey from 2 GR and Colonel Scott from 1 GR, but on the other side we lost three very highly regarded officers who had spent their whole service in our regiment—namely Colonel Hogg and Majors Collins and Hartwell.

At this time we marched down from Bakloh every year to spend the cold weather at Jullundur and to take part in exercises based on that station: the routine of that move may be of interest. Reveille was at 0600 hours—morning meal—strike camp—load tentage and baggage on to mules and camels; march 15 or 16 miles to next site—unload animals—pitch camp then midday meal. The officers would then spend the afternoon shooting—if there was shooting to be had—and the other ranks played football.

Our two battalions were stationed together in Bakloh during this time and this did indeed serve to reinforce the tremendous friendship between individuals and spirit in the Regiment. And it was on 19 October 1927 that we had the wonderful two battalion parade for the ceremony of dedication and unveiling of our combined Regimental and War Memorials, in the presence of the Commander-in-Chief, Field Marshal Sir William Birdwood.

May I just end on a lighter note. During this period we used to have a Sunday ladies' tea party on the Mess lawn. Bill Bailey was our batchelor CO. One Sunday one of the most senior ladies said to him, "Colonel Bailey, it's high time you were married." Well, that is not a very tactful remark to make to your senior officer, and I think Bill Bailey gave a very appropriate answer. "Madam," he said, "tell me this. Why should I buy a cow when milk is so cheap and so readily available." Indeed a very relevant question.

With which let me end

IV

The Memorial Service at St Giles' Church and Consecration of the Regimental Garden at Stoke Poges 7th June, 1949

By H. B. Kingsley

In a hurrying, uneasy and materialistic age, reeling from the effects of two World Wars, it is good to have a day of peace. A chance to pause, to remember, to—"get things straight." And there, at Stoke Poges, on 7th June, that opportunity came to those who were able to be present.

The setting was perfect. Summertime in the heart of England with sunshine after rain, and the lovely old Church, which has stood there since Norman times, surrounded by ancient yews, elms and vivid. green turf.

Ushers led the congregation to their appointed seats and soon the Church was full. Then, to the hymn "O valiant hearts, who to your glory came ..." the choir and clergy moved in slow procession from the west end of the Church and took their places, followed by the Right Reverend Dr Barne, who was for so many years Bishop of Lahore, and who, just returned to England, drove up from Eastbourne to conduct the Memorial and Consecration Services.

In an atmosphere now charged with emotion, Sir Arthur Mills read the Lesson, verses 1 to 9 of chapter 111 of the book of "The Wisdom of Solomon," those lovely words so apt to the occasion. As the senior Battalion Commander he read the same Lesson at the Memorial Service in St Oswald's Church, Bakloh, twenty-two years ago.

After the singing of the hymn "For all the Saints who from their labours rest ..." Bishop Barne made his address—which is printed *in extenso* elsewhere—and after a short prayer the procession of choir and clergy moved down the Church and out into the sunshine, followed by the congregation.

The procession then moved out of the churchyard and into the beautiful Stoke Park which contains the Gardens of Remembrance.

All this ground is full of history. The names of the men who have owned it are on record right back to the days of King Harold. Sir Edward Coke entertained Queen Elizabeth there. The present house was built by the Penn family, who founded Pennsylvania, and in the churchyard the poet Gray wrote his famous "Elegy." These are names chosen at random from the long line of famous people who knew and trod this ground. And as we, too, followed in their footsteps we could justly feel that in commemorating our dead and the long, eventful and honourable story of the Regiment in a Garden of Remembrance here, we were making our not unworthy addition to its story.

As we stood in the Garden during the Dedication Service and looked at our proud record, carved in bronze and embedded in stone, surrounded by lovely flowers and shrubs, we all felt deeply grateful to our Colonel, in whose brain the idea was born and by whose devoted energy it was carried out.

It is now indeed a haven of peace, a place of pilgrimage where, for a while, away from hurry, noise and other distractions, one can refresh oneself in remembering "the eternal verities."

When the congregation had paid their tribute in the Garden of Remembrance (some returned to it more than once) they moved to the Museum, signed their names in our "Visitors' Book," and pored over the exquisite "Roll of Honour," bound in dark green leather, bearing the crest embossed in colour and hand-painted and illuminated on vellum. It is a real work of art, and worthily encased in a glass-covered oak casket, so designed that when the key, itself a little hand-made gem, is turned the top and sides lift back together so that the book can be opened wide.

The volumes of the Regimental History stand behind this case and are supported by oak book-ends, ornamented with the regimental crest most beautifully carved.

We are all indebted to Col C. G. Borrowman who arranged for the making of these beautiful things.

It was a great disappointment that no serving Officer or man was able to be present to carry back first-hand impressions to the Centre and Battalions, but they may rest assured that they were very much in our minds, for the Garden of Remembrance commemorates all ranks of the Regiment, and, as the Bishop rightly said in his address, the bond of friendship between British and Gurkha was the firm rock on which the traditions of the Regiment were built.

B. K.

Address by the Rt Rev George Dunsford Barne, CIE, OBE, DD, VD Bishop of Lahore, 7th June, 1949

It seems a long way from St Oswald's Church, Bakloh, in the East Punjab just below Dalhousie on the lower slopes of the Himalayas, to this Garden of Remembrance here in Stoke Poges, somewhere near the central heart of England.

It seems a long time since Lord Birdwood unveiled the Regimental Memorial at Bakloh after the first World War. These twenty-two intervening years were destined to record an even larger number of British Officers, Gurkha Officers, and other ranks who gave their lives in the service of the Empire, and died gallantly to defeat aggression and to enable men to live in peace.

Yes, it is a long way and a long time, but there is something about the dedication service to-day which defeats distance and time and gathers up in remembrance and thanks giving the ninety years of regimental history, during which British and Gurkhas have fought side by side in battle and lived together, as comrades and friends in times of peace.

This Garden of Remembrance is a memorial of courage in

action which bids us stand bareheaded as we call to mind many a glorious deed of valour; but it is also something more. It is a tribute to thousands of British and Gurkha Officers and other ranks, who have, during the last ninety years, made and fashioned the traditions of the Regiment, and made it possible to hand them over to the new régime. The Regiment goes on, determined to maintain and enhance its great tradition.

We may well be proud of all our British Officers have done for the old Indian Army: and we may well be proud also of all the Indian Officers and men have done during the many years they have been associated together. It has been a wonderful combination. I have known it personally myself in many a regimental centre. Respect and affection for each other forged on the anvil of combat and the no less exacting times of peace.

It is good to know that we in England have this memorial of our Gurkha friends with us in our keeping; *klema eis aei* as the Greeks used to say, "a possession for ever." We would like them to know that this Garden of Remembrance will always be the peculiar responsibility of those whose home is in this Island, but whose adventuring took them overseas to forge an unbreakable link with the men of Nepal, whose proud motto is "better to die than be a coward." They may rest assured that, for all the six thousand miles, Bakloh and Stoke Poges are for ever joined together with ties which distance and time will be powerless to sever.

And for our own people—our British folk—there must be many here who will like to think that their dear ones are not forgotten, and that they can thank God for their service, even the supreme sacrifice, in a comradeship in arms, "serving," as Winston Churchill reminded us in 1940, "an unfolding purpose," and preparing them for a greater grander life beyond the grave. "Death's truer name," Tennyson has reminded us, is "onward." And fifty years later John Buchan could stand beside his brother's grave in France and give us his vision of the future:

> "I knew you moved in ampler powers,
>   A warrior in a purer strife,

Walking that world that shall be ours
When death has called us into life."

So may this Garden of Remembrance be a remembrance: of happy days of comradeship and active service; an unfaltering reminder of our Christian hope.

The Capture of Spin Baldak Fort —1/4th GR: MAY 1919 The Story of A Ragtime Siege

The following account was written within a month of so of the event by a very young (22 year old), very junior officer who was in the front line in that battle. It is mainly of interest as an example of how personal experience can differ from official history: the illustrated weekly papers of the time ran articles (primed by data from eye witnesses) which were only one degree less ludicrous than the actual happenings themselves: but all accounts of this mighty siege gave totally wrong impressions of the operation—quite ignoring the fact that for sheer burlesque and unintentional farce few military operations could compete with this short engagement on the Afghan border.

In the year 1919 an army of 10,000 men lay encamped on a wide plain some three miles from a row of white stone pillars marking the boundary of Afghanistan. Four miles on the other side was a large fort alongside of which was a small village: sooner or later it would be the pleasant business of the 10,000 on the British side of the border to take that fort: but it must not be forgotten that surprise is one of the main principles of war, so the Higher Command—acting doubtless on the excellent principle that if you can't surprise the enemy, it is better to surprise your own side rather than no-one at all—supplied little or no information about the fort and its garrison.

It was known that the fort had an outer wall about 200 yards long and 15 feet high—within which was another wall not quite so long but a trifle higher: it was also known that these two walls were very thick and not likely to be severely damaged by the comparatively weak artillery which could be brought into action against them. There was also a hint of a ditch surrounding the outer wall. What more could anybody wish to know?

One regiment was ordered to take the south side and to advance with scaling ladders. These ladders would be placed in the ditch and the regiment would then climb down. a smart turnabout would then be executed and the ladders placed on the further side of the ditch: thus having surmounted the obstacle the ladders were to be used to climb the outer wall and then the inner wall. Once the regiment had crossed the inner wall, surely no Afghan would be so foolish as to contest ownership of the fort. The regiment—yes, it was 1/4 GR was greatly diverted by this simple plan and declared that nothing like had been seen since the taking of Jerusalem: some soldiers however are notorious grumblers and one or two officers were actually heard to complain that no plans had been made to chloroform the enemy whilst the Regiment was playing with scaling ladders.

Meanwhile the second regiment of the Brigade—the 22nd Punjabis—had a comparatively simple task: they were to attack the Eastern face of the fort where the main gate lay: all they had to do was to open the gate and walk in—or in case of any difficulty they could always fall back on the persuasive influence of a few pounds of gun cotton. A third regiment was detailed to storm a couple of low hills surmounted by towers under which lay the main mass of the fort—whilst the fourth regiment waited in reserve. A further brigade was to make a wide turning movement and attack these same hills from the East whilst the cavalry were to get right behind the fort and make any fugitives sorry that they were ever born. In the face of such a magnificent plan—so masterly yet so simple—one can only deprecate most severely the facetious enquiries of the officers of 1/4 GR and the 22nd Punjabis who asked whether any plans had been made to "take out" the Afghan garrison.

0300 hours saw that mighty army move forward to the storming of the fortress. Everything was to be done in deathly silence—not a whisper was to rouse the unsuspecting Afghans. Indeed, the only sounds were the crashing of ammunition boxes and entrenching tool Kajawas as the mules threw their loads—and the thudding of hooves as they bolted into the night: every few seconds the air was split by the yells of some officer urging the men to greater silence or the despairing call of some NCO who had lost his section. A sound as of corrugated iron being dropped from a great height denoted that the scaling ladders were being loaded onto AT carts: with these few exceptions, no-one would have had an inkling that several thousand armed men were pressing forward to the fray.

As the vanguard passed the white stone pillars the sun rose on the doomed fortress and the garrison began to realise that it was about time to do something. The Afghan commander was a man of mettle and he acted quickly: if he were to die holding the fort, the others should be allowed to share that honour. With this in view he collected all the inhabitants of the village that nestled against the side of the fort—men, children, dogs, horses, camels, donkeys, sheep—and by way of afterthought, women—and herded them into the fort. He then ordered his band, clad in white garments to stand with him on the tower above the gateway and to make martial and defiant music such as would turn the infidels' livers to water: this the band did and blew so nobly that the Army heard them across the plain from nearly a mile away.

Meanwhile the Army had continued its ruthless advance: the infantry were deploying, other columns were moving round the right flank and the cavalry were riding about in all directions and wondering where they were. To those in the fort the whole plain must have appeared crawling with troops: no wonder they became excited: no wonder they started discharging their pieces at a range of about 1,700 yards—so that the old .450 Martini bullets came hopping towards the front line like ducks and drakes across the sea.

The leading infantry were greatly diverted and much confusion was caused in the ranks by men running to and fro to pick up the spent bullets for souvenirs. The only person put out of countenance by this hostile display on the part of the enemy was the tame Afghan bearing a large white flag who was supposed to be acting as special envoy to the garrison.

Now it had originally been intended that this envoy should ride up to the fort fifteen minutes before the leading infantry and call upon the commander to surrender—or that failing—to send away the women and children under safe conduct. The envoy, however, thought it would be safer to advance with the battalions of infantry as bodyguard and he went forward on a skinny nag that looked like an animated towel-horse. When the shooting started he turned round and went home but on the return journey the animated towel-horse was imbued with the spirit and pace of a Derby winner: the white flag trailed on the ground, the reins were slack, the spurs were working overtime and the dust rose in clouds—whilst the commander of the hostile garrison waited in vain for the summons to surrender.

The band, clad in white garments, continued to make martial and defiant music, our infantry continued to advance—though they no longer stopped for spent bullet souvenirs, they were now within close range and the bullets were coming past at first and second bounce with the worrying noise of the typical ricochet. It was time for the Army to play its trump card.

A battery of .5 inch howitzers came into action: (it was afterwards rumoured that these guns—already considered obsolete at the time of the South African War—had barrels almost innocent of rifling and that the ammunition had been sunk and salvaged on at least one occasion): but for all their venerable antiquity the guns did all that was required. A shell fell into the fort; a huge cloud of dust arose: the band in its white garments ceased to make martial and did finest music: the guns continued to fire and raised a dense cloud of dust under which 1/4 GR and the 22nd Punjabis were enabled to close within a hundred, yards or so of the walls with trifling casualties. Here they halted for three hours awaiting the order to assault.

The commander of the fort did not stay to see the finish of the bombardment: accompanied by all the Afghan regulars in the garrison, he crept cautiously out of the back or tradesman's entrance and made a bee line for the hills and safety—pursued at some two thousand yard range by our own cavalry. Meanwhile the villagers and their horses, dogs, sheep, camels, women, hens, fighting quail and other livestock remained in the fort and wondered how much longer the bombardment was going to last.

At the same time the 1/4th Gurkhas were becoming impatient. Close reconnaissance had shown that the scaling ladders were useless being several feet too short for the thirty foot ditch, but a narrow causeway was found to lead across the ditch to a small wicket gate in the wall and it was by this gate—when the bombardment stopped—that the Regiment gained access to the fort.

Once inside, what a sight met their eyes. The artillery had done little material damage and any trained and disciplined body of troops, determined to hold out could have sheltered with perfect security in the casemates under the walls and could have inflicted great slaughter on the assaulting infantry as soon as the bombardment had ceased. Fortunately the Afghans were not strong in training, discipline or the determination to hold out. The guns had however taken a terrible toll of the villagers and their livestock and the dead and dying were all over the fort—caught before they could take refuge in the deep shelters under the walls. Earlier the spectacle of the envoy with the white flag—meant to be offering safe conduct to non-combatants but flying before the long range fire of the early morning—had seemed to be funny: now it could be seen that this stupid bungle which made an envoy of peace advance with the deploying infantry was anything but funny.

The fort was soon full of soldiers and the Brigadier and his staff were not far behind. "Fall your men in and be ready to present arms as we run up the Union Jack"—shouted the Brigade Major. The men were fallen in and amidst an impressive silence marred only by smothered curses from the Staff Captain who had got himself entangled in the halyards—they duly saluted the Union Jack, hoisted upside down. No sooner was the flag hoisted than in bustled the adjutant of the 22nd Punjabis who, halting two paces in front of the Brigade Major, saluted smartly and delivered the following momentous report. "We have captured the Fort, sir". "Thank you", said the Brigade Major, "I am glad to receive confirmation of such important information from so reliable a source".

And what of the attack of the 22nd Punjabis on the eastern face? When the order to assault was given, that doughty regiment found themselves with no scaling ladders and faced with a high wall and a closed gateway: not surprisingly and very soundly they decided to get in through the gate. Some Napoleonic brain suggested blowing it down by gunfire; a gun was brought to bear and duly discharged: the results were disappointing. Had the shell hit the gate of course there would have been much damage and a large number of 4th Gurkhas who were already inside the fort would have had the shock of their lives. Most luckily the shell had missed the gate and exploded harmlessly against the thick wall: whereupon some brave soul walked up to the gate and opened it by the simple expedient of applying pressure with the palm of the hand, thus proving that although a gate is shut it may not necessarily be locked or barred. When the gate had been thus opened, it was a comparatively simple matter for the Adjutant to walk into the fort and deliver the astonishing report referred to in the previous paragraph.

The fort was then cleaned up, the survivors made prisoner and the dead buried: a small garrison was left whilst the remainder of the troops began their weary march of seven miles back to camp. It was now seven or eight o'clock in the evening and they had been up since the previous midnight.

The Army held the fort for a month or so: during that time the defences were greatly strengthened after much hard work by the common soldiery, and the water supply was vastly improved: the fort was then returned to the Afghans—ready for storming again in the next Afghan war?

And one last note to finish all. A little varnish may perhaps have been added here, a little imagination brought to play there, but in the main the above account is pretty true to the facts and not at all an inaccurate picture of what occurred.

This is the most astonishing part of the whole show.

F. E. C. H.

Rifleman Ranbahadur Bura 1st Bn 4th Gurkha Rifles Menin Gate Memorial

Of all the regiments of the Indian Army, the Gurkhas were perhaps the most charismatic. Certainly, they regarded themselves as the elite of the sub-continent's military contingent and it was said of their British Officers that "the Gurkhas talk only to each other and the 2nd Gurkhas talk only to God". Perhaps not surprisingly, the romantic appeal of these "small, murderous Mongolians" was lost on many of their enemies. Their almost irresponsible bravery and their predilection for the use of their kukris—vicious looking curved knives—was enough to strike fear into the hearts of even the most resolute of foes. A unit with an average height of 5 foot 3 inches was not exactly suited to trench warfare (most men had to stand on tiptoe to shoot at their enemies over the parapet) and the mud and the cold were enough to get even the usually stoical hill-tribesmen down. Their main complaint, however, was their inability to get to grips with the enemy in hand to hand combat. The Gurkhas were second to none in this type of fighting, but like many other units of all nationalities they had no solution to the central dilemma of the Great War: *how to cross the bullet swept killing zone of No Man's Land?*

On 1st May 1915 occurred one of those poignantly symbolic events with which the history of the Great War is littered. Having already failed in an attack on the 27th April, the 1st and 4th Gurkhas were again ordered to assault the strong German positions of Mauser Ridge. Both battalions advanced with great determination, but at a range of 150 yards the German machine guns and artillery opened up with devastating effect. Only two small parties of the 4th Gurkhas reached the wire, which they found undamaged by the British barrage. In frustration, the brave Gurkhas tried to hack a path through the entanglements, their beloved kukris reduced to little more than ineffective wire cutters. The outcome was never in doubt. Among the Gurkhas to die on the German wire was Rifleman Ranbahadur Bura.

Khwab O Khayal

Dreams and Reflections was the title of our first Urdu reader when I went out to India in 1918. Hamish Mackay contributed this article just before his death and it is published as a tribute to his memory.

I too was amused by Boy's account of his somewhat unusual arrival in India and also by Roy Cosens' nice follow up to it in NL 36. It is, moreover, of particular interest to me because I was another of the nine score cadets on that memorable trooping and though almost 70 years have elapsed since it happened, I can still clearly see Roy greet his father on the troop train to Quetta. It is a measure of how the emerging village schoolboy that I still was, marvelled at the simplest little happenings around him.

After reaching the Cadet College I did not see a great deal of Roy Cosens. We were divided alphabetically into Right and Left Half Companies and he, naturally, was in the Right Half-Company commanded by Borrowman of the 4th Gurkhas, where in due course, some six months later, the time came for passing out and commissioning, Roy being the attractive young man he was, almost inevitably joined Borrowman's regiment and was drafted to Bakloh.

I had no such sponsor but I did have an uncle in the Indian Army and I wrote asking his advice about which regiment I should choose. He replied (and perhaps I should tell this in a whisper!) "Go for any of the first three regiments of Gurkhas and failing that go for one of the old Madras regiments which ethnologically at least you will find full of interest." He himself had done the latter and when he wrote it was from the 99th Hyderabad Contingent, the regiment of his choice then on service in Mesopotamia; one of his companions in the regiment was I believe an uncle of our Jack Masters.

But meanwhile other influences were urging me to become a Pioneer, a Corps whose dual role of infantryman and field engineer appealed to me as it had done to other soldiers, notably Field Marshal Sir Claude Jacob whose name is familiar to every member of the "Rag" who ever entered the building with his eyes open. Sir Claude considered Pioneers to be so indispensable that no expedition could be mounted in which they were not employed and the chance of their being sent on active service therefore was better than most (a medal winning lure not without its effect now that the current source, the Great War, was drawing to a close!). It did end before the year was out and there was no jubilation: we were not in it "for duration"—no wish to be released, it was our livelihood, our existence.

One agreeable feature of that Christmas of 1918 was that a small handful of us who had relatives in India able to accept us, were given leave to go to them.

In my case there was the grass-widow of the uncle in Mesopotamia. She had been appointed in Delhi to organise the employment of women's work in the War. She gave her address, I remember, as Jangi Lat Sahib Ki Kothi Ke pas, where she had set up a delightful tented camp, bright and cheerful in the warmth even of the early morning sun and as unlike the dark, heavily clouded Quetta I had left as could possible be imagined. This was the India I had heard about and read and dreamed about, seen for the first time, a romantic and fascinating India —the Delhi of the Mutiny, the marvellous Delhi of the Moguls and of long before the Moguls. And yet there was an aspect of Delhi that was absent, nor was its absence noticed! It was to be years before I ever learnt of it and then it astonished me—the New Delhi of Lutyens. In 1918 he had not laid hand on it.

But let me turn aside briefly to mention that I never even thought about Burma at this time. Had I felt any pull in that direction, as was to happen in the years to come, this certainly would have been the time to indulge it. The travelling allowance that one could earn on such a lengthy journey might have enabled me to report to my new regiment already the possessor of a useful pony, and that is something

I should dearly have liked to do. Riding I ought to say was the one thing above all else at the College—not that I excelled in, hardly that—but that I loved heart and soul—so much so that I can still remember to this day the glow of satisfaction felt on overhearing a cavalryman pay this left-handed compliment on my skill. "He has," he said, "the best seat of any infantryman I ever knew!!"

And so it came about that on one auspicious commissioning day in mid-April 1919, I was driven in a tonga at my own expense the three miles that separated the College from the Depot of the 107th Pioneers (which was away on frontier service). I reported horseless, as was expected, and also penniless (doubtless ditto) and quite inexplicably, I was totally ignorant of what had happened in the Punjab and incredibly remained in ignorance of it for a long time to come.

Perhaps I was totally disorientated and absorbed in the history of my new regiment. It was not lacking in history, in a few years to come it would celebrate its two hundredth birthday. Once upon a time it had carried colours, the remains were framed in double sheets of plate glass and were diminishing without trace. Several large lithographs in the mess were of a famous battle in which it had taken part—Seringapatam— and as for ethnology, there was no scarcity of that.

The regiment was composed of four class companies as different as Mahrattas, Pathans, Rajputana Mohamedans and Sikhs: particular sub-classes of each of them and their various methods of tackling what they had to do was fascination itself. Our four classes were (1) Yusufzai Pathans from North of Peshawar, (2) Deccanni Mahrattus from the hill regions around Poona, (3) Ranghar and Khamzada Mohamedan Rajputs from Alwar, and (4) Lobana Sikhs, craftsmen from the Punjab. Between them they covered almost the length and breadth of India and in themselves they differed greatly in their characters and habits, their abilities and skills; sometimes entertainingly, often surprisingly.

I remember for example going on a route march with the regiment soon, after I had joined it in Quetta: I marched at the rear of the last company with two handsome havildars—one at either hand. They were Pathans who had just returned from leave: I did not know them but tried as best I could to speak to them and they willingly helped me. How had they spent their time on leave? Shooting—they told me, but seemingly not with much success. What had they been trying to get? All the time though they spoke up quite readily and cheerfully, I felt myself getting more and more into difficulties because it transpired that they were not out after game but after each other—in the midst of a family blood feud in fact, each trying to destroy the other from the protection of his own tower like house: they had been at it for some weeks! And what happened now? Well now it had to stop—for time time being: it was forbidden in the Regiment and away from home!

One could not imagine the Mahrattas occupying their leaves in this manner: they were quite unlike the Pathans.

A short while after this we were shipped off to Mesopotamia for some Arab rebellion and found ourselves near Mosul. The work was mainly road making and bridge building, most easily interfered with by sniping which quickly showed up a difference between the Pathans and the Mahrattas.

Pugnacious as always, the moment sniping started, the Pathans would down tools, reach for their rifles, and search the countryside for any sign of disturbers: the Mahrattas on the other hand tried to leave them severely alone. Usually the outcome in both cases was exactly the same except that the Mahrattas in the meantime had completed their own work!

Another character distinction that existed—this time between the Mahrattas and Sikhs—was clearly demonstrated by conditions that were peculiar to Mosul—a gleaming city of soft white marble or limestone which rubs away becoming a powder white as snow which, when disturbed, hangs in the air in clouds of white smoke.

Now the Sikhs were in Mesopotamia not to spend money but to lodge it thriftily in the Punjab where it would be duly translated into nurtured and well irrigated soil: so on pay day they would troop off to the Post Office which soon had the cash winging its way safely to India.

The Mahrattas too would make their way down to the city on pay day, but not particularly to despatch money to Bombay: they had their own views on how money should be spent.

In the first place they did not like marching the two or three miles to the city enveloped in clouds of lime dust, so they hired landau carriages and drove there and back again, by now smoking cigars and doubtless having already sluiced down their gullets: and who can blame them if they tried to get through the marching column as those walking could do nothing to avoid scuffing up the clouds of dust: with their faces swathed in their head cloths they indeed looked like snowmen. No mention has yet been made of the remaining class, the RMs—but they are as deserving of remark as the rest even if they appeared less picturesque: were they perhaps more reserved? They did have every right to be—these good looking men who had been Rajputs—once upon a time the proudest of the proud and now by choice or by powerful persuasion devout followers of the prophet. The man amongst them that I remember most clearly today was Jo Hookum named for the only words he ever vouchsafed us ("whatever you say"). Jo Hookum drove a pair of mules in the AT cart and though always satisfied with whatever instructions we doled out to him I don't believe that he ever failed to find a rendezvous, and they could be tricky, particularly on pig sticking days! No wonder I used to look on his race as cavalry material (dismounted): but mention of pig sticking is to touch upon sport and that is another subject, something to be left for another time.

Poor Uncle Charlie, there certainly was something in his ethnic ideas—but what on earth possessed him to draw the line at the Fourth Gurkha Rifles! It proved beyond doubt that he had inherited the fatal family crack: now he has me worried!

IV

Joining the 4th pre-1930

From Sandhurst the path to the Indian Army was reasonably smooth. Each Cadet posted to the Indian Army had to spend his first year in India on the "Unattached List": he could apply to be attached to a British Unit of his choice, though whether the "powers that be" paid much attention to this is doubtful.

The object of this attachment was to give him some experience of the country, the people, the climatic conditions, and perhaps most importantly, the chance of starting to learn the language before being posted.

The final posting of the Cadet to his Indian Army unit was naturally by AHQ, but this again could sometimes be influenced by the young Officer if he had friends already in that Unit and could get them to make application for him.

A number of Units, when they knew of a young Officer's interest, would tell him to come and visit them for a few days. If they liked him they could apply for him to be posted to them in due course, but if they did not consider him suitable he would be informed that there was no vacancy at that time. In most Gurkha Units in small stations with small populations this vetting was important as incompatability could cause trouble.

Personally I was extremely lucky to be posted to the 1st Battalion The Black Watch. They were extremely kind to me and treated me (almost!) as one of their own Officers. In fact they were at that time short of Officers due to leave, ex-Regimental employ, Courses etc. and I had the honour of commanding one of their Rifle Companies for several months, or perhaps I should more accurately say, my Company Sergeant Major did!

It was my good fortune to have, at that time, a relation who was on the Viceroy's Staff in Delhi who had been in the same Indian Cavalry Regiment as General Sir Arthur Mills, who had himself recently completed command of the 2nd Battalion. My relation mentioned my wish to join the 4th and they suggested that I pay a visit to Bakloh to let them see me and I, needless to say, jumped at the invitation.

Those of us who have had our first view of Bakloh from the foothills as one approached it—just a few buildings peeping over a high steep ridge and facing out over the miles and miles of the plains—rather wondered what sort of a place it could be.

In those days, before the motor road to Bakloh had been constructed, all vehicles travelling on the road from Pathankot to Dalhousie had to stop at Dunera and from there on travel was one way only, working to timings. Refreshments were available at Dunera.

Passengers for Bakloh took the Dalhousie bus as far as Tunnihutti where one quit the bus and took to feet, horse or mule. The Regiment had kindly sent down one of their Officer's chargers for me to ride, a coolie carried my case and we started the ascent. As I have indicated earlier, the Black Watch had been very good to me and my Company Commander, on going on leave, had left me his horse which acted as Charger and Polo pony and I had been attempting to play polo in the Regiment. Now, the animal on which I was mounted, appearing to be placid, I started practising polo shots using my cane in place of the polo stick. The pony was not showing any signs of disapproval when it suddenly took off and bolted; not a very pleasant situation on a narrow hillside path with a considerable drop on one side. We had a battle for some way until I finally succeeded in reducing him to a more sedate pace and managed to clock in at the Mess in a fairly reasonable state. I came to learn some time later that the animal in question had been known to bolt before this. I rather suspected that it was put at my disposal on this occasion "to try me out", but never confirmed it ... anyway they did have a vacancy for me!

A motor road to and from Bakloh to Dalhousie made a great difference to our lives. Admittedly one could get from Bakloh to Dalhousie by using hill paths—and the distance, as far as I can remember, was less than half that by main road; the return journey was considerably quicker than the climb up. There was a Club and a small golf course there.

During the periods that we were stationed in Bakloh, we always moved down to the Jullundur area for the winter months for sub-unit and unit training, which, without a proper road from Bakloh was not simple, with all the heavy and bulky loads having to be manhandled or pack loaded to wheeled transport on the main road. As a matter of fact, we always took the War Memorial on these moves down to Jullundur in the winter; and whilst on this subject, I wonder whether all Officers know the story that the 2nd Battalion's War Memorial Bell cracked on the day that the Battalion suffered so severely in North Africa.

For the move down, the Battalion moved by route march on main roads with reasonable distances between camping places. This allowed those interested, after setting up camp and normal routine, to get out for an evening shoot with a view to augmenting the Mess supper.

I remember that for one year on this move down, we were supplied with camel transport for a portion of our stores. Our route that year entailed crossing the Beas River. The majority of the camels managed to embark on the flat-bottomed boats safely and were then made to fold up in the strange way camels do, and sit down on the boat. A few, however, flatly refused to go on board: this was, however, overcome by their being made to sit on firm ground near the boat, their folded knees were then tied, large strong bamboo poles passed under their bodies and the camel drivers then lifted them bodily on board the boat. Those who have ever had anything to do with dealing with camels will know how they demonstrated their dislike of this sort of treatment!

J. W. A. L.

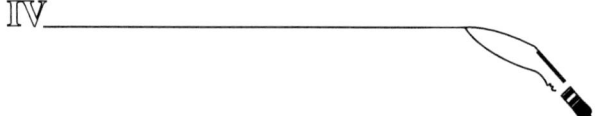

The Frontier Scouts

By Beetle Lowis

North West Frontier problems faced India from the time of the defeat of the Sikhs in the Punjab and fears of Russian penetration from that direction have been with us since then. The Frontier can be divided into three parts—in the far North are the Hindu Kush tribes, hardy but not truculent; to the South the Zhob and the Nekran, gave little trouble and, if left to themselves, the locals ran their affairs themselves: the area between was the trouble spot, as it had been since the time of Alexander the Great, the inhabitants—Moslem fanatics—considering no man their master. The country is inhospitable and unproductive, leading to the population being predators.

Two methods of control were considered: first, the Close Border policy, tried till the end of the 19th century, was to control the plains but to leave the hills and mountains to the tribes. If the tribes became a nuisance by raiding, killing or abducting, they were subjected to punitive expeditions to punish them but the end result was seldom really effective. The second method considered was the Forward policy which entailed occupying and administering all the area up to the Durand Line, the Internationally agreed boundary with Afghanistan. It was soon obvious that this second policy, to be successful, would involve considerable armed forces, the cost of which would be beyond the resources of India. A compromise policy was therefore adopted, an Administrative Border was set up to control and administer law and order, and from this border up to the Durand Line, was to be known as Tribal Territory: the Army was kept back, mainly within the Administrative Border, while the Tribal Territory was dealt with by Political Agents with the help of an armed and disciplined force. This resulted in the raising and training of the Frontier Corps—Militias and Scouts of various. Units from Chitral in the North to Baluchistan in the South. The main troubles coming from the central area, i.e. Waziristan. This was divided into two; North and South Waziristan, and the forces for these were Tochi Scouts for the North and The South Waziristan Scouts. I myself served with the latter.

Having joined the 2nd Battalion in October 1929, we moved up to Razmak in December of that year to relieve our 1st Battalion. During 1930/31, the India Congress Party caused a certain amount of trouble in the Frontier through the person of Fakir of Ipi, and this entailed columns having to be sent out to pacity or punish various areas. On these column we were sometimes assisted by the South Waziristan Scouts and I was most impressed with the men, their fitness and methods.

Some years later, on my way to a course, I had to change trains and while waiting for my connection I got into conversation with another officer. I discovered that he was the Adjutant of the South Waziristan Scouts. I was most interested and questioned him about the Unit and their life and how one could get to serve with them. He told me that if I was genuinely interested he would make a note of it and when there was a vacancy he would let me know. He was as good as his word and not very much later he wrote to say that there was to be a vacancy in May 1937.

The SWS were composed of three Wings, each Wing being about equal in numbers to a Battalion of the IA. They were lightly armed with rifles only, but there were post defence MMGs in the forts. The men wore greyish shirts, outside their khaki shorts, and pagris. In winter, in place of shorts, they wore partog 9 (baggy mussulman trousers of the same material as their shirts). On their legs and feet, they wore half hose and chapplis. British Officers wore the same. For equipment, they carried a bandolier of 50 rounds, .303 and a belt with two pouches, each with 10 rounds—70 rounds per man. We wore a revolver on a leather shoulder strap, and 15 rounds. Being lazy I allowed my Orderly to carry my water bottle! Each man also carried a water bottle and a light haversack with his own choice food for 24 hours. Education was basic! The scout had to be able to read figures so that he could recognise his rifle.

The wings were dispersed over an area of responsibility with

Unit HQ and one Wing at Jandola—the lowest in attitude; one Wing at Sararoga and Ladha, and the third Wing at Sarwekai and Tiarza. The Wings were changed in locations regularly. The country was barren but fairly level in general. Temperatures were high in summer but pleasant in winter. Sararogha and Sarwekai were a bit higher but still hot in summer. The ground was very broken—steep with some vegetation, but fairly sparse. Ladha and Tiarza were the highest forts with reasonable temperatures. Tiarza was subject to snow sometimes in winter.

One of the greatest difficulties in administration in the Unit was the tribal problem. Of the total strength, the division between Administered and Tribal tribes was never less than 2 to 1. Platoons were tribal and their commander of the same tribe. Companies, however, were of mixed tribes and the Company. Commander of a tribe not represented in the Company. Guards were never solely of one tribe. It sounds complicated, but the result was successful.

As mentioned earlier, the Scouts were administered by the Political Service and paid by them. We were said, by jealous friends, to have joined the Scouts for certain reasons—to gather enough money to pay off our debts or to have time to work for the Staff College or to achieve fitness.

Another advantage of Political administration was that the financial regulations were more reasonable than with the Military. For instance, when I joined the SWS, our only method of communication when out was by helio or flag when in visual contact, but when out of visual contact, the only other method, believe it or not, was by pigeon. Whenever we went out on patrol, we always had a signaller who carried a basket on his back containing four, trained pigeons and one had to remember to release them on our way home at a reasonable distance from the fort, so that they were kept in practice! The Commandant to improve this, went to America and with the necessary authority, purchased some "man-pack" wireless sets, which gave surprisingly good service as long as hills between did not cause too much blanketing. We were therefore the first units to have w/t at Regimental signal level. The same Commandant also modernised our transport. At that time, we only had a few ancient

Albion lorries used mainly for moving heavy loads. He replaced them with vehicles which were virtually buses. He had steel protection placed under the engine area and a strip along the sides deep enough to give reasonable protection to passengers when bending forward. These precautions certainly paid their way as I found out.

Shortly before finishing my time with the SWS, I had to go out to one of the Forts to relieve another Officer. On my way from HQ to his Fort, bringing some Scouts as well, I noticed about half a dozen tribesmen sitting under trees, carrying rifles as usual, but somehow I got the feeling that they were up to no good. When I reached my destination, I asked the Officer I was relieving how he proposed to go to Jandola and he said he was taking his car which needed a service. I advised him to travel in the lorry with the Scouts and have his car serviced at some other time and told him the reason. He said it was just imagination and he would take his car. As I was senior to him, I threw my weight about and ordered him to get into the lorry. On their way back, they were in fact fired at for some distance at fairly close range. As far as I can remember, only three Scouts were slightly injured by flying splinters.

Our work with the Scouts could be described basically as "showing the flag". We were responsible for getting around and seeing that all was well and quiet. This was called "gashting". It was carried out on foot and cross-country, at speed. I believe our normal speed was in the region of 5 mph and our gashts were anything up to 20 miles or over.

Life in general was pleasant enough, though anyone who did not like being on his own would not have enjoyed it much. One did sometimes spend quite long periods on ones own. Accommodation was on the whole as adequate as it could be in a stone fort, the exemption being at SWS HQ in Jandola. There, the Mess and quarters were definitely first class. An earlier Commandant had decided that with all the hard living in other places, the ante-room in the HQ Mess must be as nearly as possible of pleasant, well-furnished, drawing room as in a private house—which it was. The remaining rooms were functional and as "male" as a normal Mess or Club—leather armchairs and all.

Now, as to the men themselves, I must admit that I had never previously trusted them, but after three years in close proximity to them, I have softened somewhat. I believe that if at any time the Frontier blew up and turned against us, our Scouts, or at least a majority, would not turn. They might possibly desert or push us out, but they would not shoot or knife us. Up to a point, this was indicated by an experience which happened very soon after I had joined the 3WS. I was told to go out and surround and search a small village where an outlaw was thought to be hiding. We surrounded the village, sent for the headman and told him our intentions. My orderly and I went together on the search. At each small stone hut, with narrow low door, my orderly pushed me out of the way and went in first. He was unarmed while I had my pistol.

They mostly had a good sense of humour—if somewhat broad—and they were religious: on more than one occasion, when under fire, which was not too serious, I have seen them at a time of prayer, drop back individually and pray, probably at speed! One of their less pleasant habits is that of the blood feud—a life for a life. It is very fully practised in tribal territory. I had one fine old Subedar, a Malik Din Khel Afridi, whose nickname was "tarbour"—Pushtu for cousin; he, having disposed of most of his in blood feuds. It was his habit, when due for leave, to come up to his Wing Commander and suggest that this year he would like to leave six days early (or late), so that his actual date of move was not known to the important relatives—his date of return was also known to him only! He was a very great character and a good friend (but I would hate to be his enemy).

Talking to the Pathan Officers, they had one objection to our methods. They said "Why do you only stay three years (sometimes five but that seldom) with us? The first year you are pretty useless, in the second you learn quite well and after three years, when you are really useful, you leave!

In the field, the British Officer who does not consult his Scout Subedar, is very foolish. They have years of experience, a natural eye for ground and, for the tribal ones they have been doing this sort of thing all their lives.

I find that the GB did not support the Scouts with officer postings in the last years of British India. In fact, since 1919, there have been only 11 officers seconded from Gurkha Regiments compared with 130 from other regiments of IA. Despite that, I enjoyed myself greatly during my tour.

Lionel Peter Collins

Brigadier L. P. Collins, CB, CSI, DSO, OBE, died peacefully at his home in Fleet on the 27th September, 1957 and, with his death, there has passed a great gentleman, a fine sportsman and a distinguished soldier who was in large measure the architect of the traditions which the Regiment has inherited from the 1914–18 war.

He joined the 1st Battalion in 1902 and was its Adjutant in the years immediately preceding World War I, and the many times during which he commanded the battalion included the Battle of Neuve Chapelle and the evacuation from Gallipoli.

After twenty years' service with the Regiment, he was transferred to the 1/2nd Goorkhas of which he became CO in 1924. The climax of his outstanding regimental career was the great service which he rendered to the Indian Army as the first Commandant of what was then familiarly known as "India's Sandhurst"—of the Indian Military Academy at Debra Dun which is now well-established as India's National Defence Academy. After holding this important appointment for four years, he retired in 1936.

His great service to the Regiment and to India was recognised not only by the four honours awarded to him but also by his appointment as ADC to His Majesty King George V in 1934.

Maj-General J. R. Hartwell writes: "The story of Peter's twenty years with the 1st Battalion is in essence the story of the battalion during those critical years. It is recorded in our Regimental History, so I will not recapitulate it here. I saw little of him when, for a very short time, we both served with the 2nd Gurkhas, but it was impossible not to be struck with the immense influence he exercised and the deep affection with which he was regarded by the entire regiment.

"In 1928 he relinquished command to do a short spell as AMS at Army Headquarters, from which he went as first Commandant of the embryo IMA. There could have been no happier selection. One only has to mention his name to those whose character, upbringing and instruction were in his care—(one of whom is now Colonel of the Fourth)—to realise the spirit in which they regarded him, and undoubtedly the Indian Army of the last war owed much to the start given by him to the junior King's Commissioned Indian Officers. I have no doubt that it still owes him much to-day.

"It was sometimes said of Lionel Peter Collins that 'he lacked ambition.' Of personal ambition he had none—of that I am sure. But selfless ambition he had in plenty—ambition to find out what best he could give, and freely and gladly to give it to others ... ambition, although quite unconscious, to set an example and show a way of life which others might care to follow. And he had too an aura of physical and moral courage, in battle one felt braver and steadier near him.

"All who knew and loved Peter, and they are very many, will remember him as a very gallant Christian gentleman."

Maj-General D. T. Cowan adds his tribute in these words: "Convinced that the formation of an Indian Military Academy was long overdue, Peter Collins was determined that the experiment would succeed, and he imbued his sub ordinates with his enthusiasm. Those of us who took part as members of his team appreciate how much we owed to his broad-minded idealism and unostentatious example. No 'showman', modesty, simplicity and tolerance were his outstanding characteristics.

"He will be affectionately and gratefully remembered by a large circle of British, Indian and Pakistani Officers."

IV

High Scoring Feat by L. P. Collins

By E. W. Swanton

We reproduce this article by kind permission of the Editor of the *Daily Telegraph*, in whose journal it appeared on the 23rd July, 1956—a privilege which we gratefully acknowledge. Its author writes: "I too think the matter will be of interest to your readers."—*Ed.*

I wrote in a commentary earlier in the summer of the extraordinary feat of L. P. Collins, who in India in 1904 made two hundreds in a match three times within the space of ten days. One would like to know more, I said.

One now knows considerably more. Indeed from the correspondence my note evoked it would be possible to write a short biography of Brigadier L. P. Collins, CB, CSI, DSO, OBE, late of the Gurkha Brigade.

The Brigade tour in which these wonderful things happened embraced Ambala, Meerut, Cawnpore and Bareilly. The opposition in one of the matches was provided by the Green jackets, whose cricket reputation in Service circles is, of course, second to none.

The game flourished greatly in India in those days. It was indeed the Army who really planted the seed of Indian cricket. The wickets were good and fast, either matting or grass, and from the number of university and county players in the teams it is probably fair to describe the standard of play as "high-class club."

Brig Collins, writing from Fleet, answers my question as to the quality of bowling. It was, he says modestly, "good to indifferent, as is the way of club cricket." In one of the two-day matches he says, "I made rather over 200 not out in the first innings and rather over 100 not out in the second."

The feat could clearly have been performed only by someone

who was not merely a very good batsman but also a young one, very strong and very fit. Brig Collins was in fact a distinguished all-round games-player. From Marlborough, his old school, Mr J. S. Maples sends these details. He was a triple colour for cricket, hockey and rackets before going up to Oxford, where he won Blues for cricket (1899) and hockey.

He was the first Commander of the Indian Military Academy, and an ADC to King George V.

Not the least interesting thing about this short excursion into cricket history is the number of people who remembered and thought it worth while writing about the events of more than half a century ago.

1935—A year in the life of a subaltern, half a century ago

By Frank Nangle

In January 1935, as a subaltern aged 24 with five years' service, I was the Quartermaster of the First Battalion, stationed at Malakand, having arrived there the previous October. The Battalion was divided between three main locations. One company was in the fort at Dargai, guarding the rail head at the foot of the road leading up to the Malakand Pass five miles away. Another company was in the fort at Chakdara, ten miles further on, guarding the bridge over the Swat river which gave access to the tribal territories of Dir and beyond. The rest of the Battalion was in Malakand itself, a somewhat ramshackle fort strung out along the ridge which divided the Peshawar Vale from the valley of the Swat river. While this dispersion entailed heavy guard duties for the men it added interest to the work of the Quartermaster. Periodic visits to Dargai and

Chakdara were carried out on horseback and provided pleasant breaks from the office.

The climate in January and February was excellent, brisk sunny days with frosty nights and snow on the mountains beyond the Swat river. The recreational facilities for a frontier station were good. In Malakand itself there was a parade ground which also did duty as a rough hockey and football ground, in addition to a couple of, tennis courts and a squash court. Some miles away between Malakand and Chakdara there was a polo ground where from time to time, by courtesy of the Political Agent and the local tribesmen, we were able to play polo, with more enthusiasm than skill. There was also a certain amount of rough shooting to be had and in due season fishing for Mahseer in the Swat river at Chahdara. The main disadvantage of Malakand was its comparative isolation and the lack of the social amenities of a large cantonment.

That January Archie Best the Political Agent organised a chichor shoot in the foothills beyond the far bank of the Swat river where ancient Graeco Buddhist ruins stimulated the imagination. The shoot was memorable not so much for the size of the bag but for the sense of excitement engendered from operating in an area normally closed to members of the garrison, where there was always a chance of a local tribesman taking a pot shot at one.

In February I was lucky enough to be included as a guest in one of the Waii of Swat's even more memorable duck shoots. The day started with a drive of about forty miles to the venue of the shoot bear Saidu, the capital of Swat, through normally forbidden territory and past ancient Buddhist sites and the ruins of a fort associated with Alexander the Great. The setting for the shoot was impressive, being at a place where the Swat Valley widened out into a considerable plain. This was covered with small flooded paddy fields which together gave the appearance of a large shallow lake. The whole was ringed by snow covered mountains dominated to the north by those of Swat Kohistan which rose to about twenty thousand feet. The shoot was conducted almost as a military operation under the personal control of the Wali himself who was a remarkable character and a very fine shot.

Towards the end of the month we were sharply reminded of what being stationed on the North West Frontier was all about with the opening of the Loe Agra operation in the Malakand Agency by the Nowshera Brigade under the command of the future Field Marshal Alexander. Although the First Battalion only took a peripheral part in the operation, which is described in Chapter XVII of the Regimental History, it provided company detachments in support of the Brigade during the next couple of months. This operation which naturally added considerably to the amount and interest of my work as Quartermaster was finally completed by the middle of April, but not before the murder of the Political Agent, allegedly by one of his own escort.

With the hot weather starting, the seasonal adjustments to the routines of the Battalion were being made. British Officers due for furlough were leaving for the UK and the leave parties of the Gurkha ranks were getting ready for their return on leave to Nepal via Bakloh. Wilfred Oldham and I had for some time been planning to spend our privilege leave on a trek through Chitral and Gilgit to Kashmir. After the celebrations for King George V's Jubilee in May we set out on the 2nd June. In addition to Wilfred and myself our party consisted of my orderly Kamansing Gurung, who had been with me on a previous trek, Wilfred's orderly Jitbahadur Thapa and a Pathan orderly from the Malakand Levies, by name Shaida, who had been on the same trek with my brother three or four years previously. The first stage from Malakand to Dir was by chartered lorry, carrying ourselves, baggage and basic provisions for six weeks, together with a couple of scallywags from the Dir Levies as escort.

On the following day the trek started in earnest, with the crossing of the snow covered Lowari Pass on foot, following the same route taken by the 2nd Battalion when part of the Chitral Relief Force in 1895. The next six weeks were sheer delight, full of interest and incident. We were fortunate in having the blessing of the Political Agent in Malakand, who included Chitral in his charge and in Gilgit the support of Willie Weallens who was then commanding the Gilgit Scouts. In consequence we were treated as favoured guests wherever we went and met a number of interesting characters. The landscape through which we travelled was always magnificent and at times breathtakingly spectacular with views of Tirich Mir, Rakaposhi and Nanga Pargat, all over 25,000 feet high. The trek ended at Bandipura on the Wular Lake where we transferred to a Kashmiri boat in which we were hauled up the Jhelum river to Srinagar. By then it was the middle of July and uncomfortably hot and sticky, so we moved on up to Gulmarg and finished our leave in a round of golf, picnics and parties. The favourite dance tune at that time was "Smoke gets in your eyes".

Returning to regimental duty and the comparative confinement of Malakand was not altogether welcomed after the freedom of the previous two months. However it was not for long as I was lucky enough to be detailed for secondment to the Gurkha Recruiting Depot at Kunraghat. Having handed over the duties of Quartermaster to Ram Rattan Rana, an incomparable QM Jemedar and having bought a second hand T model Chevrolet, I set out to drive the eleven hundred miles to Kunraghat. From Nowshera to Cawnpore, three quarters of the journey, was along the Grand Trunk Road. The drive was not without incident but Kaman Sing and I with two dogs and a mountain of luggage, arrived safely after nine days, one breakdown and two river crossings on local sailing boats.

David has already written about the Recruiting Depot in Newsletter No 37, so I will not go into details about it. Suffice to say that I found the work at the Depot fascinating, that I learnt more about Gurkhas there than anywhere else and that my six months' secondment as an ARO for Gurkhas was one of the most pleasant periods of my service. So ended what was for me a memorable year.

IV

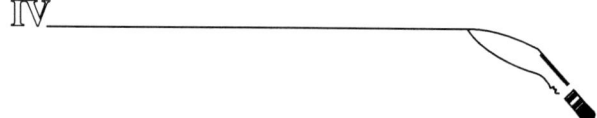

My first visit to Nepal

By H. B. Kingsley

In 1906, the year in which I joined the 4th Gurkha Rifles, Nepal was practically *terra incognita*—a country whose borders were closed to foreign visitors. It was in this year that the Regiment was honoured by the appointment of HE the Maharajah of Nepal as its Honorary Colonel, and in the following year Colonel Philip Carnegy, the Commanding Officer of our 2nd Battalion, was invited to visit Kathmandu, accompanied by Captain B. U. Nicolay of our 1st Battalion, in order to inspect the British Resident's escort. This unexpected privilege was doubly welcome because it enabled them, on behalf of the Regiment, to present to the Maharajah his Colonel's Sword which had been specially forged and appropriately engraved by Wilkinson, the world-renowned sword makers. I remember well the excitement in Bakloh when this invitation was received, and the keen interest with which we all followed Colonel Carnegy's account of his visit on his return. Little did I dream that it would be my privilege to visit Nepal before I grew much older! Yet, in the very next year, what had not even been an idle dream became a reality.

In 1908 I had the good fortune to take the Rifle Team of the 2nd Battalion down to Meerut to compete at the BPRA meeting. There, I had the good fortune to meet the British Resident in Nepal, Colonel Jack Manners-Smith, VC, who, being himself an ex-5th Gurkha, naturally took a keen interest in the shooting of the Gurkha Brigade teams. The upshot of that chance meeting was that he applied for me to be sent to Kathmandu for six months in 1909 to train his Escort. You can imagine how delighted I was when Colonel Carnegy readily agreed, and off I went in April with bearer, syce and chestnut pony.

I detrained at Raxaul where I was hospitably entertained by the local railway office. When night fell I was put to bed in a comfortable dhooli and carried away into the night and the jungle. I was quickly rocked to sleep until, some hours later, I awoke and found that the dhooli had ceased moving. Pulling the curtains aside I looked into the darkness; I could see no sign of the dhooli bearers and wondered if I had been left as a meal for a hungry tiger! Looking back, however, I saw them all seated round a huge fire: having a happy meal together. Eventually, we moved on and I fell asleep again.

When I awoke, we had reached the Rest House at Bimphedi where everything was ready for me. We were now in the hills, with lovely views all around and houses dotted about among the fields. After a bath and breakfast I mounted my pony and rode on through wonderful hills, followed by the pack ponies carrying my luggage. For those days, I was "travelling light", but this still allowed me a uniform case, cabin trunk and one or two suit-cases! The road was easy going—a wide well-maintained hill track, which, here and there, had been cut into quite precipitous cliffs Two features, which I vividly recall, were the orchids growing on trees and the pylons of the newly constructed cable rope-way. We slept that night in Sisagarbi Rest House (sometimes known, I think, as Chisapanigarhi), from where the views were even more beautiful than Bhimphedi.

On the third day I rode over the Chandragiri Pass from where the track wound steeply down the mountain range to Thankote in the Valley of Nepal. There an open carriage, like a landau, was awaiting me; I discovered later that the Maharajah had some very handsome vehicles and that these had been transported over the hills in sections by porters and assembled in Kathmandu. At Thankote, the hill track gave way to a smooth road surfaced with well-rolled chips of *bajri*.

After a pleasant drive of 5 or 6 miles, I reached the Residency, where I received a very warm welcome from the Resident and Mrs Manners-Smith and their three small daughters—(the fourth was still a baby in arms).

I forgot to mention earlier that the Resident had asked me to bring up from Raxaul a fine horse—a bay waler which he had recently acquired. He mounted it at once for a canter round the Residency compound and, to the laughing delight of his small daughters, it promptly started to buck and very nearly gave him a toss. However, after he had dismounted, the three little girls climbed on and the horse behaved beautifully! The children were very keen on riding, and we had a scamper together almost daily during my time there. I soon made friends with them. In those days my family name of "Kingsley" was hyphened to a preceding "Bell", and it was not long before they adopted me as "Brother Bilkins", I am still in touch with them and they still call me by that name.

The Residency was a charming house built of brick, with a tiled roof, and surrounded by lovely gardens, which included a perfect lawn behind the house and a grass tennis court. Its compound was a park of several acres well supplied with beautiful trees. The Residency Surgeon, Major Burden, who was a bachelor, lived in a nice bungalow adjoining the Residency. He and the British Head Clerk at the Residency Office were the only other Europeans in Kathmandu and, in those days, there were, of course, no Americans. I lived in a charming little bungalow facing the Residency and at some distance from it, but I had all my meals with the family.

The Escort consisted of six cavalry sowars and ninety-four infantrymen, under command of a Subedar. All of them were Rajputs from the Indian Army. It is interesting to recall that when the first British Resident went to Nepal in 1815, under the terms of the Peace Treaty after the war between our two countries, he had an escort of 1,000. The barracks and stables were at the far side of the road running past the compound of the Residency, from which they were hidden by trees.

My main duty was the maintenance of the highest standard of smartness on parade and guard duty. It was an easy task. The men were happy and their discipline was excellent, moreover, the fact that they were Infantrymen and not Riflemen posed no problems because only five years had elapsed since I had left Sandhurst and joined The Gloucestershire Regiment (appropriately, on St Patrick's Day!) for my year's attachment before joining the 4th Gurkha Rifles. Once a week we did a route march (for the good of our health), but there was no field training; in fact the only other training off the parade ground was putting them through the annual musketry course on the rifle range, which was only a short distance from the barracks. During my time, there was no Ceremonial Parade, though there was always a Guard of Honour when the Maharajah, Sir Chandra Shamsher Jang Bahadur, visited the Residency. He and his sons were on very friendly terms with the Resident and his family. After the official reception, formality ceased and he would take the baby from the Ayah and play with it. For me it was an enchanting and unforgettable experience, and an education for a young officer in a Gurkha Regiment.

Kathmandu was full of interest. Accompanied by Major Burden I visited all the sights of the city and in Patan and Bhatgaon. There was a profusion of shrines and temples of varying size and architectural beauty, with ornately carved window frames and doors. The sculpture was also of very fine craftsmanship, and there was a wonderful variety of stone statues of Gods and Kings, mostly guarding the temples or flanking the stone stairways ascending to their carved porticos. And there was the marvellous Buddhist Shrine of Bodhnath. Looking back, my only regret is that, at that early age, my interest in archaeology was elementary and I did not learn the age of these splendours, nor who had made them and whom the statues represented.

We rode; we played tennis and bathed and had a grand time; occasionally we went shooting, though the shikar was nothing to write home about. In June we moved up to the Resident's bungalow at Kakani, which was about six miles from Kathmandu and perched on the hills forming the western boundary of the Valley of Nepal. From there we could see the great peaks of Kanchen-junga and Dhaulagiri and, in the far distance, the peak of Mt Everest. Below us, a great river wound its way westward through forest-clad hills and we longed to follow its course into forbidden country. Leeches swarmed in the undergrowth and, when we went for our walks, we had to keep a wary eye on them.

In Kathmandu we used to visit the Maharajah in the Singha Durbar, a magnificent building both architecturally and inside. We were always greeted with laughter as we went through the "Hall of Mirrors", which one associates more with a fun fair than a palace, with its concave and convex mirrors distorting the human frame into grotesque and amusing shapes. There was a splendid library well furnished with handsomely bound volumes of Shakespeare, Macaulay and almost all the great writers, and it was obvious that many of the books were frequently read.

On one occasion—the only one on which I was required to wear my full dress uniform—we attended a great Durbar, presided over by the King of Nepal, and I had never seen such splendid precious stones. The King and the Maharajah wore them on their chests, shoulders, sleeves, and even on the back of their robes.

Living with such a delightful family, almost as one of them, made me feel as if I were at home, and it was a sad day for me when I had to say Good-bye. But, two years later, it led to another unforgettable visit to quite a different part of Nepal. The Maharajah of Nepal invited HM King George V to a big game shoot after the Coronation Durbar in Delhi and, by great good luck, the Maharajah asked for me to go and help with the arrangements.

A Royal shoot in Nepal

By H. B. Kingsley

Two years after my first visit to Nepal, the Coronation Durbar for HM King George V was held in Delhi, and, on its conclusion in December, 1911, the King went to Nepal, as the guest of HH. The Maharaja; to shoot in the Terai. By great good luck, I was one of those whose services had been requested by the Maharaja to help with the arrangements for the shoot. The other two, both of whom like myself had done a tour of duty in Kathmandu training the British Resident's Escort, were Major Dopping-Heppenstal of the 1st KGO Gurkha Rifles and Captain Orton of the 39th Garhwal Rifles.

The three of us arrived well ahead of the royal party, and I was greatly impressed by the transformation which had taken place in what was naturally a wilderness of dense forest and jungle with, here and there, wide open stretches of rice fields. A motor road, some 60 miles long, had been made through the forest from railhead to the shooting camp on the banks of the Rapti river. To make the camp site the forest trees had been felled, the roots removed, a lovely lawn laid down and canna lilies planted along the river banks. For the King and his Secretary, Lord Stamfordham, a charming shooting lodge had been built and the rest of the party each had a very nicely furnished EP tent to himself. A separate camp, close at hand, but well-screened by unfelled trees, had been pitched for the Camp Guard and the retinue.

Our first task was to arrange the furniture in the shooting lodge and EP tents, and we were also responsible for the security of the camp including, after the King arrived, visiting the sentries at night. My chief job in connection with the shoots was to see that lunch was ready at the appointed time and place; and this had its hazards. On one occasion I discovered a vast swarm of bees immediately over the table and, though not protectively equipped, I had to take immediate action to remove it. On another occasion, the Guard suddenly shinned up the surrounding trees with their rifles cocked; the reason was that they had seen a large rhino approaching and, as these formidable beasts always charge at anything white, the men thought that he would go for the table-cloth! However, to my relief, he ignored everything and passed on.

On the first morning, the Resident's wife, Mrs Manners-Smith, with her three little daughters, and Lady McMahon, wife of the Foreign Secretary, with her daughter, came out on their elephants to watch the sport; but they returned to their own camp before lunch. The King immediately noticed their absence and, insisted they should lunch with us in future. This had some amusing results. On the next day, the 7-year-old, towards the end of lunch; rose from her, place, walked round and, putting her hand on the King's shoulder, said "I've had too much lunch." When the King put his arm round her as if to lift her she said "You may lift me but you mustn't bend me!"

All sorts of stories were bandied round the table and many of them, about people he knew in various walks of life, were capped by the King. This evidence of the wide range of his acquaintances did not escape the notice of Lady McMahon, a delightful Irishwoman, as she sat beside him. One day, during a pause in the conversation, she turned to him and said, "Sir, did you ever come across one Jonathan Darby, of Leap Castle in the King's County?" The King repeated the name thoughtfully: "Darby? ... Jonathan Darby? No, why?" "Well, Sir," replied Lady McMahon, "he was a terrific dandy and every so often he would go over to London, see what was the latest in gent's wear, buy it, take the night boat back to Kingston and, next morning, he would peacock up and down Grafton Street showing it off to the Natives. One year, it was white spats. He was just turning to make his third walk down Grafton Street when a filthy little corner-boy crept out of the shadows, touched his cap and said, 'Oi beg pardon, yer Honour, but the layshte little tayshte of yer dhrawers is comin' down .'" The King was delighted with the story, told with a real Irish brogue, and the whole party joined him in roars of laughter before he remarked: "That caps all our stories. We must now go and shoot."

Each day, the guns and beaters were divided into two parties, and these went off to separate beats as soon as the shikaris reported where kills had been found. My recollection is that there were 250 elephants acting as beaters for the King's party. It was my good fortune always to accompany his party, and I had a "front seat view" of all the sport, though I had to scamper off from the morning shoot to the lunch rendezvous to see that all was in order before the lunch interval occurred.

The guns rode in howdahs with a loader in the back seat, and the rest of us on pads. On arrival near the site of the reported kill, guns and beaters formed a circle around it. Then the beater-elephants advanced and moved to and fro trampling the bush down to make wide paths, on which the tiger would be seen by the guns when it emerged from cover. When all was ready, a couple of staunch and well trained elephants were ridden into the bush by their mahouts to rout out the tiger. This was the critical moment, and you can imagine the tension which prevailed; no one knew where or when (or, indeed if) the tiger would emerge and, when it did, it always streaked across the cleared swathes at high speed. It required a steady nerve and a good shot to get a kill. As everyone knows, the King was a magnificent shot; but there was no question of leaving a tiger for him; it was every man for himself and, although we all hoped that the first tiger would fall to his gun, it was one of the others who bagged. him. However, a little later, the King scored a right-and-left, and nobody equalled that.

Even as a mere spectator, I had my "moment". It occurred when a tiger leapt on to the head of the elephant next to mine and, as the assaulted elephant (not unnaturally) made a hasty retreat, the tiger leapt on to my elephant's rump. Luckily for me, he used it only as a springboard and streaked off into the jungle without making a meal of me. I confess that I was more than a little frightened, and all the more so because I had no gun!!

On Christmas Day, the King and the Maharaja exchanged presents. The gifts to the Maharaja included a number of modern army rifles with a copious supply of ammunition, and he gave the King a male and female of almost every species of wild animal in Nepal. The one exception of this pairing was a Tibetan wild horse, for which they had been unable to capture a mate. And was he wild?! It took six men to control him as he was paraded round for our inspection. In addition, the King received some exquisite examples of Chinese craftmanship and art.

Each night, the King invited some members of the party to dine with him, and I had the great privilege of being included on three occasions. On the last of these, he gave me a signed photograph of himself and a gold tie-pin bearing his initial surmounted by a crown set with diamonds. This occurred on the last night of his visit. Being the most insignificant member of the party, I was the last to take my leave and, as he shook hands, he most kindly thanked me for what I had done and added, "I expect, young man, that you think it is fine to be a King, but you are the lucky one. You can now go off to your comfortable bed and drop off to care-free sleep. But there" (pointing to Lord Stamfordham) "is Arthur Biggs who, the moment your back is turned, will say, 'Papers, Sir' and keep me up until after midnight!"

The shoot was a complete success and the King and his friends couldn't say enough to show their great appreciation of all that had been done for them. For me it was an unforgettable experience, beyond my wildest dreams, and I shall always remain grateful to the Maharaja for inviting me to take part in this historic occasion.

After the departure of the royal party to join Queen Mary in Calcutta, the Resident's party stayed on for a few days, and I remained with it. This time I was included among the guns, and this provided a wonderful climax to my enjoyment because I managed to shoot a rhino. I presented his head to our regimental Mess in Bakloh. Little could I guess that, 58 years later, "my" rhino would be the humble companion of the King's rhino (whose head was presented by him to his own regiment) in the Officer's Mess of our joint 14 Gorkha Training Centre in Subathu.

Before I left the Regiment, I was again to have the rare privilege of a visit to Nepal. This third visit occurred in 1931 when I went to Kathmandu, with a deputation from both our battalions, to present a sword to the Regiment's Honorary Colonel, HH the Maharaja Sir Bhim Shamsher Jang Bahadur Rana who had succeeded HH Sir Chandra in the previous year. An account of this memorable visit is given in our Regimental History (Vol 11 pp 71–73).

Today a visit to Nepal is no longer a rare privilege. Tourism plays an important part in its economy. But it is still unspoilt, still a land of mystery, of beauty, and of happy smiling folk. Pray God that it may long continue to be "just that", as I first knew it and loved it 60 years ago.

IV

Kipling's India

By Allan M. Arnott

This article appeared in *The Kipling Journal* of June 1964. The following extracts are reproduced by kind permission of The Kipling Society. The quotations are from Kipling's book of verse.

In 1907 India was still the land of *"ponies, guns and traps"* before the days of motor-cars, telephones, typewriters, etc. On arrival I joined the Cameronians in the hill station of Chakrata. Then, at the beginning of October, the Regiment marched all the way to Cawnpore, a distance of about 250 miles, which took nearly a month. The routine was exactly as portrayed in *Route Marchin'*. In those days there was no tarmac on the Grand Trunk Road and the dust was awful, but still *"there's worser things than marchin' from Umballa to Cawnpore"*, especially *"a little front of Christmas time an' just behind the Rains"*.

At the end of my year's attachment I received my posting to the 4th Gurkha Rifles, with its own permanent home at Bakloh, 4,500 feet up in the Himalayas, just 15 miles from the hill station of Dalhousie, which Kipling knew well. From the main line station of Amritsar, with its golden temple of the Sikhs, a branch line went to Pathankot, at the base of the hills, and from there the rest of the journey was made by "mail" or "special" tonga. This was a sort of low dog-cart, with two seats facing backwards. The pole had an iron crossbar, or curricle, the ends of which fitted into a notch in the saddle of each pony, and so there was always a constant jangle. Ponies were changed every four miles, the average speed over the whole journey being about 6 mph. But once into the hills it was a hard pull up for the poor ponies, and at the end of their stage they were in a muck sweat. The tonga journey to Simla as described in *As the bell clinks* is splendid. Kipling must have done this journey frequently. But it was the same for all the other roads to the hill stations.

Life was very pleasant with our two Battalions in our little home in the hills. Under an energetic CO we worked hard in the hot weather at Hill Warfare, in preparation for the chance of active service in the NW Frontier, and in the winter we marched down to the Plains for large or small scale manoeuvres. But especially we were exceedingly fortunate to take part in the Delhi Durbar of November 1911. This was surely the greatest pageant that India, or indeed any other country, has ever seen. What a kaleidoscope of colour, with thousands of troops parading in full-dress uniform, the red and blue of the British Infantry, Cavalry, and Artillery; the khaki and scarlet of the Punjab Frontier, Force (The Piffers), the green of the Rifle and Gurkha Regiments. Then the Royal Garden Party held in the marble palaces of the Moghul Kings in the old red sandstone Fort, when Their Majesties went out to a little marble kiosk on the Wall, and showed themselves to a crowd of half a million Indians milling about on the sand between the base of the wall and the river Jumna. We all lived in camps, Their Majesties in the Royal Camp, the camps of the troops with not a peg out of place, the camps of the Ruling Princes, which were lit up with coloured lights in the evening—there were even camps for the visitors. This town was set in such historic surroundings, between the Kashmir Gate and the Ridge, both the scene of such desperate fighting in the Mutiny.

Life was not all work. There was "*three days casual on the bust*", ten days' station leave, two months' privilege leave in India, and eight months' furlough every three or four years. As we lived in the hills, privilege leave to avoid the hot weather was not a necessity and was frowned on, except for big game shooting. Leave to a hill station was not granted except to married Officers, the Adjutant quoting:

> *Pleasant the snaffle of Courtship, improving to manners and carriage.*
> *But the colt who is wise will abstain from the terrible thorn-bit of marriage.*

Perhaps there was something of this mood on the long march back from manoeuvres at Delhi in 1913. All the married Officers had taken the train home to spend Christmas with their wives and families, leaving us youngsters to march the Regiment back. Christmas was deadly. It recalled the lines:

> *For "if faint and forced the laughter", and if sadness*
>   *follow after,*
> *We are richer for one mocking Christmas past.*

Next morning my great friend said "This is awful. Let's take *three days casual on the bust*, and go to Lahore for Christmas Week. I know two very pretty girls there, and we have received an invitation to join them." That was good enough for me.

Lahore, the capital of the Punjab, undergoes a complete transformation in Christmas Week. The Governor is "At Home" to his Civil Service, as a return for hospitality received during his visits of inspection all over the Province. The grounds of Government House were panoplied with large "Swiss Chalet" tents for his visitors, and every house in the Civil Lines was the same. So too the Regimental Messes in the Cantonment. There was another large camp at the Club, with its beautiful lawns and gardens, the trees festooned with fairy lights. A splendid series of entertainments was laid on. A Ball at Government House, another at the Club, Races and Polo tournaments with Regimental Bands in attendance, thédansants and picnics in full measure. Then an hour before dinner the Club bar was a rendezvous for old friends, with stories to swap and news to give. We were all made honorary members of the Club on writing our names in the book and giving our present addresses. Later on, the bill came in *"for little cards for little drinks"* that Kipling tells of.

In the mornings we would go shopping in the Mall (every Indian Cantonment has a Mall) and bazaar, where the ladies could get ribbons, *"twelve button gloves, short sixes eke"* to replace casualties at the dances.

It will be no surprise when I mention that within a year I was engaged to be married. And then the problem arose of how to find the means to maintain a wife. *"Sleery's pay was very modest"* and

TALES FROM BAKLOH

so was mine. And like Sleery, I put the problem to my in-laws.

> *So they recognised the business, and to feed and*
> *clothe the bride*
> *Got him made a Something Something somewhere on*
> *the Bombay side.*
> *Anyhow, the billet carried pay enough for him to*
> *marry—*
> *As the artless Sleery put it: "Just the thing for me and*
> *Carrie."*

In my case the appointment was to the Burma Military Police. A year later I was married in Mandalay, and we spent a year's honeymoon in a tiny outpost in the Southern Shan States, miles from anywhere. I think *Mandalay* is one of the most charming poems Kipling ever wrote. It gives such a true and delightful picture of Burma. I have been a widower now for over twenty-five years and I frequently repeat to myself: "*I've a neater, sweeter maiden in a cleaner greener land.*"

I was still serving with the Burma Military Police when the World War broke out in 1914, and we were all chafing to get back to our regiments, but the Inspector-General of Police was adamant that no one would be allowed to go without a replacement which, of course, AHQ India would not supply. So it was not until 1917 that I was able to return to India. I was posted to our 1st Battalion, which was then in Waziristan, where it had just had a very severe fight with the tribesmen, in which two officers and ninety-two Gurkha other ranks were killed and such heavy casualties were inflicted on the tribesmen that they regarded the encounter as a defeat. Although we advanced farther into the hills and destroyed a number of towers there was no more serious fighting.

Kipling has a lot to say of the North West Frontier and again his description rings true:

> *There is rock to the left, and rock to the right, and low*
> *lean thorn between,*

> *And ye may hear a breach-block snick where never a
> man is seen.*

As soon as the battalion returned to Bakloh I was posted to my own battalion in Mesopotamia, a country that Kipling never visited.

After the war I was back in Bakloh. We now had two children. On the arrival of Mark 2, I quoted in a letter to my wife from the *Ballad of East and West*:

> *And two have come back to Fort Bakloh, where there
> went forth but one.*

In 1922 I was very fortunate in being appointed Military Adviser to the Punjab States, looking after and training the small armies of the Ruling Chiefs. Here was an India that the average officer (British or Indian Army) did not know existed. The States lay off the beaten track, and the Princes maintained a feudal rule untrammelled by officialdom.

Occasionally a Chief would misbehave, when we would get a repetition of *A Legend of the Foreign Office*, when

> *Things were lively for a week in the State of Kolazai.*

After this fascinating tour of duty, I rejoined my battalion and went with it to the North West Frontier, this time to the healthy outpost of Razmak, returning to Bakloh after two years there.

And finally, retirement and that long look back towards the land which I had known as Kipling's India, until the panorama of Bombay dipped below the horizon of the Indian Ocean.

> *The Injian Ocean sets an' smiles*
> *So sof', so bright, so bloomin' blue;*
> *There arn't a wave for miles and miles*
> *Excep' the jiggle of the screw.*
> *The things that was which I'ave seen,*
> *In barrick, camp, an' action too,*

I tells them over to myself,
An' sometimes wonders if they're true.

Experiencing the peculiar

We hear many tales of people having peculiar experiences in India and perhaps this account of one of my own may lead other members to tell us of some even more interesting and peculiar events experienced by them. I have already described one peculiar experience when I saw an exhibition of firewalking (see P. P. under his name Ed.): and also another when a mountain valley deity near Bakloh answered my prayers for success in shikar.

The phenomenon that I am now about to describe took place in the holy city of Hardwar. I was doing an attachment with the 3/5th Gurkhas at the time, and the battalion was stationed in Dehra Dun in process of being disbanded. Hardwar, where the holy river Ganges emerges from the hills is, of course, a great place of pilgrimage, and the year that this event took place was one of the twelve-yearly pilgrimage years of special significance. So I and three others of the 3/5th decided to go by car to Hardwar and have a look.

Even in ordinary years Hardwar attracts an enormous number of pilgrims during the special holy time of year and on this particular twelfth-yearly holy day these must have numbered the best part of a million. So the four of us in the car found ourselves pretty well jammed in an enormous crush of people in a narrow street in the town. It was an open car with no hood and I was seated in the right hand back seat behind the driver, one Campbell by name. Beside me on the other back seat was Loupy Leonard, or just Loupy. I have forgotten the name of the fourth member of our party seated beside the driver.

We were just managing to make progress very, very slowly through the dense crowd in the narrow street when I saw, just ahead of the car bonnet, on my side of the car, a fakir: he was stark naked except for a thin coating of pale grey ash. In one hand he held a number of long thin bladed knives. I saw him take a knife and stick it all the way through his left forearm from the inside to the outside. He then changed the knives to his other hand and stuck a knife in the same way through his right forearm. He then stuck a knife right through his left leg, half way between the knee and the thigh, from the inside to the outside. He then did the same to his right leg. By this time, he was coming up just about level with the rear door of the car, when I saw him pull out his tongue and stick a knife through his tongue from the top downwards. And then I saw him take his last knife and stick it through his head. It went in just above his ear on one side and came out just above his ear on the other. And then he disappeared into the crowd behind the car. In none of these insertions was there any sign of blood nor did anyone in the crowd that jostled appear to be in the least little bit interested.

I can remember Loupy saying "Oh, my God, did you see what that chap did?" and we all four exactly agreed on what we had seen. I happened to meet Loupy (I beg your pardon, I should say Brigadier Leonard) some forty or more years later in Cheltenham when we compared old memories and he agreed exactly with the account that I have just given; so I am not just imagining things. It really did happen.

There is just one other point in regard to these peculiar experiences that I would like to mention. This particular peculiar experience and the other firewalking one sometimes make me wonder whether we are really justified in casting doubt on the credibility of certain other peculiar phenomena that we have heard about in India. After all, if one fakir can survive the sticking of knives through his arms, legs, tongue and head, with no sign of discomfort or bleeding, why should another not be capable of doing the rope trick, throwing a rope towards the sky, climbing up it and disappearing into the air? I ask you. But be that as it may, I am sure that many others have had equally or even more, peculiar experiences in India than the one that I have just described. One reason for my telling of my experience is the hope that it may induce these others also to tell of theirs.
F. E. C. H.

Lieutenant General W. D. A. Lentaigne, CB, CBE, DSO

Colonel of the Regiment 1950–1955 Died in his 56th year on the 24th June, 1955

We are privileged to introduce this appreciation of Joe Lentaigne's great service with the tribute which has been paid to him by Admiral The Earl of Mountbatten of Burma, KG, PC, GSCI, GCIE, GCVO, KCB, DSO.

Although I had known Larry Lentaigne most of my time in the Navy, I had never met his brother Joe until I came out to the South-East Asia Command. He was one of the six Brigadiers chosen by Orde Wingate to command the Long Range Penetration Brigades for the 1944 Operations behind the Japanese lines. Wingate himself introduced me to Joe Lentaigne when I visited his 111 Indian Infantry Brigade.

All the Brigadiers were outstanding men in every way; indeed, if they hadn't been, Wingate would never have chosen them, but I remember forming the early impression that Joe Lentaigne was the pick of the bunch. When on 24th March, 1944, Wingate was unfortunately killed in an aircrash in Burma, my first reaction was that Joe Lentaigne would be the man to succeed him. I found this view shared by all the responsible Generals concerned and so he was immediately appointed.

No more difficult task could be imagined than to take over such a very personal command as Wingate's. Yet Joe rose to the occasion and did it wonderfully—as all the world knows.

In 1947, when I was Viceroy of India, I was particularly anxious that Senior Officers in the British Services should remain on in India and Pakistan to help the newly divided Forces of these two countries. India suffered a particular loss in that the famous Staff College at Quetta was located in Pakistan. This meant setting up a new Staff

College—and Wellington in the South of India was chosen. At my suggestion it was made an Inter-service Staff College—Navy, Army and Air Force. The choice of the first Commandant was clearly of the utmost importance; I was delighted when Joe Lentaigne's name was put forward and strongly recommended the Government of India to accept him. So he went to Wellington and created from nothing an Inter-service Staff College which, by common consent, is one of the finest in the world. So high did they value his services that he was continuously pressed to stay on and finally did no less than seven years on the job.

I had asked him to come and see me when he got home, and I believe that almost the last letter he wrote was one to arrange an interview with me.

His passing will be mourned by his many friends, both in this country and in India—for he did a wonderful job for both.

Mountbatten of Burma

"Young David"

By E. D. Murray

Although it is by reason of my recent appointment as Liaison Officer for the Brigade of Gurkhas that I have been asked to write this tribute to Colonel R. A. N. Davidson on his retirement, no-one could detach David from the Fourth; and so it is that I find myself harking back to my earliest recollection of him.

The year was 1933 when, through the wise counsels of "Uncle Arthur" and "Colonel Scotty" in 1926–29, the two separate Battalions were fast cementing themselves into the oneness of "The Regiment" and David and his fellow Adjutant Jim Goldney were collaborating in the compilation of Regimental Standing Orders as we remember them. The occasion was a 1st Battalion Dusehra *nautch* at the conclusion of which—(I recollect it with surprising clarity!)—aseraphic David, still dressed as a *maruni*, was borne in triumph on a stretcher to Travers' bungalow, his hair (as usual on these occasions) like a cock's comb, and his voice weakly crying: "Hooray!"

Nearly 12 years were to pass before I next received any real news of David. This news, which came from officers of many regiments, British, Gurkha and Indian, who had been with David during the years of his captivity, was invariably accompanied by the highest praise of his steadfast loyalty and courage and of his constant and cheerful inspiration throughout the appalling experiences of Japanese brutality endured by the luckless prisoners who had starved and slaved alongside of him on the Siamese "railway of death."

I did not see him again until 1948 when I revisited Bakloh where he was commanding the Regimental Centre. Though slightly grey, he looked little older than the "Young David" of 1933. His greeting was typical: "But this is an occasion, old boy! We must split a bottle of the best!" So down we went together to the Mess cellar, where we discovered the last two remaining bottles of Bubbly, covered with the dust of years. The labels hardly indicated that it was "the best," but that night, drinking together in the old dining room, with the Junk and the Memorial Bell among the plate on the long mahogany table and the Rifle Brigade Shield on a wall from which B.K.'s rhino gazed at us with its sardonic stare, the contents certainly bubbled and, by reason of David's effervescent presence, tasted even better than the best.

To my mind it is fitting that David, to whom the Regiment and the men of the Regiment owe so much, should have been the last of our British Commandants and the last of the "Old Ones" to leave, and we know from Raj Bir Chopra, who almost immediately took over from him the reins of command, how happily and graciously they were handed over.

In March 1948, his mission of goodwill completed, David went to Malaya to command the British Gurkha Regimental Centre where his knowledge and influence quickly smoothed out the many jagged edges which inevitably existed so shortly after the inception of this new Brigade. By nature a master of tact, he dealt with all difficulties in his natural manner of infectiously cheerful optimism, with the result that erstwhile antagonists caught the same cheery and optimistic mood.

Two years later, to the great delight of himself and all his associates, he was appointed Chief Recruiting Officer in India of the Brigade. Here he was in his element, for he had real contact with the Gurkha of every description—the raw recruits coming straight from their villages in the hills of Nepal, the recruiters and the Depot staff and the leave men travelling from and back to Malaya, the old pensioners many of whom had served with him, and the widows and wives and mothers coming down from the hills to draw their pensions or family allotments. And he was also able to establish the most friendly relations and co-operation with his partners at the Indian Recruiting Depot at Kunraghat. He enjoyed every minute of it; but it was no easy job. He arrived just as the Western Depot was about to move to Lehra; he played a major part in the recent establishment of the Eastern Depot at Jalapahar; he was closely involved in the negotiations which have led to the transfer of both these Depots across the border into Nepal, and was responsible for the preliminary arrangements connected with the establishment of these Depots on Nepalese soil.

The debt owed to him by the Brigade of Gurkhas has yet to be realised to the full. We have so much to thank him for.

And now, after 33 years of devoted and unsparing service to the Regiment, to the Gurkha and, finally, to the Brigade of Gurkhas David has retired, and will shortly join the ranks of the *buros* in England where his many friends are eagerly waiting to greet him.

Aiyu! Sidharne bela bhayo! Hajurle gariako bes bho!

Alas! The time of departure has come! Well and truly have you done your work!

A Piper Remembers

By Andrew Gow

(This article is derived from a letter sent by the author, who now lives in New South Wales, to Lt-Col John Masters last year. *Ed*)

You will be puzzled why I, a complete stranger, should write to you. There are two reasons—firstly to congratulate you on all your books (and, most of all, your autobiography); and secondly because of my own connection with the 4th Prince of Wales' Own Gurkha Rifles in Bakloh.

You may have seen in your Officers' Mess Album a photograph of the Pipers of 1st and 2nd Battalions of your Regiment. On their right stands a Pipe Corporal of the Highland Light Infantry. I am that man. I was sent up to Bakloh in March 1932 at the request of your Commanding Officer (Lt-Col Ninian Graeme) to my Commanding Officer (Col McCallum, DSO) of the 2nd HLI to bring the Pipes and Drums of your Regiment's two battalions up to a higher standard. My instructions were particularly concerned with the Pipers because Drums and Bugles were not in my line apart from their drill.

I think that your 1st Battalion was on the frontier, but they sent their band down for instruction. Your 2nd Battalion had recently returned from Razmak, where I was soon to serve in the Razmak Brigade under Brigadier Mills, DSO, who was, I think, an ex 2/4 Gurkha officer like yourself.

After getting off the railway at Pathankot I got on a bus—the usual ramshackle vehicle one saw in India in those days. I was put down at some point on the roadway which, as far as I could see, led nowhere but was evidently well known to the bus driver and about a dozen Gurkhas dressed in little pill-box caps, black jackets and hose, and white shorts. There followed the greatest yabbering, pushing and shoving to get a share in carting my gear from the bus up a steep khud track to the lower parade ground. I was taken to the Officers' Mess, where I was met by Major D. M. Murray-Lyon, DSO, MC, a former Major in the 2nd Highland Light Infantry who used to be a piper himself as a younger officer. He showed me where I was to be billeted and introduced me to Mr Adams, the Bandmaster—and what a wonderful man he was. I loved to hear him talk of the old army days—of the Delhi Durbar and other events. His patience and encouragement with young bandsmen were an inspiration to me.

I had been sent up to do a job, and I had the satisfaction of leaving both bands more proficient than they were when I arrived. The time limit was the biggest problem, so I had to give the seniors most practice so that they could impart it after I had gone. Mostly I was left to my own devices because Major Murray-Lyon was a busy man and could only see us at short intervals.

The trained piper knew the correct notes of the tunes and, in some degree, the intricate movements before and after the melody notes. So, I would play (say) "Glenogh Highlanders" Quickstep, his quick ear caught the melody, and in a little while he would be playing it; though he might be able to say the name, he would describe it to the younger ones as: "Number 11 March" (or whatever number he decided). They would squat in a circle, and I would accompany one on the chanter; then on to the next one; finally all together. Time was nothing to them if they were learning, and I never appreciated an audience more.

It was always a proud moment for me when I led the Pipe Majors round your Officers' Mess table on your weekly Guest Night. I shall always remember the look of affection on their faces as I played the Pibroch round the table and, after handing my pipes to the Mess Havildar, took the quaich of good Scotch whisky from Col Graeme, gave the toast in the Highland way, drank it and marched slowly but with a dignified bearing back into the ante-room. Sometimes a show would be put on after dinner on the Mess lawn, when the Gurkhas would give Nepalese dances, in which some would be dressed as women; they looked so feminine that only a Gurkha or one of yourselves could tell the difference.

Col Graeme and his officers were most kind and helpful to me—

for instance, I had my meals in the Officers' Mess Library. Knowing the set-up in some British regiments, I thought that this was one of the nicest acts ever done to me, for I sometimes experienced very different treatment in my soldiering days (*not* in the HLI, in which we were treated far above the usual run of those days), so you will realise how I felt when I was allowed this great privilege. Being a bookish man, particularly for Army history, I felt I was in a veritable literary paradise, and I would peruse old military journals piled on top of the book cupboards.

At that period I was completing a rough layman's History of the Pipers of the 71st and 74th Highlanders, which I nearly finished before I left Bakloh. On my discharge from the HLI in 1934, I presented it to the Regiment.

As I read your last book, *The Road Past Mandalay*, your superb description of the scenic beauties of the Himalayas took me back in memory to Bakloh—to that wide enclosed verandah looking out towards the West, with the sun sinking far beyond the plains, through which the Five Rivers glinted their courses beyond the foot-hills silhouetted against the sinking sun. All of it a brilliant picture which will always be young in my mind.

I remember too my many walks along the khud sides past the Gurkha Officers' Mess and the married quarters. I loved those early morning walks, with the sun rising on all the beauty of the hills; and, around every bend in the track, there would be another view as often as not more wonderful than the last.

It was not uncommon to see a small group of Gurkhas with their "sacrificial" tools of trade—one goat, one kukri, one sapling and a piece of rope. I thought, and still think, that this was as efficient as the twentieth century method—*and* much cheaper. Anyhow, the Gurkhas loved it.

I joined the army as a Boy Piper at the age of 15 in 1919. It seems a long time now since I stepped off the troopship at Bombay in January 1921. I found a country which was to whet my appetite for new discoveries such as I never dreamt of and which I have carried with me ever since I departed its shores in 1934. Like yourself, I have seen India from the soldier's point of view, and have had the good with the bad, and I am happy to say that one unforgettable assignment in my career—one which I would not swop for anything—was my visit to the 4th PWO Gurkha Rifles in Bakloh.

My Biography of Nihility
or
How Hamish helped Britain to lose her Empire

I'll tell you every thing I can—
There's little to relate;
For what can happen in a span
Spent sitting on a gate?

To go back to the beginning—I was conceived, as I calculate, on Malabar Hill, Bombay, in the closing year of the last century, which may have fore-determined my returning to India (and also perhaps my seeking a wife there, for Mesha was born at Parel, the Mofussil adjoining Indabar.)

We both had grandparents living in India, Mesha's grandfather being Presidency Senior Chaplain in Madras—as my father was in Bombay. He, my father, married the daughter of a Colonel in the HEI Company's service who was the son-in-law of General Dobbie, the GOC Madras (from whom also came he of the sword and Bible in Malta—and our own Nangles!)

Both Dobbies, grandfather and father, had served India in the RN, the former being killed at Pondicherry in 1761, so that my inclination to return may have been implanted long before Malabar Hill, and too much can be made of such prenatal influences, for though my grandfather served at Lucknow in the Mutiny, I never bothered to stop off there. But from earliest consciousness we all of us knew what we were to do. Mother had decided that: she knew what her brothers had done and had liked doing, and what had suited them must probably suit us. Not a bad plan.

What can a boy know about life or about anything until long after he has begun? Eye on the ball from the beginning, no shilly-shallying.

By and large it worked out pretty well.

We went to the village school at first in Holland where we were at the time and later in Scotland; something I tended to play down as a Cadet instead of proclaiming it proudly—for had not the Napiers done the same for the same reasons?

We went on to Woolwich or Sandhurst or the University (as budding Imperial foresters), I being sent to Sandhurst's then Indian overflow college at Quetta.

We had all been keen Scouts (good training for movement in the jungle) and those of us concerned keen Home Guardsmen or whatever they were called.

I was commissioned from Quetta into the 107th Pioneers, a Regiment in which (as I discovered AFTER I had selected and joined it) another of the family had served before me.

A word here about the old Indian Pioneer Regiments for they are not understood now in this country where the term has been applied to Corps of Military labourers. In India they were the elite of the Army—Gurkhas not excepted. Pioneer Regiments were organised, equipped and trained to fight as infantry but in addition they were skilled engineers with a complement of craftsmen and specialist tools and stores. No Force or Frontier Expedition was ever assembled without a Pioneer Regiment and consequently they saw more service than most. They offered a full and interesting life and were eagerly sought after.

Sadly the war had concluded when I joined but disturbances continued—the 3rd Afghan War and then the Arab rebellion on the fringes of both of whi ch we were employed, at least under conditions of active service, in the Bolan Pass, on the East Persian Cordon and in Mesopotamia which offered detachment duty, lots of variety and a great deal of fun.

At the end of all this I got married much to the disappointment of my CO who said I ought to have gone to Staff College first—but that was something I never did, much preferring pig-sticking and hunting!

Agra, Poona, Nowshera; and then the Red Shirt Movement began—the tribesmen revolted, invaded Peshawar and were denied their grazing grounds on the Kajuri Plain until they submitted. But meanwhile Burma had rebelled and I applied to join the Military Police Force there, source of worthwhile pickings for impecunious officers as well as of excitement and romantic surroundings.

After two years, and just as I was emerging from the red by living on the Chinese Frontier, all Pioneer Regiments were disbanded to the regret of every Indian General since and I being posted to the 4th Gurkhas had to return to Bakloh, which I reached in plenty of time for the Faqir of IPI's insurrection in Waziristan. While still in Waziristan I was asked to return to Burma: I had quitted it unwillingly but now it was not without misgivings that I went back—misgivings that grew as the threat of war grew nearer.

I kicked myself for a fool but need not have done so for the gods can be good, wonderfully, even to fools; and suddenly, dramatically, the Japs actually invaded our backwater.

Again I was on the far eastern Frontier, not as a Military Policeman, though, but as a Burma Rifleman, expecting the enemy to attack Kentung. He did not and we were recalled hurriedly to meet him on the Sittang only to become involved in that humilating withdrawal that ended at Imphal, which I have to confess I reached before my wife did!

This was followed by a very interesting assignment in the Chin Hills but early in the following year I was given command of the 4th Battalion. And the rest you know.

Much of it was very pleasant idleness. Where I wonder does one learn soldiering—or does one? And what, I wonder, would Staff College have led to? An AQ job somewhere which I should have hated.

I suppose something seeps in through the skin in surroundings and situations that have grown familiar, as the Bradford man said of money—"I don't make it, I just picks it oop."

A little through reading, perhaps, watching other men work or scraps you hear them let fall. Mostly that—men like M. L. and Marjoribanks (a Pioneer). One such remark I set a lot of store by was:

"If it's a fine day take your cloak with you." It was said by a shepherd in the Home Guard.

And so on and so on. Amen.

J. N. M.

Hugh Moule at Rawalpindi

By Arthur Panter

It is a privilege to be asked to write a few words about Hugh Moule, just as it was a privilege to serve for a time under his command in the years following the battalion's return to India from Italy.

Colonel Moule took over command from Colonel Stone as the 10th Indian Division, still under Denys Reid, took up its new dual role in Rawalpindi, as North West Frontier Reserve and as the Internal Security Force in that area.

About this time, I was promoted from IO to Adjutant (chiefly, it seemed, on the grounds that I couldn't find the missing War Diary of the latter part of the Italian campaign!) and David Henry was promoted to Quartermaster. If my memory serves me correctly George Inglis was second in command and other Company commanders at various times were Bob Crichton, Dixie Dean, Eric Stretton, Maurice Biggs, Busty Hayes, Monty Metcalfe, Arthur Davey and John Emerson-Baker. Bill Turner was around for a time and among a full supporting cast were various people with walking-on parts like Peter Attack for whom, though we did not know it then, a high military destiny was reserved!

These were some of the ingredients in Hugh Moule's Rawalpindi command. He knew that this was for an "interim period" and that ultimately David Davidson would be taking over.

Hugh Moule's style was that of the heroic rather than the solid and patient and he emerged quite quickly as, possibly, the most dashing of the 10th Brigade battalion commanders at that time.

The Division was undergoing training for frontier warfare and regularly marching out on daily manoeuvres (TEWTs and JEWTs* were now history) picketing hills from a central column.

Hugh with great panache would address the battalion in the late afternoon, (as ready with appreciative as with adverse criticism), see the companies on the march, drive with me in his jeep ahead of the troops, ostensibly to catch up on office work, but in fact to have a quick gin and tonic before taking the salute as the column marched back into the lines.

Not only was the battalion particularly happy during that period but it was again emerging as a unit respected throughout the division. This was reflected on a murderous Brigade exercise in August 1946 (117° in the shade) when scores of unacclimatised Enniskillens, and many Baluchis too had to be evacuated with heat-exhaustion to Pindi hospital. Hugh was able to say that not one of the Gurkhas had faltered throughout the march.

On occasions like that, Hugh Moule seemed to go out of his way to affect the non-hero. Not for him the role of the last man to take his boots off or to accept an early mug, of tea! But those who knew him got the special message and the sort of leadership it spelt out. Strangely enough, when David Davidson took over, the style was reversed though both were equally appreciated and equally effective.

Hugh Moule had a style and humour of his own certainly. He affected always to be up against "Sod's Law". He affected to be deafened by the pipes in mess dinners, to be no enthusiast for the Highland sound: indeed he pretended to see Scottishness, Welshness or Irishness as a source of emotionalism which contrasted with what we now call "cool". Certainly at the dances and balls which were then on the increase, we were treated to much Irish Dancing by the "Skins" and certainly Hugh Moule enjoyed disliking it.

* June Exercise without trees.

First, Jill Crichton arrived and Bob withdrew, presumably to some local villa or bungalow. Then, on a memorable morning, Hugh appeared in my office with a telegram. His wife had arrived in Bombay with the children! Pleasure and concern played across the Rex Harrison-like features! The world was changing!

Well—we all saw him off to Bombay. The party began at the Officers' Club and was continued at the Rawalpindi Railway Station Restaurant where an elderly retiring general, who was catching the same train, was buying sentimental drinks for everyone in sight at an enormous rate. There were tears in his eyes.

"Hold on a bit, Sir," said Hugh. "No need to go at it like a bull at a gate! I've got a couple of bottles of gin in my bag!"

"Don't worry!" said the General, "we can get some more at Lahore!"

Subsequently, Hugh's wife arrived at Rawalpindi and, like Jill, became a delightful part of battalion life.

When David Davidson arrived, Hugh Moule stepped down to the second-in-command position with that particular style and grace which characterised him. He was loyal and supportive and as a result of that concern, David, long years as a prisoner, was able to emerge as the powerful leader he was.

Hugh was a regular soldier, Sandhurst-trained in peacetime. But he was untypical. He loved to remind one of a life outside barracks and bugles. There was his Shakespeare period for instance, when he would delight to be seen at breakfast with King Lear or Hamlet propped up against the coffee pot. "Damned marvellous stuff this you know—this chap could certainly write!" and he'd treat us to a piece of dialogue from the bard whilst we edged away to our more mundane interests.

He was a delightful man, tall, angular and with the sudden charm of the nicer old Etonians. But he was fair and honest and certainly not lacking in imagination. A great companion, and, I must repeat, as gracious in stepping down to the position of second-in-command as he was stepping up to don the cloak of leader.

I shall always remember Hugh Moule and Rawalpindi with both affection and admiration.

POW on the Siam Burma Railway

Robert and Tony have asked me to give you some comments on life as a POW on the Japanese railway to connect Siam with Burma. You should read them in conjunction with "Some experiences of Prisoners of War" given in Appendix 11 of Volume III of our History, so ably compiled by Hamish. After 40 years, alas, memory for details does not serve, and many years ago I destroyed the jottings on which I made them soon afterwards. Maybe there's a moral in this!

The start was inauspicious because after surrender the very first order the Japanese gave was "Asians here: Europeans there" thus frustrating the intention of the officers to stand by their Indian ranks in captivity. Treatment by their front line troops was reasonably correct; but very degrading on being interviewed by the Kempei Tai (Military Police) in the former leprosy barracks near Johore Bahru. A few of us were beaten up, to help our memories, with steel cored dog whips, tied to trees through the night during which it rained tightening up the cords. Not a pleasant foretaste of "things to come".

We were sent back in lorries by stages to Kuala Lumpur where we were herded into part of Pudu Gaol, incidentally having the best accommodation of the whole $3\frac{1}{2}$ years, as it was a British built prison for criminals.

Recently, it was the scene of hanging of two convicted white drug smugglers for which Malaysia still retains the death penalty. Two officers chose to sleep on the "drop" during our eight months there in order to relieve the overcrowding, with no ill effect on their dreams. The food provided was minimal: broken and husked rice with a minute portion of Kong Kang, a Chinese edible weed comparable to carrot tops, twice a day, with one issue of tea dust. Nothing else, not even salt. No wonder we worried at first about the absence of an urge to go to the "loo"; the MO's told us not to report sick until we had had an unsuccessful absence of nine days. There were a few doctors and dentists amongst us, but all their medicines and equipment were taken off them at surrender and nothing replaced. The Japanese consider a sick or wounded man a definite liability, tending to hinder military operations and unworthy of spending other than the minimum of effort to cure or even attend. Work consisted mainly of clearing up various areas of the town and at this time the Japanese were not too vicious in their treatment.

At the end of October 1942 all fit men were taken in overcrowded cattle trucks, up to Nong Pladuk in Siam, the base for the railway being constructed over the Three Pagodas Pass to join up with the line being built from Burma. Here our guards were Koreans under Japanese NCOs and officers who were cruel and sadistic to say the least, and who themselves were treated very badly by their Japanese Superiors; no-one was allowed to become more than a Lance Cpl. Work was hard and continuous, but just bearable, during the period along the plain. Once the line took to the hills, engineering difficulties arose and they found themselves well behind the schedule laid down by AHQ in Tokyo. A "speedo" was ordered and the railway completion date advanced to end November 1943. This involved work hours up to sixty at a stretch through heat and rain, and frequently "to make up numbers" the sick from the hospital were ordered to be carried out on stretchers, and lay there all day through all weathers. No amount of complaining to the Japanese, on the score of appalling man-managements, elicited other than "there are plenty more where you came from" and this of course included officers who had also had to work as coolies. These events went on until the railway was finished and joined up with that from Burma; even then maintenance parties had to be left along its entire length. It had cost 17,500 white POWs their lives out of 45,000 employed; whilst 50,000 coolies, who were administered and accommodated separately, died. These numbers speak for themselves of the utter callousness and complete waste of human life and resources involved in this utterly futile engineering feat.

A single line in many areas travelling through jungle and long the river course was an ideal target for the Allied aircraft, who waited until a considerable amount of rolling stock collected above several bridges and then effectively bombed them denying the use of the whole system for weeks on end. We had complete air superiority in this far distant theatre of their so called "Co-Prosperity Sphere".

Various aspects of life include these comments: food consisted of two meals a day based on the same broken and husked rice with occasional local vegetables and sometimes a little meat. The trouble with rice only is it makes you feel satisfied for a short while after eating, but soon, you are hungry again and had to wait a long time to the next meal. Most of us though still enjoy good quality rice to this day, even after having nothing else for so long. Containers of rice were slung on bamboo poles for outside parties.

Accommodation consisted of huts approximately 110 yards long and holding about 200 men, constructed of bamboo poles, the ridge pole being about 30 feet high and roof cambered steeply. The whole was thatched with dried palm leaves called attap; they rotted in wet weather, drying to tinder in the sun, but were usually weatherproof, unless failing to overlap sections.

Clothing was "non est" for working parties, most wearing G-strings only and staying very brown in consequence. In camp the minimum of over-patched garments were worn specially so since no replacements were available.

Medical facilities and equipment did not exist at all having been confiscated on surrender. Jungle ulcers frequently resulted in amputations, without anaesthetic, using any sterilized knife and even razor blades on occasion. Excellent descriptions of the medical side and its complications are set out in Dr Robert Hardie's "The Burma-Siam Railway", based on his personal notes successfully recovered after the war and immensely recommended as informative reading.

Discipline and morale kept very high amongst everyone, as life itself depended on maintaining them as such. Everyone realising that the few basic unwritten rules had to be obeyed on mutual help and general good behaviour. Any grousing or grumbling was stamped on immediately, before it led to depression, which had to be avoided at all costs. I would stress how good the other ranks particularly were to one another, denying themselves in support of pals.

Punishments and Brutality. Escaping was impossible, those who did try were all caught quickly and executed after the equivalent of a Court Martial. There were thousands of miles to go before reaching Allied lines and almost every movement gave you away to locals, rewarded with large sums of paper money by the Japanese. Some of the tortures by the Kempei Tai were too horrible to even hint at, for those unlucky enough to be suspected or caught: few lived to tell of their ordeals. An example of brutal camp punishment was that given to three officers of a pay collecting party from well up-river who were caught with written accounts of the latest war news at one of the down country camps owning a secret set; they were all beaten to death with heavy bamboo poles and their bodies thrown into the latrines. They had, though, given nothing away as to the source. Lesser punishments were long hours standing to attention outside the guard room day and night, with nothing to eat or drink.

Recreational activities were nil. Everyone was far too exhausted each day to do other than try to rest on return to camp.

Health for the most part was dependent upon avoiding the many tropical fevers and deficiency diseases, also cholera and dysentery, brought on by inadequate food, infected water and excessive hard work. Very few of us escaped without acquiring several of them, time and again.

There was no mail until the final year when a trickle was allowed through. We sent our first printed postcards only after $2\frac{1}{2}$ years, and then merely one a quarter. One copy of a local Siamese newspaper in English was given to POW Camp HQ occasionally; it was naturally censored heavily before printing. We did have a wireless set in most of the camps I was in; being Adjutant in most of them I was able to keep contact with the main one, run by two Rubber Planters brothers, during any moves. Many were the expedients for keeping it secret, listening in only very occasionally and giving out the news sparingly, saying it had come in through working parties' contacts with locals. Now and then a dead battery had to be exchanged with a live one off a Japanese lorry.

We had one issue of Red Cross personal parcels during the whole $3\frac{1}{2}$ years and that on the basis of one between ten men, minus the cigarettes which the guards took beforehand. Being most concentrated, and our tummies being unused to such delicacies, dire results ensued.

On one occasion early in 1945 a German Red Cross representative visited us. He spoke English and appeared dismayed at what he saw and what we had to tell him. However, nothing changed as a result of it and no-one further came.

Personalities, of all the prisoners and few locals I met, four stand out vividly; the first was Lt Col Philip Toosey, RA, commanding 135 Fd Regt, who was Commandant of Tamarkam and Nong Pladuk camps from October 1942 to January 1945 and again the final camp in French Indo-China through to release. In private life he was an executive member of Baring Brothers and the Liverpool Cotton Exchange, and after the war was made a Knight Bachelor for his services to them. He was superb in his handling of the Japanese and Koreans, also POWs, specially in troubled times, which he summed up afterwards in saying "I felt I had a mission not only to save as many lives as possible, but also to maintain human dignity in those ghastly circumstances".

The second was Captain David Boyle of the Argyll and Sutherland Highlanders, Toosey's Adjutant in Tamarkam and joint Adjutant with me at Nong Pladuk and the final camp. He taught himself Japanese early on and was quite invaluable in sorting awkward situations, being completely fearless. Curiously, we came together again a few days before he died, through Hamish, as he was then a Colonel and an inspired and beloved commandant of Princess Louise Scottish Hospital for ex-Servicemen and women at Erskine, Bishopton in Renfrewshire, to which Hamish had recently been admitted on a permanent basis. Alas, there was time for an exchange of letters only before he "crossed the Bar".

A curiously remarkable Siamese merchant from Kanchanburi, where one of our plains camps was situated, is the third man. His name was Boon Pong Sirivejjabhandu, known to all by his first two names only. He was an underground agent and a captain in the

Free Siam Army. He supplied many camps at the Southern end of the railway with such rations as the Japanese allowed; also at great personal risk cashed cheques with which he brough in secret and badly needed medical supplies for the hospital and also advanced money against any remaining personal valuables for the same purpose, which he scrupulously redeemed after the War. He was awarded the George Medal for his services and courage.

The last was a Briton, Ken Gairdner, who had married a Siamese woman and had retired in Bangkok permanently. He was the focus of a communications system from us to the outside world, initially organised by him through a lorry driver in the RASC who drove the Japanese NCOs into the nearest town each week, Bampong; through him to his own senior officer in Nong Pladuk camp. Alas, this officer was killed in an Allied air raid on the camp, and the job fell on me as Adjutant to continue sending the reports on our life and conditions. These were hidden by the driver in certain specified pre-arranged places and picked up by Ken Gairdner's house servant, who had previously placed Ken's report for us on world and war happenings, at the same place. Ken was in an internment camp and allowed his wireless and comparative freedom, his wife was not interned, or restricted in any way and was friendly with the wife of the French Consul at Saigon, who passed our news to the outside world by diplomatic means. The curious fact was that the servant, in our eyes, stood out as being unusual in the extreme: he was Chinese, wore a white solar topee, had a large prominent wart on his face and dressed in semi-European clothes. Yet to Asian and Japanese eyes in particular, he could not have aroused suspicion, since he was never questioned, let alone picked up!

Finally, came the news from a Japanese officer that the war was over and, I echo the aforementioned Dr Robert Hardie's diary 17th August 1945: "one's emotions were almost numb, after such long suppression of hopes and fears. One could hardly realise that the moment for which one had waited with such desperate but such doubtful hopes had come at last. It was over: we were free again and would soon be in touch with the outside world, home. It was almost impossible to grasp. At such a moment surely one should feel some overwhelming emotion; one just felt rather numb, rather shaky and rather inclined to sob. 'Human deeds have their tears and mortality touches the heart'; Virgil's Aeneid—that nebulous expression of half-comprehended emotion seemed exactly to express one's feeling, as one tried to grasp what had happened ... and as one thought of friends who had earlier looked forward to the same release but had found a different one: men who had died in hospital, in despair or snuffed out suddenly like the miner from Dalkeith, that night in February 1943". Then again, the Gunner Officer who on reaching home included "those who had experienced the most terrible of ironies: wives who had re-married and sweethearts who had not waited: regarding those they loved as not only missing, but probably dead".

R. A. N. D.

Prisoners of War in Italy

These are only the recollections of one person, in three camps out of many, but they are probably representative of the majority.

We flew from Benghazi to the heel of Italy, and thence by train to Camp 66 at Capua, near Naples. This was a collection of wooden huts, surrounded by barbed wire, and next to a larger compound occupied by British troops.

It was supposed to be a short stay transit camp, but the Italians were overwhelmed by prisoners in mid 1942, and we lived there for five and a half months, overcrowded, with inadequate washing and latrine facilities, bitten badly by fleas, bed bugs, mosquitoes and flies, and assuming a forced hilarity to overcome boredom and depression. Boards on trestles, coir-filled "biscuits" and blankets were our bedding. But however depressing and debilitating our camp life may have been, it bore no comparison with the misery of life under the Japs.

The Geneva Convention required the segregation of nationalities but in this Camp, apart from British Officers, we had nearly all our own GOs, Indian VCOs from various units, a Rhodesian, some South Africans, a Jugoslav and one or two Free French.

We soon discovered that even officers could be dishonest. Scarce soap left in a basin or freshly washed underwear drying on a line disappeared if not watched. We also found that senior officers could be as niggly as children over very petty things.

Every Camp had its escape committee (and probably, also, one or more "stool pigeons", who kept the enemy informed) and there were two unsuccessful escape attempts here, both of which resulted in the virtual murder, by shooting at close range on the ground, of two BOs and a BOR.

We received Red Cross parcels only at irregular intervals, but those we had were vital, as the Italian food was poor and insufficient. There were no recreational facilities, and playing Bridge or fashioning mugs out of Red Cross tins were the only diversions. About once a week they let us out for walks in the countryside, surrounded by guards. There were two roll calls a day.

In November 42 we were moved North by train to Camp 17, Rezzanello, a 19th century castle on a hillside near Piacenza. This was a great improvement: our guards were northerners, and better built and clothed than the scruffy little swarthy Neapolitans, we had only three or four to a room, decent beds with sheets and blankets, BOR prisoners who acted as batmen, and the wherewithal to produce amateur concerts; Red Cross parcels arrived more regularly and were centralised in the kitchen and prepared with our rations by British cooks. Our only forms of exercise were walking round a small courtyard or playing volleyball in it.

We were allowed to write one post card and one letter a week and they and the replies from home usually arrived, through the blessed Red Cross. Each Camp had its own newsrag, compiled from scraps of information; and we received Italian newspapers, which we read with several grains of salt. All mail was censored and the covers of books were often ripped off, but occasional messages still got through before the Camp Censor had seen it, and some of us learned to copy the Censor's stamp with a paint brush.

In March 43 we were moved again, to a new Camp near

Fontanellato (No 49) in the plains near Parma. It had been built by the Church pre-war as an orphanage, and was a four storey brick building. We were joined by officers from other Camps and eventually rose to about 620 souls.

We were given a largish field at the back of the building to use as an exercise ground, and there we held athletics meetings, boxing tests, Rugger and Soccer games and various other sports, with machine guns covering us from watch towers. We were also allowed out for walks once a week, under guard and on parole.

The Comandante believed that if we were given enough to do we would keep out of trouble, so we were allowed much in the way of art requisites and materials for plays and concerts. Exercise, art, reading, lectures, cards, studying languages, and producing and taking part in concerts were the best ways to keep cheerful. With the addition of Red Cross parcels, food was sufficient, and centrally cooked by BORs.

Five officers made clever and daring escapes, two on one night and three more some 72 hours later, but all were recaptured within a few days and spent a month in solitary confinement. All of us knew they had gone but, in spite of two careful roll calls a day and checks at night, we managed to conceal it from the Italians for about three days.

We had always taken the mickey out of the Italians whenever possible, but they were fairly free with their bullets and we knew they could always have the last laugh. During the Dieppe raid, in 1942, the Canadians were said to have tied the hands of the German prisoners to stop them escaping and, for a while, the Italians threatened to do the same to us.

In each Camp there were British Medical Officers, with limited facilities, while the seriously sick or injured were treated by Italian doctors or hospitals.

The Senior British Officer had organised us into a Battalion of five companies and, following the fall of Mussolini in July 43, prepared us for a possible exodus. In some way he managed to obtain reliable information from outside, and so was ready when Badoglio signed his Armistice on 8th September '44. Some Camps were surrounded by the Germans before their inmates could escape, but we left the Camp next day, just half an hour before the Huns arrived. Our subsequent adventures were described in the last issue.

R. N. D. W.

Brigadier Harold Bell Kingsley, CIE, DSO

President of our Association, March 1959–April 1970 Died in his 85th year on the 15th April 1970

Harold Kingsley, who will always be affectionately remembered as "B-K", came of a military family. His grandfather had retired as a Major in the North Staffordshire Regiment; his father commanded the old 67th (2nd Battalion, the Royal Hampshire Regiment) at the capture of Mandalay in 1886, and his uncle who was a Sherwood Forester was killed in the Crimea at the Battle of Alma; his elder brother died in 1909 when Adjutant of the newly raised 2/10 Gurkha Rifles.

He was born in Tipperary on the 23rd December, 1885 and, though educated in England at Harpenden Preparatory School and Bedford Modern School, his home remained there until he was commissioned from Sandhurst in 1905, and it was there that he gained his love of shooting, hunting and fishing.

Even in his boyhood he had set his heart on joining a Gurkha Regiment. This ambition had considerable bearing on his career at Sandhurst, into which he passed in the lowly place of 126th. He passed out 13th which assured him of acceptance in the Indian Army. During his year on the Unattached List with the Gloucestershire

Regiment (which, appropriately, he joined on St Patrick's Day, 1905) he was stationed at Ambala and Subathu, and met our 2nd Battalion on manoeuvres. Its CO at that time was Colonel Philip Camegy who, as a subaltern had been in the 2nd Hampshires when B-K's father was commanding it. This naturally resulted in a request to be allowed to join the Regiment, and he was duly posted to the 2nd Battalion in August, 1906.

Three years later he went to Kathmandu for six months to train the British Resident's escort. This led to his services being requested by the Maharaja of Nepal in connection with arrangements at the shooting camps prior to, and during, the visit to Nepal of HM King George V after the Coronation Durbar in 1911. His own most interesting account of these two assignments has been published in our News Letters Nos. 20 and 21.

In 1912, he became Adjutant of the 2nd Battalion and was holding this appointment when it went to Mesopotamia in February, 1916. The battalion joined the 35th Brigade, which had been reduced by casualties and sickness to a strength of 750. In May, the Brigade was taken over by Brigadier "Wiggy" Thomson, MC, a Seaforth Highlander in his late thirties, who selected him as his Staff Captain. In February of the following year, when the fighting on the River Hai was at its height, the Brigade Major was killed and B-K succeeded him, of the happy and efficient partnership which prevailed in 35th Brigade, the constant success which attended its operations speaks for itself.

In 1918, on the conclusion of active operations in Mesopotamia, he rejoined the battalion as its Second-in-Command and accompanied it to Salonica and, subsequently, to the Caucasus and Turkey. When the battalion returned to Bakloh in November, 1920, after four and a half years overseas, he was one of the only four officers who had sailed with it to Basra in February, 1916.

His outstanding service was recognised by the award of the DSO and Mention in Despatches in 1917, and a second "Mention" in 1918.

In November, 1921, he was transferred to the 1st Battalion as its Second-in-Command. He joined the battalion in Waziristan, and the part which he played in the operations at Makin and in connection with the abandonment of Wana in 1923 was again recognised by his receiving Mention in Despatches.

In the following year, when the battalion was in Bakloh, he commanded the detachment of two companies hastily summoned to Nabha in aid of the civil power. The furnishing of this aid reached a critical pitch when a mob, 6,000 strong, approached Jaito with the object of seizing its shrine. After the State troops and police had suffered several casualties to no avail in their attempt to halt the mob, our detachment was called upon to take action. Using the minimum force (35 rounds of controlled fire), the situation was quickly brought under control. For his humane and effective services, B-K received the appreciation of the Government of India.

Those were the days when the 1st Battalion gained a high reputation at football and hockey, and this was extended to tennis when, in 1926, he partnered Rorie Hartwell to win the Doubles in the Army Tennis Championships at Delhi.

In 1929 he became CO of the 1st Battalion, which he commanded for four years in Waziristan, Bakloh and Peshawar. In 1931 he again visited Nepal at the head of the deputation which, on behalf of the Regiment, presented a sword to the Maharaja who, in succession to his brother, had been appointed Honorary Colonel of the Regiment in the previous year. His 25 years' service in the Regiment ended in 1933 with his appointment as Deputy Military Secretary at Army Headquarters.

To quote his own words from a personal letter: "My life in the Regiment, with its glorious traditions, has been one of complete happiness in which I have made many and lasting friendships. I had the good fortune to serve in both battalions and, when I left, my heart was too full for words."

After three years at AHQ, he became the Indian Military Academy's Second Commandant in succession to Brigadier L. P. Collins, DSO. Again we quote from one of his letters: "The imprint of Peter Collins" personality on everyone—British Officers and NCO's, and Cadets alike—was plain to see. The Academy pulsated with youth, energy and ambition, and the whole atmosphere was one of a happy home in which the good name of the Academy was paramount. It was a sad day when I said 'Goodbye' to such a happy life in such a lovely place". How fully he maintained that high standard is evident from the lasting affection and respect of his old Cadets, many of whom have gained high distinction in their army careers.

Materially, he also made a lasting contribution. "I was much impressed", he wrote, "by a description of a library which had been built at Oundle School, and applied to AHQ to have a similar library built at the IMA." His request was turned down by the Commander-in-Chief on the grounds of finance; but, shortly after this, the Finance Member of the Viceroy's Council visited the IMA. Needless to say, B-K won, and the Library was not only built on the lines of the one at Oundle, but the Foundation Stone was laid by the C-in-C. He also designed the garden of the Commandant's House which was cleared out of rough ground and completed under his supervision and is still being beautifully maintained.

In the King's Birthday Honours in 1939, he received the well-merited award of the CIE.

On his retirement in June 1939, he and Olive Kingsley did a leisurely tour via Colombo, Penang, Bangkok, Saigon, Singapore, Java, Australia, New Zealand, Fiji and Honolulu on their way home. War broke out as they reached Los Angeles, and he promptly sent cables to AHQ and the India Office, which elicited no reply. He therefore telephoned to New York for a passage to England, and was allocated one early in October. They spent the intervening month touring in America and Canada.

On arrival in England, he again referred to the India Office for orders, only to be informed that he was in a "pool". He decided to fend for himself by writing to General Bartholomew, the GOC Northern Command, whom he had known in Delhi. The reply came by telephone: "Come here at once", the immediate outcome being that he was sent to Morpeth in Northumberland with orders to create an office as "Quartering Commandant, Northumberland" and to requisition whatever accommodation was needed. Not exactly an easy assignment!

Two days later he was in business again with a staff of one clerk (obtained through the Labour Exchange), a good supply of stationery (by personal purchase), and his HQ in a bedroom of The Queen's Head Hotel. Within the space of a week he had made his number with the local military commander, been provided with a car and two local ATS drivers, requisitioned a small building as an office, and recruited a large land owner, who knew everyone, as his assistant.

From that promising start things soon got moving—two more clerks and a couple of typists, a fully trained Estate Agent and Valuer, a move into a larger office in Gosforth, and (not least in importance) Honorary Membership and a bedroom in the Northern Counties Club in Newcastle.

"My war work", he wrote, "consisted of requisitioning castles, mansions and buildings of every sort. I ought to have been the most hated man in the county, but I was overwhelmed with kindness and hospitality by the owners, who willingly gave what I asked of them. For this, the credit goes to the troops who behaved admirably". Meanwhile, Olive spent the war years as an ARP Warden in Hampshire with her house full of evacuees.

B-K's "working life", which had covered 40 eventful years, ended in June, 1945, but 3 years later he was "back with the Regiment" in its Officers' Association which he has served so faithfully, first as Uncle Arthur's Vice-President and, since 1959, as our President an office which actively filled his life with joyful purpose "to the end of the road".

I very much regret that I have been unable to obtain personal tributes by individuals in time for their inclusion in this issue of our News Letter. They will be published in our News Letter next year.

A. M. L. H

Looking back

By Mrs James MacKirdy

Mrs James MacKirdy—whose late husband Jim joined the regiment in 1919—transferred to 5 RGR in 1937—and retired as a Brigadier: her son also served in the Fifth during the War and she now lives with her daughter in Ashtead.

I first went to India in 1924—we had been married about three weeks and my family thought I was going into awful danger. The 2/4 Gurkhas were then stationed on the Frontier—so it meant, after the CO's permission, that I lived in Army Mansions in Peshawar. We were not considered married, as the marriage age was 30 in those days. So for seven years we lived "in sin" according to the Army rules. That was recalled by Jim on our Golden Wedding Anniversary—which was three weeks before he died.

I soon settled into the life and enjoyed the new surroundings. Peshawar was a grand place to spend life and the Mall there was lovely in the March/April days: masses of roses had been planted along the roadside—I wonder if they are still there.

The husbands came down to Peshawar when possible, at the weekends, and we were able to ring up and have a natter in the evenings. There would be a string of wives waiting for calls after dinner. I think Major Massey's wife was the only other wife in Army Mansions, others stayed in the Deans Hotel. Colonel Mills was commanding the 2/4 Battalion at that time.

Soon after having got into the swim of things, Jim was sent off on a course in Wellington for three months. I was allowed to go as long as Jim paid all expenses incurred. We stayed in an hotel in Conoor—it was a lovely spot and the climate was very kind in the hot weather. We had our own room where we fed and we even got some of our boxes from storage in Bombay, which we later lost somewhere on the railway between Wellington and Peshawar. We were unable to claim insurance on them—I forget now why—but it was something to do with not declaring everything. Anyway the Babu knew the contents more or less. It worried me at first when we got back to Peshawar, but I came to the conclusion that silver trays and tea services were not the main things in life.

Whilst in Conoor, Jim sent for his side car and motorbike from England, as we wanted to travel back to Peshawar that way. It was during the monsoon, so we had an awful lot of floods to contend with. We stayed mostly in Dak Bungalows, but once we stayed in a marvellous Hotel in Indore. We were practically the only guests—we had no bearer to look after us, but I remember we were well looked after. The motorbike gave up the ghost just outside Nowshera and we found a tonga wallah who was prepared to attach the motorbike to his tonga with his pagree. Jim sat on the bike and I rode in the tonga and that is how we arrived at Army Mansions!

I suppose it was August by then and I was the only inhabitant for some time. Eventually, an Air Force wife returned, and then another wife who slept on the verandah. It was not long since the Molly Ellis abduction and this wife used to tie a piece of string round her toe and her husband had the other end round his waist, so if anyone came to abduct her he would feel the tug. I myself slept in the heat of my bedroom.

Gradually all the wives returned and life started its social whirl—tennis at the Club, dances on Saturday evenings and, most important of all, curry lunch at the Club! My next-door neighbours at Army Mansions were the Auchinlecks—he was 2-i/c of the 1st Punjabis. We became great friends and then met up again when he was an instructor at Quetta Staff College.

I stayed in Peshawar until April, when Jim took me up to Murree where our son was born in May. I had an excellent bearer by then who stayed with us until we finally left India in 1947. I hated leaving then—all my servants became my friends, although I only spoke very "kutcha" Hindustani.

I went to Bakloh in September, having been given the Massey's bungalow to live in. Charles Borrowman and his sister, Jean Miller, were prepared to assist and were very kind in helping me to start housekeeping in India. I fed with them for some time until the boxes that had been left in store arrived from Bombay. By the time the Bn was due back, I was in control.

On the day of the arrival I went down to the bottom of the hill to meet them—Jim was Quarter Master and was very occupied. I had never seen camels "en masse" before, but it was very interesting. We eventually got home, to find Hamish, our son, had been well looked after.

I do not know if the swimming pool is still in Bakloh—in my day it was not used much, except by me and perhaps Jean Miller. The men used to go and wash in it we discovered, so naturally we gave up swimming when we discovered that.

The servant who went with the bungalow kept cows and every morning, at about 7, he would bring his cows and I would go and watch him wash them in "pinke" and see him milk them. The idea was that my son was getting germ free milk.

We eventually moved from the Massey's bungalow to the Nye's—they were in Nepal at this time. The Bell-Kingsleys took over the Massey's—they had been married whilst he was on leave. The social life in Bakloh started up, dinner parties and tennis on the Mess courts, with, I think, a monthly tea party on the Mess Verandah.

I remember going up the water line with Jim—it had to be inspected every so often—I did not mind the walk up the hill, but coming down was much worse because I got cramp in the muscles of my leg. We had an orderly with us to carry our lunch. He wore a hole in the heel of his sock and I was tickled to death that he turned his sock round and had the holey heel on the top of his ankle.

There was a memorable and amusing incident in 1926. The 1st Bn won the All India Tennis Cup and on Mess night the husbands drank it in well and proper. The wives were not invited. I was in bed and heard funny noises—it was Jim returning—he only had the handle of his lamp in his hand and had fallen down somewhere! I laughed. The next morning there was a large gathering of the officers on our verandah to have a hair of the dog that had bitten them!

We decided in 1927 that it was time I went home. I was very sorry to leave but it was a thrill to see my family again.

We did, however, return to Bakloh in 1936 to spend Christmas with the Goldneys and as the road had been made by then we motored all the way up, which was very thrilling. We had come from Jhelum, where Jim was Staff Captain.

Captain W. G. Walker VC
4th Gurkha Rifles

(later 4th Prince of Wales's Own Gurkha Rifles)

Date of Action	Campaign
22nd April 1903	Somaliland

William George Walker was born in Naini Tal, India, on 29th May 1863, the son of Deputy Surgeon General W. Walker, Indian Medical Service. He was educated at Haileybury and St John's College, Oxford, where he obtained an Arts degree and was commissioned into the Suffolk Regiment on 29th August 1885. He was promoted Lieutenant on 28th May 1887 and joined the 1st Battalion, 4th Goorkha Regiment in that year, seeing service with it in the second Miranzai Expedition 1891-92, and the Waziristan Expedition 1894-95.

In 1903, Captain Walker was serving with the Bikanir Camel Corps in the Somaliland Field Force and was present at the actions at Daratoleh and Jidballi. It was after the action at Daratoleh and while serving with the Berbera Bohottle Flying Column, that Captain Walker was awarded the Victoria Cross. The citation in the London Gazette of 7th August 1903 reads:

"During the return of Major Gough's column to Donop on the 22nd April last, after the action at Daratoleh, the rear-guard got considerably in rear of the column, owing to the thick bush, and to having to hold their ground while wounded men were being placed on camels. At this time Captain Bruce was shot through the body from a distance of about 20 yards, and fell on the path unable to move.

Captains Walker and Rolland, two men of the 2nd Battalion King's African Rifles, one Sikh and one Somali of the Camel corps were with him when he fell.

In the meantime the column being unaware of what had happened were getting further away. Captain Rolland then ran back some 500 yards and returned with assistance to bring off Captain Bruce, while Captain Walker and the men remained with that Officer, endeavouring to keep off the enemy, who were all round in the thick bush. This they succeeded in doing, though not before Captain Bruce was hit a second time, and the Sikh wounded. But for the gallant conduct displayed by these Officers and men, Captain Bruce must have fallen into the hands of the enemy".

In 1904, W. G. Walker, now a Lieutenant Colonel, returned to the 1st Battalion, 4th Gurkha Rifles. In 1907 he was transferred to the 1st Gurkha Rifles and spent two years with that Regiment before rejoining the 4th in 1909. He was appointed Commandant of the 1st Battalion 4th Gurkha Rifles in 1910 and after a short spell, as Inspector of Imperial Service Troops, Bombay, sailed with the battalion for Suez on 26th August 1914 on the British India Steamship Company's ship "Baroda", becoming the first unit of the Indian Army to leave India for service in the Great War. The battalion then formed part of the Indian Expeditionary Force "A". This force was composed of two Divisions, the 3rd (Lahore) Division, and the 7th (Meerut) Division.

Soon after arrival in Egypt, Colonel Walker acted in Command of the Sirhind Brigade of Lahore Division as the Brigadier had already gone to France, where the Brigade followed in 1914. He was confirmed as General Officer Commanding Sirhind Brigade in January 1915 and Brigadier General commanding both the Sirhind and Jullundur Brigades later the same year. He was promoted Major General in January 1916 and commanded the 2nd (British) Division in France. He retired in 1919, having been made CB in 1914 and Mentioned in Despatches three times.

On 23rd February 1907, he married in Melbourne, Australia, Margaret Alice Elaine Molesworth, daughter of Judge H Molesworth, by whom he had a son and daughter. He died at Seaford, Sussex on 16th February 1936, aged 72.

On Shikar in the CP

By Hamish Mackay

I once again direct my pen to the story of those former days in India before the age of the Great War occurred to upset the world.

Already then it appears to have been characteristic of Englishmen wherever they might be to seek out and slay such wild animals as they could find and even their absorption into the excitements of Empire Building merely whetted their appetites for their natural sport by providing new and strange varieties to seek out and hunt down. Fresh species could still be found in Asia and later still in Africa. It was not difficult to attach encouraging labels to the sports proving not only that it helped the local native populations but that it positively saved them from destruction?

I have to admit that I carry a sufficiency of English blood in my Highland veins to feel in sympathy with their enjoyment of what they do: but perhaps it is not merely a likeness between the English and their near neighbours. There could be more to it than that and I think that there is. I believe that if we studied the matter properly we would discover that these tastes are common to all mankind the world over to a greater or lesser degree depending on opportunity or need or other circumstances.

For the Briton an appointment to a career in India was largely the prospect of an uncomfortable existence through long periods of extreme heat and frequent drenching monsoon rains, compensated by at least a month or two of kindly climate when all nature smiled on the wretched exile and invited him to make the most of it. Then it was that he indulged his natural desires stalking the wariest or the most surefooted creatures in the world over cliff-like mountain rocks or through the wild gardens and cathedral-like aisles of the forest. If the land lent itself to speed (and most of India does in spite of the checks in its surface and acres of cactus) then the game might be changed from patient trailing to galloping madly and often dangerously after your prey. Nowhere else in the wide world could such a variety be found in such delightful surroundings and attended by such interest and comfort and companionship and pleasure: that is what made it all worthwhile.

Naturally one could not rely on these joys being available just when one wanted them—local conditions such as small wars could occur to prevent them being possible or being enjoyed: and there were also Great Wars to upset the rhythmn of the years—indulgencies then had to be put aside. No-one ever did quench them entirely—they were regarded more as temporary interferences with the serious business of life, that of dealing death to the pachyderms and the pigs and goats of high places and the great cats of the jungles, the beasts that we professed so to love and admire.

When I was posted to India near the close of the First Great War, regiments were still absent from their own home stations camping in strange surroundings, their old timers gone, some never to return, some sequestered by the state for skills and knowledge that was required elsewhere: some were men of a kind that seemed peculiar to India, replicas of the Stringer Lawrences and Bindon Bloods (the men who took and helped hold it).

One such there still was on the books of the Regiment to which I was posted, the 107th Pioneers: never seen, he was a mysterious man. We knew a lot about him by hearsay, about his prowess in the jungle as a tiger hunter, to us he was the Corbett of that age: but not a jungle man only, he was also an ardent and skilful sticker of pigs as well as a fisherman and a shot—the beau-ideal soldier and sportsman. Soldier? Yes, a would-be disappointed soldier! It was one of those things. When war broke out he was on duty in Assam: he was required there and forbidden to leave and so when the Regiment sailed to France and later to Mesopotamia he was left to fight bow and arrow battles and attack hill forts held by naked savages, the complete waste it might be thought of a good man. But could we not be mistaken in these views?

I have a strange and persistent feeling that the reason why the Naga was our staunchest and most faithful friend and ally throughout our second Great War against the deadly Japanese was largely because of the influence that men like Coote and his kind had excercised over them during the first. It was a case of sheer character and a limpid sterling personality disseminating itself imperceptibly through an observant and understanding people who knew their worth. The gods of war no less than other celestial deities work in mysterious ways their wonders to perform.

Yes, Coote was the name of our Pioneer who fought with Nagas and who served them: Mervyn Chuddleigh Coote who all of us at once knew when at last he did come back to us must be the grandson or great grandson of that Coote who with Clive had won us India, everything about him proclaimed it: he didn't know what selfishness was, never thought about himself but only about his subalterns: was not his motto "Be the cost what it may"? Did his birds not swim on the pebble of his signet ring? An Anglo-Irishman with the qualities of both.

His immediate aim was to make us, newcomers to the land, see and know and love India, the fields and the countryside, not the hill stations: those he despised as places to be avoided; the tigers of the hill stations he would tell us were far more dangerous than the tigers of the jungle and they were the ultimate aim for us. He wanted each one of us to acquire the skill and to enjoy the exhilaration of shooting his own tiger in its natural habitat. We were the wettest tyros, dangerous even if trusted with an airgun, so it was a long deliberate task he set himself demanding infinite care and patience. He would not allow bad habits to creep in and there was a fascination in it.

In the beginning he delighted us by having us all out every weekend to search out the duck jheels and the partridge runs to accustom us to handling sporting weapons properly so that we did not look and never were a menace to companions or others and incidentally we learnt a lot about the ways of wild life.

At the time Coote was reviewing the Mess Armoury. I remember his advertising for and purchasing two 577's heavy duty weapons, one having a longer two and a half inch chamber than the other, able to take a heavier cartridge capable of stopping a buffalo or a charging bison which really felt like approaching business. All these weapons were handled and practised with till our shoulders were black and blue and then at last came a day in the hot weather when the first of us started off for the Central Provinces where Coote had rented blocks of forest where tiger might be expected to be found. He was already there making a reconnaissance of the ground.

He took us to the CP individually for a month at a time. I was in luck as the first one to go, told to report to him with my kit and equipment at the forest block of Balaghat on a date in the hot weather of 1921 from Meerut where the Regiment was at the time, North of Delhi. Balaghat was a famous haunt of tigers in the heart of the jungle. Coote went ahead to reconnoitre the area and lay out the camp site. I followed by train to Nagpur almost at the Centre of Central India and then turned north by train and finally by bullock cart conveying my tent and gear along a silent forest track to the rendezvous. A more enchanting spot could hardly be imagined. Everything was new and strange to me even the melodious bird calls. The jungle was not immense here nor very thick but rather like wild park land.

Coote's tent shaded by a leafy tree had a slight movement of air through it as could be seen from an odd eddy of smoke from an earth pit outside it. Coote hearing the bullock cart came out to meet me—and so started the most wonderful month that I had ever experienced till then.

Imagine Corbett as your constant companion, telling you his stories in all their richness and variety, never telling you what to do or how to do it but continuing to do it along with you as though he was glad of your companionship and help.

The day began before dawn: after a mug of tea we would start off on our separate plans as arranged the night before seated with a night cap by a sparkling fire till we almost fell asleep. Each day produced its own adventure almost anything that happened was an adventure real or imagined. Remember the crocodiles? A brisk bubbling river ran through the block and nothing was more delicious on a really hot day than to strip off and plunge into its coolness. One day I did so and was returning to pick up a shirt and pants and gun when a pair of eyes floated round a bend in the river towards where I was headed for. If I panicked and floundered back to the beach I had just left I could easily escape but must alert the beast and must remain naked and unarmed; it did not yet appear to have noticed me: if I continued as I was going with long, quiet strokes I might gain the bank I wanted to get to without disturbing it. I'd try. Some little way further on the wicked triangular eyes again swung into view—this time directly towards me. It did not increase its pace, perhaps it did not even have to. I prayed and plunged on. Then, striking a stone perhaps, it cocked an eye! Was it an eye? It was not: it was a leaf on a twig of a broken branch—but I was a nervous wreck.

But that recalls another occasion when with further to go I had set out earlier and there was but little light to see by in the forest. After some time I came across an enormous boulder: boulders were infrequent there and I thought to clamber on it and rest there—I didn't like sitting on the ground—too many creepy crawlies to say nothing of snakes which could be found there—whereas rocks are usually free of them. I'd spend half an hour there and push on in better light. I approached the boulder and reached out to find a handhold when it emitted a violent snort and heaving itself to its feet galloped heavily off into the jungle leaving me shaking on the flat floor, heart pounding heavily. It was a bull bison I was offering to mount—could have been fair game in other circumstances but these were not quite suitable.

But what about tigers? Was it not tigers that we were after? I did walk into one one day: it was totally unheeding of me, only twenty or so paces away and never raised its head or looked my way: the easiest shot in the world but I didn't attempt a shot. That worried me afterwards; why hadn't I shot? Had I funked it? Or was my inaction tactical? As I explained to my own satisfaction?

The thing is that the season was unusual: tigers were not behaving naturally. There was a lot of drumming going on in the villages and it upset tigers causing them to depart from their beats. We blamed the drumming and Gandhi who was being difficult at this time: the drumming may have been in support of the Gandhi movement but it was inconceivable that it was done to spoil tiger shooting: but the tigers were restless and did not behave ordinarily. Coote was out daily watching them, trying to read the clues of their reactions to the leads he gave them.

At last he set up a night watch for me at a place we thought we could lure one to. It was successful but only I think because she (it was a tigress) was young and foolish. I studied her a long time unwilling to destroy her: but why should I let her destroy my buffalo calf who stood up to her courageously (and what would my servants think of one who was so scared of shooting)? She lay down beside her, victim on the bank of the stream and I shot her through the heart where she lay, totally relaxed: she bent through the air in an arc like a golden meteor and fell back on to the stream bank and never twitched a muscle.

A few days later, after discussion Coote mounted a drive in which three tigers emerged: Coote shot one, another padded directly underneath me and I shot it through the spine. It fell and never moved and I never again in my life wanted to shoot a tiger. A mark of a great shikari used to be known as a Nowshermar—a killer of nine tigers—two were more than enough for me.

I remember years afterwards travelling with a friend on the little platform of an underground coach in London and telling him the story. In reply he said that he was taking up photography—when we were joined by a third passenger, an African gentleman who must have heard me say, "Well, I too have decided to kill no more?"

Upon which his eyes grew large, he edged for the door and left us at the next stop.

Coote's story ought not to stop there; there was so much more to him. He took several of us through the CP "course"—always with the same memorable results, but that was merely one aspect of his rich, generous personality. He was laid to rest at last happily in a Christian garden where his forebears may lie in the Maharashtra although I did hear that he'd been a Buddhist (if not a Hindu). I saw that in camp he never failed to observe the common Christian practices—but we never spoke about these things.

One curious incident occurred long afterwards. When I finally had to quit India I took passage by way of Rangoon and Singapore: Rangoon in order to return our faithful Karen girl to her parents from whom she had been separated for seven years, and Singapore in order to visit Hugh who was stationed there. The second part of the journey by Catalina aircraft—that one luxurious flying machine in which one could parade the deck and view the countryside below. There the tropical blueness of the sea is only surpassed by the greens that adorn the jungle. I gazed and gazed on it and may have remarked on it to a lady who appeared like myself to be drinking it in: "Yes," she replied "that was what my husband loved and doted on." Something in the way she spoke so moved us that hesitating I ventured, "His name was not by any chance Mervyn Chuddleigh Coote?" "Yes," she replied, "that was his name."

She was returning to New Zealand where she had left her family.

It was like a miracle.

IV

Jungle Jims

By Jim Marley

In 1945 I was in HQ 115 Brigade which was the Gurkha Training Brigade comprising 14 GR, 38 GR, 56 GR and 710 GR. The late Brian Foster, who instigated the annual Wessex Gurkha Lunch at the Watersplash Hotel, Brockenhurst, was QM of 56 GR. 115 Brigade HQ was situated at the village of Mohand between Dehra Dun and Saharanpur and was on the edge of the Viceroy's Shooting Block.

Jim Corbett, with the honorary rank of Colonel, was attached to the Brigade and billeted in Brigade HQ. He will be known to most as the author of "Maneaters of Kumaon", "Maneating leopard of Rudraprayag" and "My India". His home was in Naini Tal and the Corbett National Park is named in his memory. He had also spent much time in Kenya. The purpose of his attachment was to make one familiar enough with the jungle so that if need be life could be sustained. He had an unsurpassed knowledge of the jungle and its inhabitants but was delightfully modest about his achievements.

After a while I joined 14 GR where our Tony Andrews was a member. He and I were fortunate enough to be selected to join Jim Corbett for his jungle course. This lasted for a week and I do not think it stopped raining once. Maintaining a fire in the rain proved very difficult and all meals took at least $1\frac{1}{2}$ hours to prepare.

The first principle he impressed on us was to maintain direction and to note compass points before setting out; if trail blazing, to use the same leaf throughout if possible onto bend bushes in the direction of travel.

On our first morning we were told of three officers on a recce near our camp, one of whom died of thirst and the other two were in extremis, contrasted with 14 men who lived 14 days in the jungle and were fitter at the end of it. The first three were within a few feet of a water vine, which contained enough liquid to have sustained them as long as necessary.

We did several trips in the jungle and up nullahs where we saw fresh tiger tracks. On one occasion we found fresh leopard tracks passing through where we had camped for the night, on another I recall seeing scuffle marks on the ground and Jim Corbett pointed to a nearby tree and said he would find sambhur hairs on the tree. He had interpreted the marks as those of a tiger jumping on to a sambhur whose reaction is to run for the nearest tree to try to brush the tiger off his back. He knew from the slightest mark the age and the sex of the tiger. He could imitate the mating call of a tigress; but refrained from doing it in our presence, in case, it was misinterpreted by a nearby tiger.

On our trips out Jim Corbett would point out plants and trees and tell us of their attributes; for example:

Water Vine:
A grenade-like bark; when cut the sap runs upwards so it is necessary to make two cuts quickly and drain out the section. This would produce about half a pint from two feet.

Udal:
The bark when stripped will produce innumerable bandages.

Minphal:
A pomegranate like fruit which could drug fish or wash clothes.

Malu:
Can get rope from inside of the bark and the leaf is useful for roofing or cooking.

Liquorice Fern Creeper:
Liquorice from root, tea from dried leaf. The seed called "ratti" is used as a gold standard weight. It induces conjunctivitis. The pounded seed with a drop of Aqua milk sap makes a deadly blood poison.

Neem:
The Bark when infused gives a type of quinine for fever and can also be made into a toothbrush; the leaves when infused make a poultice for sores. The nuts and berries when dried give oil for burning.

Daun:
The small green berry can produce high explosive (I do not have the recipe in case anyone has any ideas) and a red dye.

Mango:
The bark produces a green dye. Jim Corbett recommended adding where possible, to all dyes, ferrous sulphate (rusty nails) or failing that salt, or alum.

Numerous other plants were pointed out which could, produce dyes, alleviate dysentery, purify blood, make tea, powder, soap, pegs and the like.

Also, of course, many roots, or fruits which are edible, and others that were not edible, e.g. lily bulbs and fungi. As a test of poison one should slice off and put between teeth and lower lip; if irritant discard.

He was of course conversant with pests such as ticks, leeches and scorpions and how to deal with them and also snake bite. He also gave tips on how to deal with nuisances such as prickly heat (coconut oil), dhobi itch and trench foot.

Other useful tips included how to kill game such as sambhur and carry it on a mule and how to treat biltong, how to extract salt from salt licks.

Another useful accomplishment was how to find dry tinder and how to light a fire with it, as it did not stop raining for the whole week this became more and more desirable.

When we got back to the relative comfort of a 14 GR tent I recall suggesting to Tony, as it was raining more heavily than usual, that we should go outside and have a snooze!

All in all it was the most interesting week I have ever spent, and though I would no longer wish to be deposited in a jungle without support I finished the course fully confident of an ability to survive.

The above was compiled from my notes and diaries written at the time.

I. M. S. Days: A Doctor Remembers

By Lieut Colonel Sydney Heard, MBE, IMS (Retired)
—one time RMO with 1/4 GR

I applied to join the Indian Medical Service in the summer of 1938 and there followed a three month refresher course in tropical medicine, entomology and military hygiene. Whilst still in London, together with those joining the RAMC, we were also put through our paces in equitation by the Riding Master of the Household Cavalry at Hyde Park Barracks and then square bashing in Aldershot. Those of us who satisfied the board of retired generals at the India Office were given our postings in just enough time to kit ourselves out. My first posting was to the Indian Military Hospital, Jullundur. Phyl and I, like several of those taking up their first appointment in the Service, had been married recently, and we set off by the troopship Lancashire for Karachi.

We arrived at Jullundur Junction having travelled overnight to pick up the Punjab mail at Lahore. The dawn was just breaking so our first impression of Indian life was gained in Lahore Station. A few hours later we were met at Jullundur Junction by Sub-Assistant Surgeon Jemadar Udham Singh. We were accompanied from Karachi by our bearer Wahid-u-Din who for many years had served an old, and recently retired, friend. Together they had seen service in the first world war and the North West Frontier. On special occasions Wahid wore his decorations with great pride.

Udham Singh was a big man with a greying beard. He wore

a light tropical uniform, puttees and his rank was shown by two shoulder pips and his service by the letters IMD, the Indian Medical Department. He was accompanied by three men in charge of two tongas and a bullock cart and thus equipped our little convoy set off for the Jubilee Hotel some five miles away in Jullundur cantonment.

Udham Singh was to become my main guide and tutor in introducing me to a new life so different from the last several years serving on the staff of Charing Cross Hospital in London. After a week or two, we were allocated Bungalow No 90 next door to the 5th/1st Punjab Mess. This Regiment was manned by Sikhs and PMs, all big men whose band gave proof of their power well into the night, once a week on Guest nights. All the Officers were British. Most troops, however, at that time were Dogras with their 10th/17th Training Battalion and 11th/17th Territorials. Behind Bungalow 90 were the cavalry lines occupied by the 2nd Royal Lancers (Gardiner's Horse). On the far side of the cantonment was a battalion of the East Yorkshire Regiment. At first there were no Gurkhas in the station.

On the morning following our arrival Udharn Singh arrived at the Hotel and conducted me to the IMH to report to the OC. I soon found him to be a sad disgruntled man. This was understandable. A Parsee, he had been looking forward for years to retirement and reunion with his French wife and son in Paris, but the political situation in Europe had obliged him to be retained. The second in command (and the only other IMS Officer) was Lieutenant Colonel Lahiri, likewise recalled from retirement. His wife and family were away somewhere in their homeland, elsewhere in India. He accepted this with quiet resignation and I saw little of him as he kept to himself caring for recovery patients several blocks away from the acute medical and surgical wards which had been allocated to me. As I had no practical experience in tropical medicine and no knowledge of any Indian language, Udham Singh became a close friend and loyal colleague. My allocation of duties increased rapidly. The Colonel seldom left his office. The early morning MI room soon introduced me to the essential language of diagnosis—"Ek, do, tin bolo" replaced the phrase "Say 99". In addition to the acute wards, I was soon put in charge of the cantonment Civil Hospital and the Family and Child Welfare Hospital, and was appointed area MOH as well as Anti-malaria Officer. This last job together in association with the Regional Recruiting Medical Officer, Captain Sayed IMS took me out into the surrounding villages. As my assistant I had Kushi Mohammed, a civilian clerk who supervised the various methods of controlling the mosquito population.

The villagers showed me much kindness and having been graded by the Indian Army as a specialist in obstetrics and gynaecology I was particularly pleased to be called in increasingly to advise and later treat their women folk, especially in difficult childbirth.

My first acquaintances with Gurkhas were somewhat unusual. It must have been in about April 1939 that a Gurkha Naik reported sick at the early morning medical inspection. He had been sent by Colonel Borrowman who, with his charming wife, was staying in Jullundur. The patient had lobar pneumonia and was admitted immediately. He recognised the tell-tale rusty sputum of pneumonia and was convinced that he would die. In Charing Cross Hospital I had been using a new drug — Prontosil which had been discovered in Germany. The English firm, May & Baker, had improved on this by producing sulpha-pyridine, known then as M do B 693. Though it had unpleasant side effects, it was active against the relevant germ. Pneumonia patients did not usually die from respiratory causes but from heart failure resulting from the toxins released by the disease and which build up daily. Therefore the shorter the illness the greater the chance of recovery. The Hospital had just received its first small consignment of the drug so here was a chance to put it to proof. At first, the patient refused to take the tablets, "What was the point" he said, "I shall die anyway". Some of the other patients encouraged him in this belief.

As usual Udham Singh came to the rescue. The whole ward became a pantomime. Bets were placed on the outcome with the odds heavily against me, but my first Gurkha patient survived and the remarkable news spread. It must be strange to the modern generation that for the first fifteen years of my medical career no true antibiotic had been available since the properties of penicillin, though discovered in the late 1920s, were not developed until demanded by the pressures of war.

It was at about the same time that the Colonel sent for me. "Ah, Heard" he said, "The Lahore District ENT Surgeon is visiting us next week. There are a number of cadets at the KGRIM School to have their tonsils and adenoids removed. You will be giving the anaesthetics". The day before Major Perez RAMC was due, there arrived six sturdy but snuffly Gurkha teenagers. I will not go into the medical details but without adequate and suitable apparatus it is not easy for a surgeon and an anaesthetist to operate down the same throat, particularly by the so called open method where, in a hot dry climate, an anaesthetic like ether volatalises so as to reach not only the patient but all others in the theatre. However, we managed and all went well and a further six boys arrived a month later.

The King George Royal Indian Military School was situated on the Grand Trunk road near the Station. I wonder whether it still exists? I am sure that the knackers yard just opposite, which was part of my duty to inspect, is a place of the past.

One morning, still in 1939, the CO sent for me again. "Sit down" he said. This was a bad sign. "I have just received a telegram from the ADMS, Lahore. Perhaps you would like to read it". I read "Detail one Officer to report to OC Bakloh to accompany 1st/4th Gurkha Regiment to Waziristan, and return on completion of duty". "Mind you are back in three or four days" said the Colonel "we have some IHC recruits joining us and I want you to smarten them up with their drill".

A fortnight later the ADMS, Bannu, was to ignore the second part of the Lahore District Order!

IV

More IMS Days

*By Lt Col Sydney Heard MBE IMS (Retd),
one time RMO 1/4 GR continues*

The march from Bakloh to Pathankot took several days. On the first day we stopped to visit a retired Gurkha Officer who had set up home a few miles down the road. I understood nothing of the lively conversation which took place, which meant little as every day brought a new experience including my first introduction to tea being boiled up with milk, sugar and spices in a copper urn.

While on the march the CO practised road protection in a very different environment from that which we were to meet in Waziristan. I was reminded of my schooldays translating from the Latin Caesar's invasion of Gaul and could not help noticing how similar were modern tactics to those of 2,000 years previously. On the last day we were all soaked by a storm such as I had never witnessed before. Our only protection was provided by ground sheets. Lightning seemed to flash every few seconds, whilst the thunder reverberating round the hills was continuous. The rain stopped as quickly as it had arrived, but it left the camp at Pathankot several inches deep in water. I mentioned to the CO that I had read somewhere in Medical Regulations for the Army in India that in adverse conditions a Medical Officer could recommend a rum ration. This suggestion gave me a somewhat undeserved measure of popularity. The following morning we set off by broad gauge railway for Mari Indus. At about midday the CO had the train stopped at a station where the Battalion took a meal. Seeing trestle tables and chairs set up on a railway platform for the convenience of the Officers was yet another new experience.

Mari Indus was a desolate spot where the broad gauge railway ended and where we were transferred to what was known as the Heat Stroke Express. Ahead of the small engine was an open truck to take the blast of any bomb placed on the line. At the side of the engine's cabin there had been constructed a cage in which the driver sat, presumably because it was too hot to be behind the boiler and at the same time giving a better out-look. The first coaches were for the mules, which were entrained with considerable reluctance. At the end of the train a carriage was reserved for me and the Battalion medical equipment. Just as we were about to set off the door of the carriage was opened and a maund block of ice was skated across the floor of the compartment. Halfway to Bannu we stopped at a place called Laki Mowat. It could hardly be called a Station but was at a point were double lines enabled trains to pass. The only building in sight was a small hut at the side of the line. Why do I remember this insignificant incident? Inside the hut and on the wall was an advertisement for a well known brand of cigarettes. It depicted an attractive young woman and it so happened that she was a professional photographer's model whom I had treated while in London.

We set off again, and by this time half the ice had melted and water was sloshing about the floor. At Bannu we were met by the CO in charge of the advance party, with a ready supply of spiced sweet tea. Although hot, it was remarkably refreshing.

Hoping to catch the train back to Marl Indus and hence to Jullundur as ordered, I reported to the ADMS Bannu where I could hand over medical equipment for my relief. "There is no relief," said the RAMC Colonel, "you will proceed with the Battalion." I pointed out that this was contrary to the order of Lahore District, but the Colonel stressed that further advance without a Medical Officer would be impossible and thus it was that we set off on the march to Mir Ali. On the first night we camped on a rough plateau of ground, mainly broken rocks surrounded by small hills. On the way I had one problem, I had been supplied with a motor Ambulance driven by a Naik in the RIASC. At one point the road curved through a narrow gorge, and the CO thought it was wise, as well as good training, to avoid this defile by cutting across rocks and thus avoid a possible ambush. This precaution was, of course, impossible in the case of the motor Ambulance. Should I stay with the Battalion or accompany the driver with the medical equipment, without which I would be of little use? I decided upon the latter course.

Reaching the end of the gorge we waited, and it was with some relief that I saw the first troops advancing over the hill through which the road had been cut. Though no shot was fired thus began my first possible experience of encountering enemy action. Nevertheless, I think the CO was pleased to get away from the unprotected spot where we spent our first night. The following morning we set off on our march to Mir Ali.

Mir Ali was a permanent camp set on an all too rare area of level ground above and about half a mile from the Bannu to Razmak road and from which it was reached by a narrow winding track. To the right of this track and on the side of a rocky hill was a single out-post surrounded by a stone wall. From the apex of the small building which it enclosed, wire mesh was stretched downwards to the wall so that grenades flung over into the small compound at night hopefully would roll back on to the attackers. The camp itself had one or two permanent buildings but was mainly tented. With hills on three sides there was an open view across a valley through which ran the river Tochi and which the road traversed by means of a ford. Of this we shall hear more later.

At the junction of the track leading to the camp and the road itself was a small out-post manned by a signaller equipped with a field telephone so that messages could be passed from the camp to casual passing traffic such as an armoured car and vice-versa.

The camp was surrounded by a low dry wall. At dusk machine-gun posts were set up behind this wall, their fire directed and fixed on points from which it was anticipated attacks might be made. To each gun was attached a small light in such a way as to illuminate the sights without being visible to a potential enemy. On the first evening of our stay I saw a group of Gurkha officers gathered together and discussing the siting and direction of fire to be most effective. Imagine my surprise when, on approaching, I found them listening with respectful interest to advice being given to them by my bearer Wahid-u-Din who was no stranger to Mir Ali.

After an uncomfortable night in our new surroundings the next morning began early with more training. I was directed to a rocky hillock about a quarter of a mile away outside the camp perimeter and in charge of the Band to practise stretcher drill. Using my meagre vocabulary I directed several stretcher parties to the top of the mound. They had reached the summit while I was still negotiating large boulders at the base.

On joining them I asked for volunteers to act as patients for the return journey. Fortunately the "patients" were fit men and hopefully I was able to instill in their minds that gentleness as well as speed was essential in the care of the wounded. Having repeated this exercise several times I was approached by an NCO who saluted and said something unintelligible to me. Continuing the drill the same NCO saluted again and repeated whatever he was trying to convey to me. At that point Bingle appeared deploying some men on a nearby slope and I asked him to act as interpreter. He laughed, saying, "If you don't let these men fall out soon, they're going to burst their bladders."

There was one big celebration whilst in Mir Ali because for the first time for many years the 1st and 2nd Battalions came together and thus I met other members of the Regiment. I can't remember when I first met Freddie Harrison, but he was certainly in Command when most of the Battalion set off in the direction of Razmak. Reaching the River Tochi, although the water was shallow, the bed was composed of loose shingle. This was no great problem except for the motor Ambulance. Here was a dilemma. There was no cover, and Freddie wanted to get the troops over as quickly as possible in order to deploy them. The Ambulance driver felt sure that without chains and perhaps even with them, the vehicle would become stuck during the crossing, and in this opinion I backed him up. Freddie wanted me to advance with the troops but I felt reluctant to leave the driver on his own, fitting on chains entirely unprotected, and in any case what use would a doctor be without his equipment? Freddie seemed to think that I was reluctant to get my legs wet, and he, being mounted, sent his horse back to pick me up. The outcome was that the syce and I helped the driver to fit on chains, and I crossed the river mounted, together with the ambulance and the syce as a passenger. Arriving on the far bank

I had a good ticking off but Freddie and I remained friends. From thereon training was at an end and road protection was practised in earnest. Two platoons advanced, one on each side of the road ahead, whilst the main body advanced, sending on in turn two platoons, thus staggering cover from the raised ground bordering the road. We arrived at our destination some hours later at Bichikachki. To my surprise, and on arrival, I was greeted by an RAMC Captain. "George", I said, "What are you doing here?" "I'm here to relieve you", he replied. George Dunkerton and I were medical students together at University, though we had gone on to different hospitals and had not seen each other for four or five years. I introduced George to Freddie, handed over my medical equipment, and then according to some, lost my presence of mind. Being within an hour or so of sunset, I decided to make a dash back to Mir Ali. Knowing that we would need chains to cross the river, I had them fitted on before we left Bichikachki. Travelling along a rough road at full throttle, as was inevitable, links in for other trains which might be on the line, or points switched against us, as at this time normal signals were not operating.

On the second morning we came to a small town between Gorakhpur and Lucknow, whose name I forget.

There was a large crowd dancing and shouting on the platform and we could see more people crowding round the station entrance.

As the train stopped, one man seemed to be trying desperately to enter our cond Jullundur. Clearly, we could not tramp back on our own (as it was?) several days' march to Bannu, but one day I heard that an armoured convoy was passing through from Razmak. No longer having medical equipment, together with Wahid and personal belongings, we found our way down the track to the road junction where a 4th Gurkha was on duty at the Field Telephone Post. We waited for about half an hour for the expected convoy, when there appeared from nowhere, as unsavoury a bunch of tribesmen as one could wish to meet.

The capture of Officers as hostages was a profitable pursuit, but it occurred to me afterwards that again they thought that I was some kind of lunatic decoy, especially as I was obviously unarmed.

The ever resourceful Wahid who, having thought he would only be away from Jullundur for a few days was still dressed in obvious Mohammedan garb. Somehow he conveyed to these murderous-looking gentlemen that I was a doctor, whereupon the apparent leader of the gang mimed to me that one of its number was suffering from a severe toothache. Fortunately I had with me an Army box of medicines known as No 1 to 10 (old soldiers will remember the famous No 9s). I handed out some tablets of aspirin. Wahid and I then took advantage of the situation and beat a rapid retreat to the Camp. A few days later an armoured convoy did pass through on its way to Bannu and thence by the heat-stroke express to Mari Indus we linked up with the broad gauge railway back to Jullundur. Reporting to the CO of the Hospital I was greeted with the words—"Where on earth have you been?". Rejoining me from Bakloh whence I had sent Wahid to accompany her back, Phyl's greeting was somewhat different. "Do you know", she asked, "that you are going to be a father?"

A month or so later I returned to Waziristan as MO to the 5th/1st Punjab Regiment. The attractive advertisement at Laki Mowat was no longer there.

About six years after these events, Freddie Harrison was passing through New Delhi on his way to take up Command of a Brigade in Burma and stayed with us overnight. He asked Phyl if he might leave one or two superfluous items of his kit in our care. In 1945, the Japanese War being over, Phyl and our two daughters Ann and Alison, then aged six and four respectively, returned to Guernsey. I stayed on until after Independence and in 1948 I rejoined the family, sending on as many of our belongings as I could pack unaided, Wahid with his son having safely made his way to Pakistan.

Settling in a new home, left intact after the German occupation of the Channel Islands, Phyl and I sorted out the trunks and packing cases which duly arrived in Guernsey. Amongst their contents we found a dusty kit bag which I did not recognise but inside we found some discarded clothing and a row of medals: they included

Freddie Harrison's Military Cross it was through this discovery that Phyl and I were reunited with old as well as meeting new friends in the 4th Gurkha Rifles.

More Memories of India

By Mrs James MacKirdy whose late husband joined 4GR in 1919—transferred to 5RGR in 1937—and retired as a Brigadier

When I was married it was a time of unrest in India and although much of it was kept away from the wives, nevertheless an old servant of my mother's was convinced that I was going to be murdered. Life on the other hand was interesting—New Delhi was being built and Gandhi was a force to be taken very seriously and I read what I could in the papers. I have subsequently seen the film "Gandhi" and did not feel that it portrayed" us in a good light. I am so thankful that we have all learned to live together regardless of race—but it is taking a long time—indeed when I first went to Peshawar no Indian was allowed to join the Club—and I know that Jim would have been delighted with the changes that have taken place.

I think that our time at Staff College was the most interesting: there was such a variety of regiments represented there; I particularly remember Christmas 1933 when there was a big College Ball at Quetta with the officers wearing their different mess uniforms. We had someone from the Indian Navy staying with us and it really was a magnificent "do". The Viceroy and Lady Willingdon came up to Quetta in that first year. We had just faced a ten per cent cut in pay and as we had a son in England and a small daughter with us, we were hard pressed—but no-one went on strike! Lady Willingdon was reputed to have said that she did not want wives to wear the same dress twice if she was meeting them—which was a little difficult.

From Staff College after leave we went to Jhelum—a dear little station. Jim had returned to India and I had to leave my children with my mother and sister: it was very heart breaking. In fact, when the time came to see me off at the station I had filled my pockets with pennies and as the train pulled out I threw handfuls to them so that they were so occupied in scrambling for the money that they couldn't see my tears.

I was taking out a new car and after Jim had met me in Bombay we drove to Jhelum. It was on the way there that I saw the Taj Mahal—unfortunately not at night but even so by day a thing of great beauty. On arrival we discovered Jhelum to be a very happy station: the club had several good tennis courts and there was a golf course with the river near by.

One of Jim's regular duties as Staff Captain was to read the lesson in church once a month and I recall that he used to try it out on me the night before! The golf was fun, we had "browns" not greens—just well rolled earth—mutti. I wonder how it looks today. I also won a cup at tennis—playing with an Indian lady in a sari, which was quite an innovation.

After some eight months Jim was posted to Loralai in the Sind Desert as Brigade Major: it was very hot weather and he went by car and had to cross the River Indus by ferry. I had developed a most dreadful thirst and with no water in the flask and Jim refusing to let me drink the brightly coloured bottled stuff on sale to the locals I was eventually saved when the ferry Captain kindly invited us to his cabin for cold drinks.

Loralai is a lovely little spot surrounded by desert—the houses and gardens had been there many years and were all very attractive. It was at that time only the Headquarters of the Brigade—all the troops were at Fort Sandeman—and therefore the HQ was often away on exercises. During the rainy season the desert is covered with beautiful wild flowers and tulips.

In '38 I was due to go home to see the children and had been busy knitting hard for them: Indian wool was very cheap, three or four annas an ounce. I had run out and wanted some more—the Brigade was out on exercise so I suggested to a friend that we should go to Quetta on the Indian bus—some sixty miles away. Now one of the 2/4th officers Jim Goldney and his family was at Staff College so a signal was sent asking if they would put us up. Thus accommodation was offered and off we went. We sat in front near the Indian driver and masses of locals were packed in behind with their sheep and goats: how we enjoyed it!

Halfway along the road a British Regiment was stationed and having been notified of our trip were ready to give us lunch in the Mess. Between there and Quetta the engine of the bus began to fail but we eventually arrived and all was well. I got my wool, we had our hair done and then returned to Loralai by the expedience of my friend pretending to a garage that her husband was contemplating purchase of a car and then we were taken in a lovely new model back to Loralai.

Meanwhile Jim had returned to station and I was in great disgrace: he said that I could have caused an international incident and I suppose that had we been fired upon it could have been so. In time, however, I was forgiven and prepared to go home. Jim followed in March '39 for a scheduled six months' leave but before that was up war broke out, the leave was cancelled and he travelled back to India with a hundred other officers whose leave was similarly curtailed. I was not to see Jim again for another six years—save for a few hours in Bombay en route for New Zealand where my daughter and I spent five years and made many friends. We eventually returned to India in '45, the war in Europe being over before our land fall in Bombay once again.

IV

Major-General Sir Arthur Mordaunt Mills CB, DSO

Colonel of the Regiment 1935–1950
Founder of the Officers' Association in April 1947,
and its President until 1959.
Died in his 86th year on the 8th October 1964

In 1959 we asked Uncle Arthur to send a record of his service. His reply was typical:

> *A. M. M. Obit. According to your behest, Freddy.*
> *Punch 26th Jan. 1949: "Come blow your horn".*
> *I'll live my life as well I may*
> *If only men will let me;*
> *And when my bones are laid away*
> *Let all the world forget me.*

By The Colonel of the Regiment, Lieutenant-General Moti Sagar

It was only towards the end of 1947 that we in India established our first link with General Sir Arthur Mills. In accordance with his wish, his Regiment was handed over intact by the British officers to the Indian officers at the time of the Constitutional change-over. Every single item of silver, every penny in the finds and all assets of the Regiment were complete. All outstanding bills had been cleared in full. This had not happened in any other Regiment of the Indian Army. So, it was with a feeling of gratitude and friendship that the senior Indians posted to the Regiment wrote to Sir Arthur for advice and guidance in Regimental affairs. His letters to each one of us, whom he had never seen or met, were so full, so detailed and so comprehensive. It was he who guided us and helped is to be established firmly in the Regiment. It was at this stage and due to his foresight, his friendship, his comradeship, his advice and guidance, and above all his love for the Regiment, that the foundations of an everlasting friendship and fellowship were laid between the past and the present. These were further strengthened by his letters, his advice and guidance throughout these seventeen years till the time of his death.

He inspired us by his impartiality, his devotion to the cause of the Regiment, his mental robustness and, in spite of his age, his physical fitness expressed so clearly in his wise and clear decisions and bold handwriting.

The privilege of meeting him fell only to the lot of a few of us— Raj Bir, Nalin and myself. The impact of his personality was there right through the Regiment, for his thoughts were for the Regiment. It was he who conceived the idea and established the Regimental Garden of Remembrance at Stoke Poges — a unique institution.

A brave and gallant soldier, a fine administrator, an outstanding leader, a clear thinker, always ready to take a bold decision, a friend, a comrade, a guide and adviser, his love for the Regiment was second to none; he was the supreme architect of the bonds of friendship between us in India and all of you abroad.

In paying a tribute to him, I know I am voicing the feelings of us all when I say that he was a missionary, in fact, a crusader in the cause of the Regiment. He lived for the Regiment and he died for it.

*By The President of our Officers' Association,
Brigadier H. B. Kingsley*

By the death of Sir Arthur Mills, his family, the Regiment, its Officers' Association, and his many friends in other walks of life have suffered an irreparable loss.

It was in 1924, as a Brevet Lieutenant-Colonel of twenty-four years' service and with his DSO carrying two bars as eloquent testimony to his success as a leader and to his courage in battle, that he was suddenly posted to the Regiment as Second-in-Command of our 2nd Battalion. To come as he did from a famous Indian Cavalry Regiment to a Battalion of Gurkhas was an abrupt change, but he took it in his stride, immediately identifying himself with all our ways so completely that when, after a break of eight months with the 3rd QAO Gurkha Rifles, he rejoined the 2nd Battalion as its Commanding Officer in February 1926, it was hard to realize that he had served in the Regiment for only one year.

It so happened that this appointment coincided with the stationing of the two battalions together in Bakloh after twelve years of separation during which the "regimental spirit" had worn a bit thin. To Arthur Mills the unity of the two battalions was a matter of essential import and, with himself and Henry Scott at the helm, it was most happily restored; and, thanks in no small measure to his leadership and guidance as Colonel of the Regiment from 1935 to 1950, it has never been broken.

When he left the Regiment for higher office in 1929 he was respected and held in affectionate regard by us all. Even so, his appointment as Colonel of the Regiment in 1935 caused some raising of odd eyebrows. In the event, no regiment has ever had a better leader, for it is no exaggeration to say that thereafter The Regiment became his life's work.

When India gained her independence and the Regiment was assimilated into her army, he set himself to the task of ensuring that it should be handed over to the custody of its new Indian Officers in the old tradition, and of forging a strong link binding the Past with the Present in brotherhood.

How splendidly he achieved his purpose!

In April 1947, he had already inaugurated our Officers' Association of which all serving officers are members; and, in the same year, he conceived the idea of a Regimental Memorial on English soil—our Garden of Remembrance which belongs to the Regiment in perpetuity. With similar vision, he inaugurated our annual Remembrance Day with its Memorial Service and Pilgrimage to the Regiment's shrine where those who fell in battle in past wars are commemorated. Each year, at the Memorial Service their memory is hallowed and their near relations take comfort. He also initiated the Personal Memorials which commemorate those who have died since 1945.

It was through his foresight and under his direction that the Third Volume of our Regiment's history was published in 1952. He also established our annual News Letter as a truly *regimental* journal which he himself edited for its first three years. And it was owing to his constant interest in the welfare of the Regiment's widows and pensioners that the Centenary Gift of its old British Officers was devoted to their cause.

It is indeed to his great qualities as a man and a friend—to his fore sight, energy, thoughtfulness for others and unremitting care, that we owe the happy relationship which exists between the Present and the Past. To all of us, whether in or of the Regiment, he was known and will be remembered as "Uncle Arthur"—a sure sign of the esteem and affection in which he was held and is still held by us all in grateful memory of a gallant soldier, an inspired leader, a great gentleman and a true friend. I know that I speak for the Regiment, the Association and all who knew Sir Arthur in offering Lady Mills and his family our heartfelt sympathy.

From an early age Arthur Mills, whose father commanded the 37th Dogras, set his heart on being a soldier, but this ambition appeared to be finally dashed when, at the age of 16, he contracted tuberculosis and had to leave Wellington College with a medical prediction of only one more year of life. His parents sent him to the bracing Himalayan air of Gulmarg and Leh, and there he confounded the doctors. Four years later he was fighting fit and volunteered for service in the British Army, which was then being roughly handled by the Boers in South Africa.

He started his military career in the last year of Queen Victoria's reign when he joined the 3rd (Militia) Battalion, The Royal Sussex Regiment, as a Second Lieutenant in May 1900. He accompanied this battalion to South Africa in March 1901, and two months later he was given a regular commission in the 1st Battalion, The Devonshire Regiment, which was then operating as mounted infantry based on Bloemfontein and carrying out long patrol treks to seek out Boer guerrillas.

When hostilities ended in May 1902, he applied for transfer to Indian Cavalry and, in October, joined the 18th Bengal Lancers (later the 18th KGO Lancers) at Sialkot.

From Here to There

By E. J. S. Burnett

There are many ways of travelling from East to West or *vice versa*. The first time I came out East I sailed in luxury as a very young subaltern in an A Deck cabin on the port side. Just after the War I was carried both ways in the draughty bomb bay of a Liberator bomber. And last year, when I found myself in Kathmandu with a 1955 Mercedes 180 saloon and six months' leave ahead of me, I decided that the opportunity for car-borne travel from here to there was too good to be missed.

I have been often asked what plans I made before setting out on this journey. All I can say is that I wrote to the A. A. in England to get their route card, and asked a friend in Malaya to send me about £100 worth of spares, which included such things as a new battery, five new tyres, a spare set of shock absorbers, a drain plug and other mundane things, and, last but not least, a roof rack. I also successfully tempted Ian and John to be my travelling companions.

Ian is an old friend of mine, and I was delighted when he turned up in Kathmandu to join me on the trip. I met John, a "worthy" of the Foreign Office who was on his way home after three years in Peking, at the "Hotel" in Kathmandu; he has a useful knack of being able to speak languages. His impeccable Russian, Chinese (Peking dialect), French, German, Swedish, and one or two others, made it reasonably certain that we would be able to talk our way out of trouble.

At last the great day of departure dawned. By this time Ian had found important business down in Delhi and John was busy studying the "flora and fauna" of Kashmir. However, I had managed to find two other and far fairer travelling companions who wanted to get to Delhi. We left the Customs Post just outside Kathmandu at Thankot as the sun was rising on 10th October and waved goodbye to the ten or so hardy well-wishers who had kindly come to see us off.

The drive was without incident until we got as far as Amlekhganj, the beginning—or is it the end?—of the Nepal Railway. The road was said to be impassable between there and the border for a car which only had two-wheel drive. I had made arrangements for a railway flat to take us down to the Indian border but none was available. Rather than sit there and wait, I decided we should chance it and go by road. Six hours later, after considerable physical effort by my two companions in the form of pulling out large boulders from underneath the car and pushing it through five or six muddy streams, we reached Birganj where we spent the night. In the morning, as the road was under 10 feet of water in places between Birganj and Sagauli (where the treaty of 1816 was signed), we got the car loaded on to an Indian Railway flat and steamed off.

At Sagauli there are no arrangements for loading or unloading vehicles, so with the help of a dozen coolies we lifted the car from the flat on to the railway platform and, much to the horror of the Stationmaster, drove down his platform and out through the gate; and off we went for our crossing of the Ganges.

In this part of the world this crossing is always an interesting operation. The way you do it is to search around until you find a local country boat which is looking for cargo. You then persuade the crew that it would be a good idea to take your car across to the other side and you haggle over the price. Having brought these negotiations to a reasonable conclusion, all you have to do is to find a couple of bits of wood which you put between the boat and shore, shut your eyes and drive on! If you manage to do this without breaking the planks or going over into the water on the far side you are mighty lucky. You then persuade the captain and his crew to cast off and make for the farther shore. Now this sounds terribly easy, but normally the distance you have to travel is about nine miles, and the length of time this takes you depends on the gods and the river Ganges. If you are in luck, the crossing takes about four hours, but I always seem to be unlucky. This time we managed to do it in just under 12.

At the far side we got off the boat without incident, and drove to Benares, and on to Agra where we arrived early the following morning rather dirty and certainly bad-tempered after an all-night drive. After breakfast and a much needed bath and change of clothes we set off for the Taj Mahal, where I took an hour's sleep on the delightfully cool marble whilst the others were sight-seeing. (They were Americans!)

On our way to Delhi, after nearly drowning the car in crossing two flooded breaks on the trunk road, we came to a third, some 800 yards wide and with the water window-high—and you can't expect even a Mercedes to drive through that—so we searched around and found an empty 5-ton diesel lorry on which we embussed, car and all, and successfully ploughed our way through. We eventually drove into Delhi as it was getting dark.

There I dropped the two "temporary members" and met up again with Ian and John. After five days in Delhi, most of which we spent trying to persuade each other that it was time we left, we finally agreed that that time had come. So, after two hours of hard labour trying to fit everything into the car—it's amazing how much room whisky, gin, beer, dinner jackets, bedding, spare petrol tins and what-have-you take up—we set off at 4 o'clock in the afternoon.

We arrived at the border between India and Pakistan just after midnight to find it was closed, so we slept in the Waiting Room. The following day, at about 11 o'clock, after the Customs people had looked into our transistor radio to make certain that we weren't smuggling gold, we were allowed into Pakistan. We had a quick lunch at Faletti's in Lahore and then pushed on through Multan for Quetta. That night we slept on the new barrage being built on the River Indus. We woke up covered in sand, which was still blowing a storm all over us, and surrounded by an inquisitive camel herd. We then tried to cook ourselves breakfast, which we ate—sand and all. This was the first and last meal we attempted to cook for ourselves until Ian and I slept in the snow on that famous Pass just south of Innsbruck in Austria.

On arrival in Quetta, our next port of call, the car and ourselves were thoroughly serviced. By the time we left Quetta our way of life had settled down to two hours' driving and four hours' sleeping, the first two hours in the back seat and the next two in the seat next to the driver. Anybody who drove for more than two hours at a stretch was considered offside; it was amazing how well this system worked. Our food at this stage of the journey consisted of local bread or biscuit, cheese, onions, tomatoes and local fruit, and beer. Most evenings just as it was getting dark, we opened our cocktail bar, and while the man at the back fixed up martinis and a little something to eat, the wireless blared forth—sometimes Communist propaganda from Russia, sometimes hot dance music from Cairo. And so we bumped on our weary way through Persia. The roads there are heavily corrugated and can either be taken at high speed, if the car is travelling light or, if in the overloaded state of ours, at around 20 mph. About five days after leaving Quetta we found ourselves in the holy city of Meshed in north-east Persia. From there we pushed westward to Teheran to find that we had arrived in time for the Shah's birthday, which we celebrated by giving the car a minor overhaul (in particular the shock absorbers!). Meanwhile we were well looked after by members of the Embassy Staff and sampled some Persian night life.

Seventy miles after leaving Teheran we discovered we were

heading along the road to Iraq instead of Turkey, so back we came and started again. This time we went off in the right direction and drove steadily for Tabriz. In the course of this drive we ran into our first snowstorm; apparently on one occasion, while Ian was driving and John and I were sleeping the sleep of the just, all four wheels locked and the car tobogganed down a steep snow-clad hill. By the time we got to Tabriz the clutch bearing had given up the ghost. It was two o'clock in the morning and freezing and raining at the same time. We found a friendly petrol station and slept the night on the floor of the manager's office. We had to leave before the manager arrived and after some exciting driving we discovered a garage which claimed to be Mercedes agents and did us proud. They dropped the engine and replaced the bearing in about four hours, and we were off again to Turkey just after lunch. We arrived on the Persian/Turkish border on a bright frosty moonlight night at about 3 am, to be greeted by a very ferocious and moustachioed Persian sentry accompanied by one of those very large "man-eating" sheepdogs which are common in the area and are used for fighting off the wolves (*and* unwelcome visitors).

After considerable discussion in many languages, none of which were known by the sentry (or the dog), we managed to persuade the Customs Post to permit us to park the car and settled, down in it for the night. The sentry wandered off but the large ferocious brute continued its suspicious watch. None of us were prepared to take the risk of getting out of the car until Ian was eventually impelled by the call of nature to face the ferocious beast—but not before he had armed himself with a pocket full of sugar. As he anxiously got out, he threw a lump to the hound which it immediately gobbled up. It then accompanied Ian who kept feeding it with sugar; but, whenever he stopped, it made a playful grab at his leg. Eventually he realized that though it stood three feet high it was only a puppy, and that we were free to roam. John then went searching for a room for us to sleep in. As he opened one door he came face to face with the sentry who promptly struck him on the hip with his rifle butt. John, taken completely aback, managed to blurt out an anguished protest of "I'm a DIPLOMAT!"—and, for his pains, promptly had his face slapped. An ugly situation was saved by the shrieks of laughter which came from the darkness behind him, and diplomatic immunity was restored. In the end John and Ian slept in the car in their sleeping bags, and I slept in mine on the cement floor just by the car. The large but now friendly hound cuddled up close and kept me warm for the night.

The following morning we went through the usual Customs formalities and drove on to Erzerum. Before getting there just as it was getting dark, we saw by the side of the road a forlorn Englishman with a deflated Vespa motor cycle. We pulled up (it was our cocktail hour anyway) to ask him how he was, and we got a long tale of woe on the terrible roads ahead of us, the fact that he had a puncture and his pump didn't work, and many other calamities. With some difficulty we managed to find our virginal footpump, took it out of its original trappings and used it for the first and last time of our unpunctured trip. Having solaced our motor cyclist with free air and coffee (or was it a martini?), we bade him farewell.

In due course we arrived at Trabizon on the Black Sea coast to find it a town which had no petrol. We were told that the way to get it was, for some inscrutable reason, to go to the Fire Station and get a chit; we would then be permitted to draw the amount stated when the next load of petrol arrived in about three or four days' time. In some dismay, we set off to do some sight-seeing, and shortly saw what we were looking for—a petrol pump inside the grounds of a large engineering establishment. In we went and asked them if they could provide us with some. To cut a long story short, thanks to John's fluent French, we left with a full tank of petrol which cost us nothing. From Trabizon to Samsun the road follows the coast, which is very attractive and all the more so because the Black Sea, in our opinion, is bluer than the Mediterranean.

That evening in Samsun we had a wonderful meal of grilled fish and grilled meat followed by grilled meat again! This was all washed down with local wine, and to top it off, just as we were getting into the car, we saw a man selling hot chestnuts. We just couldn't resist them and bought a large bagful. The overnight drive to Ankara was full of thrills, because by that time we were out of brake-linings (the drive to a hotel in Ankara had its moments too!). We spent a couple of nights there whilst the brakes were being relined before pushing on to Istanbul.

We had quite a time during our 10 days in Istanbul. We stayed at Park Oteli; we visited Sansofi, the odd night club; we had the original Turkish bath which has been going for a thousand or more years and, during the whole of its life, has never been modernized. But our regular port of call whilst in Istanbul was the Bulgarian Consulate. After a week of trying to persuade them to give a visa we realized that they were not prepared to play, and as we were not at that time allowed to travel through Greece we booked the car on an Italian ship sailing to Brindisi. It was here that we said *au revoir* to John who had to hurry back to the Foreign Office by air. Whilst waiting for the ship we sampled some glorious fresh lobsters from the Bosphorus and a fair share of Turkish champagne.

On the trip to Brindisi we met up with a most amusing Italian lawyer, Alberto by name, who had been on a case in Istanbul. He had one foot encased in plaster, and it was only after we had known him for some time that we discovered that the broken ankle was due to drinking vodka. By the time we arrived in Brindisi we had agreed to take Alberto to Sicily to check up on a prospective wife's property. Being a very sensible man, he wanted to make certain she was worth as much money as she said. And so we found ourselves in southern Sicily, pretending to be three Englishmen interested in grottoes. We arrived in a delightful village, somewhere to the south-west of Syracuse, which belonged to the prospective wife and with it went half a county's worth of olive groves and a number of grottoes which we duly inspected. With his doubts so agreeably resolved, Alberto was taking no chances and when we eventually got to Florence, his home town, we were never introduced to the wealthy fiancée!

We drove to Florence *via* Naples and Rome up the west coast of Italy. *En route* we threw coins into the fountain, but as they were Persian and Turkish currency of doubtful value they didn't bring us much luck. We witnessed Pope John taking over his Vicarage

(I think this is the correct expression) and had a very good meal in a café just off the Square at Siena, the town famous for its annual horse race. Firenza is a town we thoroughly enjoyed, and we only wished we could have stayed longer. It was here that we said goodbye to Alberto, the Vice-Consul for Monaco.

The drive from Florence to Austria took us a brief 12 hours and when we arrived in Austria our thoughts immediately turned to skiing. We spent the night at Lermos. The following morning we made enquiries about snow, to find that the only possibility nearby was the Zugspitz, so off we went. We had three glorious days of skiing (or should I say attempts at skiing?) before we decided that it was really time for us to head for England. We drove back into Austria again from Germany and then straight on through Switzerland, all in a day. We spent long enough in Stuttgart to get the car serviced and to sample the apple cider. The size of the repair bill for the car decided us against any further incursions into Germany, so we headed for Paris *via* Luxemburg in late November.

Whilst getting to know our way around the gay city, we found ourselves near the Folies Bergères. We decided that this was a "must" so far as Ian's education was concerned, and as we were on an economy campaign we decided to have dinner in a nearby restaurant and then go in the cheapest seats. We bought our tickets and were shown to our seats just as the show started. To our surprise, instead of being tucked away in a far corner, the girl led us down the centre aisle of the plush seats of the stalls, and it was not until we reached the second row that she pulled down two little dicky seats for us. It was incredible, we were so close that we couldn't see the wood for the trees, and it took at least three minutes before we realized that the seats were cheap because we were part of the show. I don't know if any of you people have been on the stage there but it's really quite a thing!

After a good final party in Paris, we drove to Calais and reached Dover on the evening of 7th December. I dropped Ian off at his club in London and pushed down to Southampton to see my brother. He was out.

It Happened in Budapest

A diplomatic denouement

By Leslie Fry

It was a gay scene that night when, for the first time on record, the Regimental Marches of the 4th Gurkhas were piped round at the table of Her Majesty's Minister—indeed, I fancy of *any* Minister—to Hungary.

This is the tale of it.

The Netherlands Minister, doyen of the Western and "neutral" Diplomatic Corps in Hungary, was about to retire. He and his wife had been close friends of ours and, since I was next in time to have presented my credentials, the mantle of Western doyen was about to fall on me. On both counts I determined to dine him out as nearly to the tradition of Bakloh as Budapest admits.

So we gave a dinner party for all Heads of NATO Missions—and none of your black tie affairs: "full evening dress and decorations" was the order of dress—the first such sartorial elegance that Budapest, blighted by Communism, had seen for many a year. I understand that some of my colleagues dashed off to Vienna to buy tail coats and white waistcoats and ties; and certainly some of the ladies found the excuse for adding a new gown to their wardrobes irresistible.

It was a gay scene as, dinner over, we sat there sipping our port—19 of us, replete and resplendent. Suddenly the doors were opened and in marched the Piper to play a programme of my careful choosing. True, the piping may not have measured up to the critical approval of—say—Murray-Lyon, but my standards are not so high, and *nothing* could detract from the near miracle of having any piper at all playing round a Budapest table—to say nothing of the electrifying shock that the unexpected swirl of pipe and swing of kilt must have administered to my guests. Subsequently I congratulated them on their admirable composure: clearly the affairs of NATO, in Hungary at least (*pace* Monty), were in steady hands. But I did not divulge the further delights that I held in store for them. In diplomatic as in military operations, there is nothing like the element of surprise.

The ladies withdrew, the port had been round and round, the ladies had powdered; we joined them in the drawing-room. When coffee and liqueurs had been served, I invited our guests "to another entertainment" in the Yellow Salon.

Crash! In marched the full band—Drum Major, Drums, Pipers an' A'—almost taking the roof off. The chandeliers positively quivered. So did my guests. This was indeed Ecstasy in Budapest. Counter-marching was succeeded by a sword dance, a foursome reel and other Scottish dances for full 20 minutes. By then the enthusiastic interest of my guests had been so fully aroused that, when the band withdrew to the dining-room for supper, there was a discreet but persistent edging off in that direction by a number of their male members. I can only suppose that they wished to enquire into the finer points of Highland dancing and grace notes. But where, I hear you ask, did I get the Pipers? When my colleagues put that same question to me, I was happy to reply that the resources of HM's Legation were virtually unlimited, at which the Turkish Minister gravely congratulated me on my harem.

What a happy chance it was that the departure of our good friend of the Netherlands coincided with a professional engagement in Budapest of "The Girl Pipers of Dagenham."

IV

Round the World in Eighty-five Days

By Jack Masters

A travelogue extracted by "Passepartout" from the letters of Jack Masters

Every time the News Letter reaches me I realize with a start that I have failed to make the deadline with up-to-date news; and then, by the next time, I have forgotten again. So I am now going to write up some news that is recent as of this date (27th April 1961).

On 6th November I set off with commissions for half a dozen pieces, plus other possibles. Unfortunately Barbara could not come with me, as someone had to be home for the kids' Christmas holidays. I went to Spain first, very briefly, mainly in order to fix up our accommodation for the summer of 1961. Then up to London for a hectic series of meetings with agent, publishers, and some of the people who had helped me with advice and recollections and research for the autobiography—notably Michael Roberts, whose BM I was in 1942–43, before Joe hauled me away and made me a Chindit. On 20th November I flew from London to Karachi in a Boeing 707, via Frankfurt, Vienna, Istanbul, and Beirut, arriving at 2.30 am I then had to catch a plane up to Rawalpindi. However, I was very well looked after by myrmidons of Maj-Gen Shahid Hamid, lately MGO of Pakistan and now Director General of Small Industries, who was at Sandhurst with me.

The next morning early I went off in a Pakistani Information Service car, with driver and bear-leader, to have a look at the Frontier. (One of the articles I was to write was called "Kipling's Frontier, Then and Now.") Via Kohat and Bannu we reached DIK. On the following five days we travelled consecutively to Bannu, to stay with the PA, Commander Izzat Awan; up to Wana, via Jandola and Sarwekai; back to Tank and through to Kohat; to Parachinar and back to Kohat; and finally to Peshawar to catch the noon plane to Karachi, where I had an important appointment with President Mohammed Ayub Khan.

The Frontier was remarkable. In physical ways so little had changed. The Powindahs were coming down from Afghanistan. Men still strode the roads and hills with rifles on their shoulders. The Shahur Tangi looked as menacing as ever. The poplars were a wonderful pale yellow in the cold sunlight of Wana. The South Waziristan Scouts still roamed the hills and drank eggnog in the mess; and they had shot a fine *gud* just as I arrived in Wana. Izzat is a frontier PA in the best tradition, tough and big in mazri pyjamas and shirt, smoking a pipe and carrying a shot gun—we shot a couple of partridge. The buses and lorries still grind up and down, loaded to the tonsils with goats and armed men.

Under the surface everything has changed. The advent of an Islamic government, and other factors, have turned the Mahsuds' and Wazirs' attention to education. I watched classes of small boys very close to the scene of the 1st Battalion's great Palosina battle of the first war. At Wana, much against my will, I was treated as a visiting VIP of the first magnitude, and hundreds of boys from six to seventeen were out on parade (the elders with rifles, others with sticks); to gymnastic exhibitions; to visitors' books ... . They learn and speak English poetry at the age of thirteen. They are exceedingly intelligent people, and have seen that there is a better life than sticking a knife into your neighbour. All the Tank bazaar is run by Mahsuds, very polite, and good salesmen. The Czech engineers working on a dam on the Gumal River near Gulkach can travel anywhere, without escort, day or night. The Pathans working on the big dam system near Peshawar have been so good and so quick to learn new trades and skills, that the West German Government is talking of importing 10,000 of them to Germany. The Frontier, though not yet quite a tourist resort, is not far from it.

After a spell in Karachi, and another in Pindi, when I tried to get some writing done, I went on to India, flying down from Lahore in a DC 8 of Indian Airlines. Here my jobs were to write something about what has happened to India in the past fifteen years, since Independence; and about the Indian Army today. In pursuit of these two aims—I hung around Delhi for a time, meeting old friends such as the Sawhnys (he is ex-RIN), Baigs (he is Marshal of the Diplomatic Corps), and others. Apart from Moti Sagar, who most kindly put me up in his house, I visited and reminisced and (gently) caroused with Bogey Sen, the CGS (who had been at Quetta with me); Drag Dhargalkar, the MGO, and Hari Badhwar, GOC 1 Armd Div, who had both been my students at Camberley in 1947; Banerji, the MS, also a Quetta friend ... . In their capable hands and under their auspices I went first to Jhansi, to visit the 1st Armoured Division. I had a very full programme, as beside the guest night at the headquarters mess, a young officer of the 5th Gorkhas was being married, and I attended the wedding; the Central India Horse invited me to a formal breakfast—it was the only time available—because my great-uncle had commanded the regiment at the, end of the last century. The 2/3rd Gorkhas produced pipers in full dress, on the CIH Lawn at 8 am.

Next I took the train to Kalka, and was met at dawn by Sohan Lal, and escorted up to Subathu. Satish Sabharwal and his officers overwhelmed me with kindness during a stay of about a day and a half. I see he mentioned that I taught them how to make some cocktails; this is true, but he did not mention that we also hauled a couple of dozen wine bottles out of the cellars and tested whether any of them were still drinkable. They weren't, but it took us a long time to find out.

Down to Kalka again at night, right after a *bara khana*, and on to Delhi, where I arrived in time to have a quick breakfast at Moti's house, shave, and at once set off in the car with him and the family for Dehra Dun. At Dehra we were lodged in the Commandant's (Nanavati's) House, and a magnificent young man in 3rd Guards uniform made me feel I had strayed into Buckingham Palace by mistake ... it wasn't that he acted superior-like—far from it; but I carried only what clothes I could on a round-the-world trip, and a dinner jacket was not among them—not very surprisingly, as I don't own one. An amusing play in the evening was followed by a dinner party at Nanavati's, talk until late, and sleep. The next morning I watched the Passing Out Parade, which was certainly as good as any at the RMC in my day. Afterwards Moti took me to see the Chetwode Hall, where are hung most of the old King's Colours—which have, of course, been replaced by President's Colours. The continuity of the Indian Army, and its sense of its past, were very moving.

I could not stay for lunch but drove back to Delhi with General Dhargalkar, and up at dawn the next morning to fly to Khajuraho, in Bandelkhand, to see the temples there, and fly back the same evening. The airstrip at Panna, where the plane lands, looks as though it had been made by and for Chindits; perhaps I am wrong, but the atmosphere of the jungle, the dusty teak leaves, and the steep little ghats, was very redolent of 1943–44.

That about completed my movements in India. It was a most interesting and heart-warming experience. As I wrote in my article on the Indian Army today, it seemed to me that the sepoy and NCO has improved since the days of the Raj. He is better educated, more alert, and more independent, while retaining the basic qualities which made him what he was. The senior officers are of a quality that would be remarkable in any army. The hospitality, and the goodwill towards ex-BOs, is simply miraculous.

On 23rd December I flew down to Singapore in a BOAC Comet, with a brief stop at Rangoon. I had an article to write on Singapore, and since I know nothing about it, except what I had seen in a 24-hour stop in 1938, I set to work to make contacts among police, business, and army circles. Here I was very much helped by Martin Fuller, with the 2nd Goorkhas, and young Michael Roberts, with the 10th; and by Dick Hull, the C-in-C, who had been Commandant at Camberley in my time there. I ate enormous lunches with Chinese tin tycoons; visited the professor in charge of the political science school; went up the Singapore River and round the harbor in a police launch; sailed out to one of the oil islands and had a look at that; and visited two Gurkha battalions.

On New Year's Eve I discovered that Bruce Douglas was in Singapore, and also David, passing through on a trip to Hong Kong. For the rest of my stay in Singapore Bruce and Audrey took over. We danced, dined, visited a little island out in the bay (it rained), inspected the Bukit Timah primeval forest preserve, and carried out the ancient tourist custom of photographing a rubber tree. On 8th January, still in pouring rain, they took me to the airport, where, after much too hurried farewells, I took off in a QANTAS 707 for Bangkok.

My main goal here was not Bangkok itself, but the ruins at Angkor, in Cambodia, which were to be the subject of another article. So I flew to Siem Reap and duly visited them. They are very impressive, and doubly interesting to me as I had so recently visited Khajuraho. Khajuraho and Angkor are of roughly the same period—eleventh century AD—and both represent a late flowering of a Hindu art form, native in India, imported into Cambodia. At Khajuraho the original vitality was the over-powering impression (that, and a joyful, epically wholehearted eroticism), so that the towering masses of stone seemed to live and breathe still with the energy of the original models. At Angkor there is much more formalism, and conscious "art." Still, it is an impressive place, particularly Angkor Thom, the ancient Khmer capital, which has not been so thoroughly excavated and renovated as Angkor Wat, so that the ruins seem to live in and with the jungle that has crawled all over them since their abandonment.

On to Tokyo, in a Pan Am 707, via Hong Kong, where the plane stopped for a couple of hours—gathering its strength, perhaps, for the dash to Tokyo, which we reached in 2 hours 41 minutes for a new record, reaching a speed of 810 mph. Barbara and I had originally planned to meet in Hawaii, but by now I was getting weary of travelling, so I went straight home instead, flying to San Francisco via Honolulu, and then crossing the continent by train. As my friends will suspect, I am fond of trains, and here the car and the plane are strangling them, so I wanted to take such a trip while it was still possible. So I boarded the California Zephyr on 26th January at 10 am, just two hours before I had left Tokyo the same day (having crossed the International Date Line), changed trains at Chicago, and arrived home on the Twentieth Century Limited at 80 mph all the way, through a blizzard, on 29th January.

The Caribbean Cruise

By Bunny Burnett

Shortly after the issue of NL 12, A. M. Arnott received the passenger list for his Hellenic cruise last April, and sent us the following appreciation: "*I see there is a Miss Bonus (top deck stateroom with shower). She might produce a Dividend; on the other hand she might produce a little bonus, which would have to be shown on the other side of the Profit and Loss Statement. I am in a dormitory for eleven men in the bows, but there is a counter-attraction of a dormitory for twenty-five girls next door. I am looking forward to the trip.*" So far, so promising. But, in so far as we were concerned, that ended the correspondence, and McNab's subsequent letters have given us no inkling of how he fared in his fortnight's gambol on the Ægean pools.

Irrespective of the wealth of Miss Bonus and the attractions of that neighbouring dormitory, we are lucky to have McNab still with us because, during a summer holiday on the Isle of Mull, he had *"one rather exciting experience in my 9-ft. sailing dinghy. It was blowing hard with fierce squalls, and was just like riding a fresh self-willed young horse. On the way back, about a quarter mile from the jetty, a moment's carelessness, and I was in the water. However, the boat floated so I was able to hang on. After about half an hour, when I was beginning to feel that I had had enough, Commander Mackenzie, a retired Naval Officer who is also 74 and lives in a cottage at the end of the jetty, rowed out and towed me in. After a double whisky and a hot bath I was able to drive back to my hotel none the worse. But it took some explaining to my grandchildren after my reiterated advice: 'When sailing, never relax even for a moment.' Anyway, we had a grand holiday, with both sea and fresh water fishing as well as sailing."*

In December McNab moved into what he bought as *"a rather dilapidated cottage with no sanitation but with a fine view across the village green to Belvoir Castle. I have grazing rights on the green and, when I have paid for all the alterations and decorating, I will probably be reduced to grazing there myself"* (which leads us to suppose that he failed to draw that Dividend).

He is not alone in his aquatic escapade, because E. J. S. Burnett enjoyed an even more exciting experience in the water of the Caribbean.

Following his arrival home by car from Kathmandu[1] and five skiing weeks in Austria, Bunny caught a banana boat at Southampton bound for Barbados. There he embarked as the only "1st Class passenger" for a 400-mile trip, costing £4, on an old motor-boat of about 105 tons carrying cargo and passengers between the islands. *"The ship had a crew of twelve—all of them West Indians including the Captain. The trip was uneventful until we left Montserrat, where we picked up an American woman and two 2nd Class passengers, making a total complement of sixteen."*

"After an hour's steaming there was a muffled bang from the funnel, and I went below with the Captain to find out what had gone

---

[1] "From Here to There" (NL No 12)

wrong. We were greeted by sheets of flame coming from the engine room hatch, so I dashed off to my cabin where there was a small fire extinguisher. This I ceremoniously emptied into the flames, and then shouted for people to form a chain of buckets. There was no response; I looked round and discovered that I was shouting to myself."

"I shot back to my cabin, pulled on a sweater, grabbed my travellers' cheques and passport and rushed up on deck, remembering that there was a dinghy up for'ard. There I found the American passenger (looking more bewildered than frightened) but no dinghy. By this time the flames had virtually divided the ship in half. I looked over the side, to see three of the crew in the dinghy; they had launched it so quickly that they had forgotten to put any oars into the boat. In response to their shouts I chucked the odd ladder and a number of spare spars, that were lying about on deck, into the sea—(not so much to help them, but because I reckoned that they might come in useful for us to hang on to!) The next thing I saw was the Captain and the rest of the crew in the ship's lifeboat rowing away through the smoke as fast as they could go. I shouted to them to come back, as there was still a woman on board (and me!) only to be informed, in no uncertain terms, that they weren't coming anywhere near the ship as it was likely to blow up at any moment. I asked my companion-in-distress if she could swim, and was very relieved when she said she could. I therefore persuaded her, rather forcibly, to jump overboard and swim for it, and then rapidly followed suit, thinking, just before I jumped, that this really shouldn't happen to me when I was on leave.

"In times of necessity it's amazing how quickly and how far you can swim, and we soon found ourselves on board the now overcrowded lifeboat which had five oars of various shapes and sizes. After rowing to the dinghy, we handed over two of the smaller ones and evened up numbers a bit between the two boats. By this time it was nearly 3 o'clock in the afternoon; the wind had got up a bit and the waves were about five-footers from peak to trough. It was just like my luck to find myself sitting next to an outsize oar, so I had it to pull as we rowed back towards Montserrat, which was some ten miles away; those who weren't rowing were busily baling with their shoes. After an hour or so an aircraft of the Leeward Islands Air Transport circled the ship, which by this time had drifted a long way but was still visible, burning fiercely, and with the odd explosion occurring from time to time. Unfortunately the pilot did not spot us."

"We rowed on for another hour, when a searching American flying boat spotted us and dropped a couple of marker flares before flying off. On and on we rowed until, just as it was getting dark and much to our relief, a sailing fishing craft, which had come out to look for us, took us in tow. About a mile from shore a small motor-boat took over, and we finally hit the beach a bit before 10 o'clock that night. I was very kindly taken away by the manager of the airline to his bungalow. He had been flying the aircraft which first spotted the burning boat and told me that, when he saw the mass of flames and one lifeboat hanging end up from a davit, he thought that all on board had perished. He and his wife were wonderful hosts. As he was the same size as myself, even down to shoes, he very kindly lent me a complete set of clothes to wear. On the following day I had to attend a Court of Inquiry at which it transpired that the engineer on duty at the time had failed to turn off the main fuel supply when the fire started."

"Two days later I was given a free flight to my destination, Antigua. The American woman was again a fellow passenger, she turned out to be the wife of the editor of a well-known American magazine, with many wealthy and kind-hearted American friends living for the season in Antigua, who not only looked after me very well but also gave me all the sailing I wanted."

IV

Reminiscences of a 4th Gurkha Wife

By Jean McCutcheon (nee Mercer)

From my earliest days I used to hear stories of Bakloh from my grandparents, Colonel and Mrs C. A. Mercer. He had been Commandant of the 1st Battalion from 1890 until 1898. My grandmother spent many happy years in No 6 Bungalow in Bakloh and loved it.

I went to India as a small child when my father, Major Allan Mercer was with the Supply and Transport Department in Loralai, Baluchistan. My brother Eric and I were there for about a year and, incidentally, we lived in the bungalow which later became the Mess of the 2nd Battalion in 1939–41.

During the war I was a Red Cross VAD in a military hospital in Sevenoaks. It was there that I met Donald McCutcheon who had come home on "Stiff Leave" and was discovered to be quite ill. I was pleased to find a 4th Gurkha in my hospital and we soon found that we had much in common! Not the least being that he knew my brother whom I had not seen for six years. In April 1946 Donald and I were married and a few months later I was on my way to India in an unconverted troopship where I shared a cabin with eleven other women, our only luxury being one small mirror on the bulkhead.

I arrived in Bombay where Donald met me and we set off next day on a troop train for the journey north. I had my first experience of being an army wife in India when I had to go down the train to administer first aid to a newly arrived British soldier who had been unwisely sunbathing and was badly burnt. At Pathankote we got a taxi to go up the hill and I was reminded of stories by my grandmother of two-day journeys by pony or tonga.

And so at last to Bakloh. It looked beautiful and no doubt still does. I loved it and soon we were settled in our bungalow—No 4. It was a few days before Christmas and there was a marvellous party for the children in the Mess, followed by a very amusing pantomime which included a song requesting kindness for our four footed friend in the swamp. Hamish Mackay gave me a tour of the Mess building and showed me the pictures of all the previous commandants, some of whom were my great-uncles by marriage. My grandmother brought out several of her sisters and some of them married officers of the Regiment ... Phillip Carnegy, George Frost and also George Rogers of the 1st Gurkhas.

Shortly after I arrived I had the honour of being dined in as a new bride. This was, of course, a wonderful experience which I very much appreciated, and which confirmed the stories that I had heard about the pipers playing round the table.

I settled down to try and manage our bungalow and the servants, not knowing a word of the language, but we coped very well! The bearer, Fazal Din, was a gem and the khansamah, Gharib Shah, had been bearer to my great-uncle George Frost during the 1914 War and proudly told me that he had been to Bath and London.

We were expecting our first baby in May 1947, so arrangements had been made for me to go up to Dalhousie in April and stay at Stiffles Hotel. Daphne Allen, Lester's wife, had been up there for some time and had a young baby, so she was great company. Because of the withdrawal of British troops from India there was no British battalion in Dalhousie and therefore the BMH had no family department open. So our daughter was born in the civilian Cottage Hospital.

Soon we were back in our bungalow, but things were changing. The other wives and children had all gone home except for Misha Mackay and her daughters. Misha was working hard in the Bakloh hospital but found time to visit me and the baby, and I was immensely grateful for her advice and support in what was beginning to be a rather alarming time, as Gurdaspur was one of the eleven districts in dispute between India and Pakistan.

In August Padre Tony Fell came up to Bakloh on a pastoral visit and so we were able to have our baby, Margaret, christened in St Oswald's Church. At the end of the service Padre Fell deconsecrated the Church as in view of Independence it was unlikely that it would be used for Christian worship again, and its future was uncertain. It seemed like the end of an era. Almost exactly fifty years before my Aunt Jess Rawlins was married to Phillip Carnegy in the little Church, not long after it had been built.

A little later on a quiet peaceful afternoon, the whole bungalow started to shake and became full of dust ... it was my first earthquake! Very alarmed, I snatched Margaret from her cot and dashed out on to the lawn. I had always thought that when the war was over nothing could be more frightening than air-raids, but I think that an earthquake is worse, as at least in a raid you know that there is someone up there dropping bombs on you, but an earthquake is very eerie. Tremors went on for several days. One could hear them coming with a noise like an express train and screams from the bazaar below the bungalow. We were all very lucky as they were mild tremors and there was hardly any damage.

Now Donald heard that he would be returning to England on transfer to the Royal Artillery, as the Regiment was one of those selected to be retained in the Indian Army.

We packed up our possessions which we had unpacked so happily a few months before and moved into the dak bungalow. Life was now becoming difficult. There was no mail, no ready cash and no baby food. These vital supplies were only obtained when small convoys managed to get through to Lahore and forage for what they could find. The monsoon had started with rain and hail battering on the tin roof and thunder rolling round the hills. There was no reception on our battery wireless and very limited food as the rain had damaged the crops, except for bhoota which, together with tinned mutton, we had for most of our meals. I kept aside a box of tinned food against our journey home, which was a necessary precaution.

Donald was out on patrols much of the time, so of course I was alone with the baby.

One evening Bhaje ayah rushed in and said that the baby's cot was full of water. Sure enough the roof had leaked and Margaret was awash. The bearer lit a large fire and I tried to think what to do to ward off chills. The old remedy of a spoonful of whisky—in her bottle—seemed the best answer, and it worked. She slept soundly and woke the next morning with no ill-effects, apart from a hangover!

I was very glad to see any of the remaining officers who took it in turn to come round of an evening to see if we were all right, and to check that two riflemen were on duty on the verandah. How lovely it is at Stoke Poges each year to meet so many of these friends, now a little more mature—but so are we all.

To go ahead for a moment. In 1975 we took Margaret and her fiancé, Paul Solon, to Stoke Poges and she re-met many of those who had been at her christening. By coincidence her fiancé (now husband) came from the Malvern area and his family knew the Harrisons and the Dorrells. A small world.

A very sad memory that I have was looking out from the mess verandah and seeing the smoke, each column being a village in the plains being burnt.

We left Bakloh in October—a sad day. Very early in the morning we set off by truck with a Gurkha escort. There was a small but moving ceremony when we were given farewell garlands on leaving the 2nd Battalion parade ground.

When we stopped at Dunera, I was amazed to notice in the rest-house a small table with a pile of beautifully preserved periodicals with my grandmother's initials, HEM, in her writing on the covers. These had obviously been there for nearly fifty years.

There were no trains from Pathankote so we travelled to Lahore by road. The journey was not a happy one and the scenes on and around the Grand Trunk Road, between Amritsar and Lahore, are best forgotten. Arriving at Lahore Station, where there was a pathetic sea of refugees, we were told by the RTO that no more families were to go eastward and cross into India, so therefore we could not get to Bombay. This made me realise that partition was now a fact. We were told that we could get a train the next morning for Karachi, where there was a transit camp. We stayed the night at the Braganza Hotel, which I always remember as providing the luxury of a proper bath. The first since I had arrived in India.

The next morning we boarded the train and were given a "coupé" with our luggage stacked around us. We then proceeded across the dusty plains of the Punjab and the Scinde desert to Karachi. In addition to ourselves the train was crowded with refugees, with many riding on the roofs and buffers of the carriages. We did not leave our compartment until we reached our destination, as every station was past Oswald's Church. At the end of the service Padre Fell de-consecrated the Church as in view of Independence it was unlikely that it would be used for Christian worship again, and its future was uncertain. It seemed like the end of an era. Almost exactly fifty years before my Aunt Jess Rawlins was married to Phillip Carnegy in the little Church, not long after it had been built.

A little later on a quiet peaceful afternoon, the shops that I had not seen for years. I was actually able to buy the first nylon stockings that I had ever seen.

Our wait in the camp was caused by the fact that, ships were filling up in Bombay and only had a few berths left for us in Karachi. Eventually we boarded the "Empire Trooper". It was a slow and not very comfortable voyage, the lounges and saloons being so crowded that most of our waking hours were spent sitting on the stairs. In fact, the Captain remarked that he never thought the day would come when his First Class passengers would be sitting on the stairs. However, we were on our way and arrived at Tilbury in a cold November fog, only a year after I had left Southampton with such high hopes for life in Bakloh.

IV

Obituaries

Colonel R. A. N. Davidson MBE

By Dicky Day

Colonel Davidson—"David"—died on 13th November 1991 at the age of 89. With his death, the Brigade of Gurkhas and the Gurkha Brigade in India, lost one of its best loved and respected figures. David seemed to have discovered the secret of eternal youth, boyish charm and great gentleness. Underneath that kind and gentle exterior, lay courage of a level rarely seen, and one of the most competent officers whose whole life was devoted to Gurkhas. He spoke flawless Gurkhali, and on a visit to his old Regiment, he did so and the speech he made is already legend.

After leaving Cheltenham, he was commissioned in the General List and joined the 1st Bn 4th Prince of Wales's Own Gurkha Rifles in March 1923; he was Adjutant 1930–1934. He accompanied the Regimental Deputation to the Maharajah of Nepal at Kathmandu in 1931. He attended Staff College 1936–1937, and the Japanese War found David in Malaya as Brigade Major 22 Indian Brigade. After much fighting and hardship he was captured on 1st February 1942 and taken to Kuala Lumpur, where he was subjected to constant interrogation. To aid his memory he was, on numerous occasions, tied to a tree and flogged unmercifully with steel corded dog whips—and then left hanging in the tree through the night on his ropes. Life was so degrading, and tortures for defaulters so beastly they cannot be described. When all prisoners from his camp, who were able to walk, were sent up to the Siam Railway, David accompanied them and was elected by his fellow prisoners to be Camp Adjutant—chosen by them because of his so evident personal qualities. He was a man given responsibility for, not only protecting those in his charge in the course of his normal duties, but also for co-ordinating operations of intelligence and clandestine communications, contact outside the camp, and the concealment of ingenious home-made wireless sets. Discovery was followed by severe torture—some were beaten to death with bamboo poles and their bodies cast into the latrines. He was made an MBE for these "special services".

(It is worthy of mention that one of David's brothers and a few companions slipped into Singapore Harbour in 1943 and in one night of glorious revenge sank 36,000 tons of Japanese shipping—depicted in the Australian made film "The Heroes", shown on British TV recently.)

After the War, in April 1946, David took over command of the 2nd Bn, and finally in 1948, took over command of the Regimental Centre at Bakloh (Punjab), with the task of handing over the Regiment to the newly appointed Indian Officers and establishing goodwill between the old and the new. He was so successful that his goodwill and close liaison abounds to this day. The measure of this success is evidenced by the text chosen by (the then) Colonel Rajbir Chopra to open the first issue of the Indian Regimental Newsletter:

"He is like a man which built a house, and digged deep, and laid the foundation on a rock; and when the flood arose, the stream beat vehemently upon that house, and could not shake it; for it was founded on a rock."

David then transferred to the British Brigade of Gurkhas, and became Recruiting Officer in Darjeeling, North India, where he became a great favourite of the tea planters. To this day, the surviving planters remember his "*Pun nautch*" (a Nepalese dance) performed on a table top at the New Year Ball.

He then moved to Malaya as Colonel, Brigade of Gurkhas, the first holder of a new appointment carrying great influence. Before ultimate retirement, he served in the Malayan Police HQ in a special liaison and intelligence role.

On return to the UK, David was for many years Secretary, then President of the 4th PWO Gurkha Rifles Officers' Association, an inspiration to all. He was Honorary Remembrancer of his old school—Cheltenham—and gave dedicated service in the appointment.

Kind and gallant, full of laughter, deeply loyal, David will be remembered with deep respect and great affection by all who knew him.

Jai Gorakh, David!

1857–1957

By John Masters

(World Copyright Reserved)

The past is inherent in the present, whether we wish it so or not, whether that past is dark or bright. This is true on all planes of experience. There are the obvious, material facts—the commanding eyes in the portrait on the wall (long dulled in death) peer into the glass held by the lively young man leaning against the mantelpiece: the 1957 wife swears softly, under her breath, and in Hindi, as she stumbles mad-eyed the dank and airless 1887 bungalow built, she is sure, by some round 4th Gorkha major as a dungeon for insubordinate bats: the subadar's son plays football on a field built and levelled by the sweat of the subadar's father.

There are less obvious and non-material realities, which are more important, for one day the portrait will fade and one day, mercifully, the bungalow will fall down; but there will not come a day when a commanding officer of the 4th Gorkhas is not aware that his actions and even his character are being shaped by the actions and characters of Tytler, King Harman, Grant, Mills, Lentaigne ... Kulpatti and Rannu and Durgia inhabit the JCO's Mess as permanent parts of its spirit, guiding its discipline and giving depth to the human relationships formed there. Sarbdhan Bura, dying of his wounds on the bank of the Euphrates, does not really give his life at some stated number of years after the nameless sepoys of Ambeyla, for both gifts are fresh in our hands, both equally timeless.

This union of past and present became an almost palpable reality during the centenary celebrations in Bakloh this October. It shone on all of us, and perhaps in all of us, like sunlight above mist, giving a diffused and universal light in which strangers recognized each other as old friends, warming the chill out of old bones and the shyness out of young hearts and, most mysteriously, drying up nostalgia—for we, who had thought that we were returning to Bakloh, found that in fact we had never left.

Nothing important has changed. The Bakloh ridge still stands green and chequered with its houses and barracks against the farther slopes of Dalhousie and Dhayenkund, its unchangeableness merely emphasized by a few pylons marching across its flank, a new road here, an improved water pump there. The Gorkha officers have not changed, remaining obstinately their cheerful and masterful selves under whatever set of initials various kindly sirkars have chosen to classify them—the current one being JCO. Nor have the riflemen changed, nor the NCOs, nor the Mess orderlies, nor the shopkeepers in the bazaar, nor the wide-eyed babies surveying the excitement from the looped blanket on their mothers' backs.

Nor have the officers changed; and here logic must stop short at the edge of a cliff, for there is no adequate link here between the past and the present, such as is obvious in the case of the riflemen, the shopkeepers, and the rocks of the Bakloh ridge. The officers are of a different race from those who founded the Regiment in 1857, and their homes are far from the homes of all those who guarded and guided it and at last handed it over to a newly independent nation in 1947. That handover was brief and hurried, though instinct with the special goodwill charged upon all concerned (both Indian and British) by a fine old English gentleman in Godalming; and the goodwill was ardently translated into reality because every one of us knew that our old gentleman, in that time and place, stood above all race, all politics, all compromise, and spoke for the undying Regiment from a certainty of right, and thereby shaped the conflicts and heartaches of the time into a frame for the greatness of the decisions. So a few corporals of the New Guard—Moti Sagar, Raj Bir, Suresh Pandit, Nalin—spent a brief while in the company of a few corporals of the Old Guard—Hamish Mackay, David, the Boy, Bill Mills. Then the physical link was broken. But in Bakloh these October days of the centenary we saw that the officers of the 4th Gorkhas have not changed at all. They are efficient, but wear their efficiency with a light heart and a sparkling wit. They are courteous and hospitable, but not with a host's anxiety, for they turn the guest into a friend before he has hung up his hat. The youngest second lieutenant and the colonel in command share a smile and a snap and an easy confidence which will handle matters in battlefield, bar or boudoir. This is by no means so in all regiments of the Indian or any other army, and never was. How many times have we admired the efficiency of some, and wondered who would die first in their company—their enemies, by bullets; or their friends, by boredom? Or gone laughing into battle with others, the best of good fellows, the laughter congealing on our faces when (too late) the correction to their operation order reached us—"For NORTH read SOUTH throughout"?

But the distinct and distinctive spirit of the 4th Gorkhas is the same, nuance for nuance, light for light. Think back now to those few hurried moments of contact between the Old Guard and the New Guard in the press of events perhaps the most momentous in India's long history; reflect that only a handful of officers, now majors and above, even saw the old Indian Army, and they not the old 4th Gorkhas; accept my testimony that the New Guard is specifically of the pattern of the old 4th—not the old 2nd, or 3rd, or 5th ... and turn to other subjects, for, as I have said, logic and the ordinary processes of reasoning face a cliff here.

Among these friends, illumined by this light, we celebrated the hundredth anniversary. We of the past were not there to make an official inspection of the present, still less to write a report on How Things Are Today. This is fortunate, because our view was limited by several factors: by the heavy curtains of rain which hung across

Bakloh throughout the festivities, descending on the morning of the first day and rising on the evening of the last; by the golden colour of awakened memories and the matching tint in the glasses heaped upon, over, and round us; by the pace, which was a steady dog-trot from function to function, holding raincoat, umbrella, cameras and, of course, a filled glass—a pace which had put this inhabitant of sleepy old New York into a cross-eyed coma by bedtime (4 am) on the first day.

It is not even my purpose to write an account of the festivities, though I feel I ought, in the interests of history, to give the true facts about one or two matters which have become the subject of widespread and ill-informed rumour. First, the lady did not fall into the ditch, as has been hinted; she was testing the depth of water in it, from which she would readily be able to calculate the total flow and hence the rate of rainfall, information which she had promised to forward to our editor. Secondly—officers of the 2nd Gooorkhas never oversleep; this one was wide awake all the time they were shooting off guns at his ear and setting fire to his bedclothes in their efforts, as they supposed, to arouse him; he was merely trying to recall the last four lines of Henry V's speech before Agincourt, and rose from his bed as soon as they had come to him, remarking to one and all on the singular aptness of Bacon's thought and expression. Thirdly—the *buro* did not come back to the mess (the fifth time) merely to kiss the tiger, as some have thought; he came back to kiss *everybody*, but when he saw that the CO of the 1st Battalion was first in line he just kissed the tiger and hurried back to his bungalow, causing, not unnaturally, some speculation. Finally—the brigadier recently seen mushing across Madras behind a sled team of twenty-four matched huskies is not any brigadier of ours; ours have all been counted and found more or less correct, even the one who has taken to wearing a U.S. Marine Corps hat in bed.

Well, it was fun; but hilarity should not blind the critical faculties, especially in a 4th Gorkha, and behind the comradeship and the laughter ringing us we saw infantrymen as well turned out, as lithe and flexible and fast on parade as ever they had been and, in my opinion, rather better drilled. We saw, in Bakloh and on our way through India, an opening-out and a flowering of latent capacities which, in the old time, would have lain dormant because there was not the present urgent need for them. We saw the Gorkha in his traditional nautches, and in others that reflected a power of growth and adaptation which in the old time we were perhaps unwilling to foster, in our passionate love of the Gorkha as he was, of his basic mountain simplicity. We saw a Regiment which, led by its new officers and guided by the old spirit of service, is moving steadily forward into the modern world.

1857–1957 ... and on the fourth day it was over and we went down the hill, the visitors all, returning to our places of retirement, of work, of duty. The title of this reflection, those eight numerals and the dash between, supposes that there is some finality here, that at this point history comes to a stop, that here there is a mark on the page and one can say, we've reached the end, the present. There is no such end, or mark. In those few days the present took shape in a physical reality of union with the past. And now the focus must be turned forward, not pointing toward 2057 or any other specific date, but peering in the direction of the flow of time, along the flight of the arrow into the darkness of the future, all ahead vividly dark, all behind lit by the passage of the flaming arrow. We know where we have come from. In such a time as this of the centenary we must try to see where we are going.

Technical and technological pressure, already in strong force, is increasing every day on these armed and disciplined servants of the people whom we call soldiers. The more technical an arm is the closer it now stands to the end of its existence. The pilots of the Battle of Britain and those young men who drove the bombers through fiery skies to Mohne and Rangoon are near the end of their short line. There will be no continuity between them and their replacements—a row of buttons in the cellar of their nation's chief politician. All the way down the list this is so, and not only in the armed services: where a man's particular skill has been technical or scientific, to that extent it and he are doomed, for the techniques are advancing to swallow him. In the armed services only the infantryman will remain—in fewer numbers certainly, but standing where he always stood, in the centre; for the infantry does not deal, in essence, with techniques but with people. The pride of an infantry officer is not that he can use his slide rule faster than the next, but that he can lift human nature above fear and selfishness. This is an area in which, by definition, no machine can function, and until a universal peace descends on the world I think that our Regiment will continue its forward flight.

But again—in what direction will this flight be, in terms of 1857–1957? We cannot know; but it is folly to suppose that it will necessarily be a continuation of the past. Soldiers are the arms of civil policy, and India's needs are not those of England or the United States. The uncontrollable monsters of scientific advance threaten to destroy the world, and the threat, like the heat of nuclear fission, fuses the most diverse views into union. It is possible that the New Guard and their Regiment may one day find themselves aligned against the Old Guard and their country; and we can only pray, not presume, that it will not reach the point of battle. Whatever happens, we have the past to guide us, speaking now to us from the first date of the title. 1857—a struggle which could be seen as a war for independence?—a conflict of doubt in the mind of every patriotic Indian? ... at the last, resolution that a soldier must hold faith with his freely given oath of allegiance. Whatever the course of the future relations between nation and nation every man who has worn the uniform of the 4th Gorkhas will always respect every other who upholds that faith.

Here, as in so many other cases where a man is trying to say something deep and simple, yet can only find words that seem shallow and complicated, he finds that his thought has already been stated. When his subject is the vast one of nations and peoples whose differing purposes could lead them away from the memory of their comradeship and the privileges of their common humanity, he will usually find that one particular quotation will say all that he wants to say, and imply more. The fact that the phrases are among the most powerful and direct in the English language is something; the fact that the man who made them was himself a giant in love, suffering, and duty is far more. He was speaking about a Civil War, but with the change of a word here and there his meaning is aimed directly at all of us, now and for all time—*"With malice toward none; with charity for all; with firmness in the right, as God gives us to see the right, let us strive on to finish the work we are in; to bind up the nation's wounds; to care for him who shall have borne the battle, and for his widow and orphan—to do all which may achieve and cherish a just and lasting peace among ourselves and with all nations."*

The arrow flies and only one thing is certain—that soon enough, in terms of the continuity of the Regiment, the last of the Old Guard will go to his grave. We leave one memorial in the garden at Stoke Poges, another in the spirit of the 4th Gorkhas, and two headstones are enough for any infantryman to carry in his pack. The pipes and drums are marching ahead of us, and now we are loaded with garlands as we file past the sons and brothers of our flesh who stand, arms raised to us, against the pale sky on the Bakloh ridge. One day each of them will follow us, as the arrow flies. The drums and pipes will march on, speaking harshly of duty to youth, comforting maturity with familiarity, turned mellow at the last—to others, only drums and pipes; to us, the music of the Regiment.

The Battle of Sittang Bridge, Burma February 1942

On the 8th December 1941 Japan entered the war and on the 20th January 1942 invaded Southern Burma.

By the 20th February, 17th Indian Infantry Division had blown the bridge over the Bilin River. Pursued by the Japanese 33rd and 55th Divisions they started to withdraw to the Sittang River to prevent the Japanese 33rd Division, in particular, reaching the bridge first, which would have allowed them free access to Rangoon.

The railway bridge over the Sittang River, fast flowing and 600–1,000 yards wide, had been adapted to carry vehicles and prepared for demolition. Troops defending the bridgehead had suffered severe casualties during a fighting retreat over many days. By 22nd February the Divisional Commander decided that he had little choice but to order the demolition of the bridge with the knowledge that two thirds of his division would be stranded on the far bank.

The bridge was destroyed, by the Maler Kotla Sappers and Miners, early in the morning of the 23rd February. They had suffered severe casualties preparing the bridge for demolition, and could only guarantee a degree of success when it was blown in the darkness. At the time, elements of the 1st Battalion 4th Prince of Wales's Own Gurkha Rifles were still on the bridge at the western end. On the eastern side of the river, "C" Company, 2DWR and the remnants of 1/3GR continued the fight to prevent the Japanese securing the bridgehead. This allowed many members of the Division to continue to cross the river by ropes attached to the bridge and rafts made from anything that would float. Some were lucky enough to be carried in one large Sampan, which made five trips. Others were less fortunate and had to swim.

By the end of the battle a large part of the Division had been lost, either killed, drowned, or prisoners of the Japanese. The remainder arrived on the west bank with little or no equipment and only some with their personal weapons where they were re-equipped as well as possible before being reformed into units to continue the fighting.

The demolition of the bridge was undoubtedly the greatest disaster in the epic fighting withdrawal of the small British force in Burma. Mostly on foot, it covered nearly 1,000 miles in three and a half months, in the face of a superior enemy and, cut off from outside assistance, was the longest retreat in the history of the British Army. Only on the borders of India were the Japanese finally held.

By Dicky Day

The foregoing is a very brief synopsis. Nearly all the units involved have "Sittang 1942" as a Battle Honour. Almost the only exception is the Fourth (1/4GR) and it was always a puzzle and a source of some anger that when a choice had to be made another 1942 action was selected. Because of the confused nature of the fighting, and the appalling casualties, accounts of the action are sparse, and nearly all differ. Certainly our own 4GR history is lacking detail and accuracy. (As the bridgehead defences were being overrun "I whistled up 2 Companies and restored the situation". The troops in question were "D" Coy 1/4GR and "D" Coy of the Dukes under command). The best account is surely that written by General James Lunt.

Through the years Bruce Kinloch 1/3GR and I have kept in touch with the pious hope that one day we should be able to put together a reasonable record, of a battle in which the Gurkha Battalions fought like tigers and suffered enormous casualties in just two days. When we reformed at Pegu, 1/3rd and 2/5th were amalgamated as "5/3"GR, and were about half the strength of Battalions. 1/7th and 3/7th amalgamated as 7GR at almost a Battalion strength. 1/4th remained as a unit. Of 12 Battalions of infantry, there remained 80 British Officers, 69 Indian and Gurkha Officers and 3,335 other ranks, whose total armament was 1,420 rifles, 56 LMG's and 63 Tommy guns.

In the opening hours of the battle, the bridgehead was closely invested by the Japanese, but the situation was relieved by a counter attack by D Coy of the Dukes, and D Coy 1/4th, who then, under great pressure, held the east end of the bridge. At 09.30 on the 23rd February, the Japs got on to the railway line with an MMG enfilading the whole length of the bridge, resisting all attempt by D Coy to dislodge them.

D Coy then attacked towards the 1/3rd Companies under Bruce Kinloch, who were holding high ground to the left, with some success, cleaning out the Japs, only to be halted in the confusion by murderous fire from 1/3GR. To this day I believe that if we had had a bugle (we had buglers) and sounded the "Cease Fire" it would have given us a moment's respite and enabled us to link up with 1/3GR. This gave me the reputation amongst those who came later to the war of being mildly insane, but it has to be remembered that then we knew our bugle calls, had no wireless communication, and runners rarely survived.

Out of ammunition, with no command contact, we came back across the bridge at 05.00 hours the next day the 24th and were still on the west end of the bridge, when it was blown at 05.30 hours (times from General Lunt).

Tim Carew, in his account, wrote "The 1/4th Gurkhas fought like hell to save the day, but in the end did not succeed."

A Nature Ramble in the Woods

By Major P. F. Bromfield MC and Major D. S. Day

Introduction

Last year, Bromo (Major P. F. Bromfield MC) paid me a long overdue visit from South Africa. He stayed with me for several days, and one of the topics of conversation was a small private war we conducted together (as OCs A & D Coys) over a period of several days in 1942, after the fall of Pegu. This was covered in the short sentence in Volume III of the History "the missing A and D Companies eventually rejoined at Natalin".

Bromo and I hope the following will add a little to history, even if there may be some conflict with existing records!

Prelude. Ambala 1941

Our new Colonel was somewhat irreverently looked upon by we young officers as a trifle eccentric, although his ability to drive his Morris Eight into a railway wagon was much admired. One day, Bromo and I were having a quiet beer together in the otherwise empty Mess, when the Colonel came in, cornered us, and abruptly demanded to know how we would handle a cavalry charge against us.

Although very junior, both Bromo and I had acquired Certificate "A" and Part I of "B" in our respective School OTC units, so were aware in 1941 that there were things called Tanks and Armoured Cars, and that Cavalry had been abandoned due to the problems of providing the correct grade of oats. Therefore we believed, not unnaturally, that we were having our legs pulled, prior to being blasted for drinking beer when we should have been on evening parade. The alternative was that eccentricity was attaining new high levels.

We were sharply disabused of the former thought, and were not courageous enough to hint at the latter.

There and then we attended a COURSE OF INSTRUCTION—DEFENCE AGAINST CAVALRY ATTACKS. The essence of the Course was simple. When facing a cavalry charge we were to form extended line, adopt the prone position, and shoot the riders—"horses will then jump over the line, as no horse will jump on a man". (Verbatim recollection PFB/DSD)

Obviously we were excellent students awarded the "D" qualification, as the Colonel ignored our beer drinking misdeamour, and bought us one apiece.

Eventually, we made our escape to the Sirhind Club where two lovely QA's (even at this distance in time, Penny and Pat!) were awaiting us, and we regaled them and other subalterns with our latest story. It caused minimal surprise, as only a few days previously the Station had been entertained by one of our Companies conducting a drill parade on the sloping and quite high roof of the Garrison Cinema. This was at the time the Colonel was training us to be parachute troops.

Pegu, Burma 1942

Withdrawing from Pegu after the furious battle through the town, we were faced by the mandatory Jap road block—one of great strength. 7th Armoured Bde broke through, and went on, but the door closed firmly after them. Things were a trifle rough. We have a clear memory of that wonderful, imperturbable Roy

Cosens calmly drilling, under fire, a very shaky platoon in order to pull them together. John Collard, way out on a limb somewhere needed assistance badly. He had a message pad but had mislaid his pencil! However, with the initiative inborn in all 1/4th Officers, he pricked his finger, and wrote a brief message in blood. Dramatic but practical. (John, please confirm, both of us recall this clearly). No wonder John went on to win an excellent MC and to command the Green Howards.

Previously before daylight, we had also had problems, with what was thought to be Jap scouts wearing luminous shoulder patches. These turned out to be a very bright type of firefly, which were not sitting on the Japs' shoulders, and were impervious to 303 ammunition.

None of us at Company level had any maps. No doubt at top level there were some, but at lower levels the only ones we ever received covered the area we had retired from the previous week. Fortunately, at a very early stage on the Bilin river I had found in a village school a Standard Phillip's Atlas—the thin one in a red oil cloth cover, and had extracted from it the single page covering the whole of Burma. Astonishingly, it proved invaluable. (Everyone will recall the story of the Rifleman (of 1/3rd?) who made his way alone from the Sittang to Imphal navigating by a plan of the London Underground system. At least I had the right page of the atlas).

And so 1/4th GR was committed to a full scale attack to clear the road block. An attack on the axis of the Pegu/Hlegu/Rangoon road, which ran roughly east to west A & D Companies right north of the road, CD and HQ centre and left to the south, followed by what was left of the rest of the Pegu defenders.

History records that finding it impossible to break through, our forces in the centre and left went further south, around the block, and continued their retreat in the direction of Rangoon, and that A and D Companies found a soft spot and went straight through.

Reality

A and D Companies were stuck on their own on what had been the right flank, feeling rather lonely and a little unhappy. They had met strong resistance on their advance to the Road Block, and were finally stopped by a Jap strong point in a house close to the Block, just north of the road. It proved impossible to silence the pair of MMGs (NOT an Infantry Gun as recorded) by small arms fire, so the DS answer was to get within grenade range. All very difficult, but eventually achieved. The only problem which then arose was that we had no grenades, and unfortunately Bromo had lost his elephant gun at the Sittang. However, with the aid of 2″ mortar bombs—with or without a mortar?—Bromo succeeded in wrecking the place. Even then, the survivors were led out in attack by a mortally wounded Jap Officer waving his sword.

All of this held us up for several hours, and we were under constantly increasing pressure from our left, as the remainder of our troops had gone around the block to the South (as mentioned earlier) and were moving back the 20 miles or so to Takkyan crossroads outside Rangoon. A and D were now on their own, unable to get forward or to the left, with no food, very short of ammunition, and short of a couple of days' sleep.

The only soft spot was backwards from whence we had come, and there we went, with no immediate follow up from the enemy. No doubt they were nonplussed by a British unit moving backwards even deeper into Jap held territory.

Having thus disengaged, we turned North into the foothills of the Pegu Yomas, then West in the general direction of Rangoon. (Remember we had no maps, and neither of us can recall that any compasses were available). We were in pretty thick jungle, but there were a few isolated villages, and tracks made by humans and animal paths. But in order to continue to head in the direction that, in the general opinion was the right one, we frequently had to cut our way through dense bamboo, and the rise and fall of the terrain was suitable for a Khud race.

Cavalry Charge—Pegu Yomas 1942

Happily everyone agreed that even in Burma the sun sets in the west, and there was general belief that if we were to proceed in that direction long enough we would bisect the Rangoon-Prome road which was one of the only two highways shown clearly on my School Atlas. On reaching the road, we could enquire from any English speaking Burmese we met which way we should proceed in order to meet up with the rest of the British Forces. Thus completing a masterly operation. (We were unaware that Rangoon had fallen).

At first we encountered one or two small Japanese patrols, which were dealt with, allowing us to proceed peacefully afterwards, without let or hindrance other than the considerable obstacles provided by nature. We entered a long narrow valley, fairly high in the hills, with relatively little jungle. A Coy were leading, Bromo himself ahead, when they suddenly found themselves faced by a Japanese soldier sitting on a nice horse, for moments absolutely still. We were many miles from anywhere, and equally far from any scene of conflict except that engendered by our own presence. We failed miserably to arrest the horse and its rider, who sprang to life and galloped away.

We then proceeded with more caution, and discovered ahead a complete village, obviously long established, occupied by a Jap mounted unit. The houses were raised, Burmese fashion, whilst below them there were cellar like excavations, full of horses. In other words, a bamboo version of old cavalry lines, horses below, troopers above. It was all quite astonishing. (In retrospect, no doubt the Jap unit had been there for months—long before their attack upon Burma—awaiting the time to move west and cut off south—north L of C. A sort of sleeping commando.

Realising that the lone Scout either had or would advise them in due course that they had visitors, we caused them as much upset as possible, and then continued westward with all possible speed.

However, before we were out of the valley they were after us, and overtaking rapidly, so clearly we had to do something. And here the Japs had made a grievous mistake, as they had chosen to attack the only two officers in the whole army who, within the previous twelve months, had attended a course of instruction—DEFENCE AGAINST CAVALRY ATTACK.

With no fuss we formed extended line, as extended and as straight as the topography permitted, and adopted the prone position. Bless his heart, our Colonel was proved absolutely correct. The horses jumped over us, and no-one, but no-one, was trodden on.

It is for consideration that this was the last cavalry charge faced by a British unit. If so, it rounds off history quite neatly, because it is reasonably certain that the last cavalry charge by a British Unit was made a little over a month earlier by a gallant troop of the BFF, led by a British Officer, sword in hand. Sadly, the officer, an old Burmese hand, was killed. I cannot remember his name.

Blue Elephants—somewhere north of HLEGU 1942

We continued on our way the next day, unmolested, and made fair progress. We were naturally a trifle peckish, as it was by now several days since we had eaten, but happily water in numerous streams was readily available. Late in the afternoon, I was leading (Bromo and I took turns so that one of us would at all times select the route), when, emerging from very thick jungle, I looked down from the high point we had reached onto a river bed where Japs were watering elephants, which had been temporarily unloaded. They had been carrying what looked like artillery pieces.

However, the main problem was that the elephants were all bright blue. My feeling was that bright blue elephants were something that in our state of health would not be good for us, so conducted a wide detour. As soon as we could be considered safe Bromo was advised of the reason for the detour. Bromo had spent much of his life in Rhodesia, amongst elephants, but professed himself unaware of any species that were bright blue. However, he agreed that a detour was justified, even for grey elephants.

The next morning we met a solitary Burmese, who agreed to point us in the direction of the Rangoon-Prome road. Our joint command of English, Swahili, Khaskura and Urdu in the event resulted in "Road" being the only word understood by our Burmese friend.

We proceeded on our way, and after much exertion reached a

road, which proved to be the Pegu-Rangoon road running roughly east to west, and not the intended south-north Rangoon-Prome road. We had travelled in a gigantic horseshoe.

There was no sign of life of any sort on the road, so we marched off towards Rangoon to reach the town of Hlegu after a mile or so. The town was deserted, and the bridge carrying the road over a sizeable river had been blow up. There was not a soul about—I cannot even recall a stray dog or any animal, and it was quite eerie.

(Rangoon some 20 miles west had fallen and our army was retreating towards Prome)

Neither of us can remember how we crossed the blown up bridge—but clearly we did so, and proceeded on our way ...

"Our two missing Companies rejoined at Natalin ...
(Vol III of the History)

It is perhaps worth recording that we had then been some 4–5 days without much sleep and no food

Epilogue—England circa 1958

Only my orderlies, 3600 Sunar Gurung and Wazirsing Gurung and I had actually seen the blue elephants. Although I reported them, the only response I was ever aware of was a reference in a rare Div Sitrep to possible previously unknown supplies of alcohol, as an officer had seen blue elephants.

In the 1950's, I was staying in a Country Club in Surrey, to find in the bar one evening Billy Williams, whose brother lived in the district. Over a drink with "Elephant" Bill of Burmese fame, I timidly mentioned my blue elephants. He evinced no surprise, and explained that in certain areas in Burma there was a lot of clay in the beds of the Chaungs, the elephants took a mud bath, and as the sun dried them rapidly they were caked with blue clay.

The End of the Road—1st Bn in Burma 1942

Continuing Colonel Lentaigne's account of operations as written to General Sir Arthur Mills—Colonel of the Regiment at home in the UK: dated July 1942.

Extract 2

PROME—KYAUKSE—MONYWA—
SHWEYGYN—MANIPUR

Thereafter we had a let up and withdrew slowly northwards across miles and miles of paddy stubble till we reached the PROME area. We had little or no chance to refit as there was very little left after Rangoon had fallen, and in fact our armament and MT was arbitrarily reduced by half to re-arm other units and create a reserve.

On the 29th, however, the Battalion marched back towards PROME, and I was sent for to div for special orders. Here I had better describe the ground etc. PROME is a fairly large civil HQ and city on the left (east) bank of the IRRAWADDY. It is at the top of a gorge about ten miles long where the river forces its way through a jungle clad hill area. The Rangoon road goes south along the river bank for ten miles and then turns SE to run five miles or so through the hills till it reaches the paddy plains and the railway at PAUNGDE. From here road and railway run side by side southwards. Northwards from PAUNGDE the railway runs almost due north along the paddy plain and along the eastern edge of the jungle clad hills across which the road runs to the river and then along its bank. At the north end of the hills the railway turns left (west) and runs into PROME where it ends. When I got to div I was told that two Bdes were to hold the city and that the Armd Bde and five motorised BI Bns were to go south to PAUNGDE, beat up the Japs and drive them northwards in the plain. The Battalion with a squadron of tanks was to go down to the

SIMINIZEI area but along the railway line and act as a stop. It was hoped that between us and mechanised column there would be a big killing. I pushed off down a track parallel to the railway with the bn embussed and went into harbour just as it was getting dark the MT going back and leaving me completely on foot except for mortars and a cooking pot pony. Next day I heard sounds of battle to the south in the morning and patrolled southwards for ten miles with infantry almost to PAUNGDE. I did not use my tanks as they would have blown bells going on to the west over the hills. My patrols came back with a few BORs who reported that the mechanised column had not been able to clear PAUNGDE and had withdrawn northwards up the road. These men were in a very bad way, the only one who was at all coherent being a white Russian about whom I was rather suspicious. Towards dusk a Liaison Officer came along to tell me to get to hell back again. Mechanised force had failed in the south and on withdrawing had struck a series of road blocks at SCHWEDAUNG, where they had lost pretty heavily fighting their way back. I accordingly returned and found that my Bde were holding a continuation of the PROME position to the east and I was to extend it backwards to the north across the PROME-PAUNGDALE road as a reformed left flank. The Japs and traitor Burmans had apparently mortared the Royal Marines in their improvised gunboats from the west bank and forced them to withdraw upstream. They had then crossed the river in native boats and put down road blocks in rear of the mechanised force.

Next day we dug in hard and after dark I sent out A Coy to AINGGYAUNG with a squadron of tanks in support at PAUNGDALE. Next day the tanks were withdrawn but A Coy were joined by some Burma Frontier Force (Gurkhas). Enemy air were active all that day but failed I think to spot the fact that our positions were extended so much to the east.

At 0100 hrs on the next day (2 Apr) a very strong column of Japs came along to our position from the direction of PAUNGDALE. They were marching in columns of twelves shouting and talking with no protection whatsoever. Our fellows let into them at fifty yards in the bright moonlight with all they had got. I'd acquired two Vickers guns with seven belts between them and they fired the lot in a swinging traverse while my mortars got some first class targets. The Japs fanned out across the paddy fields and started to shell us with mortars and infantry guns. I was quite happy except for a turning movement that might develop round my left: my only reserve was the Pioneer platoon (20 odd strong) and the Support platoon (3 Brens and 20 odd men). I was rather worried about A Coy out in the blue at AINGGYAUNG, but BROMFIELD in command of them was a first class officer. At 0300 hrs a Liaison Officer came to my HQ with orders for me to hop it at 0330 across country NW and rejoin the MANDALAY road about five miles north of its junction with the PROME-PAUNGDALE road. He knew that the rest of the Bde and Div were also going back, but did not know when or how. I went to the phone to try and get details but it was knocked out by a lucky hit just before I got to it. I only had 25 minutes to get cracking so sent back Vickers, Mortars and Administrative transport which consisted of some pack animals, some carts and a little MT, and fixed up for a lay back about 600 yds in rear to be held by HQ Coy. I sent out orders by the Adjutant (Mountford), 2 i/c (Cosens) and Signalling Officer (Whitbread) because communication to Coys was only by runner and I was frightened that they might make a mess of verbal orders when we were in such close contact. Hardly had they gone, leaving me alone at HQ, when a runner from my right Coy came in to say that the Battalion on my right had withdrawn and that the Japs were beginning to work round that flank. At the same time I saw powerful headlights coming up across country from the SE which might have meant tanks or anything. I strung out the support platoon in penny packets with their Brens as right flank protection and, with 200 yards start of the FDLs, legged it at 0330 hrs. The Coys all clocked in at the lay back which was formed by Signals, Pioneers and Administrative personnel, I closed them and sent them back up a track which I give as the axis and then followed with the HQ lay back acting as rear guard. The Jap never followed up at all! Company commands told me that the men had had the time of their lives and then after busting up the Jap column, several of them had sneaked forward with grenades and tommy guns shikaring Japs hiding in hollows and behind bunds. A mortar or infantry gun on a mule had been shot up on the road and individuals and small parties of Japs made repeated efforts to get to it. A 2″ mortar got the range to an inch and got off 36 effective rounds at 36 different parties who were trying to rescue it.

Things were pretty confused at the RV but my QM had drummed up some hot tea and all ranks got a good drink. The reserve Brigade were holding a division lay back just in front of our Tea Point. The Jap started shelling the area and I realised that the source of the headlights I'd seen coming up must have been the Jap artillery, so I got our guns onto a map shoot at what I reckoned to be their obvious position and the shelling stopped. We then got orders to march north along the road and very soon met A Coy coming in from the East full of good cheer. Almost at the same time as our battle began an identical column of Japs had come up the road towards them at AINGGYAUNG from the direction of SINMIZWE. A Coy gave them all they had at 100 yards from a semi-circular position and, when the Jap mortars opened after ten minutes, hopped back half a mile to another position where they stayed till dawn unmolested. At first light an NCO went out about half a mile clear of the road to call in a section standing patrol that had been posted to watch a vale that came up from the south on their flank. This NCO and the section counted 80 bullock carts of dead being humped back. Neither the company nor the BFF had a single casualty! They realised or assumed that the division had withdrawn as the noise of battle had stopped, so withdrew to PAUNGDALE whence a Jeep patrol was sent west towards our late positions and luckily spotted a small Jap cavalry patrol which they shot up. They then withdrew NW across country and rejoined us. We marched 30 miles that day and entered the dry zone teak forest, very hot and airless. I heard later that a Jap column from across the River IRRAWADDY came to within three miles of the road about 12 miles north of PROME and then turned back. I think that the column that bumped us was an inner encircling movement which did not expect to find our flank so far East, while the column that A Coy smartened up was the eastern jaw of a wider encirclement that failed to connect and so the western jaw was ordered to halt and retire. The frontal attack had come in earlier in the evening on the outskirts of PROME and its success had resulted in the hurried orders for our withdrawal.

The next day we marched back a further 30 miles and were subjected to frequent air attacks. During the day I bumped into Geoff Lowsley with a Burma Battalion who had come across from the East with their division. We were lucky from the air, as we were able to spot when they intended to bomb (they dropped sheets of black paper to mark the target area, then circled to come in on a shallow dive bomb) and by quick deployment and the order "sut" when we heard the whistle of the bombs got away with it. Other units were not so lucky. Later in the day some fighters dive machine gunned and dropped hand grenades but once again our luck was in. We got some tea etc at 2200 hrs and an hour's rest and embussed at 2300 hrs for an all night run northwards, debussing at 0700 hrs the following morning. After two hours' rest, tea and biscuits, we got down once more to digging a Brigade defensive position through which the rest of the force gradually withdrew. On the fifth day we ourselves withdrew to another Brigade harbour. The plot now was that our Corps was to hold an east and west line of defenced harbours, each of one or two Brigades, and about ten miles apart. If the Jap attacked any one of them then the two on the flanks were to wheel in behind him and do him dirt.

We got into our harbour, KOKKOGAW, sent out infantry patrols 12 miles to the south and dug ourselves in. Almost at once our patrols bumped the enemy and that afternoon we had several patrol skirmishes. About 9 pm, a bald headed attack came in on us from the south across open paddy fields. This was not on my front which was east and NE, but gradually the Jap worked all round the harbour and all night long put in attacks supported by mortar and shelling. On our front he never came to close contact as my patrols outside the FDLs ambushed him every time, whereupon he would attack their positions like hell, then stop and scratch himself when he found nothing there. They did, however, penetrate in two other sectors and my reserve (the Pioneer platoon) was put in to stuff up a hole on another Battalion's front, which they did successfully. At another point a troop of 25 pdrs had to fire over open sights to hold the perimeter. At first light a squadron of tanks went out and cleared the air, whereupon our fighting patrols re-established themselves to a depth of two to three miles. We had to do the odd spot of cleaning up inside the nest where a few snipers had penetrated and had tried to create alarm and despondency by use of red tracer etc fired in all directions during darkness.

At about midday the Brigadier came over to my HQ with the report that a village—THADODAN —outside one of the other Battalion's fronts had been found to hold an enemy harbour, but they could not spare the men to deal with them. By readjusting my line I got B Coy (BRODRICK PITTARD; HILLARD having gone to hospital at PROME with his toe blown off) ready for this party supported by nine tanks. They went into the village two platoons up, with six tanks with the forward platoons. The three remaining tanks went up outside the village ready to beat up anything they flushed. I stayed with the Tank HQ where I was in W/T touch with all concerned and Bde HQ. Our people found the village more or less deserted but the tanks on the outside started screaming that they had located the enemy in a narrow deep vale running down from the village into a wide, sandy, dry vale bed. All the tanks thereupon cleared off and sat round the mouth of this vale where it joined the big vale, like cats round a mouse hole. They would not "go in" as they were scared of an A/Tk gun which they thought was there. They then all started to scream for the infantry to come and bolt the enemy. I went up to the village and found the reserve platoon of B Coy who had heard nowt of what the tanks were doing. I collected them and took them on a detour round to the main vale, and up along it to the mouth of the subsidiary vale. Brodrick Pittard and his lads then bombed their way up this vale while I collected a second platoon to stop the far end, and the third to be ready to go in from a flank. The plan worked really well and what were not killed in the vale bolted over the open and were wiped out by the tanks who had been joined by another squadron and in all got about 20 Brownings to work. Brodrick Pittard, whilst working up the vale, came across a telephone wire which he promptly cut. Almost immediately the Jap guns opened up and started to feel forward. I saw the line they were working on and cleared it of our men, advising the tanks to keep clear too, but they reckoned their armour was proof and stayed put. When the show was over I told Brodrick Pittard to rally the Company and stand by for further orders, while I cracked off myself to Tank HQ and W/T Bde that the job was done. On my way I met Mountford (the Adjutant) who I had left wounded at Bn HQ, who had come back with the rumour that I had been killed, Brodrick Pittard was missing and the Company badly chewed up. I told him all was OK and to hang around keeping an eye on the show till I returned. I warned him of the shelling. Brigadier told me to close down and on my way back I was charged by the Tanks going flat out. Apparently a lucky hit had blown the tracks of one of them and had set fire to a can of petrol they were foolishly carrying on the rack at the back. Mountford had run forward to help the crew get out and the next shell shattered both his arms. The tanks picked him up and came in. I collected B and went back to Bn via Bde to report. The MO took off Mountford's right arm and sent him back by ambulance. Unfortunately he died that night from loss of blood under a second operation. He was a first class Adjutant and the best officer by far in the whole Battalion. I felt his loss a lot, particularly as we were now very short of BOs and for the rest of the show I carried on without an Adjutant, which was a bit of a strain.

All that night the Jap kept up pressure, but his attacks were very half-hearted affairs. B were very unlucky in this scrap as they lost two GOs killed and a third wounded. Only one other man was killed, and their total casualties were twelve.

Next day we could not locate the Jap anywhere, but his air came over three times and gave us a pasting with HE and incendiary. These were all concentrated on my sector, but I lost very few men as we were well dug in. Unfortunately, however, the QM was wounded in the ribs and had to be evacuated. Our Administration was all in a village which took the first raid, only two men (manning Bren guns) being hit. We got our MT and A transport carts out as also about half the mules and the ammunition. A slit trench full of 3" Mortar bombs, however, started to go off through a thatched roof being blown onto it and I had to call off our people, with the result that several wretched mules were burnt to death and we lost all our cooking pots for about the third time. However, we had by then learnt to cook in kerosene oil tins, gurrahs taken from villages and corrugated iron sheets for chapathis.

It was now obvious that the Jap had bypassed us and heavy attacks were going in on the Burma division on our right (west) in the YENNANGYAUNG oil field area, so once again our division started to withdraw. Chinese began to roll up at this stage from sundry directions and our Brigade and the Chinese did rear-fighting till everything was clear, when we did 125 miles by MT in twenty four hours over the most atrocious road, the first 30 odd miles being a metre gauge railway embankment from which the railway lines had been torn up. B Coy on debussing were attacked by Jap fighters with machine guns and hand grenades, but drove them off with no casualties.

We only halted for a few days in this locality when the Chinese took a knock to the east and forced us to withdraw north again. Once more the Brigade took up a rear guard position at KYAUKSE to cover the withdrawal of the division across the Irrawaddy by the AVA Bridge. Here we were on the right of the Brigade position with our FDLs along the line of an irrigation channel. The Jap had got tanks by this so I went to the canal headworks, monkeyed with the sluices and got the channel flowing. By breaching it we were able to flood the paddy stubble in front of our FDLs and make it tank-proof. This worked well, but it brought out hundreds of snakes. One man was bitten but we managed to save him. Here the Brigade had a tank regiment with a troop of 25 pdrs and an 8 gun 25 pdr battery under command.

The honours this time went to BILL WILLIAMS' lot who bore the brunt of the Jap attack. The Jap went baldheaded at them astride the main road through some very thick stuff and drove in their forward Company. However, the LIMBU-RAIS counter-attacked at first light and laid out close on five hundred. We on their right really only got the edge of the attack but had some fun with their westerly encirclement column. A platoon patrol five miles out to the south west spotted a Jap battalion go into a village. They got the news back and a troop of tanks went out with an armoured OP. Twelve 25-pounders shelled the Japs out of the village and the four tanks and the platoon played with them in the open till they bolted into another village, when the guns repeated the dose. We reckoned that the Japs lost 500 in this party.

We got orders to "beat it" at 1800 hrs, got clear without much trouble and bussed back over the AVA Bridge which went up that night.

The Army now took up positions East and West along the right bank of the IRRAWADDY, with the Chinese across the river at MANDALAY. The Mongols were the right Brigade of our DIVISION. The day after we got into position at about 0900 hrs, news came that BURDIV HQ had been shot up at MONYWA and the Japs had got the town. There was no news of the BURDIV Brigade across the CHINDWIN and their other two Brigades were still crossing the IRRAWADDY. The "MONGOL HORDE" were placed under command of "BURDIV". There was only MT to lift half a battalion, which had to be found by taking all the vehicles of unit transport (approximately two 3-tonners per battalion for all purposes, eg Mortars, ammunition, cooks, tools etc—we had no bedding).

I was told to start the ball rolling, so "jeeped" westward with my runner and a Tommy-gunner, leaving the left wing to embus and follow on. When I got there I found DIV HQ badly shaken, the first of their Brigades arriving after an all night march, very tired and dispirited, and another Brigade from our Division arriving by train. They put this Brigade in to go westwards and try to clear the town while they concentrated their own two Brigades and our Battalion behind them.

Just before dark FLOSSIE COSENS rolled up with the rest of the Battalion (the lorries having done two trips) and we went into harbour to protect DIV HQ and all the odds and ends. At 0200 hours I was put under command of one of the Burma Brigades and we marched west at 0600 hours.

The plot was for our sister Brigade from our Division to continue pressure on MONYWAS from the EAST, one Burma Battalion to go round to the NORTH and take the Japs in flank and rear, and the Brigade to which I was attached to follow up westwards in reserve.

The turning Brigade did a grand chukka but never put in an attack. Our sister Brigade worked up to the outskirts of the town and then stopped. My new Brigade was then ordered to go through and clear the town, attacking "two-up", we on the left. My start-line was 100 yards in length, my first objective, the centre of the town, one MILE in length, my final objective a mark on the map NORTH of the town; to this day I do not know if it was a marsh or a hill. No artillery support was allowed as the whereabouts of the turning Brigade were unknown and I might shoot them up.

So off we went, "one-up", intending to fan out to "two-up" when the front widened. Within five minutes I saw that the Battalion on my right flank had disappeared, which was more or less what I had expected. However, we pushed against the Jap front and soon found a soft spot which we bust by mortar concentration. I then went back to get the two reserve companies ready to go through but one was delayed as the Jap fired the houses at my selected point of attack, which showed that he was windy. Before the fires had died down enough for our fellows to go through, the Brigadier came up to say the attack was "off", as they had found a way round. We had lost fifty men in the leading Company and I reckon that the break-in and mopping up would have resulted in another four hundred casualties (75% and more of the Battalion). Still, it was worth it as until then I had thought our only hope was to break a way through.

At 2100 hours I broke contact, went back three miles the way I came and then "rear-guarded" through the night, fetching up at ALONE, exactly eight miles from where I had started, by the direct route. Spent the day trying to get food, water etc for the men and started marching at 0900 hours as rear-guard. A squadron of tanks, however, arrived with orders from Corps to lift the Battalion back to our own Brigade and DIVISION. Half the battalion went off direct in lorries and I stayed with the other half and went back twenty miles to the tank harbour where we had four hours' sleep. We then marched again as rear-guard with tanks covering us until another batch of lorries lifted us back forty odd miles to where I found our Brigade embussing. We went straight on all that day and night and debussed at a place called PINGYAUNG at about 0500 hours. Here we halted three or four days while the whole force went through, then marched twenty miles by night and bussed another twenty five that day to SHWEYGYN ferry on the CHINDWIN.

The road was a very Kachha track through teak forest littered with broken down vehicles of every description. At dark we went into Brigade harbour in the jungle about five miles from the ferry and heard that BILL WILLIAMS' push, who had led the column, had actually got to the ferry in the dark. At morning "stand-to" I heard mortar and LMG fire from the direction of the ferry and went down and woke up Brigade HQ.

RONNIE CAMERON jeeped off to find out what had happened and we waited. Apparently the ferry was guarded by an Indian battalion of which one Company had been evacuated ex RANGOON, one Company had been taken across the river the previous day, a third Company was out cutting firewood for the river steamers and one Company and HQ Coy were on the job. Near them was BILL WILLIAMS' lot, dossed down exactly where they had debussed at 2200 hours.

At first light the Japs rushed BILL WILLIAMS' battalion and got two of the posts that overlooked the ferry-head, which was in a basin surrounded by a ring of conglomerate jungle-clad hills, all more or less knife edges except at a few points. DIV HQ, about two miles from the basin, ordered RONNIE to piquet and hold the nala running from them down to the basin and to make good the hills overlooking the basin. This would enable everything either to pass down the nala into the basin on to the ferry boats and away or, in the worst case, to destroy all vehicles and guns and get men away up a goat track which ran from near DIV HQ NORTH and parallel with the river.

RONNIE gave his own battalion the job of piqueting the Nala and us the job of sweeping the basin clean. The Jap, finding that the basin was not entirely in his hands, decided to encircle it and started to work up the Nala connecting us with the basin. RONNIE's battalion were late in coming up so he reversed the roles and gave me the job of piqueting. I put in "B" Coy, (BRODRICK PITTARD) and "C" (SMART, who had now returned) and just got them there in the nick of time. By using the Mortars flat out I blasted the Jap off a key ridge and got "C" up onto it. After that it was fairly easy to hold our positions as both "B" and "C" were able to give good targets to the Mortar. Meanwhile, RONNIE's crowd were still slow in coming on and BILL WILLIAMS was having considerable trouble in hanging on in the basin. However, the BOFORS AA guns did first class work shooting Japs off the skyline. The sweep through the basin never came off and towards dark DIV decided to burn everything and hop it up the goat track. I think the chief point was that the ferry boat crews would not face it and in any event, it would have taken two to three days to clear all the tanks, guns and MT, during which the Jap would have been heavily reinforced.

I was ordered to stand by and go like smoke when I got the tip. All the people in the basin streamed through me and then RONNIE came along and told me to go. I cracked off the light signal for my first lot to come off and then shot back to the next corner and banged off another light signal. Going strong round the bend to poop off another I found 4000 troops of sorts concentrated in the Nala bed patiently waiting for the track to clear in front of them. I put out stops and prayed hard that the Jap would not follow up; he did NOT and we stayed there till 0400 hours. One Jap with a tommy-gun could have killed thousands. The block was caused by a mountain battery and L of C troops with their mules heavily overloaded and unable to see where they were going.

All night we were almost deafened by exploding ammunition and lit up brilliantly by blazing lorries, but up the deep jungle-covered side Nala where the goat track twisted its tortuous way it was pitch dark. When we eventually moved off and day came, we found the track littered with kit and a mule over the Khud every ten yards. We did ten miles of this, beating along stragglers from the armoured Brigade, who had to march for the first time in months, and then got to a place on the river bank where the steamers could lift us off. And that was the end of our fighting.

We then marched across the hills and jungles of the BURMA-ASSAM frontier till we reached the moderate civilisation of MANIPUR. These last marches were in many ways the worst.

There was little water, long distances, steep gradients and at the end Monsoon rain which converted the earth track into a slippery slide, very difficult to climb with the modern, nailless boot. The whole route was fouled by refugees and stinking corpses every few yards, which made breathing almost impossible.

The Battalion manhandled all its Brens and their magazines throughout the whole campaign at all times. On the march we manhandled our three 2" mortars and one 3", all with 36 rounds each. In addition we had to carry the QM (MILNE) and another man for long distances, the former having fallen forty feet over the Khud and the latter being incapable of walking through dysentery. The last march was thirty miles in rain. A climb 5000 feet followed by a drop of 4000 feet and we did it without a single fall out. The men throughout the show were first class.

Our casualties were:

British Officers
Killed: MOUNTFORD
Wounded: FLACK, HAWKINS, VAN MAURIK.
          HILLARD, COLLARD, DAY, MILNE.

Gurkha Officers
Killed: PADAMBAHADUR, SHERBAHADUR,
           DILBAHADUR
Wounded: SARBAJIT, GANGARAM, NARSING.

GORs
Killed: 40
Wounded: 114
Missing: 185.

The missing are a mixed bag. Many are definitely dead, some must be prisoners, others were evacuated to hospital and may have died of wounds or illness. A few got cut off in action and got through from BURMA with refugees.

Our casualties were the lowest of any battalion in the Army; in great part due to luck and in part due to care in avoiding unnecessary losses. Discipline prevented others. In general, discipline was bad in the force in almost every respect, but we kept a very high standard going all the time and so saved ourselves a steady drain of avoidable casualties.

The big surprise of the war was Jem RAMDARSAN (RANNU's grandson): I made him Pioneer Jem, but he never had a chance to pioneer. He rejoined us from a field works course on the eve of sailing and all our pioneers gear went west in the dump.

His platoon then acquired an LMG from God knows where and proceeded to take a hand in battle. At the PEGU road block they did first rate work and were then officially recognised. Later, as our strength went down, I incorporated the AA and the support platoons under them until at one time they were a commando of RAMDARSAN, 60 men and no less than 10 LMGs of various types and ages. Rough stuff was their speciality and they never flinched at anything. The pioneers were a pretty grim lot, all ex-bandsmen, all tough and collectively with all the guts in the world. AGAM also did first class work in charge of the mortars.

The Battalion lived up to its old motto of always being first class on service. We never ran and always did the job given us. "PUNCH" COWAN, "BILL" SLIM and General ALEXANDER told us, and several times, that we were the "stud ducks in the puddle" and our Brigade became a byword in the Burma Army—"If 48 (the Gurkha Brigade) is on the job, then all is well". The tanks and gunners always wanted to be with us, as also British Infantry.

Trooping

By Patrick Lumley

I arrived in Bakloh early in June 1942 and by the end of the month was told that I would be going to the 1st Battalion.

During the next week, I learned that the draft would consist of six other BOs and two hundred recruits.

Of the BOs, A. B. D. Scott, Alec Lock and Doug Irvine were in the nineteen to twenty years age group and J. Lister, Curly Lloyd and Frank Westcott, slightly older than myself, at twenty-two to twenty six years.

All six had more experience of India than myself, having been a longer time at the RC as well as having done a six month OTS course, against my short two month course. But I was senior officer by virtue of commissioned service in England.

There were no NCOs in the party and I was relieved to hear two Jemadars Manbahadur Gurung and Basantbir Gurung would be going with us.

It was about the 7th July, in the early afternoon, we paraded in pouring rain at the embussing point. Jem Basantbir arrived late and Col Owens promptly put him under open arrest.

The journey down to Pathankot was uneventful. The Colonel had told me to watch the road, and if there was any sign of it being washed away, to de-buss and allow the buses to negotiate the awkward sections unloaded.

We had to do this four times on the way, and I must say that under arrest or not, Basantbir proved himself to be a great asset and continued to be so for the next two weeks.

At Pathankot, the recruits loaded the large amount of stores on to the train and settled themselves for the journey. It did not seem to me that they would be very comfortable, but there were no complaints. The train left late that night, the next day was unremarkable and the following morning we reached Lucknow.

We waited about four hours in Lucknow, during which time the Railway Transport Officer told me that some civil disturbance was causing disruption on the railways. This did not affect us at the time and the following morning we arrived at Gorakhpur. One recruit left the train at this point and we did not see him again.

Shortly after leaving Gorakhpur the train stopped again. The reason for this was that a section of the track was missing. The train was on an embankment and the surrounding fields were flooded. At Basantbir's suggestion, we fished around in the shallow water and found the missing section, two rails with sleepers all intact. It seemed that the saboteurs had simply removed the bolts from the fish-plates and heaved the section of track over the embankment.

We decided that we had enough men to lift this piece of track—as I recall it was about forty feet long—back into position.

In the light of my subsequent experience, I now feel that this was a very risky operation. If any of the men had slipped on the steep embankment and let his share of the load fall, some of the men could have been seriously hurt. However, at that time no such thoughts bothered us and the rail was soon back in place. We did not find the fish-plates but the train crawled over the repaired section quite safely.

While we were replacing the track, the saboteurs were removing more track further down the line. While we were attending to this second obstacle, civilian passengers in the front three coaches on the train started to leave us. All had gone by that night.

By the time we reach Siwan, it was getting dark and we decided to wait there until daylight.

We decided to mount a guard and agreed that eighteen men with six patrolling and twelve stood down would be sufficient. The GOs paraded the guard and explained their duties. The men not on the first watch were ordered to unload their rifles. In doing so, one man sent a round through the glass roof of the station. It made an impressive noise and brought down a hail of abuse on the unfortunate offenders's head.

At this stage my own knowledge of Gurkhali was limited to asking the men if they had taken tea or food and if all was well. Fortunately I did not get any negative replies or I would have been stumped.

The next morning as we were preparing to move, the District Magistrate arrived and told me that he was going to keep us in the area for local protection. I replied that I was under orders to proceed towards Calcutta. He said that he had jurisdiction over all troops in the area and ordered me to stay. I said that I was sorry not to comply, but as we were simply passing through, I did not think that we could be classed as troops in his area. We then saluted each other, shook hands and the train moved off.

We had two more cases of fishing for railway track. While

working on the second section, we could see a party of men working on the line further down. I told Alec Lock to take six men and stop them. I also reminded him of one of the few things I had learned at OTS, namely that we were not allowed to fire on civilians unless authorised to do so by the District Commissioner, or someone of similar status.

Alec set off and we soon heard the sound of rifle fire, the party returned and reported that the saboteurs had dispersed. I started to remonstrate with Alec regarding the shooting, but as he had only fired over the heads of the rioters, I did not press the point.

I am not sure exactly where the next setback occurred, it must have been near Chapra. The railway crossed a river over a narrow but steep gorge. Here a section of track was removed and dumped at the bottom of the gorge. There was no choice but to return to Siwan, slowly, the engine pushing the train. There we spent the night.

We heard that the rioting was getting worse. There did not appear to be any trains on the line, but this was not confirmed as the telegraph lines were cut.

In the morning, the locomotive which had been unhitched so as to place it at the front of the train, was missing. The Magistrate came and told us that as the locomotive was not available, we might as well stay in his district for the present. I apologised again and said that I would have to get back to Lucknow for further orders.

No one could tell us where the engine was, but we eventually found it in a shed. It had steam up, but it was chained to another engine which was quite cold. I asked the station master to find a key for the padlock. He told me that the key was with the driver, who had gone home, having completed his tour of duty. I said that he, or someone else must produce a key and another driver. Frank Westcott suggested that we should shoot the lock open. Of course, the lock could have been cut with a hack saw, but shooting (which probably would not have worked) seemed more dramatic. Anyway, the threat of shooting was enough to get us the promise of a key and an engine driver.

After consultation with the guard, we posted two riflemen in the engine cab to support the driver and fireman, paid our respects to the Magistrate and started off.

We travelled slowly, being aware that various sections of the track had been laid by ourselves and could easily be put out of alignment.

We moved slowly, not stopping at stations but keeping a look out for other trains which might be on the line, or points switched against us, as at this time normal signals were not operating.

On the second morning we came to a small town between Gorakhpur and Lucknow, whose name I forget.

There was a large crowd dancing and shouting on the platform and we could see more people crowding round the station entrance.

As the train stopped, one man seemed to be trying desperately to enter our compartment. Being stark naked, he did not appear to pose much of a threat to us, so we opened the door cautiously to allow him and no one else in. We gave him a blanket and discovered he was the local Police Inspector, who had been trying to quell the riot single handed.

The station was a mess. Broken windows, smashed doors and furniture and tickets scattered about like confetti. No railway employees were to be seen.

We posted riflemen at the windows of the train facing away from the platform and also on the platform, two to each carriage door. My idea was for them to stand quietly at ease, observing the crowd, hoping that this would have a calming effect. I was not sure how well the GOs had understood my instructions, nevertheless they were smoothly carried out and the crowd near the train ceased their demonstrating.

We had a short conference and Frank offered to take a small party on a "Show the Flag" march, through the town.

We assembled thirty men, unarmed except for Kukris and Frank's pistol, and agreed that he should not be away more than an hour and a half.

The party duly returned. Frank reported that after some initial hostility, one man received a cut across the abdomen, the cut was not deep, but had the desired effect and there was no further trouble.

The situation was now quiet, so we moved on, arriving with the Police Inspector in Lucknow that evening.

Our friend the RTO met us and told us that the laws regarding firing on rioters had been relaxed and that local commanders could now open fire if they considered it to be necessary. I told him that we had already anticipated this order.

We were put in a rest camp, where we stayed for three days. We did not try to arrange any entertainment for the troops who were quite happy washing clothes and resting.

During this time Jem Manbahadur developed a fever and had to go into hospital. We arranged for him to return to Bakloh as soon as he was fit to travel.

On the fourth day we assembled at the station ready to continue. After seeing the draft settled in the train, I saw that a tall Major had joined our group of BOs.

None of us had previously met Roy Cosens, although we knew him by reputation. I was more than pleased when he told us that he would take charge of the draft for the rest of the journey.

Long Range Penetration Group Dec 1942–May 1943

Trevor Braham in his book "Himalayan Odyssey" in writing about Gurkhas—he was climbing in Nepal—says: "I soon began to distinguish differences between tribes, each speaking their own dialect. The Tamangs of the lower valleys, the Chettris from whom most of the Gurkha soldiers are drawn, the Gurungs of Central Nepal and the Newars of the upper and trading classes." Perhaps Braham had been fêted by a recruiting party from the 9th Gurkhas?

T. M. L.

Copy of Diary Notes made between December 1942–May 1943 by Colonel F. R. S. Cosens, 4th P.W.O. Gurkha Rifles, commander of the LONG RANGE PENETRATION GROUP.

Since the beginning of 1942 the Japs had had matters all their own way in Burma. The army in Burma under the command of (then) General Alexander had carried out a delaying action of about 1,000 miles, against much superior Japanese forces and for most of the time with no air cover. Since the monsoon started in May 1942 the Japs had made no effort to extend their zone of occupation over the thousands of square miles of inaccessible mountain and jungle, so the British forces had a welcome respite in which to recover, reorganise and get down to serious training. The monsoon rainfall reaches 200 inches in five months in many places, but despite this the experienced units and new reinforcements carried out continuous training, drenched by day yet lacking a change of clothes and mosquito nets.

The Southern front leading up to Chittagong, along the west coast of the Arakan, was only held by patrols and little signs of enemy occupation were seen. In order to boost morale and to give the Japanese high command something to worry about it was decided to send 14 Div to occupy the Arakan down as far as Akyab. To guard the left or eastern flank of the Div the first of the LRPGs was organised. I was ordered to report to Gen Lloyd (later killed in an air crash) and was given two state forces battalions from Tripura state. About 15% Assam-born Gurkhas and other Lushais, Nagas and Assamese. Running to the sea is the Kaladan river, which ends at Akyab and rises 300 miles north in the Chin Hills. The idea was to hold the river line in order that ample warning could be given should the Japs react by a flank attack against the Division moving south-east down the Arakan.

I had to draw cash (no paper money) to cover estimated expenses on hiring of boats, local food purchases, pay of porters, etc. Maps were few and large areas of the country to be covered were marked "unsurveyed dense jungle". The route followed was 85 miles to the Sangu River, 30 miles over a 4,000 foot range (the border between Burma and India) then 90 miles down the Kaladan River into Burma. In peace time the Sangu River was only navigated for a few miles by river-side villagers, for fishing. The fishermen and sampan owners were loath to accept service with the Army as the unsavoury reputation of the Japs had already reached their ears. However, money was forthcoming and terms favourable to all were accepted. One unit was despatched on 8 Dec, with orders to proceed as far as possible and to establish a forward base. Force HQ and the second battalion followed on 15 Dec. In the first few miles progress was simple and uninterrupted. The river was low, the current slight and pools were deep.

Then followed a series of rapids. In each case everything had to be unloaded and carried over huge rocks whilst the boats were pushed and pulled up against the current. Progress was maintained at about 15 miles a day. Steep hills covered with impenetrable forests ran right down to the water's edge. Jungle fowl and barking deer were seen in plenty and quite a few were shot by rifles. Anyhow, aiming from a rocking dug-out or sampan isn't easy. At the advanced base deep patrols were sent out, but drew a blank. We crossed the Burma border over the range of hills on Christmas Day 1942, and we were the first to re-enter Burma since the Spring retreat. The event was celebrated by bully beef a la bamboo shoot, backed by rice and washed down by very potent zu cum rum. Occasional songs had to be cut to the minimum. The first view of the Kaladan River was a thrill. It flows in flat country with an appreciable river traffic of dug-outs and sampans. Here another base was organised and villages approached for hiring of 85 sampans and some fast dug-outs for reconnaissance purposes. The political officer with the Force, an Anglo-Burmese, organised his own intelligence service from local villages and these provided light screens for the main force. The food problem was difficult, but grenades kept us going with fish.

On 10 January 1943 the first move was made to a former provincial outpost named Paletwa. All troops travelled by boat with no boots, equipment on the floor of the boats and weapons loaded and held across their knees in case of ambush. It was uncertain whether Paletwa was occupied or not but when we arrived we were told that one week previously a Japanese patrol had been there and had murdered all the local born Gurkhas in public.

(Here to deviate. Utmost secrecy had been ordered over the whole expedition. No-one was able to tell their families about anything.

We just faded out and left wives and others without a clue as to what was happening. When we got to Paletwa I sent a letter to my wife who was a cypherette in Lucknow and to my sister in Shillong, who was Commandant of the Women's Forces on the border. In two successive letters I said I was with an anaemic Scottish couple. This caused much head scratching, but a large map in Brigade HQ in Lucknow showed PALETWA).

Paletwa was turned into a strongly defended base and stocked up with reserves of food and ammunition. At Paletwa, (82 miles from Akyab) the river is tidal; and tides and thick river fogs caused much communication trouble at night. 38 Miles south of Paletwa is the large town of Kyaokbil overlooked by a long, high and steep hill. This is a local holy place as the hill was surmounted by a pagoda, a Hindu temple and a Muslim masjid. The hill was reported to be strongly held by Japs and was the final objective ordered by Divisional HQ. The assault was fixed for the night 20 Jan 1943. Nights were chilly, but all we had were jerseys plus blankets for the evacuation of casualties. As I was uncertain of the fighting ability (or reliability) of the two battalions, I approached through dense bush right across the front of the Jap positions on the hill. Luckily we were not seen and I got the force backed on to the river, at the south end of the hill, whilst the Japs were expecting us from the north. If any troops felt like running away there was nowhere to go except for the 300 yard wide river, a Mahomedan school teacher gallantly acted as guide, as he had had some of his family killed by Japs. The assault went in with complete surprise and the whole hill except for the tip occupied by the pagoda was captured in two hours. (We later buried 38 Japs and lost 1 Gurkha jemadar and 5 troops).

The state of affairs continued for about three days. We built a small airstrip for the visits of General Lloyd who was pleased with everything and told me to pull out across the river (i.e. west side) when ready. I later went and did a recce for a suitable beach away from Jap view and found a suitable place across a chaung. This chaung was about 3 feet deep. The withdrawal from close contact was ordered for 8 pm the next night. As both battalions had had a lot of malaria I ordered that all ranks would take their shorts off and tie them to their equipment so that they would have dry pants when across the river. At mid-day that same day I started getting malarial shivers and wasn't too well by the evening. Anyhow, the pull out went off without a hitch and I came to the chaung with the last platoon to find it DRY. The tide was out (this episode went into the official history as "the bare-bum withdrawal".) When we were all across the river I collapsed and was saved by a European M.O. who found I had a 106° temperature.

The force then concentrated at Paletwa for some weeks, covering large distances by patrols. Eventually we were ordered back to railhead owing to the approach of the monsoon during which Sangu River becomes quite impassable. It was all a very interesting experience. We beat the first Chindit raid by two months but as the Arakan campaign was a failure no publicity was forthcoming. (The above article was sent to me by Brig Ted Hughes. We are grateful to him. Ed)

F. R. S. C.

Tuitum Saddle 22.3.44

By G. L. Aitchison

It was the fourteenth day of the Jap advance in force on Imphal, and I thought that my only problem was B Coy's defensive perimeter at Tongzang. The Bn had already retreated forty miles from Kennedy Peak back to Tongzang, Jap 214 White Tiger Regiment having achieved surprise and success. It was essential that B Coy's perimeter and bunkers be well-sited, strong and secure.

Colonel Oldham thought the perimeter was too small; I replied that if he would get down into a slit trench and have a Bren Gunner's view, he would see that the fields of fire were excellent. To move the bunkers forward would lose the benefit of the reverse slope.

Furthermore a larger position would thin out the dannert wire, and Jap fieldcraft was so good they would probably get through. B Coy preferred and trusted close wire. The CO then said the bunkers were not strong enough to withstand a direct hit. I replied that the surrounding hills were like the waves of a choppy sea. Accurate artillery fire from different heights over intervening ridges was notoriously difficult, and a direct hit was therefore unlikely.

We went into the BOs' Mess and I was immediately proved wrong. The Mess sustained a direct hit. Fortunately the Mess was the strongest edifice we had ever used, built by an engineer unit now evacuated to Imphal. The crash as the shell landed hurt the ear drums, dust rose in clouds and universal darkness covered all. Yet so strong was the roof that no one was hurt, not even a cut or a bruise; except Davies who was eating cornflakes and condensed milk, and swallowed the spoon.

It had seemed a long day and I hoped to turn in early ready for stand to at 3.00 am. Since the Japs invariably attacked at night, we usually "stood to" between 2.00 am and 3.00 am. And next morning the CO, who still had reservations, might order B Coy to rub it out and do it all again.

Then the CO ordered me to get B Coy, in full marching order, carrying all it possessed, up to Tuitum Saddle and report to Major Fairgreave, 2 i/c 1/10th GR. The perimeter became someone else's problem. I never found out who.

I was dressed to look as much like a GOR as possible, carrying an SMLE rifle, ten rounds in the magazine, nothing up the spout, wearing black issue boots, denim battle dress (inefficiently dyed jungle green, trousers a different shade from blouse) full pack, two bandoliers of .303 around the waist, two filled Bren magazines in one webbing pouch, grenades in the other, hideous but practical issue spectacles, face blacked and a Gurkha hat. Steel helmets had long been abandoned. I had no binoculars: the men could see with naked eye and tell me quicker than I could focus binoculars. 4 GR believed that officers should do all that the men did and more, like carrying full packs and ammo. There was another school of thought that this made the officer needlessly exhausted. We never took our packs off, they became part of us. However, I was of course cosseted: I never dug a shovelful of my own slit trench. My orderly's job was to carry chagals of water; dripping through the canvas, by latent heat of evaporation, the water was deliciously cold. I never imposed water discipline while on the move, as did some officers trained in NWFP. The men drank all they could and more at dawn, forcing it down. If by good fortune water was available on the march, the men were free to drink in an orderly fashion.

By 2000 hours B Coy was filing out of the perimeter straight up the khudside in the dark. To our left the Tiddim Road twisted and turned up the steep gradient of the "chocolate staircase", so called because in the wet season the road surface looked like melted chocolate.

B Coy leading men met 1/10th GR out-posts and exchanged the softly whispered recognition signal "Cheeet". Such was my nervous tension that I thought only a few minutes had gone by since leaving Oldham; I was astonished to find that it was midnight and the approach march had taken four hours.

Fairgreave had two rifle companies about 300 yards below the crest; he was sitting under a sheet of corrugated iron propped up by a stick, all his men similarly protected. He politely invited us to help ourselves from piles of CGI sheets beside the Tiddim Road. The bedrock was too close to the surface to dig slit trenches. The enemy were firing grenade dischargers. Fortunately the Jap grenade was a poor weapon and a sheet of CGI gave full protection.

Fairgreave said the enemy had retaken the saddle and we would attack at dawn. His two companies would attack frontally uphill, while B Coy did a left hook and advance on the enemy along the ridge. 129 Field Arty would fire a barrage from MS 128 way down in the valley.

We all got what sleep we could and assembled on a start line before dawn, and advanced as planned. The artillery barrage came down, but a lot of their rounds fell short. Either that or the enemy managed a counter barrage. Near me Naru Pun, my orderly's cousin, had a shell all to himself and looked as though he had been run over by an HGV. Fairgreave certainly thought it was our guns falling short and was savagely rude to the FOO, who looked terribly crestfallen. He was a very young 2/Lieut with spectacles, who looked as though he ought to be back in college writing his weekly essay.

After the barrage B Coy made the crest and turned right. Enemy fire had concentrated on Fairgreave's frontal attack, and we had few casualties. The 1/10th Rifle Coys had made good progress and success was likely. I turned to check B Coy dispositions and casualties and felt as though I had been kicked twice very hard by heavy rugger boots. My webbing was cut through, pouches falling forward and pack slipping off my back. Two LMG bullets had entered the chest wall, bruised the lung, and bounced out again. I was able to carry on until the wound stiffened up.

The surviving Japs were in covered foxholes throwing their not very effective grenades. B Coy mopped them up. We could have taken at least one prisoner and I shouted "Kaidi" but a Naik turned a .45 Tommy gun on them, shouting "Teri my chikni Japani". I was annoyed because .45 ammo was in short supply.

I joined Fairgreave on the crest and he was all confidence and charisma. We discussed briefly company perimeters, when an enemy LMG fired bursts from quite far away. Nobody was hit but I was grazed on the thigh. I gave my orders to Jemadar Birsuba. Where was the incomparable Subadar Man Lal? Had he quarrelled with the Subadar Major? He was replaced by Subadar X from the Regimental Centre, the only useless GO I ever met. He knew he was useless and made no effort to interfere, but made a great show of putting a field dressing on my wound, a job which should have been left to Piper Narbahadur (Pipers doubled as medical orderlies).

We occupied old slit trenches which were shallow and unsatisfactory, and tried to improve them with stone parapets. QM 1/10th arrived in a Jeep with barbed wire, anti-tank mines, ammo and food. Fairgreave sited the A/T mines brilliantly. Later some enemy light two-man tanks advanced over these mines and were blown up.

My wound stiffened up, it was difficult to breathe. Fairgreave ordered me to hand over to Jem Birsuba. A Jeep returned with the wounded to the ADS. I had two nights of great discomfort, breathing with difficulty. An American FAU was a godsend. With great patience he used those thin army half mattresses called "biscuits" to prop me up in a position where I could breathe and drink a little water. For me an interesting if not always agreeable 24 hours.

But B Coy had to stay put and hold the ridge. In four days they beat off three counter attacks including light tanks, then marched 24 miles to rejoin the Battalion at MS 112 and take part in breaking the road blocks back to Imphal Box. Then they bore the heat and burden of the day at Bishenpur, preventing the Jap from getting within range of Tulihel Airstrip. Between January 1942 and July 1944 B Coy sustained over two hundred casualties. They showed willing throughout.

Fairgreave got a well earned DSO. Two of our section commanders got the IDSM, not for the attack, but for beating off the counter-attacks. Jemadar Birsuba got nothing but two months later he won an MC near Bishenpur.

"D Company Commander was also Wounded"

(Colonel Oldham's Account of the Battle for pt. 5151 in N.L.39)

By Walter Halpern

I enclose some faded photographs taken with my box Brownie of scenes during what I called the "boomerang" patrol from Imphal round and about the Chin Hills to Kalemyo and back (Vol 3, page 135) in late 1942/early '43 in company with the Black Watch and Border Regt commando units and Chin Levies. We got to within three hundred yards of Kalemyo from where we shot up and 2 inch mortared the town, having earlier that day failed to get any Japs in the village of Tanan about half way between No 2 Stockade and

Kalemyo itself: about ten days later we laid an ambush for about 6/8 hours along the road north up to the head of the valley towards Tamu, but unfortunately no Japs came—only parties of Burmese travellers—one lot suffering from what Narbahadur thought was smallpox. Once out of the Imphal plain we were supplied by parachute drops all the way there and back.

After the rainy seasons patrolling in the Fort White area and numerous probes against Bash Hill and No 3 Stockade, D Company was on Hungvum Mual outpost where we were attacked most nights in moonlight by Jap patrols: we easily repulsed them but we had still not learned to hold our fire until we actually SAW not HEARD the enemy and as we had no wire we still used sharpened bamboo stakes—panjis.

Also before the 1/16th Punjabis were over-run at Milestone 52 we were shelled from the ridge to the East by a Jap troop of high velocity pompom guns: our mountain battery sent me a troop in support fairly quickly but the first OP officer was almost "blind", later to be replaced by a hawk-eyed Sikh officer who got on to the target at once though the Japs had probably withdrawn by that time.

It was in this area or further up Kennedy Peak that we heard and saw by moonlight the 1/16th Punjabis being overwhelmed at MS52: it came as a surprise when their QM came through our perimeter with some 20 stragglers on their way back to Kennedy Peak. He had succeeded in slipping through the Jap ring down into the nullah formed by the KWE LUI: this was probably where Scotty found their mules later on.

During the Pimpi/5151 operation (NL 39 article) the thing that Colonel Oldham does not mention is the fact that nobody was told about wire by the recce parties as it came as a complete shock when we saw it—although I had earlier asked the question.

The small nullah on 5151 was roughly central to our axis of advance and separated the two forward platoons of D Coy, so I had to move with either one or the other to keep in touch: I went "left"—why? I don't really know but I think I could see better on that side.

I found the left platoon just on the edge of the wire, firing away at bunker openings but unable to advance: the wire was about 2 feet high and 4 feet 6 inches deep and cross latticed. I helped L/NK Bhome Pun cut the wire in a number of places and also Tommy gunned the openings of the immediate bunkers. I believe that I hit a Jap or two. After this section had got through the wire I followed but a grenade burst behind me blowing me off my feet with some pain in head and back: picking myself up and somewhat shaken I ran forward shouting "Ayo Gurkhali" and doing as I was taught and what I had practised so often: I passed a few casualties as I ran and the next thing I recall was being on top of a bunker and what I believe was the very top of 5151 with a clear view downhill in front of me. I looked back to see who was coming up behind and found I was absolutely alone: very alarmed I was turning to go back when I was hit by a .265 in the hip through the groin. It spun me right round and I was knocked off my feet.

This time I got up and loped off downhill and back to the wire passing a fair number of casualties: somewhere below I found Narbahadur my Subadar: he enquired what had happened but the casualties themselves indicated what had befallen the left hand Platoon of D Coy. Narbahadur said that I had a lump on my head like a pigeon's egg and also my back and hip/groin wounds were becoming rather troublesome. I asked for the whereabouts of Alec Lock my number 2 and the reserve platoon but he said that he had seen no sign of them but that I should go back as he would find Lock and tell him to take over.

On my way back to Bn HQ I hoped to see Lock myself but he must have been on the right hand side of the nullah. Colonel Oldham took my report and sent me to the RAP. I must admit that I was quite glad as my wounds were getting rather painful.

The doctor (*not* Tata) gave me a morphia injection and I was put on a stretcher—bamboo poles with gunny sacking and carried back up the hill behind Pimpi. On the way I was sick (morphia does that to me) and when our shelling started, the orderlies (not Gurkhas) pitched me down the Khud as they fell flat: a tree stopped my fall and I yelled out that they were our own shells. Eventually they pulled me back on to the track and we reached the ADS: next day we were jeeped to Imphal. Here General Cowan came to see us and sent us to Shillong for treatment and rest.

I was back with the 1/4th again after a few weeks and I seem to remember that we were pushing forward from Kennedy Peak for one of the main MS52 operations: to get the feel of things I volunteered and went forward quite cheerfully from KP to do a daylight recce on MS52 and I kept on the east slope of the ridge for cover. The whole top of the 52 position had been cleared by the Japs and by our shelling, giving a clear field of fire. In fact the face of this bastion was completely bald except for tree stumps and what looked to be bunker positions.

Somewhat later I felt myself much affected by Scotty's death and was particularly moved at Comber's funeral and I noted that I began to develop an uncontrollable shaking; moreover I fell down the Khud during the night withdrawal from Kennedy Peak to Vital Corner and badly hurt my ankle. All in all I no longer felt that I was in a condition to look after the men and I asked Colonel Oldham to relieve me of command of D Coy. Home, hospital, sick-leave and back to Dhangu. I was lucky—the Japs had almost surrounded Kohima and were shelling the garrison as my ambulance—just about the last to leave finally got out.

The Guiding Light

One of our Governments after the war propounded a "Guiding Light" policy, and every time I hear that phrase my mind flashes back to Libya in May 1942.

We had recently arrived from Iraq and, after a period in Egypt, had moved up to the Libyan border, far away from the battle front. There we formed a semi-defensive position known as a "box", and erected a fairly comfortable tented camp.

Within a day or two of arrival some of us had met a peacetime friend from another unit, (Roy Railton, RIASC), who asked us round to his Mess that evening. This was a mile or two away and he gave us directions to reach it. As the terrain was mainly featureless desert, however, his instructions consisted of a certain distance on a compass bearing, in the "piece-of-cake: can't-miss-it-old-boy" tradition. But desert navigation was just what we had been training for and, after a few drinks that evening, Libya held no terrors for us.

After sundown, four officers piled into a staff car, (John Strickland, Ben Browne, Roger Werner and Ewen Kerr, I think), dispensing with the driver, and I decided to follow in a 15 hundredweight. They started with considerable elan, in approximately the right direction, and I followed their dust trail with complete assurance.

They stopped from time to time to check their bearings, but this was normal practice, and it was not until we had been going for twenty minutes or more, with no sign of the expected location, that I began to doubt my comrades' ability.

My fears were confirmed when we met a water truck, in the middle of nowhere, whose driver admitted that he was lost, and who followed behind us thereafter like a sheep. By then I had grown tired of driving on my own, following a car which became increasingly difficult to see as night came on, and I changed places with Ben at the next stop. I could now relax in the back of the staff car, reflecting comfortably that if we got lost I should not be alone.

By now it was a starlit night, and a compass was of limited use. John therefore opened the near-side door and stood on the running board, looking up at the Pole Star and directing the driver to steer vaguely in the right direction. The 15 hundredweight and the water tanker trundled along in our rear.

The effect of our stirrup cups had now worn off and our insides informed us that we ought to be eating. There was still no sign of our host's tent and we entertained thoughts of a night without food, though we were sure we could find the Battalion again in the morning.

"Left a bit ... steady ... right ... right ... straighten up ... " and other instructions continued as our guide tried to lead us in the right direction.

Then we saw the light. It was only a small one at first, but it became brighter for a bit and then stayed the same. That was surely our prospective host lighting our way. We changed course and headed for it.

It moved, but that was natural. It moved quite a lot, and funnily enough it never seemed to get any closer. We were not unduly surprised by the appearance of a light in the desert. We knew there were other troops in the area, and we were far enough back from the Gazala Line to be a little casual about open lights at times. This one looked like a pressure lamp at a distance.

We followed it hopefully for a while, with our guide still standing on the running board; and then we came to a barbed wire strand, strung loosely between picquets. Older campaigners would have stopped and wondered, but we drove blithely through a gap, towards that beckoning light.

Half a minute later we were shocked by an explosion. The light flashed in front of us, the car jumped and crashed to a halt, lurching to an angle as one wheel collapsed, and we breathed dust and acrid smoke. It was too quick for fear, but there was a stunned silence. Eventually someone said: "Are you all right, John?". Silence again, before John, still on the running board, answered: "Yes, but it's blown my ... hat off!" He climbed back into the car, unhurt but rather deaf.

We realised now that we had run over an anti-tank mine; in fact, we must have driven into a minefield through that gap in the wire. It was obviously a British field, and therefore composed of so called "Gyppy" mines. Thank goodness for that, anyhow! We should not have escaped so lightly from a German one. However, that did not alter the fact that we were firmly stuck with the things all round us, and it would be stupid to move until morning.

Ben, in the 15 hundredweight, had pulled up sharp at the explosion and he suffered no damage, although he was also in the minefield. Being too cold in the 15 hundredweight, he walked carefully along our tracks and climbed in with us.

We therefore settled down for the night, moving as little as possible in the crazily tilted car. The time passed slowly and hungrily, and at first light John and Ben climbed out through the sunshine roof and gingerly down onto the track made by one of the wheels. Seeing that it was safe the rest of us did the same, stepping like Agag, more delicately than we had ever stepped before, until we reached the wire. As Ben had driven the 15 hundredweight in, John suggested that he drive it out, and stood in front directing him as he reversed slowly. As soon as he was out of the minefield he drove back to the Battalion. Thereafter it was only a question of time until our rescuers came.

It took the experts a long time to remove the car, we heard, for there were mines close on either side and underneath it.

The strange thing was that after the crash we never saw the light again and I still wonder, at times, whether a Fifth Columnist had tried a landlubberly version of the old-time wreckers' trick with lamps.

R. N. D. W.

The 2nd Battalion from May to June 1942

By Robert Williams

Towards the end of May, 10 Bde moved by degrees, in desert formation, up to Gambut, with its progress along the Trigh Capuzzo hindered by a violent sand storm. Unfortunately, Col Weallens's station wagon chose that day to break down three or four times, none of which added to his cheerfulness. At the end of a trying journey, however, the Brigade encamped in a green valley below one of the escarpments.

From there the Bn was moved to a bleak spot, appropriately

named El Arid, in an aerodrome defence role, and after a while was shifted to Bir Arca, in a depression below Gambut Satellite 2 airfield, taking over the defence of both the latter and Satellite 1.

Bombing by day was infrequent, though we were roused early one morning by a ground-strafing plane, at which the men let go everything they had. By night, however, the Hun was a regular customer, and watches could almost be set by the first drone of his engines every evening, while an unhealthy pyrotechnics display brightened the night sky; but in spite of these thoughtful attentions our casualties were few. Bathing parties were sent off to the coast, compressors were used to assist in the feverish laying of mines, graders scraped roads through the "Box", and Roger Werner, our MTO, was kept busy dealing with broken springs and stub axles.

Shortly after battle started on the 26th a flap arose, and we moved nearer to Gambut Main, while the RAF on Satellite 2 scrambled their kites rapidly eastwards, abandoning tents and equipment, and leaving an unarmed and almost mutinous South African ground staff to fend for themselves.

B Coy was bombed that night on the 'drome, which fortunately caused more amusement than tragedy. "Slogger" Martin and Sub Sukdeo were asleep in their slit trenches when a bomb landed almost between them. It blew Sukdeo's tin hat and ground sheet off his body and deafened them both, so that they could only talk in uncontrolled roars or whispers for some time to come.

The flap died down on the 28th, and the Bn and the RAF resumed their normal activities. At the end of the month the Bde was moved west of Tobruk to El Mrassas, going by the coastal road, and was there given a day of rest in preparation for battle. Col Weallens from here took a Recce Group south, and disappeared from our ken for two whole days

On the 1st June orders were received for a sudden move south, and Ben Browne, the Adjutant, took the Bn through Acroma to Point 169. Owing to lack of guides, however, groups of the Bn became separated, and were only united next day. For this reason, Peter O'Bree, our LO with Bde, had a hectic night keeping contact between the latter and us, though how he ever found us was a mystery. We discovered next day that in our ignorance we had leaguered outside our own territory and unpleasantly close to the Hun.

For several reasons our projected night attack was cancelled. One Coy of ours and one of 4/10 Baluch were to have gone forward by night to lay Ammonal charges under the enemy guns and tanks—a suicidal idea for which Slogger Martin and B Coy had been selected. Owing to lack of explosives and the late arrival of the Bde, however, the assault did not materialise, and neither did that scheduled for the next day, on account of violent sand storm. Consequently we moved towards Bir Harmat, reaching there in bits and pieces when the storm abated. Here John Strickland assigned us positions covering two gaps in the wire, codenamed "Peter" and "Paul", where we were expected to contact the non-existent French.

During the past week the Hun had dug in his tanks and guns around Knightsbridge, lying there doggo while our guns plastered his Box, then putting his fingers to his nose and letting our troops have it.

The Bn now endured a few days of spasmodic shelling of the Box and water point, during which John Strickland and two GORs were wounded and evacuated, while Sweeper Nandoo plaintively showed a small scratch on his backside.

Throughout the next two days large enemy columns were observed to be moving west and south of us in the direction of Bir Hacheim, which was frequently bombed and shelled: but although we sent out two night patrols, under Slogger and Peter McDowell, these failed to make contact with the enemy. Division seemed far more complacent over the possibilities of outflanking than we considered healthy.

On the 4th Col Weallens made a recce for a night attack towards B180, though little opposition was expected for the Bn, which was to be in reserve. That evening, however, twenty three JU 88s subjected the Bn to a severe medium-level plastering, but fortunately no one was hurt, except in 28 Field Regt, which was still in support. During the bombing, Ben Browne and Robert Williams were sharing an L-shaped slit trench, when a bomb landed rather close and the fragments flew overhead. Ben, who was lying on his back, said: "Robert, something like a football just went over us!"

By dark we were formed up ready to approach the Start Line, when three Italian petrol lorries blundered into the wire in front of C Coy. Peter McDowall promptly knocked one out with a two Pounder, and the other two escaped. Two scared Italians were then escorted to Bde HQ, by the Bn Intelligence Officer, Robert Williams, who rejoined the Bn as it reached the Start Line.

Dixie Dean and Middleton were now back with B Echelon; Roger Werner, Ewen Kerr, Peter McDowall and C Coy at the Bir; Ronnie Smith, being Bde MG Officer, had his own command, and Peter O'Bree was still LO.

At 0250 hrs nearly 100 guns began to lay down a barrage, and the HLI and Baluch attacked some minutes later. The objectives were B204, Bir Et Tamar and B178, which were soon obtained with the minimum of opposition. This was hardly surprising, as we discovered later that the main enemy positions were further back than we had supposed, and a heavy weight of high explosive had fallen on empty desert.

As the guns opened up, Robert was in the act of contacting the Bn—in itself a slightly scary operation in the dark—when he found himself almost under the guns. Not realising they were going to explode at that moment, he nearly jumped out of his skin.

During the attack, Roger Werner had been detailed to light up a large "V" ground sign, made of sand-filled kerosene tins and pointing to the enemy position, for the benefit of our aircraft. In order to light it, he and his orderly had had to take one side of the "V" apiece. But this was not a happy procedure, because the enemy seemed disgruntled and Roger and his orderly had never dodged shells so fast. The RAF apparently knew nothing about it, for they were conspicuous by their absence.

At 0635 hrs on the 5th June a Coy of HLI was overrun by tanks, and we were ordered to be prepared to move to their assistance, though our two-pounders were still guarding "Peter" and "Paul" and didn't arrive for some time. Shortly afterwards, however, we took up a defensive position round B180 and dug ourselves in, in spite of a crowd of Royal Northumberland Fusiliers, West Yorks, Gunners and tanks, who seemed to like that area too.

During the morning both HLI and Baluch were heavily shelled: 4 RTR used our Box as a rallying and refuelling point: the GOC's order "No retrograde movement" was received from Bde, and we were told to stand by to send HQ and two rifle coys, plus four anti-tank guns, to help the HLI. This order was cancelled, however, and at 1400 hrs the remnants of the HLI withdrew into our Box, having been badly cut about.

During the afternoon the Bn Box was also quite heavily shelled: the HLI went back to Bde HQ; all unwanted transport was also sent off to B Echelon, and Robert was ordered to gather together all cooks' lorries and take them back as well. This he did, and ran straight into the arms of the Hun who, unknown to anyone at the sharp end, had outflanked and captured Bde HQ shortly before.

Some of Bde HQ had managed to escape, while Dixie Dean was well away with B Echelon, who moved eastwards, being joined by a few escapees as they went. However, Roger Werner and Middleton dropped neatly into the bag.

Meanwhile the Bn spent a restless night, being warned of impending enemy tank attacks. Digging in the rocky ground was hard, no compressors were available, and two-pounders on portees, and 25-pounders used in an anti-tank role, were horribly vulnerable to enemy tank fire.

By 1130 hrs next day the Baluch had been overrun, and with them 4 and 157 Field Regts, RA, while the Bn was shelled consistently all the day. At about 1400 hrs the shelling increased and MG fire seemed to come from all directions. Peter McDowall set a splendid example of steadiness, walking from trench to trench among the shell bursts and encouraging his men: Col Weallens appeared to ignore the fire completely: Ben Browne had been ordered to stay by the wireless set, and so saw little of the battle: Ewen Kerr's two-pounders put up a short but gallant fight against heavier guns: Ronnie Smith's machine gunners fired very effectively before they were finally closed down: Slogger Martin's B Coy was attacked from dead ground in the rear, and didn't stand much of a chance: Malcolm Grose, with A Coy, was helping the British Gunners with 25-pounders: D Coy (Sub Balbir) resisted as long as was humanly possible: Sub Gumparsad and his carriers seemed to adopt the old cavalry tactics of "Charge and be damned": Doc Dutt (who later received an MC) put up a truly magnificent show in a disused Bir, lopping off limbs by candle-light under heavy shell fire, with the, scantiest equipment, and there were several other fine exhibitions of courage which have never been recorded.

Unfortunately the wounded could not be brought to the Bir immediately, as stretcher bearers were forced to await lulls in the storm.

At about 1645 hrs several German tanks, with motorised infantry behind, approached the Box. All our supporting guns were knocked out, and small arms fire was useless against the tanks, which moved from trench to trench, spraying them all with small arms or heavier stuff, until the motorised infantry, in groups, winkled our men from their positions.

All were lined up and marched off as POWs, except Dutt and the RAP, who were left to deal with German wounded. Nevertheless, he gave our wounded preferential treatment, and yet found time to assist the Stretcher Bearer Havildar and a Naik of A Coy to escape during the night. These two NCOs, part of B Echelon, and one section of Carriers who had been covering a Gunner OP, were all that came out of the battle.

The Crossing of the Senio River— Deccmber 1944

On 15 December 2/4 GR moved once more into the hills to take part in the battle for the Senio River, which was to be the prelude to the dismal winter of 1944–45.

Some twenty five German Divisions, together with five Italian

Fascist Divisions, held a defensive line to which they had been driven when the 15 Army Group pierced the Gothic Line.

On 16 December the Battalion reached the new concentration area and immediately relieved 3/18 Garhwal Rifles, less one Company, which had patrols out and came under command of Colonel Lowis. One of the patrols, about a section in strength, had crossed to the far bank of the Senio and had established itself in a large house behind the Floodbanks, without any opposition. It was decided to exploit this piece of luck and "C" Company was to cross the Senio with orders to hold a small bridgehead.

I made a recce of the crossing point on the night of the 16th December and had been watching it quietly with Subedar Kajiman Gurung for about an hour with a section to cover us, should it be necessary, when we heard voices from the far bank. The covering section who, like myself and Kajiman, were lying in a slushy depression on the floodbank, were signalled to be silent. The voices receded into the distance and after a pause one of our section struck a match to light a cigarette. The match was quickly extinguished but it was only luck that prevented whoever it was on the other side of the river from hearing the reprimands of the remainder of the section. I closed my eyes and had a quiet word with the "Guvnor"!

The next night, the 17th December, the initial crossing, in Company strength, was effected by "C" Company by means of an unstable bridge which consisted of two long tree trunks lashed end to end and secured to either bank by rope. The trunks were below the water since the river was very high and fast flowing and very cold. Two riflemen "volunteered" to cross with a rope to secure to a tree to use as a handrail and to give some support. It was not too successful and although a few riflemen slipped off the trunks they held on to their weapons and the hand-rope.

The crossing place was obviously known to the Germans and as we deployed to approach the large house we were heavily mortared but escaped with one or two very minor casualties who elected to stay with us.

Having secured a firm base at the house between the Ceiffiano-Route 9 Road and some three hundred yards from the River Senio,

I decided that I would attack the hamlet to the West and my second objective as soon as possible, and thereby enlarge the bridgehead.

We attacked at 4 am on the morning of 18 December.

Shortly after moving forward from my Company start line, we encountered an enemy artillery/Mortar DF which ran from Route 9 (which was parallel with the Senio) to the River Senio. I halted the Company and we lay "doggo" until after the shelling had lifted.

After a respectable pause to ascertain that we had not unduly suffered we moved forward and, although the Company encountered stubborn defensive fire, the attack on the hamlet was successful. We had driven the enemy out and the position was consolidated.

One platoon under command of Havildar Harkabahadur Thapa went forward to secure the west flank of the hamlet, a second platoon secured the entrance to the hamlet from the north. This was commanded by Jemadar Rabi Gurung, an inspiration to us all. Jemadar Dilbahadur Thapa with his platoon, was held in Company Reserve in the hamlet.

With the Senio River to my rear and the information from Colonel Lowis that Maurice Biggs with "A" Company would be put across to strengthen and extend the bridgehead the following night, I felt secure.

Although I had the Gunners fire plan, I had no FOO Party and thus artillery support rested entirely with what information I could pass to Colonel Lowis in my varying situation reports.

The hamlet became known to the Battalion HQ and the Gunners as "Bustyville".

Having taken the "Bustyville" objective and consolidated, we were immediately counter-attacked but my call for Artillery assistance was answered and the Company was "boxed in" by close artillery and machine-gun supporting fire and we remained quite confident that we could hold our gains.

Several probing efforts were made during the day by enemy fighting patrols and since they were met by Harkabahadur and Rabi with some vehemence, I concluded that they were trying to establish the strength of the bridgehead.

The next night Maurice Biggs, with "A" Company, was put

across to strengthen the bridgehead and at the same time to relieve a platoon of "C" Company to take a hill feature which had been causing us some annoyance the day before, since it overlooked our positions.

Point 132 was a long, sloping hill with difficult approaches but the narrow ghylls on its flanks did provide some cover.

Colonel Lowis ordered me, in Gurkhali over the air, to attack and secure Point 132 as soon as possible. I selected Jemadar Dilbahadur Thapa for this task and a plan was made for Jemadar Rabi to move his platoon and give covering fire from the flank to Dilbahadur's platoon during the assault.

The best covered approach to the summit of Point 132 was up a deep ghyll to the east of the hill. At this stage, since we had no opportunity of a recce, the exact positions of the enemy defences were unknown to me, and a patrol which I had sent out had not returned.

I took a chance, and as first light was breaking Rabi was in position—unnoticed—and Dilbahadur was approaching a false crest to Point 132.

The weather was dank and misty but lifting and the ground was covered with a very light snow slush and, of course, was very muddy.

The false crest was rough-bouldered, fairly flat with gradually rising slopes to the summit. The few trees were by now stumps as the result of our artillery fire and there was a certain amount of low scrub.

The Assault

The initial assault was actually carried out on this false crest and it was here that Dilbahadur ran into the first outposts in their slit trenches. His approach took these outposts by surprise and the enemy was in fact preparing to "stand to" as part of their normal procedure.

Company HQ was now approaching the false crest by the west ghyll and I gave orders to Rabi to carry out his fire task.

In the gathering grey light Dilbahadur's platoon surprised the reinforcements who were moving across the open ground to the outposts and a certain amount of mortaring began on the approach routes but we were almost clear of the enemy target areas.

Enemy Strength

The enemy was about a platoon strength in all but the troops were— (we discovered later from our prisoners)—the elite 90th Light Division of the old Afrika Corps and our adversaries at Ortona on the Adriatic.

The reserve troops in this position were from the 305 Division and what we had in fact stumbled on was a Divisional Boundary.

The Hand-to-hand Battle

The attack degenerated into an all-in running fight below the summit of Point 132. There were some casualties to Dilbahadur's platoon before the final assault but he had overrun the outposts and dealt very severely with the few reinforcements.

With further covering fire from Jemidar Rabi's platoon, Dilbahadur closed for the final assault on Point 132, and the small cluster of what appeared to be cattle sheds and huts. It was from these ramshackle buildings that the remaining enemy disgorged and the platoon closed with them with their kukris and severe hand-to-hand fighting took place.

Dilbahadur's ferocious attack caused the Germans to break off and withdraw to what was obviously their pre-planned defensive position on higher ground, leaving Dilbahadur and his platoon in possession of Point 132.

Several enemy dead were lying around and five or six unwounded were taken prisoner. They were horrified and scared with the ferocity of the attack.

Consolidation took place but a counter-attack was made by the Germans almost immediately. The position was held and Rabi's platoon was moved to a flank position to counter-attack should the enemy be successful.

During the day (19 December) some sorties were made against Point 132 and "Bustyville" and both positions came under heavy mortar and artillery fire.

Point 132 became almost untenable. "C" Company was determined to hang on to what it had gained but Colonel Lowis informed me in Gurkhali that it had been decided at Divisional and other levels to withdraw us to the south of the River Senio. (I later learned that this was because the Brigade attack at Tebano on our right flank had failed and that those engaged were back on our own side of the river).

Verbal orders were given over the wireless to "A" and "C" Companies by Colonel Lowis in Gurkhali. These orders were given late in the day to avoid interception.

Subedar Kajiman Gurung recced the withdrawal route and found a place where we could wade across with the support of rope lashings found in the hamlet, taking our casualties with us. "A" Company were to cover our withdrawal and return by the log bridge.

We commenced the withdrawal at 1800 hours, with Dilbahadur and then Rabi's platoon from Point 132 directly with guides to the crossing point.

Harkabahadur covered them back to the river and then crossed with Company HQ. The withdrawal was textbook stuff and when we were clear, Maurice Biggs and "A" Company crossed by the log bridge.

The Germans were not aware of our withdrawal until next morning when they began to pound our previous positions. We watched from the security of the home side of the river as we climbed the slopes to our new Company areas.

The 2/4th were the only Unit to cross the Senio River in strength in 1944 and hold a bridgehead. Following our withdrawal, the Eighth and Fifth Armies remained in the positions throughout the winter and the Senio was not crossed again until the 9 April 1945, when the Eighth Army drove towards Bologna and the Argenta Gap. Less than a month later the Germans surrendered in Italy.

F. J. M-H.

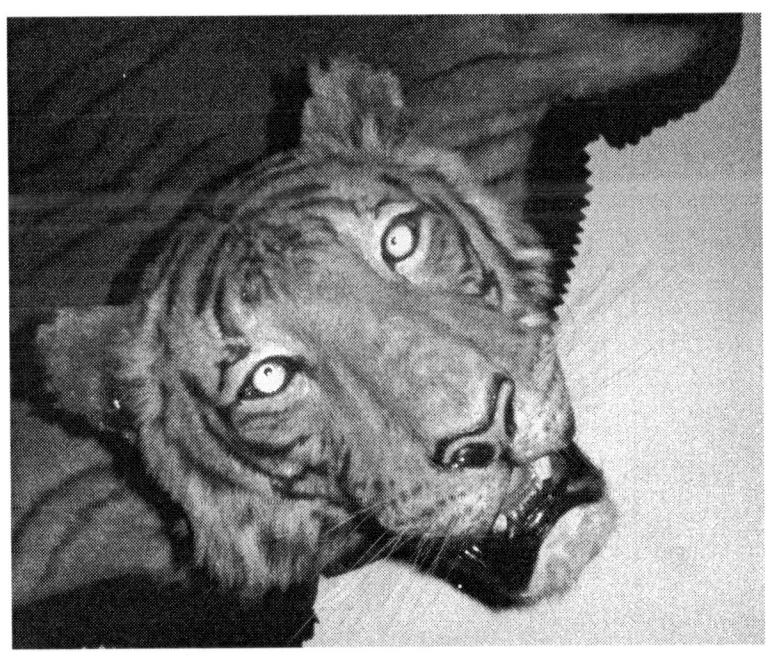

The Tiger of Bakloh

The Memorial Garden, Stoke Poges

A Regimental Piper

Hon Captain Narbahadur Gurung OBI IDM IDSM after retirement he was appointed Minister of Health in the Nepal Government

4th Bn Mules in Burma

Snow in Bakloh No 5 Bungalow

Subadar Gumparsad Gurung in review order

The Pipes and Drums, in 1885 the 4th GR were the first regiment in the Indian Army to have a pipe band.

Hon Capts Agam Gurang MBE OBI and Ramrattan Rana OBI—
Bakloh 1945

Training for war—Bakloh 1945

Mount Everest October 1970

Nauch Party—the morning after. Young soldiers dressed as women on these occasions as females were not permitted to participate

The only glockenspiel in the Indian Army, presented by the Officers' Association during the 1994 reunion

The 1914–18 War memorial. Two were purchased by all ranks of the Regiment in the 1920s

Rifle cleaning. Up until late 1946 all Gurkhas had their heads shaved apart from the top knot

Training for war in India 2005

Escape and Evasion in Italy: 1943–1945

By Robert Williams, in collaboration with Ben Browne

For the officers and men of the 2nd Bn who went to Libya so cheerfully in May 1942, three main events were shortly to change the course of their lives—the battle of the Cauldron, Italian POW camps, and escape and evasion after General Badoglio's abortive Armistice of 8th September '43. Each one is a story in itself and it may be possible to tell more next year: for the moment, however, we shall concentrate on escape and evasion.

Although most of the GOs and some of the BOs had been together in Camp 66 (Capua), they were all moved out at the end of 1942 and BOs and GOs were then split up: the GORs were already separated. Ben Browne, Roger Werner, Peter O'Bree, Ronnie Smith and Robert Williams finished in Camp 49 (Fontanellato), just north of Parma, after staying for some months in Chieti or Rezzanello. Slogger Marten, Ewen Kerr and Peter McDowall remained in Chieti; Colonel Weallens was in another Camp and Doc Dutt, our MO, had earlier been repatriated on exchange.

Immediately after the Armistice the Germans surrounded many of the Camps, including Chieti, (where Allied orders to "stay put" were followed slavishly by the Senior British Officer), so that most of their inmates had little chance of escape. However, for some reason they were slow to arrive at Fontanellato, so on 9th September '43, after several days of rumours and alarms, the Italians cut the wire and we marched out as an unarmed Battalion, about 620 strong, to a wood a few miles away, guided by Italian officers. The Germans were furious, imprisoned the Commandante, wrecked the interior of the Camp and sent out search parties, who recaptured several people. In any case, our large unit soon became too conspicuous, as more and more locals came openly to view these strange Inglesi, so we gradually split up, making off singly or in groups, in various directions, from the 11th onwards.

Marten and Kerr went to Germany, but McDowall reached Switzerland, after a gallant escape from a railway wagon. There he was interned, but sadly he died of an illness some months later. The Colonel, Werner, O'Bree and Smith were recaptured in succeeding months and also taken to Germany, where their lives became progressively more dangerous and unpleasant as the Allies advanced; we regret that we cannot remember what happened to Grose or Middleton. Ben Browne and Robert Williams crossed the lines months later and rejoined the Allies. They can therefore only speak with first-hand knowledge of their own experiences.

They had left Fontanellato separately and did not meet again for over eighteen months, when they were back in India. They both, however, moved south-westwards into the foothills of the Appenines and, while Ben found a mountain village, which kept him for many months, with an uncomfortable interlude in a charcoal burner's hut, Robert circulated in a large area in Emilia. In January '44 he moved many miles further south, to end near the Pass of Cerreto, in Apuania.

We started moving by night and hiding by day, but pi-dogs and a bright moon made night movement a farce and, by day, the farmers and shepherds found us in the woods and hedges. We had no compass and no map, no knowledge of Italian or the country's geography and, worst of all, no inkling of the people's real sympathies. Radios were scarce, and reports of Allied actions and intentions were intermittent and garbled. Feeling at first rather bewildered, we imagined the enemy everywhere. Admittedly the Germans were alert, as they had cut all communications a few days before and they and the Fascists were seeking ex-POW, but many of our fears were, in fact, groundless, although a number of people were later betrayed and recaptured, including Roger Werner. The reward for betraying an ex-POW was approximately the price of a pig!

For some months we still had British Army boots (whose heel-plates were a give-away in mud or snow), socks and battle dress obtained through the Red Cross in Camp, though some of us dyed the BD. We also had old clothing given us by the peasants, and this often produced some comic effects; but we always looked utterly British, however hard we tried, and few of us managed to hoodwink intelligent Italians for long. However, we gradually picked up Italian until a few of us could bluff the duller locals into thinking us Piedmontese, Corsicans, Neapolitans or Sardinians.

We found most families extremely friendly, especially immediately after the Armistice, though many were frightened. Every village had people who had lived, or had relatives in America, Australia or the UK. One man, hearing the name Williams, actually replied in Welsh; while a charcoal burner, alone on top of a wooded hill, addressed him in pure Cockney. One family had a son who was a POW in Germany, one with the Italian (Allied) fleet and another a POW in Washington.

There were frequent scares of Blackshirt or German patrols or large round-ups, and we were hustled away at all hours by frantic villagers, or hidden for days in cellars, stables or nearby caves. Often these were mere flaps: rumours spread and multiplied fast, and our hosts lived on their nerves even more than we did.

We were sometimes helped by priests when others were afraid to do so, and a number were tortured and shot in public for supposed or actual assistance to the British or partisans. The women's courage was also very high, and it was often they who nursed us in sickness, brought food to us in hiding or scouted an escape route ahead. Neither did the children give the game away.

The land was full of escaping men. Apart from nearly 50,000, of various nationalities, who got out of the Camps, there were many Italian deserters, who hated their King, Mussolini and the Forces, and we frequently met one or the other in woods or villages.

We always avoided towns and normally went to villages approachable only by tracks, and preferably at several thousand feet. The result was that we seldom met really educated people and knew only the life of the mountain folk, many of whom were illiterate, ignorant and opinionated.

We had little need of money at first, as the people refused payment for food. With the few Lire we sometimes received we bought vino in the pubs, and any cigarettes or tobacco available, though some of the latter was breathtaking. When we eventually received Allied money through SOE or partisans, much of it went on buying new boots. Ben got his final pair of boots from a "Free Fall" air drop, which tried hard to obliterate him first.

The families mostly produced their own cheese, grapes and vino, wheat, maize-or-chestnut flour, milk, eggs, pasta and, sometimes, pork; but when such food was unobtainable we lived on potatoes, grapes, wild strawberries or bilberries, dry bread and cheese, and sheep or goats' milk from shepherds. Coffee, tea, and even salt, were hard to come by.

We always wrote a chit and left it wherever we stayed, giving our names and numbers and asking the Allies to recognise their services. They hid it carefully because, had it been found by the Fascists or Germans, the family would have been shot or deported. Burning of complete villages was not uncommon. Some houses had an impressive list of names, many of which we knew. They later received a certificate signed by F. M. Alexander.

Several families asked us to stay in hiding until the Allies came. Some of us tried it once or twice when we were tired of walking, but we felt cornered and it frayed our nerves so badly that we never stood it for long. If it was safe, we sometimes helped outside with threshing, collecting chestnuts, or picking and treading grapes, and indoors with shredding corn cobs or making macaroni.

Our requests for shelter were often refused and we normally found that the richer the house the poorer the hospitality. Sometimes we tried as many as six places before someone accepted us. We usually slept on hay or straw in a barn, or chestnut leaves (prickles included) collected for cows' bedding, which were warmer than hay or straw. The cows wore bells and were restless, and the stench of their sealed stables was nauseous, but we were often too tired to care.

We concluded that two was the best number of people in a party, though it needed much understanding and self-control. To be alone was unwise: continued lack of moral support could affect your nerves and finally your resistance. Three together were more difficult to accommodate and feed in a poor house, while four or over were too easy to observe.

Robert and his party were once captured by two Carabinieri, but luckily they were friendly and let them go. At intervals, he was helped by an Italian engineer working for the German TODT Organisation, by two Fascist officials whom the locals dreaded, and by a Fascist Forest Guard.

Towards the end of 1943 Ben and some friends had been armed with Italian rifles but, after an abortive attempt to shoot some trying Carabinieri, the area became too hot and they had to hide their rifles and separate. At one stage he became bodyguard to a conceited partisan leader and visited a local garrison town so the man could bed his girl friend. Waiting in a pub, armed with a Sten, Ben was asked by a local if he was English, but convinced (?) his questioner that he was Corsican. Three days later, enraged Germans caught another, completely innocent, ex-POW in that town and were said to have shot him.

In February '44 Robert was taken to meet an Italian sailor of SOE, sent in to organise partisans. He had received a number of drops of arms, ammunition, clothing and money; but his band were undisciplined and arrogant and, within days of meeting them, Robert and his mate were nearly caught in a large German/Fascist round-up, and only escaped by traversing the highest snow-clad mountain in the area, then hiding in a wood for some days, fed by a splendid family.

Thereafter he contacted three British SOE officers who had been dropped nearby, formed his own small band and received a parachute drop one dark night in a high valley. Next day the valley was combed by Germans, who luckily failed to find the hidden containers. However, the members of the band got tired of playing partisans and it soon broke up. In fact, the resistance movement in much of Italy (but not all) was scrappy or ineffectual, being used mainly to pay off old scores.

Ben crossed the lines a few months earlier than Robert and had some exciting moments. He was carrying a detailed map of the German defences of La Spezia, given to him earlier by some partisans. He reached the casual and comic US Negro 92nd Division, at Barga in the Serchio valley, where, after a convivial start with the blacks, a white American had his party thrown into Livorno gaol, with pimps, prostitutes and black marketeers. Luckily, next day the British intervened.

In early December an Italian of IS 9 crossed the lines to collect ex-POW, and Robert, warned by a nearby SOE officer, joined the Italian, a RAMC Captain and a USAF Sergeant and travelled south. Marching fourteen hours a day for four days in the mountains, they crossed the lines on the fourth night, into the same Negro Division, but fortunately they were treated well. Thereafter Pietrasanta—Florence—Rome—Naples—delousing—debriefing—10 wonderful days in Naples—and home!

GOs in Captivity

By Robert Williams

After the 2nd Battalion was captured in Libya on 5/6 June 1942, the officers and men were moved by degrees to Tmimi, Derna, Barce and Benghazi, from where they were flown or shipped to Italy. Most of the BOs and GOs were then sent to a small hutted camp (No 66) at Capua near Naples, where they remained until November 1942. During this time I gave my home address, which was that of my parents, to some of the GOs.

In November the BOs and GOs were moved to separate camps, and they remained separated for a further nine months, until the Armistice signed by Gen Badoglio on 8 September 1943, when most of them managed to escape. British and Gurkhas therefore did not see each other again until they rejoined the Regiment during or after the war in Europe. Some were lucky enough to cross the lines and rejoin the Allies, some died, some reached Switzerland and were interned, and others were taken to POW camps in Germany.

When I eventually returned to England, however, it gave me great pleasure to discover that several of the GOs had each written two or three Red Cross air mail letter cards, in passable English, to my Mother, either from Italy or from their later camps in Germany, and my Mother (who I don't think had ever seen a Gurkha) had replied to them conscientiously, bless her, and had kept the GOs letters which I still have. Those who wrote were: Sub Balbir Pun, Jem Rambahadur Gharti, S. M. Naule Thapa and Sub Narbahadur Gurung.

Balbir's three letters came from: "M-Stammlager XII" (Nov 43); "Oflag VIII F" (Feb 44) and "Oflag-79" (Oct 44). Rambahadur's three were the same dates and places, plus a final delightful letter, dated 2 May 45, saying: "Dear Mother, You will feel glad to know that I am a free man now and am staying at a small comfortable place in Norfolk." (This was actually Thetford). Naule's two both came from Campo PG 63 (Dec 42 and May 43), and so did Narbahadur's.

Their introductory words varied from: "Dear Mother, I am a friend of your son Williams and belong to his unit"; "Madam Sahib, Best respects to you"; "Dear Memsahib, I am taking the liberty of writing this to you", and "My dear Mother, I am quite well and safe. I hope that you be same there". My Mother was particularly charmed by the last approach.

All asked for news of me and one, in May 43, added: "We are hoping to meet the Captain Sahib soon and all our other, friends and men whom we are missing very much". But a recurrent theme was the absence of mail from home. One wrote, in Feb 44: "I am extremely grateful for your very kind letter dated 26 Dec 43 which was the only letter that has ever reached me in the whole period of my captivity". Another said: "Kindly inform my people to send letters, to me regularly."

The poor fellows expected a lot of my Mother and I know she did what she could. "I am looking forward to get more and more news from you," said one, and: "For about some days I was getting very anxious on account of receiving no mail from you. When your mail arrived in my Camp, at that time I was greatly delighted to receive it.", and: "Reply me soon after getting this letter."

Balbir mentioned the following GOs in his Camp: Sub Sherjang,

Jem Tularam, Jem Dabel; and one GO reported that: "Sub Sukdeo Kanwar has expired in Italy hospital". One of them said: "It is believed that I have delayed to write to you, because of the air raid on my Camp. The air bombardments had taken place on 24/8/44." (I am surprised the German Censor allowed that through); and another stated stoically: "I am passing my days in Italy comfortably."

There is no doubt they were grateful to my Mother, and one ended his letter by saying: "You have done a great favour for me and I will never forget your sympathy. Yours affectionate son ... ." But let Rambahadur finish, from his "small comfortable place in Norfolk": "I am sorry, Mother, that I cannot see you, simply because I cannot get leave and some other circumstances."

NBG's Last Day

By R. P. R. C. Naidu

It was in the middle of a conference that I got a call from Chander (Lt Col Chander Sekhar) to say that NBG would be arriving by the afternoon bus and could I collect him from Tuni Hatti. I was personally thrilled at the prospect of meeting the old stalwart. The Commandant's jeep was ordered to wait for him at Tuni Hatti and bring him straight to No 19 Bungalow where I am, staying.

I remembered meeting NBG the first time in 1965 when I was in the 2nd Battalion. We were deployed for operations and it was during this period that Lal Kaji, NBG's son, a Second Lieutenant in the Battalion, decided to get married. He was given overnight's leave and he drove all the way to Western Sikkim, got married and was back in his platoon defended locality by the morning stand-to. NBG visited the Battalion a few days later—stood straight as a ramrod, balding forehead, sparkling eyes, ruddy cheeks, well groomed moustache and a very sharp and an alert mind. He talked of soldiering, junior leadership, command, Razmak, the Cauldron, Nepal, politics, the Mongolian races, the arms industry and even after he left that afternoon, his presence was felt for a long time after. He simply took us with him on a trip of days and places long passed away, when he talked.

Vikram Raghavan and I trekked the district of Syangja, Baglung and Gulmi in December 1976. At Hony Capt Budhiman's house near Syangja, I saw a most in congruous photograph—two smart Gorkhas riding horses and enjoying it too. From what I have seen of our men, they can neither ride a horse nor a bicycle. One of the men in the photograph was Budhiman's father and the other—NBG in his younger days, in the NWFP, much slimmer, but with the same confident and imperious air.

After our strenuous trek we decided to go to Kath-mandu for a few days. It was an early nippy winter morning—we were still in our sleeping bags—when there was a sharp knock on the door of our roam in the Sainik Niwas and in walked NBG, dressed immaculately in a tweed coat and tie. He gave us 45 minutes to be up and dressed and be at his place for breakfast. We both felt like vagabonds in our faded denims and jungle boots at his rather roomy house. He talked of more politics in Nepal, India, various Generals, his plan for ex-servicemen, for the Regiment, the lack of balance in our cap badge, the military attaches, old times, the present and what was to come. We finished by near lunch time and it took us a long time to digest all that he had to say.

NBG next made his presence felt at our Reunion in 1977. He arrived a few days earlier at the Second Battalion with his wife and Lal Kaji's daughter and was his usual ebullient self. The Second Battalion had some more of the old guard-Hony Capt and Sub Maj Moti Lal, MC, IDSM, Hony Capt Jum Kaji Gurung, Sub Maj Mohindra Bahadur, but NBG simply towered above them. He moved over to Bakloh and it was too small to contain him. Reminiscing with the officers and wives from the UK, meeting the grown up and married daughter of a long dead comrade, settling a point about the quarter guard. It was obvious that he had been looking forward to the Reunion and to be with the Regiment again.

Early February 1978, I got a letter from my wife from the South to say "We were seeing the Republic Day parade on the TV and suddenly there was LK's father—at the head of the ex-servicemen's contingent. He looked out of place—it seemed he was still on active service."

There was a steady drizzle at Bakloh when the jeep wheeled into No 19 and NBG jumped out even before the jeep came to a halt. The cold wind and the rain was none too pleasant, but they didn't effect NBG. "Doctors have restricted my movements, but one shouldn't take them too seriously".

We had tea and he talked of the Republic Day parade and how they can improve the organisation. He said he was going to come back again next year to attend the parade to see that improvements have been made. "I have met the Adjutant General, Gen Eric Vas, Colonel of 9 GR, and I have to meet him again when I go back to Delhi from here.", "I have to meet Gen Gill at his farm in Moga, and I have some confidential matters to discuss with him."

We went over to the JCO's mess in the evening for drinks and he just took over the place. Over rum and hot water, he talked of Bakloh then and now, the Army then and now, the welfare activities of the Indian Army as compared to that of Nepal, the unity in the Regiment irrespective of the battalions, the continuity in the Regiment whether the officers were British or Indian.

We went back to No 19 for dinner and over brandy and hot water he said that Kulpatti, the 2nd Battalion's first Sub Mai was from his village, "I am starting a collection of books and I will open a library in Sabet, our old village, in the name of Kulpatti". He brought out the brochure giving the account of our Centenary Celebrations in 1957 and pointed to our crest, "We must have the Asoka Lions on the Khukries. At the moment our crest is a body without a head. I am going to take this up." We finally went to bed at about 11 pm.

Next morning I had to leave early to attend a conference. As I was about to leave NBG popped out from the guest room, all ready, "If I did not have to go down today, I would have come up with you". No sign of fatigue or strain, nothing to suggest his eighty odd years.

As I was leaving, he said in a voice mellow with emotion, "It was a dream come true staying in No 19 as guest of the Commandant. It was something beyond my imagination."

The whole way to Dalhousie and back that late afternoon, NBG's words rang and it filled me with a sense of satisfaction in having pleased an eminent soldier of the Regiment. During that morning, K. K. Prodhan, the 2 IC, took NBG around the Battalion and he met all the officers and JCOs at tea. The impression on the officers and JCOs was tremendous. Most of the officers had not met NBG before. His colossal personality was unmistakable. K. K. Prodhan told me later that the old man really was moved going round Bakloh and more so when leaving the place—where he joined the Regiment and retired from service. One got the impression he was bidding a final farewell.

At about 10 at night Chandu rang up from Pathankot to say that NBG had collapsed in the bathroom and was admitted in the Military Hospital, Pathankot, in an unconscious state. It stunned me—just the evening before he was overflowing with life. He had plans that needed half a life time to see through and he was now in hospital. I said a silent prayer and hoped for the best. The telephone rang early morning and I somehow knew, even before picking it up, that another legendary figure had passed away into the pages of our Regimental History.

At PT, an hour and a half later, I announced the sad news to the Battalion and the shock was evident in the very audible sighs of sorrow from the four hundred odd men present. Everyone seemed to have frozen in mid breath. NBG was the same in death as in life: he just took your breath away. He certainly did not look a man spending the last day of his life at Bakloh—it was as if he was just renewing old associations. He gave no signs of ageing, or having any medical problems. He drank his rakshi and brandy that evening and was articulate till the end. With all his 80 years, senility never even suggested itself in his walk, speech, the wide ranging topics he chose to talk on, his incisive arguments, his long-term plans, his visions of the future of the Regiment, his plan for a memorial library in Nepal, honouring another luminary of the Regiment, his planned discussion on confidential matters with Gen Gill. I wonder what it could be? He died clutching the secret to himself.

Did he have a premonition of his end? On looking back, his visit to Bakloh seemed more of a farewell then a renewal of memories, his chat to the officers, JCOs and men more an "adieu" than a pep-talk—his last pilgrimage to his Regiment's Mecca. And he did patiently wait till he reached the Second Battalion, his first love as a soldier, to finally hang up his boots.

Ambush on the Frontier

By John Cross

In 1947 when it was the turn of the 1st/4th Gurkha Rifles to leave their North-West Frontier station, it left in a convoy driven by Pakistani army transport. Added to the column at the last moment were five lorry loads of Sikhs—gunners, muleteers, drivers and non-combatants—who, in direct contravention of every order pertaining to the Frontier, had been disarmed by the Pakistanis. The Sikhs and the Pathans loathed each other with a deep and bitter loathing that invited trouble. Unfortunately news of the Sikhs was leaked to the Pathans as a thousand of them ambushed the convoy, which was by then in two parts. Then the Sikhs and the three Gurkhas with them were overpowered and shot in cold blood. Although the driver was subsequently recognised, such was the chaos in higher formations, no action was taken against him.

The wonderful unit, the South Waziristan Scouts, came to the rescue and gave the Gurkhas sufficient breathing space to stop fighting, collect their belongings and find sanctuary in two local Scout forts of the Beau Geste type scattered around the Frontier. There they stayed, cramped and uncomfortable, for two days. A *laksha*, a holy war gathering of many Pathans, was waiting to slaughter the Hindu Gurkhas at their departure. The last thing anybody official wanted was trouble on the Frontier. Subterfuge, something that the Pathans understood and loved, was needed. One account of their rescue, told me after the war by the then Governor of the North-West Frontier Province, Sir Olaf Caroe, makes the more exciting reading: the regimental history of the 4th Gurkhas has a slightly different version.

In essence, what happened shortly before fresh transport was due up at the more precariously defended of the two forts to take the Gurkhas away, was, according to the Governor, that the Political Advisor, a dedicated and fluent Pushtu-speaking Englishman, went to the valley where the main part of the *laksha* was and started talking to them. He was witty and cracked jokes. The crowd gathered to hear him the better. He so dropped his voice that those on the edge could not hear. "Speak louder" they cried. "The wind is taking my voice away, come down into the valley", was the answer. Skilfully and slowly the Political Advisor took them out of sight and sound of the fort, with even the sentries following.

The transport duly arrived with tailboards down, drove into the fort and without stopping, slowly drove round and Out while men clambered in and Scouts threw the bedding rolls inside. Only as the vehicles were departing did a sentry notice and gave the alarm. The Political Advisor was completely at their mercy but so successfully had he captured their hearts, the Pathans slapped their thighs and said "Wah, there goes a man". The soldiers in the other fort also managed to get away unscathed.

According to the then CO of the 1st/4th Gurkhas in his book, *Yes, Your Excellency*, and the regimental history, the man who spoke to the Pathans was a Pathan himself, the Assistant Political Advisor and that rain had so dampened the spirits of the *laksha* that the smaller of the two forts was left alone and the larger of the two was the one whose rescue I have described. Even there, rain and boredom had dulled the Pathans' ardour. No matter, it was stirring stuff and many lives were saved by whoever that man was, with the discipline and bravery of Gurkhas and Sikhs alike in the convoy and the Scouts being unshakeable.

1/4 GR in Kohat, Gardai and Wana 1945–1947

Anecdotes, Incidents and Events by Henry Burrows

Reference is made to the following in this article:
  The Regimental history Vol III pages 508–516
  "Yes, Your Excellency" by V. E. O. Stevenson-Hamilton
  Newsletter No 38 pages 10–12 The Challenge by Ken Saxton
  Return to The North West Frontier by Ken Saxton

Kohat

1/4 GR trained for Frontier Warfare from September 1944 to October 1945 in Kohat under the command of Lieutenant Colonel R. R. Proud from the 6th Gurkha Rifles with whom he had seen a considerable amount of Frontier service. As Adjutant, I was very aware that Lieutenant Colonel Proud was a hard task master who ensured that we were well trained for duties on The North West Frontier. John Fairley and I attended an intensive two weeks' Frontier Warfare course at Thai run by the legendary Brigadier "Tochi" Barker.

One particular incident happened shortly after I had taken over from Eric Mercer (who had been my mentor and guru ever since I joined the Regiment on the 4th of October 1942). Lieutenant Colonel Proud decreed that the Battalion would proceed on a few days' exercise to put into practice the early lessons we had learnt in the skills of Frontier Warfare. He ordered that the Battalion would march at 1100 hrs. We duly paraded ready to march, with the exception of the 3-inch mortar Platoon commanded by Derek Royals, who was having a major problem trying to load his mortars onto very frisky mules. The second-in-command, Ken Walsh, duly called the Battalion to attention and I reported to the Commanding Officer that the Battalion was present and correct and ready to march, with the exception of the Mortar Platoon! Lieutenant Colonel Proud was annoyed and said something like "When I said the Battalion would march at 1100 hours we march at 1100 hours!" Off we went with poor Derek Royals and his platoon left behind.

While in Kohat Lieutenant Colonel Vivian Edgar Omar Stevenson-Hamilton (Colonel S-H from now onwards) took over from Lieutenant Colonel Proud as Commanding Officer (CO). Shortly afterwards I went off on 8 weeks leave to the UK just before the Battalion moved to Dehra Dun to be Demonstration Battalion to the Battle School, the Tactical Training Centre and the Indian Military Academy.

Gardai

I rejoined the Battalion in January 1946. Shortly after taking over "C" Company in October that year the Battalion returned to the North West Frontier but this time to Gardai, a two-battalion tented camp near the old site of Razani. This was a very different scene from Kohat. Gardai conditions were tantamount to being on active service. The enemy were the Pathans from one of the local tribes of Waziristan.

During the actual move from Dehra Dun the Battalion was commanded by Major F. A. G. Redl as Colonel S-H was on leave in the UK. Major Redl had seen a considerable amount of Frontier service himself and during the first few months in Gardai he imparted his considerable knowledge to us in his own forceful way. His orders, groups and "wash-ups" were memorable occasions. Soon after Colonel S-H returned from leave Major Redl left the battalion. A few months later, in May 1947, the Second-in Command Major R. N. D. Williams departed on longer leave. Shortly afterwards the CO had to absent himself on duty and command passed to Major W. S. Tee for a short while.

I shall never forget those ten months or so in Gardai. The whole

Battalion was involved in some two to three Road Opening Days (RODS) per week. The purpose of all this was to protect the road from Razmak to Bannu so as to allow a safe passage of motor vehicles carrying supplies. This meant getting up in the early morning when it was still dark and then leaving the secure sanctuary of our stone walled camp at first light. Once outside the camp the leading rifle companies fanned out into open formation and moved at considerable speed towards the hills and high ground on both sides of the road that they had been ordered to picket. All movement was covered by the 3 inch Mortar Platoon whose detachments leap frogged from one firing position to another.

Even in camp, life had its hazards. One of our Battalion HQ clerks was wounded in the foot while watching a football match between the Bn team and a visiting team from the South Waziristan Scouts (SWS). The football ground was outside the camp perimeter wall and covered by a detachment of 3 inch mortars but even this did not prevent the wily Pathan from having a go. On this particular occasion the reaction of the SWS supporters who were sitting fully armed on the touch line, was magnificent. Led by one of their officers they launched an attack on the snipers' position within seconds of the shots being fired.

At the beginning of July 1947, along with a few senior NCOs, I was detailed to go to Dera Ismail Khan where we were to act as referees at the various Polling Stations for the Referendum of the North West Frontier Province. We were under the control of Lieutenant Colonel George Strover of the Guides Cavalry and dispersed in small groups to man the booths of remote Polling Stations. Colonel S-H mentioned the Referendum on page 177 of his book and I endorse what he said about the booths being filled with wild looking but cheerful Pathans. It did cross my mind that, on all occasions, we were heavily outnumbered. Skinners' Horse accommodated, fed, watered and generally looked after us very well indeed. Because of the tremendous heat, we dined outside in the evenings on the Mess lawn and I was interested to observe that an armed sowar (cavalry soldier) stood behind the CO's chair throughout the dinner. The adjutant Captain Skinner (who attended the OTS in Bangalore with me) was a direct descendent of the Skinner who raised the regiment and later went on to command it.

Life did have its amusing moments in Gardai. Jimmy Evans and I had both bought small 125 cc motor cycles in Dehra Dun and brought them with us to Gardai. We kept petrol for these machines in camouflaged jerry cans outside our Wana huts. Cold water was also kept by our orderlies in similar cans. Poor Tommy Gibson, while taking his evening bath, asked his orderly for more cold water. The unsuspecting orderly borrowed one of our cans and poured petrol into Gibson's bath—with disastrous results.

While in Gardai we occasionally had contact with 1/1 GR who were in Razmak. In fact one of their young British Officers (BO) was attached to my company for frontier and language experience. John Whitehead (later to become Brigadier Whitehead ex 1GR and 7GR) was then learning Gurkhali and quickly picked up some choice swear words from one of my Gurkha Officers (GOs) who shall be nameless. Ken Saxton in his "Return to the North West Frontier 1947" mentions 1/1 GR being attacked whilst on column. This turned out to be a very unpleasant incident with five Gurkhas being wounded. However, two of them on a reverse slope were heroically rescued by a 2nd Lieutenant Peter Davis of 1/1 GR. Davis was awarded a MC for his bravery but, because of the turmoil in India at that time, the award was not announced as far as I know until 1952 when Davis was serving as a Captain with 2/7 GR in Malaya.

When the Battalion arrived in Gardai we relieved an Indian regiment and, as was the custom, rifle companies took over the outgoing unit's accommodation, parts of the perimeter wall and wire, as well as the strategically sited fortified perimeter posts complete with head cover. These posts normally contained two LMGs mounted on tripods for fixed line fire. The posts also contained boxes of reserve ammunition and 36 grenades. Every item handed over was meticulously checked but, because of the time factor, sealed boxes were very often accepted as such.

The same rules applied in mid June 1947 when we moved to Wana and handed over to a Battalion of the Frontier Force Rifles known as Piffers (Abbreviation for Punjab Irregular Frontier Force).

However, some three years later, while on leave in London, I was in for a considerable shock. I was enjoying a drink in "Bobby's Bar" at the Café Royal in Piccadilly (then the unofficial rendezvous for Gurkha Brigade Officers) and was talking to a chap, wearing a Piffer tie, about service on The North West Frontier. It soon transpired that his regiment had taken over from us at Gardai but when it came to their turn to hand over, the sealed ammunition boxes were all opened and found to contain sand.!

Wana

The move of the Battalion from Gardai to Wana is described by Colonel S-H in Chapter XVII of his book and by Ken Saxton in his article "Return to the North West Frontier 1947". I can remember it being a long, very hot 4 days' drive and feeling very thankful on our arrival. Being a Brigade camp, the whole area was much larger and more open than Gardai. The general atmosphere seemed very relaxed and we heard stories that the local Pathans never shot up the Wana Hunt because some tribal chiefs were members!

We were brigaded with a battalion of the Rajputana Rifles and a few of us attended a guest night dinner with them about the time of Independence Day. This battalion was in the throes of breaking up and dispatching its Moslem soldiers to join regiments of the new Pakistan Army. Throughout dinner we were entertained by their band and when it came to the time for the Bugle Major to request permission to march off (for the last time) the poor man did so in floods of tears. This brought home to us the awful reality and sadness of the disintegration of a fine and distinguished regiment.

The move from Wana to Manzai and Tank

The Regimental History, as well as Colonel S-H and Ken Saxton, all describe the uneventful move of the first half of the Battalion to Manzai.

TALES FROM BAKLOH

As OC "C" Company I was fully aware that we could be shot up on our way through the Shahur Tangi but had no idea that the cards were so heavily stacked against us.

Soon after we arrived in Manzai the Battalion was warned of the possibility of being flown out of the NWFP and I was appointed Emplaning Officer in addition to my duties as OC "C" Company. (I had qualified on a Unit Emplaning Officers Course at Chaklala in February 1947). Much time was then spent on working out scales and weights of kit.

From then on events have been accurately described in the Regimental History and Colonel S-H's book. As a rifle company commander I was very busy and had little idea of the problems and dilemmas facing the CO. We were all most anxious for the safety of the second half of the battalion. After hearing reports of firing in the Shahur Tangi our anxiety was increased by the arrival of two riflemen who witnessed the killing of six Gurkhas by a Pakistani naik. These two riflemen, as Colonel S-H describes in his book, had been caught in the ambush but hid in the rocks and engaged the Mahsuds looting the trucks, killing some six of them. These brave men then waited until it was dark before walking some 18 miles to Manzai where, on arrival, they had the presence of mind to lie up in our latrines (outside the perimeter wire) until it was light.

The Pakistani naik eventually arrived in Manzai. He was immediately arrested and brought before me. My Company Havildar Major, Siriparsad Gurung (better known as 002) had the presence of mind to search the naik before marching him into the company office. He found that the treacherous naik had a Pathan knife concealed behind his back. The naik was relieved of this weapon which now hangs on the wall in my house.

I can add little to what has been written in the above references about this anxious and taxing time. The ruse, twice employed by Lieutenant Colonel Chambers, CO of the SWS, for extricating "B" and "A" Companies from Chagmalai and Sarwekai respectively, was risky but very successful. I heard that in the first instance the "B" Company Gurkhas were actually covered over by tarpaulins with a few scouts standing on top of them when the lorries were driven through the ambush positions to safety in Manzai. I feel that this trust between comrades in arms could never have been achieved had not the Battalion established an excellent relationship with the SWS. Those games of football and drinking sessions with the officers certainly paid off.

Postscript

Some 45 years after Independence, through family connections, I became friendly with a Colonel R. A. Shebbear (late Guides Cavalry). Bob Shebbear (now deceased) was awarded the new Indian Army's equivalent of the Victoria Cross for extricating a Battalion of Bombay Grenadiers that he was commanding, complete with families, from Pakistan to India at the time of Partition. Whether it was the same battalion mentioned in Colonel S-H's book I was never able to determine.

I feel that great acts of bravery must have been carried out by some officers and men caught in the actual ambush area of the Shahur Tangi. By Frontier standards to have 27 killed and 26 wounded is appalling. By virtue of circumstances it was impossible to evaluate enemy casualties but there must have been some.

Sadly there were no awards for gallantry for the simple reason that the (now deceased) British Officers who survived the ordeal of the ambush were, along with a few of us alive today, pitched into the "Blood Bath of the Punjab" where conditions were hardly conducive to the writing of citations.

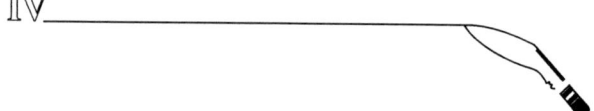

1/4 GR Amritsar October–December 1947

By Henry Burrows

Bill Tee briefly covered our stay in Amritsar in his article "The Winds of Change 1947–1949" in NL 42. However, the following may be of interest.

Shortly after our arrival at Amritsar, while still licking our wounds from the ordeal of the Shahur Tangi, the Commanding Officer (Lieutenant Colonel Stevenson-Hamilton) decreed that a Durbar should be held. Together with representatives of all ranks, I attended, which, as many will know is a democratic free-for-all whereby anybody could stand up and air their grievances. After the usual complaints about food and rations, a Rifleman stood up and asked why he was ordered to protect the lives of Muslim refugees when only a short time ago a large number of his comrades had been killed by Muslim Pathans. Before the CO could attempt to answer this direct and embarrassing question, the Subedar Major leapt to his feet and asked for permission to answer it. With a look of relief the CO agreed; whereupon the Subedar Major turned on the Rifleman and asked him "Who gives you your salt?" (in other words "who pays you?") Looking somewhat abashed, the Rifleman muttered something like "the Sahibs" and sat down. After a few days, the rifle companies were soon dispersed to areas outside the city.

As O "C" Company, I was given the task of ensuring the safe passage of thousands of Muslim refugees moving by day along the Jullundur—Amritsar road and railway lines which were some miles apart. Our responsibility stretched for about sixty miles, so my platoons engaged on either escorting or static protection duties were very thin on the ground.

Company Headquarters were established in an empty house and the platoons accommodated in tents nearby. We were fortunate in having our own well, which I tested daily with my Horrox Box and insisted on super chlorinating of all water consumed. My company area was encircled by barbed wire and very carefully guarded. The surrounding countryside was littered with the corpses of refugees and carcasses, the victims of violence, cholera, starvation and exhaustion. While performing our duties outside the camp the stench was so indescribably awful we wore scarves round our mouths and noses to keep out the swarms of flies and the choking dust.

Once, while visiting one of my platoons on railway line protection, I was testing the water from a nearby well when a refugee train halted at the small station where the platoon was on duty. Some Indian Parachute Regiment NCO's. (Muslims on their way to Pakistan) clambered down from the train and came over to where I was busy with my cups of blue coloured water. After saluting, they asked if I was poisoning the well water. I explained what I was doing and convinced them by drinking the contents of all my cups.

Chapter XX of Colonel Stevenson-Hamilton's book and the late Peter Attack's article SECOND BATTALION 1947 in NL 45 both give brilliant descriptions of the situations we were all facing. However, there were some bizarre incidents and happenings of which the following are but a few:

- The combined 1st and 2nd Battalion Nautch on the 11th October that Ken Sexton mentioned in NL 48 did produce one casualty. The late Derek Royals disappeared after the Nautch ended. Rumour had it that he was found clinging to a rope and bucket at the bottom of a very deep well!
- Due to the chaotic situation the Battalion's reserves of rum began to run low. One of my Gurkha Officers procured a small quantity of rum from a local source. That evening, with my GO's we put back a few tots. The next morning, when my orderly brought my mug of tea, I asked him to light my hurricane "butti". When he said that it was alight, I realised to my horror that I could not see.

I lay still for a few hours nursing a splitting headache until my sight returned. I had the rum confiscated forthwith.

- My annual confidential report was long overdue about the time that Bill Tee took over as CO. Being one of the first ECO's to be gazetted a Regular Commission, I was anxious for my report not to be forgotten. I approached the CO and asked if he would initiate one. Bill told me to write it myself for his signature. I did just that and apart from a few alterations, my report was typed and Bill signed it.

- When Countess Mountbatten visited Amritsar on 7th October the Battalion had to provide protection at the AMRITSAR HOTEL where she stayed. It was rumoured that on entering her bathroom one evening, she surprised one of our Rifleman enjoying a good wash.

- While driving a jeep through Amritsar I had a minor accident when crossing a small bridge with a vehicle being driven by a be-spectacled and black-moustached British Officer. He turned out to be the late Bunny Burnett who was then, I believe Commanding the 2/8 Gurkha Rifles in Lahore. The accident was fortuitous as it led to a convenient arrangement whereby we exchanged our surplus petrol for his surplus rum.

A difficult problem arose when my senior GO, Subedar Dhanlal Gurung, reported that a Nepalese woman was being held by one of the locals in a nearby village. The men felt strongly that the woman should be asked whether she was being held against her will? I sought the CO's permission to investigate the problem as it did have a bearing on C Company's morale. He agreed but did make the point that whatever the outcome I would be entirely responsible for the welfare and disposal of the unfortunate woman. Very early next morning with two platoons and a section of 3" mortars we surrounded the village under cover of darkness. At first light, accompanied by Subedar Dhanlal Gurung and Company Havildar Major Siriparsad Gurung we made our way to the headman's house. After rousing the headman, the Havildar Major explained the situation; as well as the fact that his village was surrounded.

The headman readily agreed to take us to see the Nepalese woman. Subedar Dhanlal Gurung and the CHM ascertained that she had been forcibly abducted. She quickly collected a few belongings and we escorted her out of the village and back to our company base. We had to feed the poor woman for a short while until the British Officers left the Battalion by rail for Delhi and delivered her safely to relatives/friends in the depths of that city.

I end this article by referring again to Bill Tee's "The Winds of Change" and correcting an inaccuracy. The last British Officers to leave 1/4 GR were Bill Tee, James Castle, Tom Gibson, Derek Royals, Alec Robertson, David Cotton, Malcolm Smith and myself. We all left by train for Delhi where we spent a few days before I went off on local leave accompanied by Royals, Robertson and Cotton down to Ootacamund in the Nilgiri Hills.

We met up again with the other BO's at the Connemara Hotel in Madras prior to embarking on the SS Ethiopia for Rangoon where we all joined 1/10 GR. Personally I rate the day I left 1/4 GR as one of the saddest days of my life.

Escort Duties and Safe Passage For a Million Refugees

By Peter Attack

Author's Note: I wrote this account of the Second Battalion's activities entirely from memory. It would have been preferable to have done so before David Davidson passed on because he was CO throughout the year, and could have filled in some of the blanks in my memory, or added facts of which I was unaware at the time.

I am grateful to Colonel Arun Yadav, the present CO, who has checked the Battalion's records for me but could find nothing more detailed than the sketchy account given in the Regimental History, including a list of people who served with the Battalion at some period or another during 1946–48.

The main purpose of the account is to pay tribute to the Battalion's noteworthy achievement in providing safe escort to as many as one million refugees during the period immediately following partition.

1946 had been a straightforward year. A couple of months at Dhangu, sorting things out having returned from Italy in December 1945; the move to Rawalpindi in March followed by eight months routine training for North West Frontier type operations, culminating in higher formation exercises during a notably hot summer and autumn. The Battalion acquitted itself very well indeed both in the field and at sport, particularly football.

Christmas arrived to find us in a particularly merry frame of mind because, a few days earlier, Divisional Headquarters together with our sister Brigade and supporting artillery had been despatched to the Black Mountains (north of Abbottobad) to sort out some Pathans who had been indulging in their customary festival activity of a little local pillaging. We were spared the trip for reasons unknown and were content to escape the rigours of a bleak, cold and very wet sojourn in the mountains. So, a routine peaceful year ended. 1947 was to be very different.

For John Emerson-Baker and myself, merriment ceased 1st January 1947 when David called for us and said, "They're in a bit of a mess in the mountains. The weather is bad, the single track road over the Kusulgarh Pass has become virtually impassable. You two are to go up there and set up control of movement both ways." So off we went.

It was cold; wet snow and mud to match the Somme. It was not much of a job really, although it was amazing how trade picked up on a Thursday with people coming to us for passes because they had "urgent reasons to get back to 'Pindi by Friday night, but of course we'll be back on Monday morning". It all fizzled out by the third week of January and John and I returned to the Battalion to find everyone packing up to move to Campbellpore. Funny that—I thought that we had been destined for Abbottabad, but to Campbellpore we went. I recall little of the place or of our activities there; hardly surprising really because, having unpacked, we started packing again to go to Abbottobad in the first week of March!

By now there were rumours of increasing tension in the towns and villages. On arrival at Abbottabad we were put at short notice to provide picquets on all access roads, patrols to villages in the surrounding area—to show the flag—and a mobile reserve to deal with any IS situation which might occur.

Manshera was thought to be a likely trouble spot and one company took up residence there. But the first place to blow was Haripur, at the bottom of the hill, late afternoon in mid-March. The DC, Oliver St John, took off on his own closely followed by "C" Company who were on stand-by. Things calmed down soon after darkness, but the Company remained there for some weeks in the school, adopting a low profile rather than risk provoking further violence.

Back in Abbottabad we put out picquets of platoon strength on all the approach roads in anticipation of bands of dissidents coming in from the surrounding countryside. Sure enough they came, about three or four days later, from the east—about 400–500 of them brandishing shotguns, spears, lathis and anything else that was handy. The picquet Commander told us on the radio that the mob had halted about 150 yards from the picquet but were threatening to continue their advance. We informed the DC and I was detailed off to accompany him to the scene. It was just as the picquet Commander had described. He had deployed one section across the road, complete with banner and bugler. Text book stuff. Well Trained we were in 2/4 GR.

Oliver St John was an impressive man, large in stature and full of energy.

"Come on," he said to me. "Where?" I asked. "Up there," he said pointing with his faithful walking stick. "Up there" was to the mob. "All of us?" I asked. "No, just you and I."

Now, this was not what I had been taught at Bangalore, nor had we considered such an approach during IS training within the Battalion. I was reluctant but who was I to argue with someone as important as the DC.

So we went. At about ten yards range, Oliver St John started to talk to them. "Go home," he said, "You are just being bloody fools." Muttering from the crowd and a brandishing of weapons. So he raised his voice and repeated his earlier instructions, adding a choice description of what might happen to them if they failed to obey. Still no move, and more muttering. I was beginning to be disenchanted and looked back to our platoon. The Gurkhas were watching with some amusement.

Then—he strode forward the ten yards, clouted the first four or five men with his walking stick, and repeated the order. More or less silently they slowly turned and went. A much respected man was Oliver St John.

Some days later there was more trouble, this time at Taxila on the Peshawar—'Pindi trunk road. A task for yet another company. It did not amount to much but tension in the area was high and so the company (it may have been "D") remained there.

It was the first week in June when we heard that the date of Independence was to be advanced from March 1948 to 15 August 1947, and the threat of partition was now a serious possibility. There were fears of widespread disturbances and the battalion's primary task became "showing the flag". Our area of operation changed and tactical Battalion HQ moved at fairly short notice to Khaur—main centre of the Attock oilfield. Companies were spread over a very wide area indeed, working mainly in platoon detachments. Each day they would send out patrols to surrounding villages to reassure the local population and to report back any signs of trouble.

Living conditions in the field were uncomfortable with daytime temperatures in excess of 120 °F (in the shade). For several weeks the temperature at night did not fall below 100 °F. We got blocks of ice once a week from an ice factory—but they did not last long! The rear party and families stayed in Abbattabad.

It was during June that we traded in our fifty mules for some twenty or so Bedford three-tonners. A more than fair exchange in terms of carrying capacity, and, as it turned out later in the year, the three-tonners were to prove invaluable.

It was also during this period that we learned that partition would take place but there was no news about the actual line of the border between India and the new Pakistan. There was increasing anxiety about the possibility of large scale violence, particularly in the most sensitive areas, Gurdaspur, Amritsar/Lahore to Ferozepore/Jullundur.

On the 9th August the Radcliffe Report was issued and the boundary line was announced.

Immediately, the Battalion moved about 100 miles southwards, with Battalion HQ at Pindigheb and an operational area stretching to Mari Indus and Talagang. Tension was rising rapidly and within a day or two we had rioting and arson in Pindigheb and there were reports of Hindus being killed in outlying villages. Our task now was to go to every village within our area to bring in Hindu refugees to a central camp, from which they would be moved either by road on foot or by train to refugee reception camps (still to be established) across the border, some 150 to 200 miles away. Every three tonner was employed—each carrying sixty to seventy men, women and children two or three trips a day.

Sometimes we were too late. A patrol would reach a village and find it apparently deserted. But shortly a few people would appear and the headman would be asked "Where are the Hindus? Do they wish to come away?" "No Hindus here, Sahib," would be the reply. A further search would disclose twenty or thirty bodies in the village well. Goodness knows what the residents intended to use for drinking water thereafter.

This routine continued throughout August, the violence increasing. We did not record the numbers of people brought to the safety of the central collecting point, but the total must have been in the region of 50,000. Whether or not they survived the onward move to the border I do not know, but most of them must have done.

Our most westerly Company (I cannot remember which) became involved in a different sort of sideshow. News of the widespread unrest had obviously percolated across the Indus to Waziristan, because a group of one hundred or so Pathans decided that this would be an appropriate moment to indulge in their traditional sport of looting a few villages on our side of the river between Mari Indus and Mianwali. Our Company was elected to restore the situation.

Their sudden appearance at the scene just before nightfall must have come as a nasty shock to the Pathans. After a brief exchange of fire they decided it would be safer on the other side of the river and withdrew during the night.

By the end of August there was extreme violence on both sides of the border. A rumour of a massacre of Moslems near Amritsar would provoke a reprisal on Hindus at Gujaranwala which in turn set off further killings on the Indian side of the border. Refugee columns moving in both directions (but on separate routes) were also being attacked.

When the line of the border had been announced a large force of military units had been set up to work in conjunction with the police to preserve law and order on both sides of the line. It was known as the Punjab Boundary Force, under a single command. For a variety of reasons the force was ineffectual and was disbanded on 29th August. On either 1st or 2nd September 2/4 GR was ordered to move across the border and concentrate near Jandiala, just east of Amritsar on the Amritsar—Jullundur trunk road.

I took the Battalion recce party, preceding the Battalion by about three hours. It was a long journey from Pindigheb and we passed various signs of rioting en route. We arrived late in the afternoon and, basing Battalion HQ on an unoccupied Waterway's bungalow, we allocated various areas in the surrounding fields to the rifle Companies. It was dusk by 7.00 pm; I still had no satisfactory spot for the fourth Company and reluctantly came to the conclusion they would have to bed down for at least one night on the edge of a very smelly village. At this point a jeep appeared out of the dusk bearing a Lieutenant Colonel 4 GR! He introduced himself as John Masters—of whom I had only vaguely heard. He was on his way to UK to attend Staff College, had heard we were in the area, and decided to spend the night with us. The Battalion turned up in good order at about 8.30 pm, had a meal and got a reasonable nights rest.

Next day we were briefed on our new role. It was to pick up columns of walking Moslem refugees from an overnight staging camp on the River Beas to our east and escort them to the border mid-way between Amritsar and Lahore. To avoid Amritsar itself a bypass route was devised using canal banks around the city. We could expect column strengths to be anything from 40,000 to 80,000 people—covering something like 10–15 miles of road once on the move.

We started next day. Because of the daily distances involved, David decided to commit only two Companies at a time to the task, ie day on and day off, and of these two Companies, only about half of each should be on foot at any one time, the balance moving in three tonners, swapping over periodically so that all got some rest. So, at best, there would be only about one hundred and twenty men acting as immediate close escorts, stretched over 10 miles at best but at worst (which turned out to be more often than not) they had to cover 15 miles! With the road jammed with refugees, it was not easy to move the reserves in three tonners to an incident when one occurred.

We soon got into a daily routine and all went well for the first two weeks or so, with only a few minor incidents. One irritation was to see the refugees being stripped by police at a checkpoint on the outskirts of Amritsar of any implement that could be used as a weapon for self defence. These implements/weapons being distributed later the same day to local militants for possible use against the next column of refugees!

On 19th September, David and I were at Battalion HQ in mid-afternoon. We heard automatic fire from the direction of Jandiala railway station—about 1.5 miles away. David suggested I should go to see what was happening. The firing stopped and I arrived there about 10 minutes later. A train was in the station, crammed with refugees—several hundred of them being on the roof. In the station yard lay 10 or 12 Sikh bodies, evidently hit by fire from the train. The escort on the train consisted of a young British Indian Artillery Officer and 18 NCOs and men—six at the front, six in the middle and six at the back, armed with rifles and three Brens.

The subaltern told me they had stopped for water for the engine. He saw a group of about 50 Sikhs armed with shotguns, kirpans and spears evidently intent on attacking the refugees. He gave the order to open fire and the Sikhs withdrew, leaving their dead behind.

I chatted with him for a few minutes and advised him to be extremely careful on approaching Amritsar because news of this incident would have been passed up the line immediately.

The engine driver announced that he was ready to go and off they went. That evening we heard that the train had been derailed on the outskirts of Amritsar and everyone on board had been slaughtered—about 2,500 people we guessed.

Next day was my birthday and we had a few post prandial drinks in the evening.

Escorting the columns was an appalling task. The refugees were in an awful state. Many had been on the road for 10 days or more with only whatever food they could carry plus a few vegetables gathered from the countryside. There were no medical facilities and disease was rife—cholera, dysentery, malaria *et al*. The number dying overnight at the Beas staging post increased each day—reaching about 200 per night by the end of the month. Many who could no longer walk subsided by the roadside and died there. Mothers abandoned newly born babies. The vultures, shite hawks and pie dogs were having ceaseless banquets on human flesh. The stench was indescribable and a fifteen mile column was a black swarming mass of flies—any flat surface being totally covered by them. We wore handkerchiefs or scarves round our mouths and noses to keep them out.

The soldiers remained amazingly cheerful but were becoming increasingly worried about their families who were still in Abbottabad. They knew that sooner or later the families would have to move to India by train—and they knew what happened to people on trains. What happened at Jandiala/Amritsar had also occurred on the other side of the border.

Late one afternoon a deputation of senior and junior NCOs came to see me. They told me of their worries and said that all the married men wanted to go back to Abbottabad in order to act as escorts for the families. I said that officially no one was permitted to go back across the border but, more importantly from the Battalion's standpoint, we could not spare so many people. I promised to discuss the problem with the CO.

David and I discussed the matter. He decided that we should allow a party of 10 (to be chosen from amongst themselves and to include representatives from each Company) to make their way in a 15 cwt truck and try to get through to Abbottabad. They were given enough petrol and three days' rations.

We heard a few days later that they had arrived safely—but it must have been some journey. Just to finish this part of the story—the families did move in mid-October and got through to Bakloh completely unscathed thank goodness.

Now back to Amritsar and the last days of September.

A few days earlier, and unknown to us, it had rained heavily in the mountains to our north. We awoke on the morning of 25 September to an astonishing and quite dreadful situation. Flash floods had come down from the mountains during the night. Many hundreds of square miles around us were flooded to depths varying from a foot to about three feet.

At the Beas staging post there was chaos. About 50,000–60,000 had stopped there, some 8,000–10,000 camping on a ledge somewhat lower than the surrounding countryside and on the river's edge. The flood had hit the main (Jullundur to Amritsar) railway embankment one mile to the north of the staging post—where the railway crossed the river. Half a mile or more of the embankment had been washed away and so had the 8,000 or so refugees on the river's edge. The young British Indian cavalry officer had spent much of the night rescuing people from the flood—more than twenty he had pulled out I was told. He died three days later of pneumonia.

There was no refugee movement that day or the next. The canal banks around Amritsar had burst, so we had no bypass route. The refugees were all huddled in a foot or more of water. No cooking was possible.

I drove David to a conference in Amritsar where it was decided to move a column right through the middle of the city next day.

Owing to the serious danger of militant attacks in the city, David decided to commit the entire Battalion—on foot—to protection through the city streets. Once the column had cleared the city two Companies would stand down.

At about mid-day next day the head of the column was well through the city. So far, so good. Then—in the middle of the city—a group of half a dozen Sikhs opened fire on the column with shotguns from the roof of the police station. They were not policemen! The policemen were sitting on the steps spectating!

Peter Hervey and Ben Browne were furious, as was David when the news reached him. I had never seen David really angry before, nor have I since. He jumped into the jeep and off we went to "superior HQ". I gather there was a big row. But when we returned David was able to announce that anyone who came within 100 yards of our column and showed the slightest sign of hostility would be shot without warning. This news was promulgated within Amritsar that evening.

From then on there was no serious incident in the city. But two or three days later, Peter Hervey and Ben Browne became involved in further shooting. This time on the far side of Amritsar and about three miles from the border crossing. Sugar cane came right to the edge of the road, so there was good cover for the Sikhs to spot a gap between our marching escorts, come out of the sugar cane, kill a few refugees and then scuttle back under cover. Peter identified the village they had come from, "borrowed" a Honey tank from our friendly cavalry colleagues, pointed the gun at said village and threatened to blow it to pieces unless they desisted.

Calm was restored, but we had lost a number of refugees.

The floods began to subside and in the first week of October, so did the flood of refugees.

We had time to relax a little and busied ourselves helping some of the people in remote villages who had been cut off for days by the floods. By now the countryside was mostly a sea of mud.

British officers had gradually been leaving the Battalion throughout the year, Bob Crichton and John Emerson-Baker left in July/August I believe. Now Peter Hervey, N. Q. Browne and

G. L. Harvey left. So that by the end of October only David, myself and a recently joined subaltern (possibly 2Lt E. Gee—I'm not sure) were left. Frank Wisbey was perhaps still with the rear party which had got through to Bakloh. All Companies were commanded by subedars.

On 29th October Pathans invaded Kashmir (via Abbottabad!).

We moved hurriedly to release the Gurkha Para Brigade from the area of Gurdaspur—Pathankot and westward into Jammu state.

Our task was to protect the L of C (particularly bridges) on the road (really no more than a track) through Jammu leading to Kashmir. Once again we were widely dispersed, but we were used to that and all worked well. We had no excitements and by early December we were withdrawn to Amritsar and occupied a large secondary school.

By now we were receiving increasingly irate signals from GHQ, New Delhi. Why had P I Attack not reported to Deolali for movement to UK? We ignored the first two. Then replied, "No sign of Indian officers to take over, cannot leave until they arrive." Dire threats of court martial etc. But eventually reason prevailed. On 17th December two Indian officers arrived—a Major, from Madras I believe, and a 2Lt straight out of Belgaum. Sadly, I cannot remember their names.

On 18th December I handed over the accounts, imprest, regimental funds, POL, vehicles and so on.

On 19th December I stood on the platform of Amritsar station and said goodbye to David, Kajiman, Motilal, Kumlal, Hoshiarsing and many, many others. It had been an extraordinary year—nine months of it beside David. I learned a great deal from him. I hope I practised some of it in later life.

The Second was a great Battalion. We were lucky too. Not a single casualty throughout the year—and I am sure they escorted at least a million refugees to safety.

40 Column in Burma 1944
The Lull Before the Storm

By Donald McCutcheon

This is a personal account and commentary on the first twenty-four days of the column in Burma. It was not an heroic period and you will not find much "gung ho" in it. However, I have taken it as a period in which the discomforts and, on occasion, the pleasures of life in a Chindit column can be considered without the distraction of excitement, skirmishes with the enemy, or set-piece attacks.

In just over three weeks, we covered about a hundred miles as the crow flies, but rather longer as the Chindit hopped. This may not seem fast going, but we had to accept a supply drop every five days and, because of the need to protect ourselves against sudden attack, we had to start going into harbour in the late afternoon or early evening. The first factor was dictated by the inability of the column to carry more than five days' rations. Supply crops were also time-consuming and all too frequently went well beyond the single night allowed in training back in India. The problems of the night harbour will be familiar to those who served with Frontier columns. The proposed site had to be recced, the area around searched for likely trouble spots and the whole force bedded down after defensive positions had been prepared. All of this took time and cut into that available for marching. At this stage of the campaign, we were fit and could have covered greater distances per day but for these inhibiting factors.

When we turned east from the Irrawaddy, we were given vague orders to join Morrisforce and to take care to avoid the landing strip at "Chowringhee" because there would almost certainly be inquisitive people there before long. Morrisforce had at least a head start on us, so we would have to move fast if we were to catch them up. It took us ten weeks to do so. At this stage, we had no idea who or what Morrisforce was or was doing. It was known that 4/9 GR and a thing called "Dahforce of Kachins", with British officers, were part of it. But nothing else and certainly not its area of operation.

Shortly after we left the river, we discovered our first casualty. A roll call had shown the Rfn Rambahadur Pun was missing. As matters were we could not risk delay in searching for him. He never rejoined the column.

Our first major problem was the crossing of the Shweli about 15 miles ahead. Whilst not as formidable as the Irrawaddy, the Shweli was quite an obstacle in its own right and we required equipment such as assault craft and outboard motors which were demanded from air base.

On the night of 15 March, we were to have our first supply drop which was to include a special "mail bag" with our new signals instructions and orders from 77 Brigade under whom Morrisforce and now ourselves were serving. This air drop was well executed, but came the dawn and all the tall teak trees seemed to be festooned with highly coloured "statichutes" from which our precious rations dangled out of reach. Further there was no sign of the equally precious "mail bag". After diligent efforts which included sawing, blasting and using local elephants, we found all our 'chutes and the mail bag. This recovery was going to be a problem for a few days yet as we were crossing the northern edge of the teak forests.

It is worth remembering what a column was. It was based on a large rifle company of four platoons of four sections. There was a sort of support company of three specialist platoons: Recce, three Gurkha and one Burma Rifles section, with one British and one Burrif officer; Commando/Pioneer of three Gurkha and one Indian sapper sections commanded by a sapper officer with a British officer "in support" and a Support Platoon of one section of 3 in. Mortars and one section of MMGs and occasionally life-buoy flame-throwers.

Column HQ included Communications (Royal Signals and RAF), Intelligence (Gurkha and Burma Intelligence Corps), Medical (IAMC and RAMC) sections and a very small administrative element. The total strength was about 400 all ranks and 140 mules and ponies. In our case we had a plethora of animals having taken over from 30 Column and Brigade HQ, those that they could not take with them across the river. On the move, we formed ourselves into 4 or 5 tactical groups of about 100 men and 30 mules, each of which were to a large extent self-contained units. Columns became long snakes, concertinering at every obstacle when moving through country lacking in tracks. Tailenders found it very difficult to maintain a steady pace or keep up. The alternative was for the tactical groups to move independently, more or less picking their own way, and time provided the tactical situation permitted. Although there was some loss of control and there was the risk of groups going astray, it was undoubtedly a more comfortable way of travelling. In our pursuit of Morrisforce, we unfortunately used the snake method and life at the tail became a trifle wearing and there was controversy between front and rear of the columns. Independent patrols were popular because they moved at their own speed. In the latter stages, with shorter moves and independent operations, this nuisance largely disappeared.

These early days saw the genesis of the love-hate relationship with our packs which had only simmered during training when we went fully equipped for shorter distances and time. We used standard GS packs with ammunition pouches sewn to the sides. Some had the doubtful luxury of early Everest carriers. Clumsy frames which rode heavily on the hips. The men would have preferred namlos (head ropes) but near the enemy these were restricting and dangerous. The load on pack and belt included light-weight blankets, spare clothing and personal effects to taste and, after an air drop, 5 days of "K" rations (15 packages) and one "luxury meal" meant for consumption as soon after an air drop as possible. In addition, depending on one's role or choice, there were weapons, ammunition, kukris, dahs, machetes, grenades, compasses, binoculars and the odd kitchen sink—total 70 to 80 lbs or nearly half a mule load. Everything was essential but you hated it, yet would not be parted from it. The moment of relief when you were able to doff your pack for a halt or for a night was marvellous.

You grew ten feet, floated on air and discovered the secret of levitation.

We became epicures on the American "K" ration. For those who do not know the "K" ration, it is explained that it consisted of small cans of food (eg spam, corned pork loaf, etc), biscuits, dry milk, tea, coffee, sugar, lemonade crystals, sweets, cigarettes, chewing gum and loo paper. The whole was packed in robust, waterproof cardboard containers which could be used for a fire to heat up the contents, most of which could be eaten hot or cold. There were three packs per day marked "B" for breakfast, "D" for dinner and "S" for supper. They did not differ all that much and a mistimed meal did no harm. The men happily translated these into "Bhyana", "Dinsu" and "Sham". We got to recognise the contractors and their goodies—perhaps "General Foods" gave the best sweets, "Kelloggs", the best cigarettes and somebody else the best tinned food. (Don't forget the Hershey bars!). Swapping and combining gave remarkable variety. Although far and away better than the equivalent rations supplied by our own armies, "K" was only meant for the short term and certainly not as the main ration for almost six months, even with the added and quaintly named "luxury meal" which consisted of bread, jam, bully, pork and soya link sausages, oleo margarine and V cigarettes. The general belief was that the last three were Tojo's secret weapons which nearly won him the war in Burma.

On the lighter side of life, the more intellectual among us were wont to hold philosophical discussions on the relative values of knives, forks and spoons, if some decree came out limiting us to one item only. I, personally, favoured the spoon with one side slightly sharpened, but some held this to be cheating. The longer we stayed and the worse the weather, personal comfort in harbour was a matter of lowering standards or increasing tolerance to discomfort. We had learnt about bashas, bamboo beds and Boy Scout tricks of hammering out holes for the hips, dry flat places with shelter from the elements and other niceties. But, eventually, fatigue and experience accepted wet, sloping places on any surfaces, with dry bedding unheard of.

Came the Shweli on 16 March, and we went through all the proper business for a river crossing. Recces for the crossing place, stops and forming up places, with access to the river. Tests of equipment dropped on us and so on. It all seemed to be paying off and the crossing to be successful. It was not to be. The accumulated effect of a rather long drawn out air drop, keeping men late, confusion caused by a late change in the approach route and a decision not to use outboard motors on the score of preventing noise and the misbehaviour of the mules that we had inherited, who did not care for the dark Shweli and were not responsive to their new and not very expert leaders, lead to delay and eventually we crossed over just before dawn and went into hiding, tired and a bit cross with fate.

We now began our chase of a phantom force with plenty of evidence as to its passing, but little as to its location. We also received our first orders to operate by ambush and demolition on the Bhamo-Sin road, still 40 miles to the east.

Having recovered from the Shweli crossing, we made reasonable progress through jungle and teak forests. The locals were friendly and helped us with labour and guides. At one place, a local asked us if we knew "Lindsay Thakin (sahib)". When told that we did, he was very pleased and asked us to send him his regards. John Lindsay was the Burrif officer with 30 Column.

We had made preparations for action against the Bhamo-Sin road by building up a stock of explosives which some of our spare mules were carrying. Otherwise the march through the jungles was not readily interrupted. There was a false alarm when "acting on information received", Alec Hayward and George Duckworth were sent to "snatch" the headman or "thakin" of Sikaw who was said to have been in the pay of the enemy. Light aircraft were called for to take him away for questioning. However, the bird had flown which was just as well, because the light aircraft did not turn up having been grounded at their base at Henu (White City), by enemy action.

The recce parties who had gone ahead, reported that it would not be possible to operate against the road, firstly, because it was not a motor road, but rather a track for marching troops and animal transport and, secondly, because 4/9 GR had already dealt with it. This was reported back and we were now ordered to take on the Bhamo-Namhkan road, 20 miles to the north east. So, off we set.

On 28 March, we heard of the death on active service of General Wingate and the consequential changes in command. The former was clearly a blow to us all, but the latter were incomprehensible. There must have been sound reasons for it all, but no-one seemed to command that which he was meant to.

We crossed the Bhamo-Sin road, taking full precautions because it was known to be used by enemy infantry parties. No opposition was met and we went on our way with high hopes of something at the next road (how right we were!). We were passing through a pleasant country with friendly inhabitants. There were a number of ex-Burma Army (Kachin and Gurkha) VCOs and NCOs who came to greet us and express the hope that the sarkar would prosper.

We were climbing steadily, but slowly, and the final climb up a hill called Gawbum, when we took six hours to travel four miles, was exhausting but worth it. At the top, we fell into a veritable Shangri La.

There were rolling downs like those in Kent or Sussex, clear fresh streams, bridges with quaint Chinese style roofs and eaves, fruit and cultivation. But, best of all, charming, friendly and hospitable people with whom we could relax knowing that they would give us very early warning of any Japanese movement.

This was the place and way to spend the war. However, the days of our idyll, the lull before the storm, were numbered. On 5 April we sent out patrols to recce forward to the road for safe harbours, approaches to the road and suitable places for ambushes and demolition. On 6 April, we made contact with the enemy and our idyll was over.

Irrawaddy Crossing—1945

By Bill Tee

Tony Bowyer's casual demand that, "I knock out the story of the Thabeikkyin Crossing of the Irrawaddy" landed on my astonished desk in mid December last year just about 41 years after the event. I was minded to refuse—but who can refuse Tony's charm and the lure of seeing your name in print?

As a start I re-read that part of Volume 3 of our excellent Regimental History to prompt my ageing memory and found, to my annoyance, that the historian's account differed from my memory. Let me say therefore that what I remember is, as far as I am concerned, the truth! To me it is anyway. This introduction is made by way of an apology to those of you who remember differently and, in an offhand way, to those of you who have access to official sources of information.

For our approach to Thabeikkyin we enjoyed the luxury of "marching" in large and uncomfortable military vehicles; of actually crossing the map at a discernible pace. I wonder in passing how many miles I walked in Burma; or to put it another way how many tons I carried over one mile! The unaccustomed movement across the ground gave me personally a sense of freedom, a sense of purpose and a confidence in final victory; a lifting of the spirit after long miles and hours of foot slogging through that beautiful land. Or was this illusion part of the magic conjured up by that great commander, Bill Slim? Probably he had much to do with it before the arrival and quick departure of Oliver Leese.

When we debussed in and around the ferry head—the actual village of Thabeikkyin was on the far bank—all was quiet; all was dominated by the mighty river itself. I remember thinking "thank heavens we don't have to cross that". The only unusual thing that we found was an enormous rice dump (paddy actually) behind the river bank hidden among the great teak trees that flourish in that part of Burma. The Irrawaddy dominates the place; it is wider than the length of four football pitches; it is over half a mile of deep, deep water flowing inexorably from the great hills in the north through Burma down to the sea. Both banks were raised above the river and the surrounding countryside so that lateral movement could be unseen from the far bank. The far bank was so far away that, without binoculars, we could not see people on the bank nor the detail of houses. But even if we could not see the Japs we knew darn well that they were there.

My abiding memory of soldiering in Burma is being scruffy, itchy and dirty, of being hot and thirsty; of being constantly and chronically short of water to drink or wash in. So, on that river bank long ago and miles away, quite soon small bathing and washing parties of men were organised. They splashed and swam and washed and throughly enjoyed themselves. After a time the parties became less small and less disciplined—Hamish was not looking! The Gurkhas were having a ball!

This idyllic scene was rudely shattered by that once heard never forgotten crack of bullets passing close overhead followed after an interval by the dull thump of discharge. The bullets seem all around and the thump tells of the firers' position. The inscrutable Japanese had opened up with two machine guns from the far bank. Probably they had watched us arrive, carry out our careful recces and then, with growing disbelief, had watched our unmilitary swimming parties. They were probably envious but they did give their positions away!

On our bank bare torsos and other unmentionable bits of Gurkhas fled the water up the bank into the trees shedding garments and other military impedimenta to be collected at a later time. Abruptly the horrid calico ripping clamour of overhead bullets stopped. No one was hurt; total silence reigned; even the birds and insects were quiet. Then Rfn (or were you a L/Naik at the time, Bhime?) Bhimbahadur, a dashing driver as I remember, stood up in the water, collected his clothes and without haste stepped smartly up the bank into the security of the trees. Bhimbahadur, friend of long ago, where are you now? I salute you and your sang froid.

Some time later at an "O" Group Hamish told us our immediate military futures. Mine was a shock; he had selected me (C Company—Tee) to cross the Irrawaddy ahead of all the world. I thought then (and think now) "Why me, Hamish?). In 1987 it may come as a shock to many but in those days orders were never queried! Hamish told us that we would cross that coming night without noise or preparation; without artillery or mortar cover; with no deception plan—only with surprise. Surprise was then as it still is and always had been the first principle of war. But I did feel naked as the "O" Group went on. We would cross downstream of the known Jap positions as, so Hamish told us, if we tried to cross upstream inexperienced Gurkha boatmen might drift downstream onto the enemy machine guns. Good thinking, Hamish! Some boats had been located upstream and these were to be brought down to an embarkation point in the early part of the night by Gurkha boatmen from the other Companies. The plan was simplicity itself. The boats would arrive; we would get into them; we would cross and establish a bridgehead. Easy. Bill Tomlinson had selected the embarkation point and, on the far bank, the debarkation point.

In the event the night was an utter shambles and into the bargain we got no rest or sleep. Gurkhas are not great on water (or in it—except for the Majis) and those selected to bring the boats to the embarkation point proved unequal to their task. Burmese river craft are probably still as fickle as they were 40 years ago. Some ran ashore on the way down river; others sank in shallow water and some were lost forever. Happily no men were lost. According to the plan C Company (Tee) had moved off after last light and we spent the night on tenterhooks. A few boats did arrive but they were too few and too late to get across before first light. Hamish was unmoved by all this and smiled his inscrutable smile. We would go over the next night.

So in the full light of day boats were dragged out of the river, dried out and moved to the embarkation point. Heaven knows (and possibly that idiot Lieutenant Ghote!) what the enemy thought of our tactics. They must have discounted our antics as a deception plan but, at the time, Gagan Sing, splendid Senior Subedar, was totally sure that we were on a hiding to nothing. He and I were sure that the Japs would draw the obvious conclusion—that C Company (Tee) was to cross that night from the place to which the boats had been taken. Gagan Sing had an acid sense of humour and he exercised it on me without in any way indicating to the rest of C Company that his thoughts tended towards the suicidal. So we waited behind the bank and slept if we could. We ate the hot meals that Bill Minto sent up to us. Great man, Bill.

While we waited the hours of that day long ago two gaunt Burmans approached and asked that they be allowed to help themselves from the paddy dump and in exchange offered two handfuls of scintillating, glittering rubies and amethysts and diamonds from the mines at Mawchi. The shock of seeing so much wealth in the hands of men to whom it was almost worthless is with me to this day. In those days I was young and idealistic (where today I am old and idealistic!) and I refused their offer and sent them on to Hamish. In the event my gesture saved many of us from a watery grave; for Hamish, among whose high attributes was, and probably still is, the ability to talk their own language to riverine Burmans said that they could help themselves if they would ferry us across the river. They agreed and as the official history records they went off to get their paddles. When I told Hamish of my intention to write this article in our Christmas exchange of greetings his answer was typical. "If we hadn't discovered that cache of paddy we'd never have persuaded the boatmen to put us across—did they get the paddy in the end? I'd like to know for certain that they did?" Hamish, I would like to be able to tell you but, remember, you sent me across that very wide river before I could find out!

Anyway the reputation of the Burman for duplicity proved Gagan Sing and I wrong for they duly returned that evening with their paddles and they ate with us. The fateful night drew on slowly, very slowly. Finally at whatever ungodly hour Hamish had chosen we levered ourselves gingerly into the boats. With one Burman in front and one at the other end we set off and were paddled into the Stygian darkness of the hostile night. The boats, as I remember, were long and thin, fragile and exceedingly unstable; they took five or six Gurkhas in addition to our Burman friends. We were adjured to sit still! We did not have many boats and the plan called for 4 or 5 crossings during the rest of the night to get C Company over. I did not go in the first boat; I went in the second; I would happily have gone in the last or not at all! But the Gurkhas expected me to be near the front and I could not do less than they expected. No noise, no artillery, no mortars, no aircraft, no deception in other areas. Just C Company in fragile boats crossing that mighty river less than a platoon at a time. Just surprise, the first principle of war. We crossed in elemental silence punctuated only by gurgling river noises and the thunderous noise of the paddles in the water—or was it the noise of my small heart? We planned to go in line ahead but inevitably we got separated by the current and the differing skills of the boatmen and after a short while we travelled totally alone on the running surface of the Irrawaddy. We could see the stars—no moon, no clouds, no wind. Most of the time we could not see the bank we had left nor the bank towards which we were hopefully pointed. My compass told me that we were headed roughly east but only the boatmen knew where we were really going. In situations like this body functions are reduced to a minimum; every sense is strung tight. Breathing comes lightly. The stars looked down on the puny might of C Company (Tee) as we prepared in our little boats to storm the unknown defences of Japanese power.

As the seeming eternity of time went on—in reality all of half an hour—I got to thinking that I could swim but most of C Company could only make a stroke or two. That delicious abandonment to fear and, when our landing was unopposed, almost disappointment is the core and heart of wartime soldiering. A shadow loomed ahead; yes, the shadow of land. Three more thrusts from the paddles and we hit the bank. Nothing. The Gurkhas and I moved with the speed of light up that bank. Travelling in the second boat had been no help; in the event we arrived first! Men right and left; lie still and listen. Nothing but the jungle noises that we knew as friends. Then, thanks be, the second and third boats grounded; they emptied quickly. The boats pushed off into the darkness and were gone. Two men went off on a local recce; nothing. We waited still uncertain that the boats would return. After an eternity of waiting they did and more and more of C Company (Tee) made our little bridgehead less little. Another and another wait and the whole of C Company were with us. Later boats were guided to the point of disembarkation by a shaded torch and finally the success signal was sent over the radio to Hamish. Not a single man or piece of equipment went missing on that crossing and I now record my admiration for those Burman riverine men who helped us so long ago.

Throughout the following day the other Companies passed through our bridgehead and we, in our turn, moved to the perimeter of Thabeikkyin. In fact the war went on.

That crossing long ago and far away was a single stitch in the gigantic tapestry of the war in Burma; but I was there and, at Hamish's order, C Company (Tee) were the first to cross the Irrawaddy. A tiny niche in history but mine.

The Mule that got Away

By Bill Tee

In 1941 during Hitler's War my Battalion, the 4th Battalion of the 4th Prince of Wales's Own Gurkha Rifles, was raised from the cadres sent to us by the other three Battalions of our proud Regiment. Our first task was to train recruits as they arrived from the hills of Nepal in the individual skills necessary for infantry to survive.

That done we moved away from our Regimental Centre at Bakloh in the foothills, the Siwaliks, close under the eternal snows of the Himalayas for unit training of all sorts. We were given Tommy guns and Sten guns and 3 inch mortars and 3.7 mm Howitzers, rudimentary wireless sets, a medley of vehicles including armoured carriers and other assorted hardware.

We learned how to pack ourselves, our weapons and our kit into aircraft and into landing craft and into vehicles and into trains; and we learned how to move with no transport at all; we learned how to fight in cooperation with heavy tanks and medium and light tanks and no tanks at all. We learned how to call on the air force for help and how to direct artillery fire. We learned about explosives and mines. We kept fit and we improved our individual and unit skills. We travelled extensively over the Indian sub-continent and finally joined 19th Indian Division at Conjeeveram near Madras in the Deccan. We trained to fight in deserts, on mountains, in marsh, on farmland and on plains. We were the best trained formation in the whole army but up to 1944 we were untried in battle.

In the end, in 1944, we were told that we were going to Burma by train and river boats and vehicles to fight the Japs.

We handed over our Howitzers and our Tommy guns and our carriers and nearly all our vehicles and much else besides and were issued with jungle kit (including steel helmets). Later we were sent to collect our mules from Ferozepore. We were given about 45 of these peculiar animals. I believe that our herd or bunch or whatever the collective noun applies to mules had originated in Brazil.

Gurkhas can be taught almost anything and they can readily learn the arcane skills of mule handling; but they have always been reluctant to volunteer to join Mule Transport Platoons. In our case they were detailed by other departments for this not too popular duty. In the long run these unwilling volunteers make a great success of their Mule Platoon and came to enjoy it. They went on mule handling and hygiene courses; and mule experts came to supervise our training and routines.

All went well except for No 37 mule (or was it 38? I cannot recall exactly after all these years!) He (or it) was an absolute so and so—more mulish that any other mule known to man and enormous to boot! He caused so much trouble that, having read our routine progress reports, the top mule man in all India—a Scotsman!—was sent to stay with us and to show us how to deal with No 37 (or 38). He was marvellous with mules—quite exceptional).

The other 44 mules more less ate out of his hand but even he had difficulty with No 37! I still recall on short and long route marches seeing No 37 prance round and round and round our expert without pause no matter how long the march. The expert walked stolidly forward in a straight line in a space left clear for him by the other mule handlers with his brute circling him endlessly. The expert passed the leading rein from hand to hand continuously throughout the march. But neither on the march nor in camp was No 37 ever violent with the expert. With his own handler, however, he continued his private unremitting war! No 37 could attack from both ends, biting or kicking. Unceasing vigilance was necessary to avoid injury or worse.

In the end the expert turned to Ferozepore and we, in the person of his handler, were lumbered with No 37. He terrorised the Mule Platoon; his unfortunate handler should have been awarded at the very least the CBE (Combined Beggars Efforts) for his tenacity. He led a miserable and dangerous life.

We trained on for the best part of a year and became inured to the tales of woe from the Mule Platoon; they almost exclusively concerned No 37. No matter how we tried or what we did he remained a bloody nuisance. He was in a great degree admirable in that he would not submit no matter what we did—he just would not behave as other mules do. But he remained a permanent pain in the posterior despite our admiration for his indomitable spirit.

Then we started the long tedious journey into Burma. It was in the wake of the terrible battles round Kohima and Imphal. We advanced to Chindwin without much interference from the Japs but with a great deal of interference from No 37! Reluctantly, and causing as much trouble as a hornet's nest, No 37 came with us! At every opportunity he played up causing as much mayhem as he possibly could.

Crossing the Chindwin should have been fun; it was an unopposed crossing and it gave us the long awaited opportunity of getting rid of our hated steel helmets. We were delighted to dump the lot in the deep centre of the river; they were cumbersome in the jungle, unwieldy and awkward through the thick stuff. We never wore them again during the Burma Campaign and, as I recall, no other troops in our division did either.

Back to the mules—to No 37; we planned to swim them and him

(or it) across, towed by boats powered with outboard motors. All went well from No 1 to No 36—and from 38 to 45—but 37 proved once again that his malevolent spirit was unbroken. A lot of tedious and back breaking effort was needed to get the sod across. And he (or it), at long last, managed to land a kick on his unfortunate and long suffering handler.

He, brave soul that he was, was evacuated to hospital with a knee swollen to the size of a football and was probably glad to be out of kicking or biting range at long last. The mule handler's morale fell to rock bottom and an unwilling and rebellious Gurkha took charge of our four legged fiend.

By this time I had been promoted number two to our commanding officer, Hamish MacKay, and I was among other things, in charge of transport and administration matters.

I went to Hamish and asked if I might have No 37 shot. He was getting under the skin of the Mule Platoon and his new handler was quite likely to had a nervous breakdown even if he was not hospitalised or worse by a kick or bite. Hamish, to whom all things were possible, frowned. He would not countenance that.

If we may not destroy government property, I asked Hamish, can we, please turn the sod loose in the jungle. Hamish must have seen my, desperation and realised that it did reflect moral among the mule handlers. But he still needed a lot of persuading. In the end, reluctantly, he acquiesced and I went off to break the good news to the Mule Platoon.

Next morning we gave No 37 his last feed of oats—a double portion—and he was led, as obstreperous as ever, to our foremost outpost. Pointing firmly towards the Japs, we gave him a friendly tap on this enormous rump and released him. He shot off towards the rising sun at high speed making a very rude noise. Thankfully we never saw him again.

Do you wonder that the Japs lost the war after this master stroke? I can only assume that they captured No 37 and that he hindered their war effort to an even greater extent than he had hindered ours. And yet, strange to tell, the mule handlers seemed lost without the stimulus of his presence!

The CO was again Wounded

By Tony Bowyer

In April 1945 the Japs were withdrawing from the Mandalay area and were trying desperately to re-group much further to the South. Our 98 Brigade was ordered to put a stop over their line of retreat and after some narrow escapes from ambush by the Divisional Commander of the Japanese 33rd Division (General Tanaka)—the old enemies of our 1st Battalion in the Chin Hills and Manipur, the 4th Battalion was ordered to clear the village of Magyi-ok which was evidently on the Jap route to the south.

On the night of 5th April we encountered our first rain storm which was a big surprise and made the paddy fields impassable for our vehicles on the morrow. However, on the morning of the 6th, Damarsing (D Company) made good early progress and crossed the chaung only to be held up on the far bank whereupon I was ordered to take C Company farther round the flank of the obstruction and after some fighting the Japs in front of Damarsing withdrew. D Company made progress but was finally held up on the outskirts of the village and the Battalion dug in for the night.

We were under attack for most of the night and I remember some heart-stopping moments when our bren guns jammed in the middle of frenzied attempts to clear us out: however, their attacks gradually petered out and with the dawn on the 7th April we resumed our attempt to seize the village. This was accomplished quite quickly by C and D Companies and I occupied the front edge of the settlement of about eighty houses with the usual pagodas.

We quickly began to dig in and it was soon obvious that we were completely overlooked from a prominent hill, isolated from the main range of the Shan Plateau, and we were intermittently shelled during the next few days. Movement in the open inevitably called down a round of shelling and I had a couple of narrow escapes running between my platoon positions.

At about 1100 hours I was called to the wireless set and Colonel Hamish told me that he was coming up to my position at about mid-day to discuss the next moves with myself and Steve Goodall (B Company).

When the Colonel arrived, I briefed him on the position and he insisted on taking a look outside the perimeter. I told him that the ground in front was not secure—apart from a standing patrol about 150 yards away to give early warning of any approach. Hamish thought that the presence of the two rifle companies and the sniper bodyguards who always accompanied him, would be sufficient guarantee. It was a very hot day and there was a shimmering heat haze despite the earlier rainfall.

And so the party advanced about 100 yards from the edge of the village into the scrub and bush which was quite thick on the ground. The time as far as I can recall would be about 1300 hours and the recce party consisted of the Colonel, Steve Goodall (B Company) and myself (C Company), a signaller with the wireless, two company runners and three snipers for protection.

We three officers were consulting our maps and checking bearings and at one point were facing due North—the direction from which the Japs were escaping to take up new positions well to the South. At this moment Colonel Hamish was in in the middle, with Steve Goodall a foot away to his left and myself a foot away on his right hand side.

Suddenly a single shot was fired from close range. I estimate about 25 yards at most. I remember a blinding flash and a loud bang and I really did "see stars" and my ears were burning; I felt stunned, there was an acrid smell and I thought that I had been hit on the left hand side—ie nearest to Hamish.

The three of us dropped to the ground and we were in mid-air, as it were, when a second shot arrived, kicking up a spurt of dust between Hamish and myself. My recollection is that another couple of shots were fired kicking up in front and passing between us. It was then we realised with horror—from the blood pouring from his right arm that Hamish was the one who had been hit. I had used my field dressing on a C company rifleman a couple of hours earlier, but Steve Goodall applied his own dressing to the arm and we called for stretcher bearers.

Our snipers raced into the scrub but could find no trace, not even the cartridge cases, and meanwhile we were getting Hamish back to the perimeter. Mercifully the Jap guns were silent from the overlooking hill—but it was their general practice to shift ground after a bout of shelling to confuse our counter battery fire. I simply have no recall of our move back to the perimeter—nor can I remember whether Hamish walked or was carried on a stretcher. Almost certainly he would have refused the ride! What I do remember is that the battalion was in shock and we all felt very down—probably a mixture of gloom and anger at first—then a burning desire to make the Japs pay for it.

It was typical of Hamish—when writing the Regimental History—that he should merely record on page 341 "the CO, reconnoitring the new ground was again wounded, this time so severely that he had to be evacuated".

It was his training and the fine spirit which he had impressed upon us all that enabled us to carry on, however grimly, and finish the job in Burma. It was a privilege to have served under him. He was an inspiration: how wonderful to return to Bakloh as the 4th Battalion disbanded and to find that now recovered from his wound the Commandant was none other than Hamish himself and that there was an opportunity for a fortunate few to resume service under his command. These were happy days indeed with Hamish and Mesha in Bakloh:

God Bless Them Both. They were a truly remarkable couple.

IV

Half a mile on a Good Day: 4/4 GR on the Mawchi Road

By Tony Bowyer

It was by now late April 1945 and the main columns of the 14th Army were closing rapidly on Rangoon in a desperate race to have the armour there before the monsoon broke. 19th Indian "Dagger" Division after the spectacular successes around the northern bridgehead over the Irrawaddy and at Mandalay was designated as follow-up to the chief thrust and had arrived at Toungoo in Central Burma. The Japs were retiring in substantial numbers through the Shan Hills to the east and were seeking to keep open their main escape routes so that eventually they could concentrate their forces. It was also evident that they needed to extricate thousands of their soldiers trapped on the wrong side of the Rangoon road in the jungle-clad hills of the Pegu Yomas: to this end the metalled road running east from Toungoo to the famous wolfram mines at Mawchi—some eighty miles distant and close to the Salween and the Siamese border was clearly of critical significance.

At this point 98 Brigade (2 Royal Berks; 8/12th Frontier Force and 4/4th GR) was ordered to protect the Army's left flank by pushing up the Mawchi Road and thereby securing freedom from observed artillery fire onto the main road Mandalay-Rangoon. I recall discussing this with our attached Anglo-Burman Intelligence Sgt Fitzgerald who was very dubious about such a limited aim and gave as his opinion that we should have to go all the way to Mawchi and that the Japs would contest every inch of ground. I remember being not greatly bothered at the time but subsequent experience ensured that I listened to his opinion even more carefully in the future!

The Royal Berkshires were first into action probing against a low-lying ridge studded with white pagodas astride the road at Milestone Three: they came up against unexpectedly fierce resistance and the Frontier Force were ordered to assist with an outflanking movement to turn the position. At 1 am 28th April the 8/12th crossed the Sittang bridge at Toungoo and set off up the road in bright moonlight: by 4 am the leading company was in trouble, had taken casualties and was digging in. By the following evening they were occupying a defensive position just over the bridge from Toungoo and 4/4 GR under Lieut Col John Strickland were ordered to assist the Berkshires with a move wide to the river and to the south of the road. Meanwhile the signs were not good— early identification revealed that the enemy units were part of 15 Division, a tried and experienced unit well known to the 1/4th in Northern Burma, and on the evening of 29 April the monsoon rains began with an absolute deluge.

Fighting in monsoon capes was cumbersome and restrictive and the Japs were all around us in the jungle: our first objective was to meet up with the Berkshires in a position somewhere on the river tributary and I still remember vividly the pouring rain and that kind of intuitive feeling that you are not alone—when in the darkness "C" Company bumped into the Berkshires: the password for the night was correctly given as "Biscuit" to the British sentry but from a Gurkha the sound emerged mangled and unrecognisable and the "fire-fight" was on and not easily stopped: mercifully we only took two casualties but this was not a good start and we halted for a miserable night on the ground and in the open with hats felt Gurkha tilted well forward to allow the rain to run off in torrents on to our capes.

Meanwhile the Frontier Force had succeeded in getting beyond Pagoda Ridge and we moved at daybreak to join them: there was massive evidence in the daylight of the difficulties which had faced the Berkshires in this opening phase: patrol casualties (requiring burial) strewn on tracks and enemy ambush positions which all too clearly had taken great toll at point blank range and two armoured cars with turrets blown off and overturned.

Our own advance was immediately contested and "B" Company quite quickly lost its Commander Steve Goodall who was seriously wounded by a burst of automatic fire ("B" Coy was to lose four commanders Sant, Adams, Goodall and Poole). Steve's misfortune was not to end there for when he eventually made the evacuation airstrip he was left on a stretcher in the plane under a Perspex canopy in bright sunshine for hours until it was safe to take-off: he almost fried! In addition he had lost his glasses as he was carried from the RAP and Derek Bevis had appropriated them on the grounds of greater need—having broken his own pair. At their first meeting post war in London the opening remark—"Bevis, where are my glasses?" has become part of 4/4th folklore.

Of course it was not funny at the time as soon a pattern began to emerge. The Japs were stubbornly defending the road which was often mined and strewn with obstacles: tree trunks were felled and booby traps placed at the jungle edge which bordered the road. These obstacles were often covered by machine-guns on fixed lines and the Sappers took an increasing share of the casualties. All this was time consuming and required great care—even on occasions a rope stretched across the road with blankets draped was sufficient to impose a significant delay on the advance. It was also clear that the vegetation on the jungle-clad hills was becoming more dense and the ground steeper the nearer we got to Mawchi: the Japs had excellent OPs and we were troubled by artillery whenever we moved on the road.

The climate was terrible, ranging from oppressive heat to a chilling wetness with a resultant high sickness rate and little hope of reinforcements. Mosquitoes were everywhere and seemed positively to enjoy the toxic lotion which was issued as a repellent. There was little chance of sleep as at night the enemy jitter patrols were all around probing and trying to draw fire. In these conditions the wireless sets were temperamental to say the least and it became customary to pay out signal cable as we moved forward and then to tee in with a telephone. I can still recall the dismay when "the phone rang" in the darkness and being exhorted by Bn HQ on the other end to "speak up, I can't hear you"—with a Jap patrol fluttering nearby. I remember too the sound of levers flying off enemy grenades and the quiet thud as they landed on the ground and then the seeming eternity of the wait before detonation.

It was now apparent that we were fighting two entirely different kinds of battle at the same time: there was a world of difference between the tactics deployed on the road itself by what became to be known as the "spearhead" battalion and the methods necessary for action off the road and in the surrounding thick jungles which began so abruptly at the very roadside. On the road itself the infantry battered their way forward for comparatively short distances each day, with the help of tanks, armoured cars and artillery: only very rarely was air support available. Jap positions especially as the country became hillier away from Toungoo were surprisingly setpiece with well constructed and carefully sited bunkers and the usual tree and log reinforcement to the roof: the camouflage was expert and ready to hand—the positions were very difficult to see. On one prominent spot-height there was an amazing fortress position on which "C" Company made two or three attempts at uphill, frontal assaults before eventually taking it by turning the flanks and isolating the main posts.

When we eventually gained the top—the view was breathtaking all the way back to Toungoo with the whole road under easy surveillance and an oversight for miles over the main route to Rangoon into the bargain: a superb OP and clearly well prepared for a siege with inter-connecting deep galleries and dugout shelters extending over the whole range of the hill: this was the only instance by the way where we encountered wire along this particular front. All this was to prove that the Japs were determined to hold this route open and that they had been preparing the defence for some time: perhaps as well that we had not been aware of this right from the start!

Off the road by contrast we progressed with a series of left and right hooks to get behind the opposition: it was an exhausting business—rarely could mules be taken and we had to carry heavy man packs and all our ammunition: ration deliveries from the road were not practicable and ration parties elsewhere were often in trouble as the Japs were fond of cutting the road to the rear: the men were alternately sweat-soaked and chilled to the marrow—battalion strength was down to three hundred or thereabouts and Company

HQ took its own share of the perimeter at night operating as an extra rifle section: "C" Company at this time mustered between 50 to 60 effectives and we occasionally operated in two rather than three platoon units: the only two ever-present company GO's during our spell on the road were Sub Liladhar Pun and Jem Magras Gurung: Damarsing Gurung (Kalo) having been wounded earlier, had not yet returned.

The going was very slow and often it was necessary to cut a path with Kukris: we encountered Japs in surprising places for there were no landmarks and no prominent objectives—though there were quite high hills and deep ravines: sometimes after leaving the road it would be hours before we saw the sky again and there was the pervading stench of rotting undergrowth. Water was a major problem, brackish and warm in the bottles and chagals even when obtainable: shaving was a trial for the BOs—blades at a premium and how we envied the Gurkhas the simplicity of their toilet—no beards and with clean shaven heads at that period no hair to comb: and what a contrast to our Sikh machine gunners who had a terrible time with their meticulous grooming.

Rations were generally of British compo type tins and packets rather than the American issue with the breakfast, lunch and dinner packs: when operating on the road itself efforts were always made to bring up hot meals whenever possible and the men fell into the expensive habit of "gingering up" their dal bhat with the fish, cheese and yes—the jam of the compo issue. I was not averse to doing the same myself and on several occasions was "invited to comment" on the fact that the compo was being expended at a rapid rate: one or two men also developed a liking for that bullet-hard emergency chocolate pack which we carried in our battledress and the QM noted the number of emergencies which we seemed to be experiencing. On two or three especially grim occasions as we lay sodden in the rain there was a rum issue which was of course very popular with all ranks.

Eventually after what seemed an eternity but was in fact only eleven days 98 Brigade was pulled out for a rest and the relief was 62 Bde (3/6 Raj Rif 2 Welch and 4/6 GR). We were never so pleased to move out from a location—we had by the way reached Milestone Five and to quote the title of this article—Jack Masters the GI of the Division whilst at our Bn HQ gave this as his answer to a visiting officer's question on the rate of progress—"Half a mile on a good day".

Even the relief was fraught—the only time incidentally I can recall handing over to the Raj Rif: there were about twelve of us conducting an "O" group in a small crater by the side of the road—when the Japs began firing some kind of high velocity gun over open sights and at close range—one of the rounds struck an overhanging tree and produced a devastating airburst which resulted in seven casualties: I was subsequently greeted by the Adjutant with "you look as if you've seen a ghost"!

Our rest turned out to be a spell of patrolling and watch on the main Mandalay-Rangoon road in what was to be the long wait before the start of the break-out battle and the end for the Japs in Burma.

The Frontier Force however were not so lucky and they were recalled to the Mawchi Road a week earlier than ourselves to mount a massive right hook to establish a road block ten miles behind. the Japs present position at Milestone Fifteen. This "Operation Cracker" was mule-based and fire support was restricted to the Bn mortars alone as they would be out of artillery range. This was something of a disaster and the Frontier Force were soon in difficulty and involved in hand-to-hand fighting right from the start: after two days the correct decision was made to withdraw them and 1 Assam were sent to assist them in getting back. Never, again were long hooks attempted on such a scale.

Sure enough on 26 May the 4/4th were ordered back to the road and we brought welcome relief to our friends in the 4/6th GR who similarly had a high sickness rate and were much depleted in numbers: and it was this second spell that was to prove a severe test of skills at every level: off the road it continued to be an old fashioned exercise a hard slog with navigation a nightmare—compass bearings and counting the paces—occasionally, truth to tell, requesting our own mortars to drop a smoke round or two on a given map reference and sometimes in mild despair picking what we thought to be our present position and holding our breath. Fortunately we were always "out" in our calculations but it was a dangerous gamble even though the odds were considered similar to the proverbial sack of rice in a scattered air drop!

On the road with this our second wind, the extent and determination of the Jap resistance had now been realised and units of 255 Armoured Brigade which had distinguished itself in the fighting around Meiktila were ordered to our assistance and the sight of their Shermans was quite a morale booster to the men. This Brigade (116 Regt RAC—surprisingly a Gordon Highlanders TA unit converted to armour; Royal Deccan Horse and Probyns) was very experienced in open country fighting, but the Mawchi Road was to prove very difficult for them as for us. As an interesting preliminary it was proposed that the company commander and the squadron commander should experience each other's roles! This was good in theory but my few minutes in a Sherman and the tank major's patrol with me on foot carried little conviction! Each was happy to settle for the element which he knew and more or less understood.

The nature of the ground required that the leading troop had to proceed in file up the road on virtually a one tank front: this was fine for blasting the jungle on either side with Browning and Besa but limiting in extent. The Japs also had anti-tank guns and these were easy to conceal and able to operate at virtually point-blank range: there were also problems of communication with the infantry wireless sets often not working although netted in with the tanks.

I shall never forget trying frantically to stop a Sherman of the Royal Deccan Horse advancing up to and beyond the forward section of "C" Company where a scout had spotted a suspected gun just round the next bend of the road. I fired the Verey pistol—a prearranged signal—to no avail and had just stepped on to the road (feeling twelve feet tall and very conspicuous) to look for the spring-loaded telephone on the rear of the command tank when there was a flash and a deafening roar. I was too late, the Jap gun had opened point-blank at some seventy five yards and had brewed up the leading tank. The result was absolutely horrific and the Sherman was quickly on fire with a plume of smoke and flame some fifty feet in the air and the ammunition exploding for about an hour afterwards.

The normal drill for the infantry-tank co-operation was for the move to start early in the morning when the Shermans had drawn level with the leading position of the previous day—the advancing company being responsible for forward patrolling over the first lap. The tanks were held for the night some miles back in a secure harbour area and as they moved up the roar of the engines getting ever louder soon dispelled any element of surprise: the intention was already obvious, now there could be no doubt as to the timing!

In some encounters before we had the tank support however, the Bn had better fortune and indeed in an earlier battle where "D" Coy captured two guns, Bunny Burnett (later to become Major-General Brigade of Gurkhas) won a splendid MC.

Towards the end of our second spell the going was really rough at around Milestone 19/20: there was a large expanse of densely jungle covered country intersected by very steep ravines and without tracks: the monsoon was by now in full blast and the Bn floundered and hacked its way through. At about this time all the British battalions were beset by the, repatriation of their experienced men having served the requisite time overseas (three years and four months) and there was a very tragic incident when a party of 2 Welch Regiment homeward bound was coming down from Thandaung, a peacetime hill station just north of the Mawchi Road, and was ambushed by the Japs—with an entire party of thirty wiped out.

From the outset artillery was restricted in its effect by the jungle and the lack of visibility: the Japs clearly had an early advantage with their prepared OPs on the heights and were very clever at moving their guns despite all our sound-ranging and location efforts. Many a time the comforting echoes of our concentration died away and as the reverberations in the deep valleys ended, a defiant pop proved that the Jap seventy-fives were still there. Combined statistics show that the Japs lost 22 guns in that first

19 miles but our best friends in the circumstances were not for the first time the screw guns of the Mountain Battery rather than the 25 pounders of our old friends in 115 Field Regt Ammunition deterioration and wear on the guns—apart from difficulties of observation—provided several examples of "dropping short" although our worst accident was a mortar explosion some ten feet from the barrel just alongside Bn HQ.

Our time on the road ended on 11th June: we were very glad to hand over our position to 4/6th GR and to head for the forthcoming break-out battle: (ironic to think that 19 Div contingent for the Victory Parade in Rangoon had reported the day before!) In its way the battle for the Mawchi Road was a severe test and was seen as such by the other units involved—for I have read most of their regimental histories. Physically it was exhausting and debilitating and coming with the onset of the monsoon and at a time when we were tired and dare one say when we thought that we had won—it was to bring out the best in the battalion.

The whole operation took much longer than anticipated and Sgt Fitzgerald was right up to a point—the Japs did contest every inch but we didn't have to go all the way to Mawchi—the real resistance ended at Milestone Twenty Five. 4/4 GR saw some of the hardest fighting of the campaign here and was at times at full stretch: even with the rain and nothing but flooded slit trenches elsewhere to look forward to we were still pleased to a man when we left the Mawchi Road: it was not to rank as a separate battle honour but those who took part are unlikely ever to forget it; and it seemed then—as indeed it does now—to have been quite an achievement even to have survived.

IV

"Forty Years On"

Some recollections of the 4 GR Battalions in 1945

1/4 PWO Gurkha Rifles 1945

"I challenged the staff captain by field-telephone" said Eric Mercer. "You can not be serious. We respect our mules. We like them. We know them and will miss them, but we can not pack them up like baggage and transport them to the Frontier."

"The mules must go" said the captain. "Division says so. I will try to arrange cattle trucks at Dimapur."

So the faithful animals moved at twenty-four hours notice and many days later arrived with the battalion by the barren hills of Kohat, to the consternation of brigade headquarters and to the horror of two Jemadars of the Veterinary Corps sent to inspect them. "These animals have no VH (Veterinary History) sheets," they exclaimed. "Without VH sheets they can not be Army mules." Furthermore, according to Eric Mercer's amazing memory, one of these excellent beasts developed Epizootic Lymphangitis, a foul mule disease that put them all in quarantine and did not help to endear us to the frontier clique.

Relieved in some ways to be away from the ferocity of the fighting, many men in the battalion hankered after the campaigning life on the Burma border where, despite casualties, morale had always been extraordinarily high. Here in Kohat it seemed that one had to learn soldiering all over again. Security of weapons which was never a problem in Burma was paramount here and became a tremendous problem to Colonel Proud. He introduced constant checks and an intricate disc system to placate the District and the Brigade commanders, both of whom had long service on the frontier and a reputation for severity.

Surprisingly, Colonel Proud's other main concern was to reduce the strength of the battalion. On its journey from Manipur, the battalion had collected men and casualties from Transit Camps en route and drafts of new recruits had just arrived from the Centre. Except for specialist signallers and buglers, whose numbers were sadly depleted, the criterion for retaining riflemen was: if you served even a day on operations—stay; if not—be cut, or "pruned". Many of these men who were at the peak of their training, did not want to languish in a quiet frontier cantonment and most went off to the 4/4th, no doubt to distinguish themselves in the ensueing battles. One day Henry Burrows, who had taken over from Mercer as Adjutant, put on his cap, went in to the CO's office, saluted and announced "the battalion is pruned, Sir," thus signalling the completion of our metamorphosis.

Looking back most peoples memories of 1944 are of off-duty moments, rather than of the hard frontier warfare training to which we did not take too kindly at first. Andy Kerr writes to me: "we spent most of 1945 in Kohat. I regret my memory is not good on soldiers' names now, but I do remember the great shock which went through the battalion when Subedar Dhanbahadur, one of the most popular Gurkha Officers died of a heart attack (Dhanbahadur, tough, always buoyant, awarded the MC, had suddenly become despondent as we left Burma on hearing that both his old parents had died. The men said his heart was alright, he had pined away). I remember the whole battalion lining the route of the cortege and the genuine sorrow of all ranks.

"Strangely enough, one of my memories concerns you. Three of us went to a jewellers shop in the bazaar and each bought an Omega wristlet watch. You will hardly believe this but that watch is still on my wrist 40 years later. When I bought it, it was gaining 10 seconds per day and still is. I thought it was expensive at the time!"

"Kohat was one of those places which had little to commend it and apart from the Mess and the Club, one's leisure activities were strictly limited, the hot weather being particularly tiresome. We trained early mornings and late afternoon, which made the days very long. I can remember ... our astonishment one morning when we were all lined up for a battalion inspection when the CO (by now Colonel Stevenson-Hamilton) appeared on a horse, a particularly green army charger, which bucked around all over the place with the CO grimly holding on by his eyebrows. This went on for some time. The battalion stood easy, and everyone enjoyed the performance immensely except for the CO. He eventually controlled the wild animal, cancelled the inspection and in characteristic fashion roared out in characteristic fashion "commence the march-past". This precision worked out fine until the Pipes and Drums started, whereupon the Colonel vanished from the parade ground in a cloud of dust."

Andy Kerr also recounts how one Sunday he was sitting around the small club swimming pool with Ken Welsh and Bill Young, normally a reasonably sober sort of chap, when Bill suddenly said "If I ride my bike off the high board (it was *very* high) will you and Ken just dive from it?" Andy and Ken laughed, nodded absently, and forgot about it. Half an hour later, to their horror, they saw Bill climbing up the steps with the bicycle on his shoulders. Shouting at the top of his voice, he raced the bike along the top of the board and through the air. I can still see him holding the cross bar with one hand, the handlebars with the other and pedalling furiously through the air. He emerged without a scratch, sat beside us and said "a bet is a bet". Kerr and Welsh looked at each other but knew they daren't "welsh" on the bet. Welsh went first, a sickening flat fall on to his stomach. Kerr overdid it, determined not to belly-flop and turned over in the air, ricking his back.

Perhaps we spent much of our spare time at the swimming pool, but it was not the centre of a gay social scene as in the more populous parts; there was a great shortage of ladies and some officers went to extreme lengths to attract them. Sunbathing next to the irrepressible Derek Royals, I remarked that the old shrapnel wound on his shoulder was looking rather nasty. "I have to keep it touched up" he said "the girls keep asking me how I was wounded." We half-believed him.

Henry Burrows, trying his best to be the stern peace-time Adjutant, still had time to observe the social scene and he also recalls an incident at the little club, the embarrassing predicament of a young British officer who shall remain nameless. "He was fortunate enough to become romantically involved with a young lady of the cantonment", says Henry. "Late one night, he and his lady friend slipped out of the hot club and indulged themselves with a swim in the pool which, because of the strict anti-malarial precautions was out of bounds. Refreshed and rejuvenated, they further involved themselves in an amorous embrace on the edge of the pool, when the chowkidar aroused by a noise, switched on the flood lights! The situation was exacerbated by the fact that the SSMO, the Station Senior Medical Officer, was having a small drinks party on the varandah of his flat overlooking the pool. Raucous cheers greeted the spectacle, to the chagrin of the wretched lovers".

It may seem from these few recollections that the officers of the First Fourth spent their time in Kohat roistering. Far from it; the opposite was in fact the case. It is more that these experiences were so different from Burma that they stay in the mind. The officers, British and Gurkha alike spent an inordinate amount of off-duty time with their men, perhaps too much. We built a wall between ourselves and the other people in the cantonment who we thought knew nothing of the hunger, the thirst, the danger of the years the battalion had spent in Burma, but above all they could not know of that strange comradeship that pervades a fighting unit, a Gurkha unit more than most others, which has been through thick and thin together and never given in. Too often the rum flowed freely in the hot evenings, as we fought the battles again in the Mess, the GO's Mess and outside the low brick barracks, while Subedar Major Agam Gurung, the redoubtable father-figure would recount time and again, with full sound effects, how he had man-carried the mortars all the way out of Burma. If we had not been present we listened in awe, then told our own little story.

J. M. E.

IV

The 2/4th in Italy

When Tony Bowyer wrote to me and asked me whether I would be willing to write a few lines about the 2nd Battalion in 1945 I agreed to do so but with some reluctance.

I recollect as a young man sometimes wondering what I would be doing "40 Years On" but when you have to think back on events which took place "Forty Years Ago" you begin to realise that your memory is not what it was. However, what follows are personal memories of those days using the Regimental History only as an aide memoire.

My broad recollections of "Forty Years Ago" can be summed up quite briefly by the fortitude and humour of the men, the mud and cold of an Italian winter and the searchlights playing off the clouds to lighten the darkness. It was not until April that we were able to go on the offensive and then the campaign was soon over. At the time I was commanding "A" Company of the 2nd Battalion which was in 10th Indian Brigade of the 10th Indian Division.

January 1945 saw the Battalion on the River Senio which was the winter line in Italy for the Eight Army. I can speak with fairly intimate knowledge of the Senio River as "A" Company followed "C" Company (Busty Hayes) over in mid-December 1944 and I fell into it! The Germans had left a pole and a hand-line across the river which was about forty feet across between floodbanks and in spate. A combination of the pole bouncing up and down in the swirling water and an errant hand-line was too much for my sense of equilibrium and in I went, fortunately on the upstream side which enabled me to grasp the pole. As I lay in the middle of the stream, swept horizontal by the current, and hoping that my marked chinagraph map would not fall into the hands of the enemy, I could hear muffled laughter punctuated by the odd word "Sahib" coming from those on the bank who had already crossed and had not taken part in my personal "crossing the line" ceremony. To this day I have no recollection of how I extricated myself and joined them.

We left the Senio area in February 1945 and moved as part of the Division to the hills on the extreme left of the Eight Army front. Here the names of Castel del Rio, Monte Verro and Monte Spaduro come to mind. Here we spent our time patrolling but the problems of supplying forward troops were considerable. Rations were brought up by mule who sometimes, sank to their bellies in the mud and on occasion had to be destroyed but I have nothing but admiration for the muleteers, some Indian, some Cypriot, who kept us supplied in Italy. They did a magnificent job.

One incident comes to mind about the Monte Verro/Monte Spaduro area which, on reflection, has never ceased to amuse me. There were two hills known as "twin tits". (Has anyone ever heard of two similar looking hills being called anything else in Army parlance?). I was ordered to lay mines across the face of one hill although it was believed that the enemy had already mined it. Anyway, I was given the Pioneer Havildar and some of his men to do the mining. It was very dark and when it came to laying the mines the Pioneer Havildar came up, saluted and invited me to show him where they were to be laid. At which we both marched into the supposed minefield and this having been done the mines were laid on our return with commendable speed.

It was whilst we were holding positions at Monte Verro that I learnt on the R/T that an old orderly of mine when I was commanding "B" Company in Cyprus had been killed in a forward position. This saddened me as he looked after me in an exemplary way when I first joined the 2nd Battalion.

If January, February and March 1945 were essentially months of holding static positions with frequent patrolling, morale was good and we were looking forward to movement in the Spring. This came when we moved out of the hills in April and took part in the crossings of the Sillaro, Quaderna and Idice rivers.

I recall my company advancing on tanks to go in on the right of the New Zealanders on the Quaderna and meeting up with two New Zealanders who had come out from their positions to show us where they were. This I was not expecting but information which was gratefully received from two men who belonged to what was in my opinion one of the finest fighting formations in Italy.

By 1 May the Italian campaign was over and we found ourselves in the area of Ferrara. I recall the day the war finished very well as not only did we fire off a lot of tracer and flares but I lay awake most of the night listening to a nightingale singing in a nearby tree. It sounded at the time like a symphony of peace.

It was whilst we were near Ferrara that Bob Crichton visited us from hospital for a celebration in the villa we had taken, for a mess. Sad to relate that while relieving himself at night from a first floor balcony he succeeded in falling off and went straight back to hospital.

The only occupants of this villa apart from ourselves were two Italians and their small daughter called Ada. Ada was about five, a delightful child, and loved by us all. I remember asking her one morning after breakfast if she would like a bar of chocolate and not unnaturally she said that she would. When I signed for the chocolate I was a little surprised to find that I was about the sixth person to provide her with chocolate so far that morning, including all of the Mess orderlies.

One day while we were at the villa an Italian sergeant turned up on a motor bike and said that his father owned the property. He also said that the two Italians were his father's butler and his wife and that his father would be glad to know that the house was in the care of the Fourth Gurkhas.

When we proceeded to the Gorizia area in May 1945 for possible action against the Yugoslavs some of us went in jeeps as an advance party and stopped in Venice for lunch. We managed to get a gondolier to take us to the Officers' Club and told him that we would pay him if he waited to take us back. Sadly we got lost in the narrow streets and canals and could not find him again. Whenever I have been back to Venice since the war I have always felt slightly guilty that there is someone rowing one of those boats to whom some members of the 2nd Battalion are in debt.

The Gorizia region was the scene of conflict in the First World War between the Italians and the Austrians, indeed Caporetto where the Italians were defeated was not far away. In the hills round there it was still possible to see fortifications and old equipment lying about. Our stay in Canale was memorable. It was essentially a Yugoslav village with perhaps one remaining Italian family. For the first ten days or so we went about our duties and no-one spoke to us at all. Gradually relations improved and reached a point when the Mayor had to inform his Communist masters in Belgrade that he was unable to arrange for the demonstrations that they wanted without being made to look silly. Such was the information conveyed to us by a girl in the village who was the secretary of the local Communist party.

We stayed in Canale until September 1945. When the time came for us to depart the whole village turned out to bid us farewell and we were sorry to go, for I think that we had proved that with commonsense and goodwill conflicting ideologies were no bar to friendship.

It was while we were at Canale that trips were arranged by a welfare organisation for the men to visit Venice. They were not very keen to go and I recall asking the members of one party on their return whether they had enjoyed it to be told in a rather dismissive way "that the streets are full of water!".

I then left for Gorizia en route to Naples and a course at the School of Infantry at Warminster. When I got to the transit camp in Naples I was invited by the Adjutant (an ex-3rd Gurkha) to cut cards for four jobs that had to be done—one was a good one and the other three not so good. I drew the good job which involved being British Duty Officer at a club called the "Orange Grove" somewhere in the hills round Naples. On enquiring what I had to do I was told that I would get a free meal but that my job was to make sure that the British Officers drank up when time was called and an American officer would do the same for his countrymen. It was suggested that I should talk to a New Zealander who had done the job the previous evening to find out exactly what happened. I found this chap and asked him whether he had had any problems the previous evening and he said that he had not as some while before closing time he had already been carried out anyway!

I have referred previously to the humour of the men which was always a great comfort in adversity. In "A" Company we had a

Rifleman who carried the PIAT (anti-tank) gun. This man would never be anything other than a Rifleman but he was worth the rank of Havildar from the point of view of morale. On the line of march he would keep everyone amused and although we never saw a tank up in the hills at which he could fire his PIAT, he was occasionally called on to fire it in the air when we were under attack. On such occasions the projectile used to land with a tremendous "crump", and although its trajectory was doubtful it never landed on us.

In September 1945 the Battalion moved to Salso Maggiore and in November sailed from Taranto to return to India.

These than are my memories of "Forty Years Ago" but I also remember the simple pleasure of drinking mugs of steaming tea with the men, for these were days of friendship and meeting challenges, united as we were by being Fourth Gurkhas.   M. K. B.

The 3rd Battalion in 1945

1945 was a year of change for the Battalion. At the end of 1944 we had re-assembled from leave at Shahgarh in the CP and had started training for another Chindit operation based on an air-landing near Toungoo, in south Burma and by the end of the year we were in Batavia in Java as a normal infantry battalion on "cordon and search" duties, trying to round up fanatical Indonesians. What follows is mainly anecdotal and may help to fill in the pages of the Regimental History.

1945 started with the return of leave parties from Nepal. Some, having missed their turn in the early years of the war, had not been home for some several years. Despite the flood of mukhiyas' letters they had borne this unreasonable annoyance with patience. The relaxation of restrictions in 1944 meant that the men had to take a much shorter furlough than usual at a time when the weather was normally at its worst. If memory serves, in 1944 there had been the heaviest barsat for years with roads and tracks flooded, fords impassable and buildings and bridges down. As a result many overstayed leave and most were dealt with summarily by company commanders with doubtful going to the CO for disposal. There was one case of absence of over two years! The rifleman had gone on special leave when we were back in India and had returned in the mazri shirt and khaki shorts of the time, looking like a being from another age. His story was of problems at home, the unnoticed passage of time and the final realisation of the need to go back with the crowd of returning leave parties. He had missed Waziristan, jungle training and the 1944 campaign. But he had returned and of his own free will. Jack Masters did a double-take when he read the charge sheet and dealt with the absentee in a fitting manner.

Believing that the Chindit column organisation was unwieldy Jack had reorganised the Battalion into a conventional battalion with the addition of support troop of anti-tank guns, it having been anticipated that we were to operate in an area where the Japanese could use armour. However, changes were coming. 14th Army had moved fast in Burma and the resources needed to support Chindit operations were better diverted to maintain the momentum of the main army. The Chindits were disbanded, the Battalion became a normal rifle battalion and was ordered to move to Ranchi for further orders. Jack left to go to 19 Division as GS01 and Bill Tomlinson, fresh from an attachment to the Australians in the Pacific, took over. HQ 23 Brigade, a former Chindit Brigade which had operated closely with 14th Army in north Burma was, under Brigadier Lance Perowne, acting as the holding formation for ex-Chindit units in transit for Burma. We were camped near Lohardhaga to the west of Ranchi and from our arrival in April were engaged in exercises to gain experience in the, to us new, but normal organisation.

On the Ranchi VE Day Parade our very recently acquired and unfamiliar mules expressed their dislike of the Artillery salute by gymnastics of a most reprehensible nature, attracting the comment of a Gunner officer, "Hmm. Mules not gun-trained, I see". What our mule-drivers said is best forgotten.

We were inspected by a stream of senior officers and the memory of one inspection remains. It was probably by a senior medical officer because throughout the Grand Parade one heard the low rumbling voice of Karel Martischnigg, our Czech MO, complaining, "Sir, you have not seen my latrines".

In early June we were ordered to join 5 Division somewhere in the Pegu-Yomas Rangoon area, coincidentally not very far from our earlier target of Toungoo. We packed, moved to Calcutta to embark and were fortunate to have Brigadier Ted Hughes at the quayside to speed us on our way.

The voyage round the north-eastern edge of the Bay of Bengal was uneventful. It was the first time that most of the men had been to sea and they spent their time gambolling on the forehatches like puppies.

When we reached our "greenfield" site at Mingaladon 5 Division was still engaged in containing the isolated but still defiant and dangerous pockets of Japanese in the Yomas. The Division was battle-hardened and having served from Libya to the Arakan and north Burma claimed to be the most travelled on the Allied side. Although the 2nd Battalion had been in the Division in Libya and the 1st Battalion had met them in north Burma there had been no Gurkhas in the Division until our arrival in 1945. The West Yorkshire were the only British battalion in the Division and all the other infantry battalions were, in name, regular Indian battalions. We were slightly apprehensive as to the welcome awaiting us war-raised and Gurkha newcomers from such an oddity as the Chindits. Our fears were groundless and we were soon at home in our new brigade in which our comrades were 1/1 Punjab (unofficially known as "Auchinlecks Own" since the Auk had served with them) and 4/7 Rajput Regiments.

It as now revealed that the Division had been withdrawn from the Yomas to be reinforced to prepare for Operation ZIPPER or the return to and liberation of Malaya. 23 Division from Madras were to be the assault division and we were to be the first follow up division with up to ten others British and Indian, to come later.

Combined operations training started immediately with wet-shod driving, use of scaling ladders and scrambling nets which were suspended from some vast cast-iron pipes to resemble the side of a ship. There were the usual inspections and exercises but we still had time to visit Rangoon and see the sights such as the Shwe Dagon Pagoda. This was our first sight of a city that had experienced the doubtful benefits of the Japanese Greater Far-East Asia Co Prosperity Sphere. We were not at all impressed. Although there was little war damage Rangoon was a neglected dull and drab place.

Arrangements for ZIPPER almost complete; our convoy awaited us in the Rangoon River and 23 Division were putting to sea from Madras when, suddenly, on 12th August came the news of the Japanese surrender. The tidings elicited an outburst of pyrotechnics from the Division that rivalled anything seen in the war. Orders and counter-orders issued and eventually we were ordered to Singapore, but on a more or less peace-time basis. As explained in the History, peace brought new problems not the least being the inabliity of the old colonial powers, France and Holland, to re-occupy and pacify their colonies. Of this more later; for the moment we were with very large and intact Japanese forces and a great number of helpless Allied POWs and civilian internees. We would have to "gang warily". We embarked on 30th August, split between two ships the main body of the battalion in one and the recce party with the Division recce party under the Division Machine Gun Battalion (17 Dogra) in another. The voyage was peaceful enough and Commandos were first put ashore in an unopposed landing near Penang. Next the Paras were put ashore in landing-craft near our proposed beach-head at Morib near Port Dickson. Although likewise unopposed they had the unhappy experience of meeting a sand-bank some way off-shore and having to wade to the beaches. Worse was to follow. Just as they had dried out they were recalled and had to repeat the journey in reverse order. A wet and not amused party of Paras rejoined the convoy. For our part, there were shivers as to what might have been had we been there for real.

As we sailed down the mine-swept channel between Sumatra and Malaya the Division recce party noticed that they were several ships astern of our main bodies. They were told not to worry since the organisation was such that we would be called forward at the proper time to allow us to be at our locations (in the case of our

Brigade, 161, the Cold Storage Company area) WELL before the main bodies. No such luck. Put not your faith in the Organisation. On the afternoon of 5 September the gallant recce parties were dumped on the quayside. The 3rd Battalion party was lucky to commandeer a very co-operative Chinese truck driver with truck who took us rejoicing to the Cold Storage Company to find everybody well and truly bedded down several hours gone.

We thought that our day had ended but one of the companies reported that there was a basha in their area which was a small ration store guarded by a Japanese Navy detachment. They had an interpreter with them. The company commander said that the party was refusing to move until told to go by the Royal or Japanese Navies. The 2IC was sent down to add weight to the proceedings. Fortunately a "deus ex machina" appeared in the form of a senior private of the Japanese Army on an aged bicycle. This gave the 2IC heart for here was someone he could order about. Through the interpreter the soldier was ordered to proceed forthwith to Japanese Navy HQ, not far down the road, and summon someone with sufficient Naval authority to shift the detachment and allow the liberation of Malaya to continue. Soon there appeared a perspiring Japanese senior supply petty officer on another but naval bicycle who ordered the withdrawal of the detachment, but not before a formal handing over of the stores between himself and the 2IC. There followed as solemn and punctilious a handing over as ever satisfied a military quartermaster of a variety of tinned food from sharks' fins to asparagus. The hand-over completed, a short speech of appreciation for our forbearance from the supply petty officer and the whole party moved off into the sunset. Somewhere that handing over certificate is in some archive. The brigade had exotic rations for a few days.

We moved for a short spell into the old Naval Base area in the north of the Island, enlivened by a visit from a Moderately Senior Naval Officer who asked us what we thought of ZIPPER. "Good" said Bill Tomlinson, "except for the beaches which much have been selected by an idiot. Look what happened to the Paras". The temperature dropped sharply as MSNO remarked icily that he had

had to do with the choice of beaches for that part of the operation. Silence.

During our stay on the Island we had made contact with the POWs and internees and provided a guard for the Hospital Camp at Kranji where we met Alex Masters, Jack's younger brother who had been taken with 2/1 GR and had had a bad time. In Changi we were shown the very ingenious and secret radio run by two RAF officers with power from the camp supply and spares provided by really brave Chinese helpers. The Gurkha POWs at Nee Soon seemed pleased enough to kick a football to and fro, endlessly, as was their wont when in the lines in India. The civilians were concentrated in Sime Road Camp.

We, once again, saw the deadening effects of the Greater Far-East Asia Co-Prosperity Sphere with no real war damage but neglect and lack of care everywhere.

By now plans for the evacuation and disposal of Japanese forces were drawn up. They were to be formed up in their own assembly areas in the forests north of Johore Bahru from whence they would be conducted by 1st Battalion 161 Brigade to be handed over to us at a POW stockade. After interrogation we would hand them over to the 3rd Battalion of the Brigade who would either escort them to Rempang Island to await repatriation under Japanese arrangements or hand them over to military police if they were suspected war criminals.

At the end of September the Brigade moved into position and we went to Kluang, a pleasant ex-Japanese Naval Aviation land station which was to be the site of the stockade. Our first task was to supervise the erection by Japanese labour of the stockade and in this we were helped by some US Army Sergeants who were of Japanese origin and therefore spoke Japanese. The procedure got under way; parties reached the camp for interrogation where they were graded "BLACK", potential war criminal; "GREY", doubtful and due for further interrogation and "WHITE" (the majority) with nothing against them and to go direct to Rempang Island and await a boat home to Japan.

Soon after we arrived in Kluang, Dasain was upon us and the

local peoples committee (Communists to a man and derived from the Malayan Peoples' Anti-Japanese Army) were approached to see what they could do to provide goats. There was an initial communications block. For some reason the committee said that they could provide GIRLS which, as they had seemed to have hoisted in the sacrificial nature of the occasion seemed odd. Using the vocal and manual method of interpretation the problem was finally solved and the GOATS appeared.

We remained at Kluang with our guard duties and pleasant off-duty amenities until mid-November when we were transferred to 9 Brigade of the Division who were being sent to reinforce 23 Division who were having a rough time in Java. As said before, the French and Dutch had been unable to assert immediate authority in their old colonies and the British had had to act as surrogate liberating forces. The internal situation of the old Netherland East Indies was getting steadily worse. During their occupation Japanese had nurtured anti-European feelings and after the surrender the Indonesians took it out on Allied POWs. 23 Division had suffered casualties in protecting these people from gangs of fanatical Moslems. It was later reported that Indian Divisions in Indonesia suffered more casualties there than they did in the last months in Burma.

We reached Surabaya at the end of November and disliked it from the first. Although the situation had improved slightly we were still required to carry out guard duties in a city knocked about in the recent disturbances as well as being surrounded by unwholesome marshlands. In addition there were bridges to be guarded and night patrols through apparently deserted but certainly gloomy streets where the gangs of fanatics could lurk and spring. This unpleasant and uncomfortable phase ended on 5th December when the Battalion moved in bits and pieces and a motley collection of transport to the more salubrious Batavia where the task would be to secure the Brigade perimeter and carry out "cordon and search" in the area.

Battalion Headquarters moved in the "Koningen Emma" and spent some days in the docks at Tandjoeng Priok. Here we lost two men, survivors from Chindit days, who disappeared never to be seen or heard of again. Eventually the Battalion concentrated outside Batavia at a place called Grogol in an abandoned lunatic asylum which remained our base for the rest of the year. Although the 1900 hrs curfew restricted social life this was better than Surabaya.

Just before Christmas the mess acquired a turkey cock and had to bar the mess orderlies from whistling at it to make it gobble. They had seen a BO doing this and thought it the greatest fun but nearly killed the bird.

Thus ended 1945. D. S. McC.

1945—The Break-Out and beyond

After Mandalay and the hard slog of the Mawchi Road where the Battalion encountered some of the stiffest fighting of its whole campaign, the 4/4th returned to the Rangoon Road in mid-June to participate in the Break-Out Battle.

Large numbers of Japanese were cut off in the Pegu Yomas and were due to break out to safety by crossing the Sittang River: the 4th Bn was deployed at Kywebwe and for the most part guarded the main Mandalay–Rangoon road which with the adjacent railway line formed a formidable dual obstacle which the Japanese would have to cross en route for the river: between us and the hills of the Yomas there were observation parties of "V" Force and Karen irregulars of Force 136: behind us and between road and river the fields were flooded to a depth of several feet.

I recall that "C" Company was dug in on the "reverse slope" of the small railway embankment and that the bottom of the slit trenches was permanently filled with about six inches of water. we were forbidden to move about by day and we welcomed patrol opportunities. By the end of June we knew that the Japanese on our front were the 54th Division—a hardened Arakan unit which had arrived in Burma in September 1943: and on the 28th—after a fruitless and uncomfortable first night in a platoon ambush (I had

7 Platoon with me—Jem Magras Gurung) about five miles into the Yomas along the wooded Kywemathe Track, we finally "got lucky" and a party of six Japs under a Warrant Officer came into our position and from the documents we identified 121 Regiment. What was interesting was that each soldier was carrying lengths of bamboo in preparation for the Sittang crossing; we had in fact surprised a recce party for sketch maps showed possible crossing points. There were several such encounters—but the days wore on and the waiting was deadly: my platoon "strengths" were fairly typical—13, 18 and 17 GORs; each platoon was responsible for about half a mile of railway line! Fortunately for our peace of mind we did not know the full picture—we thought at the time in terms of 6,000 Japs trapped in the Yomas—in blissful ignorance of Army HQ estimate of 19,000 and the post-war Japanese claim of 31,000!

There were moments, as I peered over the embankment into the darkness, that I imagined the entire 6,000 (or 31,000?) were about to break out through "C" Company HQ: and I imagine that every rifle company commander up and down the road was thinking the same.

We finally cracked the mystery of the date when on 19 July a Jap Nisei (American born) deserter was taken prisoner and he gave the crossing date as the night of 20th/21st July: and so it turned out. The 8/12th Frontier Force were involved and then on the 23rd the 4/4th were ordered south and thence to put in an attack on the village of Lebyingyi in which HQ of the Japanese 153rd Regiment had taken refuge.

There had been torrential rain and the whole of the country between the road/railway and the river was by now well under water and we were generally at extreme range of the supporting artillery—the guns being confined to the road. The RAF however reacted in style and Lebyingyi was more or less removed from the map and there were many Jap corpses which had been flung on to the rooftops.

Our next mission was to clear those villages on the Sittang itself which were likely crossing places and although knee-deep and sometimes waist-deep in flood water we had a field day—on the 28th of July killing 217 Japs for the loss of one man—CQMH Aitabir Pun who was shot through the mouth whilst leading a charge; Aitabir was an outstanding NCO and had been awarded the IOM.

The strength of 54 Division in our Brigade area was 8,500 and they suffered over 5,000 killed: only one recce patrol to the Sittang in the preliminary phase returned alive, they said: and the commander of 153 Regiment was killed at Lebyingyi.

The conditions in this fighting were frightful: the wells were polluted with the dead—and indeed cholera broke out: and the wounded and sick had to be taken out by mule: one of my Company HQ died from hepatitis—(the stench of death and decay was overwhelming and few of us could eat: we existed mainly on tea and very welcome it was). As in so many previous situations, the mules and their drivers—who had marched all the way from Imphal—were our mainstay. The history also records the presence amongst our orthodox MT back on the road of a Japanese 3 ton lorry inscribed "Dalhousie Transport Co."

So ended the Break-Out Battle. As Bill Slim said: "It was commonplace for all armies to issue orders for a fight to the last: the Japanese actually did it". Their suicidal perseverance in the face of such odds was truly remarkable and in this last encounter they even had their nurses and comfort girls fighting alongside them—though sorry specimens they were by this time.

On the 1st August the Battalion returned to Kywebwe where the scene was enlivened one night during the open-air showing of the "latest film" (Tommy Trinder in "Champagne Charlie" it was) when bursts of firing broke out from the nearby crossroads where my Company HQ was situated: I already had visions of a counter-attack to regain my bedding roll when it became apparent that our armoured car regiment had shot one of its own mess waiters who had walked out of the perimeter to relieve himself and had not known the password on his return.

On August 14th came the Jap surrender and officially the War was over: unfortunately there was no Japanese wireless net, and isolated units and indeed lone individuals continued to fight on.

Eventually we were given interpreters and quantities of leaflets showing the Americans taking the Jap surrender but we rarely managed to persuade any to give up: they nearly always preferred death.

With the cessation of hostilities the Burmese themselves began to line up their politics with a view to independence demands and there were hordes of dacoits terrorising the villages. I vividly recall travelling by jeep at night when the headlights would pick out shadowy figures moving in file down the side of every road and track: all of them were armed to the teeth—and arms were relatively easy to come by—for thousands had been airdropped over the countryside for use by irregulars. It was of course the start of the Civil War which to some extent is still going on in Burma today.

We all had our share of POW duties and Bunny Burnett became Commandant of a cage at Nyaunglebin—whilst our Battery Commander of 115 Field Regiment—Andrew Urquhart—took over command of the largest camp of all on the Rangoon Road.

We now moved South to Daik-U: here was our first peace-time Dushera and it was truly memorable. The MT was despatched to Mandalay Brewery and returned with oildrums full of "rum": no-one went to bed on Kalaratri (mine was a luxury billet—a door on four house-bricks) and the madals were sounding until dawn: it was here that I discovered to my cost that a mug of tea following rum from the bucket had a "topping-up" effect! Next morning General Pete Rees inspected the Battalion—and there were a lot of Hats Felt Gurkha slanted well down across the eyes—but we made it and the General was very complimentary.

The SM soon had parties working on tennis court construction—mainly with cowdung, straw, mud and water—the mixture being smoothed out and left to dry in the sun: we set up a quarter-guard and displayed our gun trophies taken on the Mawchi Road. The football and volleyball teams reformed and we began to enjoy ourselves—though there were regular call-outs for the standby company to deal with dacoits or isolated parties of Japs who were refusing to surrender: there was much violence in the surrounding countryside. I recall most mornings seeing the village constables bringing in dead dacoits—slung from ropes and mounted on poles carried on the shoulders—and there were frequent explosions bringing tragedy to children playing amongst the discarded ammunition and unexploded grenades in the jungle. Occasionally there was call to visit villages and townships a distance away and one was able to see once again some of the ground over which we had fought only months earlier: how sobering to find that places etched on the memory in a moment of battle were already overgrown with jungle and creeper—only the signal cable remained to point the way to the one time HQ. (I am reminded of the poet's epitaph on Western civilisation: "their only monument—the asphalt road and a thousand lost golf-balls").

At this time we had many friends in the outlying Karen villages and we spent several pleasant evenings with them: whilst in the Divisional area plans were afoot for a military tattoo to be held under searchlights in the Toungoo arena: the 4/4th contingent produced a toy soldier assault on a mock fort. There were visits to concert parties and to some performances by stars (Gracie Fields, Vera Lynn and Tommy Trinder amongst others): on one of these occasions an officer party travelled up by one-tonner and in accordance with regulations the driver removed the rotor arm to immobilise the vehicle: when we emerged at the end of the show—the engine had been removed in its entirety—less of course the rotor arm: a cautionary tale!

By Christmas time the Battalion was packing and getting ready to move to its last station in Burma—Kalaw in the Shan States—a place which could not be bettered and an ideal end to our travels.

I recall the last nautch at Daiku around Christmas time and the wonderfully funny and suitably coarse performance of Sigs Havildar Harinarayan, dressed as a Pathan with his pantomime camel and its filthy habits: and absolute riot: the laughter and songs of Gurkhas around roaring fires and the throb of the madals.

I for one will never forget 1945—I took over Bill Tee's "C" Company as Second-Lieutenant and stayed as Company Commander until the Disbandment Parade in late '46. Most of all, I was fortunate to have two of the finest platoon commanders in Jem Magras Gurung, MC, and Jem Damarsing Gurung—both subsequently to become Sub-Major and Hony Captains in the post-war Regiment: wonderful companions and great leaders.

Forty years on I look back with pride to those stirring days and to happy friendships in the 4/4th.

M. A. L. B.

No Names, No Pack Drill

By Robert Williams

I suppose it was that post-war feeling in Burma in 1946, but some funny things happened on the way to the Forum, although some of them were funny peculiar rather than funny ha-ha.

We went out to the range one day for some pistol practice. The officer next to me fired his .45, which made the customary noise—and the bullet dropped out of the end of the muzzle. I had a momentary mental picture of a Japanese, at whom it had been fired, bowing politely and then cutting off our heads.

The gardens in Kalaw were mostly terraced, with roughly three foot retaining walls. After one of our Guest Nights, an officer walked unsteadily out of the Mess to answer a call of nature. He walked blithely over the terrace wall, with his legs still going, as in a Tom and Jerry cartoon, fell flat on his face, remained prostrate for a minute, got up and walked back into the Mess. As far as I am aware, that particular call of nature remained unanswered.

A staff officer in Brigade HQ looked out of his bedroom window one morning, still in his pyjamas, saw a leopard and shot it from there with a .303 rifle.

The CO planned a splendid new Quarter Guard and ordered the Jap POWs to make it. They started by levelling the plinth and retaining it on the downward slopes by large tree trunks dug into the earth. I asked the Jap officer in charge how he intended to square the corners of the basha they would now build. He answered, "Pathagolas, three, four, five," or words to that effect; and I suddenly realised that if you lay out any old piece of wood three times on one side, four on another and five across the hypotenuse, you have a right-angled triangle. A schoolboy theorem at last put to good use.

Some miles away was Inle Lake, teeming with duck, and parties of BOs and GOs went there to shoot. The BOs were meticulous about taking the birds on the wing, but the GOs, sensible men, stood no such nonsense. They waited until several ducks were in line afloat and shot them in enfilade.

On this lake, each boatman propelled his dugout canoe by standing on one leg on the stern platform, and moving the single paddle by holding the top with his hands and wrapping his spare leg round the shaft. One can only imagine that "Don't drink and paddle!" was their watchword.

I believe the giraffe-necked women lived nearby, but nobody had the brass neck to display one in Kalaw.

The British battalion in Kalaw had no idea how to make themselves comfortable in a tented camp, pitching their tents on slopes and making no allowance for monsoon weather. Our CO courteously suggested that we might help, and a working party of our men spent a day or so with them, showing them how to level the plinths for tents, how to dig gutters round them and monsoon drains throughout the camp.

An officer was playing his gramophone one day and a Japanese officer, in command of a nearby working party, asked if it was the New World Symphony. We somehow did not expect the Japs in those days to recognise European classical music; but this man said he had been educated at Tokyo University.

After yet another Guest Night, an officer woke up next morning on top of his bed; with his shod feet on the pillow and his head, not surprisingly, at the other end; with his mosquito net properly tucked in all round; fully dressed in uniform—and with his pyjamas on underneath. He swore that he had not been wearing them in the Mess on the previous evening.

It was decided to hold a King's Birthday Parade, on which both we and the British Battalion should participate. As we approached the ground, the British were already on parade, and at that stage they were behaving appallingly, drilling sloppily and moving their arms and feet around in the ranks, while ostensibly at attention or properly at ease. But our steadiness and discipline acted as an extraordinary tonic and, from the moment they heard and then saw us coming, their standard improved dramatically, so that the parade passed off smoothly, in spite of the differences between our two types of drill. It was a remarkable voluntary transformation.

An officer was sent on an Air Support Course to Mingaladon Airfield, some miles from Rangoon. One evening he cadged a lift into Rangoon, had a happy night and realised, early next morning, that he had no means of returning to Mingaladon except on foot. Luckily, a brother officer knew the Officer 1/c Fire Fighting in Rangoon, remembered where he lived and woke him out of a sound sleep. Fortunately, the Fireman kept his temper and detailed a vehicle to take them. There can be few officers who have arrived (late) for the first lecture of the day in the cab of a fully-fledged fire engine.

Tamam Shud

Letter from America

By J. Masters

SOUTH MOUNTAIN ROAD,
NEW CITY, N.Y.
18th April, 1950.

MY DEAR GENERAL,

I think I told you in a previous note that I had decided to retire when the U.K. Government handed our Regiment over to India. Having no idea what to do then, I came over here to America, believing that this is still the land of opportunity; also believing, with experience to back me, that English and American ideas are in fact part of one and the same piece of timber. One end of it—the English—is solid, the other pliable. I have always thought there were Americans who would be happier in England, and *vice versa*, and now after two years here I am sure of it.

However, to go back: my decision decanted me on the shores of New York on February 9th, 1948, with my loss-of-career gratuity, my pension and a large willingness to work hard. I went over with at least one definite idea to try out—that was to take parties of rich Americans to the Himalayas for short holidays: you can fly from here and be in Ranikhet on the third afternoon! I spent a couple of months working on that and aroused a certain amount of interest in newspapers and in the travel trade, but nothing came of it finally. Meanwhile I had written a short piece satirising Hollywood's ideas about India, and this was bought and published at once by *The Atlantic*, a very high-grade highbrow magazine here. More important, a literary agent, who is also Somerset Maugham's agent, told me that I had writing talent and should think of doing it professionally. I thought about that carefully and finally decided to follow his advice. That was about April, 1948.

First I wrote an autobiographical book about pre-war life in the Indian Army. This would NOT have been my idea, but the agent thought there would be a sale for it. There wasn't!—though the publishers said it was very well written. That took me until October, '48: I had also written several articles and short stories and sold three or four. Early in '49 I embarked on my second book—the one I had wanted to do the first time. It is a story about the Indian Mutiny of 1857. The Viking Press, who are good publishers, bought an option on it when they saw my finished draft last October; and about a week ago finally paid over the rest of the advance and contracted to publish. It should come out here about September or October this year. I am doing the last major editing now: in a month or two we start trying to find an English publisher, which will not, we think, be very difficult. I am excited as I put a lot of work in it and think it is quite a new approach to India and to historical fiction in general.

Meanwhile I wangled myself a short job writing a film-scenario for the U.S. Army—a training film, "The Operations of the Reconnaissance Battalion." They make a vast number of films every year, the pay of the script writer is good and although I know nothing about film writing, I'm learning. I have also written a television script and am probably going to act as collaborator to a rich old lady who thinks she's got the makings of a tale but doesn't know how to write it. And I am hard at work on my next book, which is about the suppression of Thuggee. My basic idea is that I, as the fifth generation of my family to serve in India, have a story to tell. I plan to tell the story of the English in India in a long series of books covering one family down through the generations. The family (which I have called Savage) will have nothing to do with my own, or any other particular real family. They will be the thread of continuity running through. In telling about the thugs for instance, I am going to give my current Savage the part of William Sleeman. Since it is a novel I can make minor alterations to highlight the true facts, the feelings. It is of course an enormous field and if I run dry of ideas it will be my own fault entirely. The book will probably be called "The Dark Imagining."

As you can see I am busy and my wife is too because apart from housekeeping she types for me. We live in a pleasant house, 33 miles out of New York, and have quite by chance, fallen into an exceptionally nice community of people. Most of them are dramatists (Max Anderson who wrote "What Price Glory" is our chief), artists, writers, etc.; they are not a bit peculiar or "arty"—very kind and generous people. We are hoping to sub-let this place for the summer and go to the seaside in Maine, which is I hear rather like Cornwall. When things straighten out I want to visit India, most certainly including Bakloh and the Regiment. And England of course, where my father (late 16th Rajputs) and mother still live in Lyme Regis. But I have to keep my nose to the grindstone for some time yet. It's not easy starting a second career at the age of 34. I don't know what chance may bring any member of the Regiment to

America, but if anyone does come I hope they will remember my name and address.

My best wishes to you and to all of the Regiment, past and present.

Yours sincerely,
JACK MASTERS

Later:—In a letter of mid-July Colonel Masters writes—"My novel about the Indian Mutiny called *Nightrunners of Bengal*, has been accepted by the Literary Guild of America as their selection for February, 1951."

Our congratulations on a fine achievement.—*Ed.*

Return to India and Bugles

By John Masters

In the spring of 1963 the idea was broached between myself, the authorities at the National Broadcasting Company, and the cameraman with whom I had worked in Pakistan in early '62, that we should make a documentary for TV about India's will and ability to resist Chinese Communist aggression. I was to get the Indian Government's co-operation, to make the arrangements, to plan the programme in outline, and speak the commentary. We reached agreement among ourselves and I approached the Indian Government, at first informally through personal friends. It took some time to get the OK, but (as I learned later) powerful people in India wanted us to make the film; so, late in the summer we got the clearance and, soon after, the cameraman set off. He was to get background cover and show the difficulties of the terrain in one of the border areas attacked or threatened by the Chinese in October 1962.

Barbara and I set off from New City on September 24. Our daughter Susan is a sophomore at Stanford (no, she has not been dated by Prince William, yet)—and we had not seen the university; so we crossed the continent by train to San Francisco; spent three days looking over Stanford and, on October 1, flew to Tokyo. We left the same evening for a remote fishing village in Yamaguchi Prefecture, opposite to Korea on the Sea of Japan, and spent a week there in a Japanese inn. I worked on the final draft of the MS of my latest novel every morning; we walked every afternoon; and then (after being ceremoniously wrapped into my kimono by the maid, who was charmingly ugly and 65 years of age) we bathed, ate a huge meal and drank a lot of saké and fell back on to the pillows and to sleep. October 12, we left Tokyo and, at about 3.30 am on October 13, arrived at Delhi Airport to be met by the cameraman, Comdr Nar Singh from the Armed Forces Information Office, and Lt-Col Pyara Lall, who had been hauled out of his job of GSO 1 at the National Defence College to act as chief bear leader and liaison officer with our group.

A contractual problem which had arisen between NBC and the Government of India had to be sorted out before we could start work. The week's delay which this caused, though it seemed calamitous at the time, enabled me to meet and get to know many people who were to be important to the success of our filming; for example: Mr. Chavan, the Defence Minister; John Lall, Joint Secretary of the same Ministry; General Moochoo Chaudhuri, the Army Chief of Staff; Vice-Admiral Soman and Air-Marshal Engineer, the Navy and Air Force Chiefs; Mr. Desai, Foreign Secretary; Mr Mirchandani, Armed Forces Information Officer ... and many, many others. Under the protective and enthusiastic aegis of our good friend Lt-General Moti Sagar, we finally worked out our problems satisfactorily, and got the ball rolling with three days' shooting at the Rajputana Rifles Regimental Centre. The sequences shot here, plus what we filmed in a village some 25 miles out on the edge of Rohtak, we hope will show where the Indian soldier comes from and some of the processes that are used to turn him from a peasant or ploughboy into a soldier.

Next we went to a forward area. The cameraman had already covered some parts of the frontier zones, and now we went to another. Our first base was at 10,000 feet, whence we went out every morning at first light to 14,000 feet, and shot until about 2.30, when it was time to grab something to eat and face the road back. The road was awe-inspiring—colossal drops, collapsing cliffs, a constant stream of traffic, and all the time work in progress by hundreds and thousands of hands aided by power tools where possible. At that time, early November, it was extremely cold at those altitudes, but we were magnificently looked after by the Indian Army—a Jat battalion arranging breakfast for us one day (brought hot to the snowfield where we were working); a Dogra battalion giving us lunch; a brigade headquarters, tea. The building where we all stayed was used by many others at the same time, and Barbara was the only non-local woman within many miles. The cameraman shared our bedroom, but, as everybody slept fully dressed, that was of no inconvenience. Our administrative arrangements had been handed over to a battalion of the Regiment, which sent down an officer (2/Lieut Baldev Singh Sodhi), a cook, and orderlies for everyone, plus blankets, bedding, and all else that we could possibly need. Other formations attached LOs, so we finished up with a major, a lieutenant, Baldev, a PRO from Corps, and Pyara.

The shooting went well, in weather that was wonderful after the first three days. I kept on meeting old acquaintances or reminders of the past ... the SM of the Dogras had been in Tocol with us in 1937; a major met on the road had been a naik in the 2/11 Sikhs at the same time; five subadars were produced from the battalion which I had had under my command in the 1944 Chindit campaign; and of course there was Subadar Major and Hon Lieut Rudrabahadur Pun, who had been 7525 Nk Rudrabahadur Pun when I was Adjutant in 1940, and had been on the first list of my recommended promotions to havildar at that time. The battalion was generous beyond words to us. Best of all, we were able to attend a *bara khana* and variety show arranged for us in their lines, and stay overnight with them. At some 11,000 feet, with the wind blowing from everlasting snows, and us in a *basha* with sides made of pinned blankets, we needed the *raksi* provided, but could have done without the stove which Rudrabahadur insisted we must have. It warmed the wind a bit, but it also sent flames licking out to the ceiling and the walls. The originator and chief of this wonderful hospitality was Lt-Colonel Kale. Of the variety, I can only say that it was fun, and I wish other old *koi hais* of the Regiment could have seen it. Whereas in our times, the *nautches* were almost invariably traditional in both form and costume, most of the *nautches* are now copied from those seen in Indian films; the men wear lipstick and bright rouge make-up and very dashing European-type clothes; the "women" could get into a Cairo belly-dance without much trouble. I refer, of course, to stage shows. The *nautches* held in the lines continue in the old tradition of *Porsenges*, *Marunis* and their accompanying *Madales*, without whom no Gurkha dance would be complete.

There is no need for me to stress the tremendous natural difficulties faced by India all along this border. The attitude and morale of the Indian Army and Air Force in the face of these difficulties is most impressive and heart warming. My colleagues, American, Swiss, and one an Englishman who had never known the old Indian Army, were amazed by the cheerfulness, energy and discipline of everyone we saw. I was not amazed, but was extremely pleased to find these qualities still very much in evidence, and in many cases enhanced, from the old days.

At the end of this period we returned to Delhi and filmed sequences of Shiksha, the joint American-British-Indian Air exercise. In connection with this, and with other Air Force sequences, I spent a good deal of time with the brilliant young Air Vice-Marshal Pinto, AOC-in-C Western Air Command. Toward the end of the week, when Barbara left me to go ahead and prepare a flat in London, we went to say goodbye to Moti and Kimmie, and while there met and talked cheerfully with Lieut-General Daulet Singh, GOC-in-C Western Command. The shock that hit me about 3 o'clock on Friday November 22 was therefore all the greater to learn that Pinto and Daulat, and Lt-General Bikram Singh

(Corps Commander) and Major-General Nanavati (Divisional Commander) and Brigadier Oberoi (Brigade Commander), had all been killed, together with the pilot, in a helicopter crash in Poonch. Nalin Nanavati I had met in 1960, when I stayed a couple of days with him in Dehra Dun at the IMA, and he was a personal friend. I did not get to bed till late, to be called from New York with the news of President Kennedy's assassination. I already knew, though it was not publicised at the time, that another IAF plane was missing with nine aboard. The next day I attended the cremation of Lt-General Daulet Singh, Maj-General Nanavati and Brigadier Oberoi, at the Nigambodh Ghat, and had a chance to speak with General Pran Thapar (late 2/1 Punjab, whom many will remember, we met on the Frontier), Lt-General Kalwant Singh, the other General Thapar, of the IMS, and many many others. It seemed that every general and admiral and air marshal in India was present in the slow procession from the back of the Red Fort to the burning ghat, with the road lined by soldiers at "Rest on your Arms Reversed", and bands playing the Dead March. At the ghat I saw Mr. Nehru, and his sister, Mrs Krishna Huthee Singh. It was a tragic and tremendously oppressive day.

The next day we interviewed the Chief, General Moochoo Chaudhuri, in his office—an appointment that he kept in spite of the great pressures now on him after the disasters of Friday. I had a quick lunch with Mrs. Huthee Singh in the P.M.'s house (the old C-in-C's House) and then we left for Dehra Dun in the three hired cars which we needed to transport ourselves and our cameras, equipment and other baggage from place to place. We reached Dehra about 7 pm, and the next day started on three days' shooting at the Academy. Needless to say Maj-General Suresh Pandit of the Regiment was our mainstay and friend in all that we wanted to do, and these three days were the most pleasant of all that we spent—comfort, ease and calm, in very good sunny weather, with cold nights—it now being the end of November. On the social side, Suresh had a small family dinner party at his house on our second day—only members of the Regiment, with their wives, of course, and one officer from the 11th. This was Suresh's birthday, and his

ADC and Pop Appaya inveigled me into a plot to open a bottle of champagne. In this we were successful ... The next night all our NBC crew were guests at a reception and dinner at the officers' club—a most delightful and much appreciated gesture. Here I met and talked some time with General Rudra, whom many will remember; he was a great friend and admirer of Joe Lentaigne.

On the fourth day we drove from Dehra to Agra via Delhi, arriving again at about 7 p.m. Our work here lay with the Parachute Brigade, commanded by Brigadier Sagat Singh, who is of the Maharajah of Bikaner's family, and we spent a couple of hours that first evening arranging details with Sagat and his G 2 Air, Major Bhowani Singh of Jaipur, better known as Bubbles. What we wanted here was a para drop in front of the Taj Mahal, to symbolise in a single dramatic and colourful sequence the subject of our documentary, and scenes of field firing and training with live ammunition. The drop was arranged, and took place on the flat land directly opposite the Taj, on the other side of the river, and went off very well, though the first plane load had to circle for some time in a Jump position until we got sunlight on both the Taj and the foreground (all our show is to be shown, and was shot, in colour, and this requires strong light of the right colour temperature at all times). The second and third days we drove each morning to the Dholpur Field Firing Ranges some 35 miles south of Agra, and started work about 9 am, when the light became strong enough, finishing about 3 pm—and then the drive back, the cleaning of lenses, recharging batteries, preparation of film logs, etc. Finally, we finished, and drove straight through from the Dholpur ranges to Delhi, with a stop off in Agra to have dinner—arriving in Delhi about 1 a.m. It was a full moon, and the tomb of Akbar looked particularly impressive as we passed it.

The rest was goodbyes and thank yous—Goodbye to Moochoo, Moti, who had done more than any other one person to make our trip a success; General Raja, the DSD; Gp-Captain Datigarha, the SASO at Palam ... too many to mention; and on December 4 at 1.35 am I shook hands with Pyara and took off in a Qantas Boeing 707 for London.

It is not easy to sum up my seven weeks in India on this NBC mission. It was frequently assumed that my chief impression would be one of change, and certainly much has changed; but my chief impression was one of continuity, as I have mentioned—continuity of the Indian Army, of certain traditions of hospitality, of grace and good manners. No one could have been received with greater hospitality than Barbara and I enjoyed. We are very grateful for a wonderful experience; and, for myself, one of the most satisfying moments was that in which I was able to greet Deryck Mountford's son at our farewell party in Delhi. I had hoped to be able to invite his mother too, but she was in Kasauli and I missed her, to my great regret.

No one, officially, gave me any message to carry to anyone, but I know I can safely carry to all past members of the Regiment the good wishes of the present members; just as I took the liberty of wishing good luck to the present, from the past.

Translated with InDesign using 1627MJF specifications

Lt Col J. Masters

Lt Col John Masters died on 7 May 1983 in hospital at Alburquerqe, New Mexico, where he had received heart surgery. He was 68.

Jack Masters, as he was always known in the Regiment and Indian Army, joined the Second Battalion in October 1935, and was Adjutant to Lt Col W. R. Weallens in Iraq, Syria and Persia 1941. He took over command of the Third Battalion officially from June when Lt Col Ian Monteith was killed, actually at Shahgarh in the CP in October 1944, where it had reassembled after leave following the Second Chindit operations, and he organised its reversion to a rifle battalion basis from that of one in Special Force, when the latter was disbanded.

He was born on 26 October 1914 in Calcutta; educated at Cheltenham College Junior School and Wellington, before going to Sandhurst in 1932, destined for the Indian Army, after attachment to the First Bn. The Duke of Cornwall's Light Infantry at Razmak.

He saw active service on the North West Frontier, 1936–38, and during the Second World War in Iraq, Syria and Persia 1941; then came the Staff College at Quetta during the first half of 1942. Followed staff appointments as Brigade Major 114 Bde to Brig Michael Roberts, 10 GR, and then 111 Bde (Special Force) Chindits, in which was serving our Third Battalion, under our own Brig Joe Lentaigne in 1943. Then, when Gen Wingate was killed in March 1944, command of one Column of 111 Bde West of the Irrawaddy. In Jan 1945 after only a few months commanding the Third Battalion, he was appointed GI to 19 Indian Infantry Division commanded by Maj Gen Pete Rees. Lastly, after the War, he was on the Directing Staff at the Staff College, Camberley, 1946 and retired from the Army in 1947.

He found he did not like life in post-war England and emigrated to the USA, which he had visited and much appreciated on a pre-war long leave. There, after a few schemes on business and travel projects which proved to be non-starters, he tried freelance journalism which again was not successful.

Then he thought of the idea of a historical novel with an Indian background, and the Savage family was born. This was an immediate success from the first novel published "Nightrunners of Bengal". Altogether he wrote eight best-sellers on this theme of which "The Deceivers", "The Lotus and the Wind", "Bhowani Junction" on which a popular film was made, and "Far Far the Mountain Peak" are probably the best known.

He was inspired when he dedicated one of his later books "Himalayan Concerto" to "4th Gorkha Rifles, worthy successors of 4th Prince of Wales's Own Gurkha Rifles, all men of the Himalayas".

Though his novels brought him great success, in the Regiment and Association it is by his three volumes of his autobiography that we shall remember him best: "Bugles and a Tiger", "The Road Past Mandalay", in which his experience and description of the fighting man in action is so vivid, and "Pilgrim Son". These three combine his talent for story telling with the authenticity of history.

In spite of being based at his home in the suburbs of New York, and later at Santa Fe, Jack kept close touch with the Regiment and Association. Whenever his travels took him to India he always included a visit to one of the Battalions and was most generous in donations to any cause, usually concerned with family welfare, then current within it. He specially attended the Centenary Reunion at Bakloh in 1957 and, indeed, sent Uncle Arthur, then our Colonel, the price of a return air fare from UK to Delhi so that one of our Members might be present. This was gratefully accepted. Likewise, whenever his visits to Europe coincided with our Remembrance Day, he made a point of attending.

He and Barbara were extremely keen on physical fitness, and indulged this by trekking specially in the hills and occasionally mountains; for this in Europe, they were very fond of Spain and in particular of Ronda in Malaga, to which they returned again and again.

Jack was a very colourful personality and a staunch and loyal Fourth Gurkha on every occasion; we shall miss him acutely in the years ahead. Our sympathy and sincere condolences go to Barbara, their daughter and son, Susan and Martin.

R. A. N. D.

The Mandalay Lunch

There was an overwhelming response from former officers of the 4/4th to the suggestion that there should be a reunion to mark the fortieth anniversary of the capture of Mandalay Hill in March 1945. Preliminary soundings had shown that the number of intending diners would be close to the fifty mark and accordingly the time and venue was set for The Angel Hotel, Midhurst in Sussex, on Saturday, 30th March 1985.

In the event every officer whose address was known and who was in the UK on that date signified his intention to be present and indeed Major M. R. Strivens, MC, together with his wife, made a special trip from South Africa to be with us on the day. Major Richard Sant was unable to make it from Australia but with typical generosity sent a cheque for the wine; and the assault company FOO from 115 Field Regiment RA—Captain David Hine was present with his wife. It was also a great pleasure to meet Mrs Chris Burnett—widow of Bunny who, as all will know, literally "made it" all the way from "D" Company, 4/4th to Major General Brigade of Gurkhas: and to see again Mrs Erica Mackay McBride who travelled for the occasion from St Louis, Missouri.

In the chair as usual was the CO, Colonel Hamish Mackay, supported by Lieut Colonel John Strickland and the assembled company and their ladies. In fact every appointment in the battalion from CO to Company Officer was represented by at least one incumbent—a remarkable turn-out.

It was a wonderful, unique occasion and the years seem to have been rolled back: conversation flowed and there was a lot of laughter—though we did not forget those of all ranks "who didn't make it". The presence of so many ladies made the occasion even more delightful.

Our special guests were the President of our Association—Major Dicky Day—and the Secretary—Major Martin Fuller—together with their wives. This was to underline—courtesy aside—that this was not merely a battalion commemoration but also a proud regimental day for the Fourth Gurkhas: and to represent all those men with whom it was a privilege to serve—the guest of honour was Gurkha Major Manbahadur Rai of the 10th PMO Gurkha Rifles stationed at Church Crookham.

There were toasts from Major Bill Tee to the Regiment and to the 4/4th and to Colonel Hamish, who replied in his own inimitable way. Our President, Major Dicky Day, spoke for the guests as follows:

> "Colonel Hamish—Gentlemen. On behalf of all the guests, I thank you most sincerely for including us in this proud occasion.
>
> Fortune favours the brave—she smiled upon the Fourth Battalion of the Prince of Wales's Own Gurkha Rifles by giving it one of the finest Battalion Commanders in the Indian Army. Under him the Battalion distinguished itself—a record which includes the legendary capture of Mandalay Hill. Friendships forged in the fire and smoke of war are the closest and most enduring of all.
>
> And here Dame Fortune excelled herself, by ordaining that many of those brothers in arms survived to enjoy after the war that comradeship.
>
> I ask the guests to stand and drink with me to Colonel Hamish and the Fourth Battalion."

Officers who had signified their intention to be present included:

Col Hamish MacKay, Lt Col John Strickland, Bill Tee, Andrew Jeffrey, Bill Minto, Maurice Strivens, Alan Davies, Peter Sibree, Derek Revis, Steve Goodall, Arty Gilbert, Dicky Day, Martin Fuller, Hugh MacKay, Peter Hervey, Dudley Hall, Peter Hopwood, Alan Wiltshire, Essy Steel, John Craig, Peter Finch, Desmond Montgomery, Stewart Adam, David Hine and Tony Bowyer.

Obituaries

The following obituary appeared in *The Times*:

Colonel "Hamish" Mackay

Colonel "Hamish" Mackay, who has died aged 88, was the brilliant commander of 4/4 (Prince of Wales's Own) Gurkhas in the Battle of Mandalay Hill in March 1945 during a campaign in which he was wounded twice, awarded the DSO and Bar, and was mentioned in despatches.

When the 19th Indian (Dagger) Division reached the outskirts of Mandalay the brigade commander ordered the Royal Berkshires to take Mandalay Hill but Mackay requested that the Gurkhas should take the lead as he knew the hill and its parts. Consent was given and the Gurkhas climbed the north-eastern end of the hill in the darkness and attacked the summit at dawn supported by the Royal Berkshires.

Maj Gen "Pete" Rees, commander of the 19th Division, who did not bestow praise lightly, commended the feat which had been accomplished after a long day's march with the words "What a magnificent battalion". In the final stages one company of the Gurkhas on the crest of the hill was attacked fiercely by a large number of Japanese. Mackay sent a message to the officer commanding "Do you want any help?" "No, only breakfast, out," came the reply.

James Noble Mackay was born in Bombay in 1900, the son of the Presidency senior chaplain. After education in Holland and Scotland he was commissioned into the 107th Bombay Pioneers with whom he served in Afghanistan in 1919, Persia in 1920 and on the North-West Frontier in 1930.

The Pioneers were an elite corps in the Indian Army for they were trained to fight as infantry as well as being skilled engineers. On their disbandment he was posted to the 4th Gurkhas with whom he saw service in Waziristan.

Mackay was then asked to return to Burma, where he had earlier served for a while in the Military Police, and now joined the Burma Rifles. When the Japanese attacked in 1941 Mackay took part in the long retreat from Sittang in Imphal. His wife walked a similar distance—though not with her husband—and was awarded the Kaiser-i-Hind medal for this feat.

Mackay saw further service in the Chin Hills before taking command of 4/4 Gurkhas in Madras in April 1943. After the war Mackay commanded the Regimental Centre of the 4th (PWO) Gurkhas at Bakloh.

Hamish Mackay was a highly successful battalion commander devoted to his men as they were to him. Under his leadership they were the first to cross the Irrawaddy when the Japanese were being forced back and they distinguished themselves again in the final stages when the Japanese army was desperately trying to break out.

Mackay never attended the Staff College: staff work was alien to his nature. He excelled in field sports, notably hunting and pigsticking.

He is survived by his son and two daughters.

A Full Circle

By Janet McCarraher nee Mackay

On the 23rd March 1997, my sister and I drove on to the parade ground at Bakloh and saw a beautiful double rainbow with snow tipped mountains behind. It was magical and even more extraordinary when we later discovered that it had been the anniversary of our father, Hamish's, death.

In September 2000 I returned to Burma to visit Maymyo. A town I had left as a two-year old, in a carrier, during 1942. Thus another circle became complete.

When a family reunion was discussed a few years back in Bali, I had a great desire to visit Burma en route. Through the wonders of E-mail and The Lonely Planet Guide I contacted an agent in Rangoon who proved to be the most accommodating man ever. I explained that I wanted to stay at the Irrawaddy Flotilla Company Hotel in Rangoon, visit Mandalay, and then go on to Maymyo; and had eight days in which to do it. I left him to do the rest. On arrival at Rangoon Airport we were met by him and taken to the hotel; now modern and built in the old Flotilla Company grounds. The magic eight days began.

My conscience said no; my heart said yes. Throughout our entire visit we had experienced nothing but kindness, generosity, friendship and smiles.

My husband Malcolm and I climbed Mandalay Hill, barefoot in deference to the local religious custom, carrying photographs of Hamish, the Mandalay Bell, and the inscription written by Hamish in Burmese. These were read, and admired, by all who saw them. *"Welcome, you have come home"*. The hill is steep, covered with vegetation and rocks. However did you manage it, and in silence too? The views from the top are stunning giving a 360° view of the Irrawaddy and the surrounding plains.

Next day we drove away from the heat of the river valley, past stalls of pineapples, bananas, apples, melons, cauliflowers, dahlias, asters, gladioli and roses right up to the front door of the Candacraig in Maymyo.

I had maps, names of houses and sights to see, given me by Joanna Wright, whose father had accompanied my mother Mesha, Nanny and myself across Burma in 1942. Also from Steven Brookes who has written a book called *"Through the Jungle of Death"* whose experiences were very similar to ours.

We were shown a detailed map of Maymyo dated about 1930 with all the house names on it giving us the chance to visit every place we wanted to see. Unfortunately photocopying facilities were not available to us in Maymyo. We walked up the road to Government House where the Dorman Smiths had lived, the Baptist and Anglican churches (*in full use being a Sunday*), the swimming pool, the Botanical Gardens and the Market.

Best of all was meeting Mr Atcha, a watchmaker, who had photographs of Mandalay, the Bell and names of many of the 4th Battalion officers who had captured the hill in 1945. He spoke fondly of General Pete Rees and remembered his red neck scarf, of Bill Slim, and he corresponds with his son Lord John Slim. He spoke of the hospital train, our escape to India and where we lived. He had mended Westland Wright's watch in 1938. He can't have made that up. It was wonderful.

Never at any point was I stopped from filming, photographing, speaking to people, playing carom or marbles, and being asked into people's homes for a cup of tea.

Maymyo is a major base and there were many soldiers about. Understandably parts of the town were off limits being an army barracks, but smiles were plentiful.

We later had two lovely days in Rangoon visiting the Shwe Dragon pagoda and being shown round by a displaced student who philosophically said "It will come right. The country must allow students back to university". We visited the National Museum beautifully displayed, Scott Market where dollars were welcome, had tea at The Strand Hotel and watched ferries bustling across the Irrawaddy during a rain storm.

At no time did we feel threatened. At no time were we made to feel unwelcome. We drove past University Avenue and gave thanks to Aung San Sui Kyi and most of all, thanks to the wonderful country of rubies.

Editor's note:
Janet is the younger sister of Erica and Hugh Mackay. Their father Colonel J. N. Mackay DSO* commanded the 4th Battalion during the successful attack on Mandalay Hill in March 1945.

The Re-raising of the Fourth Battalion

By R. A. N. Davidson

Major Ran Singh and I reached Panipat Lines in Ambala at 11.00 hours on 28th February, shortly before the Colonel of the Regiment, Maj-General Moti Sagar, arrived from New Delhi. After inspecting the Guard of Honour, commanded by Captain Vijay Badhwar, he was introduced to all assembled serving and pensioned officers and JCOs and to other guests. There were many old friends and famous Regimental personalities present. To mention a few:

> From the Centre: Lt-Col Sabharwal (Commandant); Majs Tampi, Advani, Dhanpal Singh and Ran Singh; SM Rambahadur Gharti.
> From Second Battalion: Lt-Col Malhotra (CO) and the SM Hon Lieut Rudrabahadur Pun, VrC.
> From the Gorkha Sabha in Bakloh, representing pensioners Hon Lieut Babar Sing Thapa, OBI, SB, President of the Sabha (First Battalion); Sub Motiram Rana (Second Battalion); Nk Kishan Sing Rana (Third Battalion) and Jem Bishne Gurung (Fourth Battalion).
> ADC to the President of India: Hon Capt Birman Gurung, MC; from Army HQ, Maj Kale; from Corps HQ, Maj Sodhi; from Recruiting Depot, Hon Capt Motilal Gurung, MC, IDSM

The Colonel had a few words of greeting with every single person, and then went to inspect the Quarter Guard, which was graced by the Memorial Bell and Triptych of the First Battalion, who were in an operational area and had loaned these and also much silver for the Officers' Mess for the occasion—a most thoughtful and friendly gesture which was greatly appreciated by all ranks of the Fourth Battalion.

The *Bara Khana*, preceded by some welcome hospitality in the JCOs Mess, was a magnificent affair, in which no effort had been spared to perfect every detail. The whole Battalion was there. The Colonel, after a fine welcoming speech, very kindly asked me to accompany him on an informal round of the long trestle tables, talking to all and sundry as we progressed. I was much impressed by the keenness, soldierly bearing and alertness of all ranks; it was also good to find a considerable number from our sister Regiment, the First Gorkhas, whose Second Battalion had sent a large draft. Everyone was in a cheerful mood and eager to comply with "Bhat Bhajyo"; it certainly was a splendid meal which the SM Hon Capt Magras Gurung, MC, had organised.

I was to stay in the MES Inspection Bungalow with Colonel Moti and his son Ashoke, whilst his daughter Meenu stayed with the CO, Lt-Col Gurbax Singh Gill, and his wife Rajinder. We went there for a short while, and then to a football match between the CO's XI and "The Rest", appropriately ending in a draw of one goal each. Afterwards the Centre's Band, and Pipes and Drums beat Retreat in fine style. The Band had recently returned from the School of Music Pachmarhi, where they had all attended a course after the change of their instruments from high to low pitch. Their presence in Ambala for the ceremonies was very much appreciated by everyone.

That evening there was a Regimental Dinner in Mess, at which the same age-old routine was observed. Many items of silver had already been presented by individual officers and engraved with the date of re-raising: 1st March 1962. As mentioned before, the First Battalion had most kindly loaned much of their silver for the occasion, and this certainly helped to furnish adequately both dining- and ante-rooms. A considerable amount of furniture had arrived from Kartarpur, near Jullundur, where the First and Second Battalions bought so much of theirs pre-war; it was all exactly right, as were the furnishings to both rooms chosen by Kimmie, our Colonel's wife, who unfortunately could not come owing to being on family duty in New Delhi. Loyal Toasts were drunk to the Queen and the President, followed by the Toast of the Fourth Battalion given by the Colonel, after a very fine speech.

We then went on to a most creditably staged Variety Show in the Lines, comprising songs, dances, jokers and short sketches. It was almost incredible how all rehearsals, scenery and costumes had been arranged in the short time available. And so to bed around 0100 hours.

The first item on the great day, 1st March, was the reading of the Granth Sahib by the CO in his quarter. I was most honoured by being asked to be present, and very much impressed by this Ceremony. We were entertained to a buffet breakfast afterwards in their compound. Then came the full religious service in the Battalion's Mandir, to which I had also been invited. Once again I was most impressed by the solemnity and seriousness of all those attending, and there were many of all ranks, throughout its various phases. Pandit Nil Kanth, as the Senior Pandit in the Regiment, officiated, and as usual took the whole Service admirably in exactly the right religious spirit for this memorable occasion. During it, garlands of marigolds were presented, and I was extremely touched by Babar Sing's short speech and presentation of mine; it was a most friendly and heart-warming gesture, from a brother officer whom I have known and served with for forty years. Later in the Service he gave a most stirring speech to all ranks on this historic rebirth of our Fourth Battalion. A most interesting item during the Service was the carrying in, blessing by the Pandit, and then placing in its permanent position inside the Mandir of a large silver replica of a temple, which a number of returning leave men posted to the Battalion had presented. This very generous act was considered an extremely lucky omen for the Battalion on the first day of its new life. Finally, the exact moment of the Re-raising of the Fourth Battalion was announced by the ringing of the Mandalay Bell, once again in the custody of its rightful owners.

The Battalion Ceremonial Raising Day Parade was held at 1030 hours on the new Parade Ground, and attended by many spectators, military and civil, from near and far. Many stated, not once but several times, how incredibly good the drill was for a newly raised unit which had been together for a fortnight only. To this I subscribe wholeheartedly: it was of a very high standard and worthy of an old-established battalion which had been practising for a long while. All credit to everyone concerned for a splendid parade. The Colonel of the Regiment took the Salute and, after the Advance in Review Order, addressed the Battalion first in English and then Gurkhali, impressing on all ranks the magnificent history of the old Fourth Battalion and exhorting them to follow its splendid example and traditions, and to enhance the honour of the Regiment. After this, messages from a former Colonel and First President of the Officers' Association, Maj-General Sir Arthur Mills; from our President, Brigadier Kingsley and all members; and from the CO of the old Fourth Battalion, Colonel Mackay, were read out by the present CO, again first in English and then Gurkhali. The Battalion then marched past again, this time in threes, and away from the Parade Ground: it was wonderful to hear the stirring music of "Scotland the Brave" once more played for the Fourth Battalion of our Regiment.

After light refreshments in a marquee for the spectators we went to the Officers' Mess for a delicious buffet lunch, to which about fifty guests had been invited, including a very old friend of the Regiment, Lt-General Kalwant Singh.

The Colonel of the Regiment had to leave soon afterwards by road for New Delhi. As always his presence had put the finishing touch on these two memorable days of celebrations and been an inspiration to all ranks.

After tea I myself had to leave by train for Delhi, and was greatly moved by the large number of officers, JCOs and other ranks who came to the station to see me off. Whilst saying good-bye to them I realised this was probably the last time I should do so to any of our Battalions and, as the train moved down the long platform and their waving hands grew dimmer, my heart was very full. Luckily the Second Battalion's representatives were with me to lend me cheer on my way.

I Remember, I Remember

By Bill Tee

While soldiering for the King Emperor with the 4th Prince of Wales's Own Gurkha Rifles from 1939 to 1947, I was a very junior officer much in awe of my seniors; as was right and proper.

I met most of the legendary British and Gurkha officers of the Regiment who were still serving when I joined; but not Gordon Borrowman, Arthur Mills, Willie Weallens or David Murray-Lyon. Of the famous Gurkhas still active in 1939, I met all except Hotu Rana. One of these was Agam Gurung of 1/4 GR who gave it as his opinion that his British officers must have been illiterate as no 1/4 GR soldier or officer was awarded the VC at the time and place that 5 RGR were winning theirs! Wilfred Oldham was killed before he did justice to the courage of his men.

I submitted my first article to the Editor of the Newsletter in 1986 or 87 rather diffidently. Over the years since then editors have accepted my jottings and I have been surprised and pleased that many of those whom I have met at Stoke Poges have smiled their compliments in appreciation of my humble efforts. Raj Bir Chopra wrote to congratulate me! Dicky Day praised my first effort. John Strickland told me that he had enjoyed my scribbles! Pip Mogridge, the present editor, wrote to say that all members appreciated my contributions!

As I am now over seventy—the allotted span of three score years and ten—I am putting together two final contributions for Pip Mogridge's scissors and/or red pencil to forestall the failure of memory or the time when I will "cease upon the midnight with no pain". A little of what I now remember may be of passing interest to a few of those who now read Newsletters.

This, my first effort, covers the period from November 1939 to October 1944; the next will cover service in Burma and elsewhere until I transferred to 10 GR in 1947.

From Sandhurst in 1939 just after the start of Hitler's War, having been commissioned to the Indian Army List, I sailed on a troopship from Southampton to Cherbourg through a raging storm that reduced troop decks to a nauseous hell. From Cherbourg we travelled by troop train—eight horses or forty men!—to Marseilles through a despondent France to take ship for Bombay. We paused in Cairo and saw the great Archie Wavell greet his family long before he left his mark on the war and on India. After the war I read and admired his soldier's sonnet "The Madonna of the Cherries".

In Bombay on the dock side a fierce, handsome total stranger, a Punjabi Muslim, took me in charge; he served as my bearer for a few years. With other young men we entrained for Saugor to be acclimatised and knocked into shape while postings were sorted out.

4 GR had been my second choice of Regiment; the first was my father's Regiment, the Royal Irish Rifles. Choices had been made at Sandhurst. The Colonel of the RIR, General Steel, who had been junior to my father when he was senior subaltern, turned me down for lack of vacancies, so he said! My father died in Karachi of an appendicitis operation in 1922.

I am not sure now why I asked for 4 GR. I was born in Ranikhet near Almora in the hills not far from the Nepalese border. I wanted to join a Gurkha Regiment; how lucky I was!

When postings were published I found myself at the back of a scrum round a Notice Board to find out our fates. One of my friends called to me that I had been posted to the "Grinders"—the Bombay Grenadiers—my heart sank. Subsequently I took the trouble to thump Ronnie Watson. Gordon Shakespear was with us then; he (with Malcolm Cruickshank) was posted to 2 GR. Gordon was known to his Goorkhas over his long years of distinguished service as "Ceasefire Sahib"! I wonder if Gordon's son, who followed him into 2 GR, was also nicknamed Ceasefire!

I travelled through the vast plains of India into the Himalayan foothills, from Saugor to Bakloh, to join 1/4 GR. I still have the letter signed by Dermot Smart, the then Adjutant, telling of my acceptance.

1/4 GR was returning to Bakloh from Damdil on the North West Frontier and, in the interval, I was attached to their Training company. It was commanded by Captain F. E. Nangle. Much later I came to know him as Frank—his name was actually Francis—and much later still as "Bingle"; but in those first days he frightened me stiff! He was a martinet whom I called "Sir"!

I fell in love with Bakloh and am still in love more than fifty years on. What a beautiful, quiet and serene hill station it was! Crisp, sharp air blowing from the eternal snows of the high Himalayas; chukor calling from steep hill sides clothed in conifers and chil trees; sweet stream water, crystal clear and bitingly cold with mahseer to be caught—though not locally. Sunny days and cold, cold nights. The comradeship of men of a fine Regiment and everywhere Gurkhas their heads close shaven! I have read many times that part of Volume II of our Regimental History that describes the development of Bakloh. Gordon Borrowman's "Prospect" of Bakloh brings to mind happy days. The Bakloh that I knew is that shown in the 1937 photograph. Anne-Marie, my wife of twelve years, having read the first draft of this article, has suggested that we visit Bakloh in 1994 and I have written to Raj Bir Chopra abut such a visit!

When I joined the Training Company Budhe Gurung was the senior Subedar; over the long years he remained my ideal soldier; I never knew a finer. Happily we served together for many years and I enjoyed the benefit of his example. Naik Purandhoj Gurung took me in hand for weapon training and I became a marksman in those weapons with which infantry battalions of the Indian Army were then armed.

And of course Bakloh was dominated by 4 GR whose home it had been since December 1866. The impact of history and tradition in a great Regiment on the morale of the newly joined is incalculable but, without the slightest doubt, it dictates a way of life and living that upholds standards set by others in days gone by.

In due time 1/4 GR drove up the Kangra Valley from Pathankot and turned on to the winding hill road to Bakloh.

My first appointment as a one pip sprog of 19 years was to

command A and B companies of 1/4 GR! Of course the battle wise Subedars (regretfully I cannot now recall their names) did the commanding and I started to learn business from them. Shortly afterwards, in the absence on leave to get married of Derek Mountford, I acted as Adjutant, and while so employed Freddie Harrison gave me my first rocket! A low key, gentle castigation the impact of which for me, has not been equalled since!

Basantbir, Amarjang and another bright lad took time off to take me trekking through the hills and valleys of Chamba and beyond to Dharamsala, an enchanted corner of the world where I half expected Pooh Bear to appear round the next corner.

In Bakloh early one Sunday morning, while watching a football match from the raised verandah of the bungalow in which I was living, I stepped down on to the ground to get a better view. I was wearing sandals, a dressing gown, and pyjamas; to my horror I trod on the head of a krait. When the beast's tail whipped back over my foot I leapt some feet in the air. The horrid little snake must have been as surprised as I was frightened!

In September 1940 1/4 GR moved to Ambala. The Officers' Mess was set up in the Government Rest House. Here we learned much of Duties in Aid of the Civil Power and we played football. Terence Donlea was team captain, and Basantbir and Amarjang our stars.

Freddie Harrison moved on; unhappily he became a prisoner of the Japs in Malaya. In December Bobby O'Brien arrived from 8 GR to take command. He had lost an arm, I know not how. But I do know that, after the War, he played golf to a single figure handicap. I met Freddie Harrison at Stoke Poges once in the 80s but I never saw Bobby O'Brien again after I was posted away from 1/4 GR.

The late Peter O'Bree was the last British officer to join 1/4 GR from Sandhurst and my immediate senior was George Lorimer. George was not Sandhurst trained although he was a Regular. Both George and Peter moved with me to the Brigade of Gurkhas in 1947. They joined 6 GR when I went to 10 GR. I never beat George at squash and never will for, most unhappily, he is dead now!

4/4 GR was raised in Bakloh on 15th March 1941. I was posted as Quarter Master and was the first officer to join. My lack of technical knowledge was unimportant as Bhagwan Sing Thakur was my Quarter Master Jemadar.

Officers and men arrived for training from the three other battalions of the Regiment and from Training Companies. Our commanding officer was Maurice Berkeley from 7 GR. He was never really fit—he would not admit this then and now, if he should read this article, he will be livid! He left us in March 1943 to be replaced by Hamish Mackay. Maurice was a gourmet, highly intelligent, widely read, pedantically precise, a little impractical—a most civilised man.

Of those Gurkha and British officers who joined 4/4 GR at or just after its raising in Bakloh in March 1941, only six Gurkha officers (Budhe Gurung, Damar Sing Pun, Dassiram Gurung, Durge Thapa, Narbahadur Pun and Jagat Sing Gurung) and five British officers (Bill Minto, Michael Davis, Alan Davies, Dick Poole, and myself) accompanied it to Burma in October 1944. All of these survived the war although none of us were with 4/4 GR when it returned to India in 1945.

Bill Minto had been with Grindleys Bank in Bombay before he joined us; he was the only officer with any money—the rest of us were chronically hard up. Bill was the proud owner of a smart Ford coupé that stayed with him for many years! He let me drive it occasionally!

My main memory of 4/4 GR's stay in Bakloh is struggling with training programmes week by week; juggling schedules, instructors, squads, stores, equipment, ranges, parade grounds, sickness, leave and much else to ensure a cohesive effort for 800 men in groups of 10 or 12 each week. I cannot remember why I, the Quarter Master, did this work; we were few and each took his share of whatever work was going. On reflection it seems that, of the three officers trained to write complicated programmes of this sort, I was the junior; the other two were Maurice Berkeley and John Hawkins!

Six months after its raising, 4/4 GR moved on by foot and by lorry (provided by the Dalhousie Transport Company) to Hoshiapur. As Quarter Master, I was lorry borne. When negotiating one of the hairpin bends below Bakloh, the steering wheel stuck on the full turn. The driver and I wrestled with the confounded thing and freed it by main force just in time. He turned on me and told me in no uncertain terms to keep my hand off the something steering wheel! I was as frightened as he!

4/4 GR's first of many, many river crossings was over the Beas at Gurdaspur; unlike other crossings spread over the face of India and Burma in the next four years, it was a bit of a shambles! Perhaps part of the reason was that Bill Minto took over as Quarter Master after our arrival in Hoshiapur! I moved to C Company. Gurdaspur and its countryside is a delight and steeped in history. In his time Alexander of Macedon with his hoplites passed that way.

4/4 GR moved south the many miles to Ahmednagar east of Bombay; we passed through Amritsar where 1/4 GR turned out to cheer us on. From Ahmednagar, Maurice Berkeley sent me to Saugor to attend a 3in Mortar Course. I fooled the instructors and got a "D". On return I set about training the best Mortar Platoon in the Indian Army! No live ammunition of course!

The War went on. In response to stresses of internal security and seaborne threats from the Japs, 4/4 GR were moved to the Deccan by lorry—I drove 700 miles in a 15 cwt truck sharing the driving with Bob Crighton. Bob trained our Carrier Platoon—no mean feat as we had few drivers—before moving on to 2/4 GR with whom he fought in Italy.

In those days teaching Gurkhas to drive anything, even pedal bicycles, was a headache. Newly trained, happy go lucky Gurkhas let loose with 15 cwt Chevrolet lorries on public roads were a nightmare.

Teaching them to ride motor cycles was a particular pain in the posterior. We chose an enormous flat grass field so that they would not hurt themselves on landing: a single stumpy tree grew in the middle of the field. One after the other the trainees gyrated unsteadily round the field progressively narrowing the circle until nearly every one of them inevitably ran into the tree! Frustrating but comical! It was astonishing that so few drivers or passengers were hurt and that we suffered so few crashes.

We criss-crossed Southern India many, many times not only

moving camp but on a multitude of Southern Command, Corps, Divisional, Brigade and unit exercises. These exercises and moves were interspersed with individual, section, platoon and company training. Never a dull moment. Among many other places we saw Calicut, Bangalore, Trichnopoly, Kumbergaon, Secunderabad, the Kolar Gold Fields, Vizagapatam and Conjeeveram.

Conjeeveram, a holy Hindu city crammed with—to the eye of an untutored European—grotesque temples, had in an age long ago, been home to Raja Dharma Datta, an early ruler of Nepal.

Our camp, a few miles outside Conjeeveram, was horrid. We lived in tents and a few bashas made with bamboo skeletons and roofed and walled with palm fronds. The country was as flat as the proverbial pancake; it was humid, hot and wet; we were plagued by mosquitoes; our tents, pitched on loose dry sand, were located among toddy trees, and paddy fields.

We spent occasional days and nights on leave 50 odd miles away in the Connemara Hotel in Madras; it was there, while playing snooker, that a Colonel Harrison of 6 GR ordered a young officer to beat the bubbles out of a whisky and soda—a chota peg. It was a long process; single bubbles appeared out of nowhere to crawl slowly up the glass even when the drink seemed totally still. Visiting Madras made a welcome and civilising break. Some of our officers' wives lived there.

On one occasion in our Conjeeveram bivouac, a large truck loaded with 3.7 mm howitzer ammunition, caught fire. I ordered equipment, stores and men within a quarter of a mile be moved. Maurice Berkeley arrived from wherever he had been and, assessing the situation, he cancelled my order decreeing that the offending truck be unloaded. Despite the fire raging next to the ammunition, unloaded it was—the only loss being the truck itself! I had been looking forward with apprehension to the monumental bang of a truck load of ammuntion blowing up.

While we sweltered in Conjeeveram a rest camp for soldiers and officers was created in Coonoor, a delightful hill station, 200 odd miles away in the Nilgiri Hills. The Indian Staff College was located there at one time. While there I met Liz Ormston who was to become my first wife. Coonoor is a magic place half way between Mettupalaiyam on the edge of the flat plain and Ootacamund at the head of the mountain railway. It was a splendid contrast to Conjeeveram—cool, gay, bright, social and naughty.

On one of the larger exercises I contrived to get C Company lost and we were cut off. We spent a glorious 10 days behind "enemy" lines helping ourselves to what rations we could capture and generally creating mayhem. When we finally rejoined Andrew Jeffery, then the Adjutant, was extremely pert in his remarks! While our escapade lasted we had tremendous fun in the "enemy's" administrative areas redirecting his heavy traffic. One long convoy ended up nose to tail in a dead end street in Madras!

4/4 GR moved on again—early 1943 I would guess—to Renigunta and to Attur.

On the tedious drives to and fro over the vast land mass of the Deccan we were strictly adjured to keep awake, all of us at all times. One day, with down cast eyes, I was reading a book when Maurice Berkeley overtook us in the convoy; that evening he ripped me off a sizzling rocket for sleeping while on convoy! I said nothing! There was nothing to say!

Then we moved to Nilumbur on the western slopes of the Nilgiri Hills. We camped astride a mountain torrent, an enchanted place. Scraps from the central cook house filtered into a pool in the stream; from a cliff top a mass of mahseer could be seen milling about in the pool. Hamish Mackay forbade fishing with hand grenades!

On a patrol exercise from this same camp one of C Company's few swimmers, Padambahadur, was drowned. His flailing arm caused the fore sight of his slung Lee Enfield Rifle to strike the back of his head; the blow knocked him unconscious and he was swept away in the rapids. We recovered his body and buried him on the river bank with a burning sliver of sandalwood in his mouth. The sad and unlucky death of another friend. On another patrol exercise hot, sticky and exhausted we halted by a pool of translucent water. For fun and to cheer the Gurkhas up I dived head first into the pool with my equipment on. I was knocked out by a rock sticking up in the water. When I came to I saw Gagan Sing Gurung, C Company's senior subedar, with a field dressing between his teeth, swimming to my rescue. The extraordinary thing about this story is that Gagan Sing had never swum before that day and never swam again! I still have a scar to remind me of that exhausting day long ago and far away.

The tall teak trees among which we trained on the western escarpment of the Nilgiri Hills had been planted 75 years before our arrival there. The Indian Forestry Commission's work was magnificent; but what a long time to wait for results! Officers of the Commission never saw their life's work come to fruition during their life time.

During our stay in Nilumbur a king (queen?) cobra showed itself to be extremely aggressive. It was long and fat and weaved at us until, quite suddenly, it charged. We gave it pride of place and withdrew hastily. Perhaps its young were about!

In pursuance of watermanship Pete Rees, our untiring and diminutive divisional commander (always dressed totally in jungle green—even to his handkerchief, socks and underwear), organised water sports. Our only true waterman was a Maji; he was entered for the sprint. To everybody's surprise and our cheers he swam the 70 yard wide river under water, surfacing by the far bank to win comfortably from all comers!

The War still went on and in early 1944 we moved to Nasik north east of Bombay. Now airborne training was added to our repertoire of desert, mountain, open, amphibious and jungle training; until at long last we were told our fortunes. Louis Mountbatten visited us in his resplendent Admiral's uniform and, at one of those stage managed parades that he loved, he told us that we were going to Burma.

We had trained with and without vehicles and now had only a few Jeeps; we did, however, have 45 Brazilian mules—the notorious No 37 among them!

In Nasik we were also visited by Grant-Taylor, a some time Chicago cop, who taught us the psychology of killing face to face. He was a gunman in the gangster style, lightning fast on the draw.

Indian rum, a very potent tipple, was made in Nasik. Perhaps it still is!

While there I took time out to marry Liz Ormston at the Pro Cathedral in Bombay. Maurice Strivens—"Striv" to one and all then as now—was our best man. (My first choice had been a friend from Stonyhurst, Giles de Bertadano; but he was in close arrest for some trivial military offence at the critical time!). As Liz's family and I were tall, Striv stood on a shoe box for the photograph! Liz and I spent a glorious ten days in Mount Abu near Udaipur before she returned to Bombay and I to Nasik.

Later Liz visited us in Nasik and we played golf there. Gagan Sing entertained us to rum, bhat and an informal candle lit nautch. I can hear the mardles even now 50 years on! Company Havildar Major Budhibal Gurung, a giant Gurkha at five foot ten, challenged Liz to eat raw green chillies with him. Without a grimace she matched him chillie for chillie to the delight of all! Looking back I am not so sure about Liz's delight!

My second wife, Anne-marie, and I stayed with Striv and his wife in Johannesburg in 1986; he had changed hardly at all in the intervening 40 odd years.

Liz's father had been the Hong Kong & Shanghai Bank Manager in Kuala Lumpur when the Japs overran Malaya in 1942. He spent the rest of the war as their unwilling guest in Changi prison in Singapore. Liz, her mother and her sister escaped from Singapore just ahead of the beastly Japs and, after a dangerous voyage south to the Sunda Strait—where they were bombed from the air—into the Indian Ocean between Sumatra and Java, reached Bombay. Liz's father kept a diary which he hid among his soap, toothbrush and flannel in his wash bag—strictly forbidden by the Japs under pain of death—but happily, he was not found out.

In October 1944 4/4 GR left Nasik, headed for service against the Japs in Burma as part of the 19th Indian Dagger Division. We had trained over a longer period during the war than the other battalions of 4 GR and went to war much later than they did. We looked forward eagerly and with some apprehension to what was to come.

Stoke Poges House

By Tony Bowyer

April, 1982, was to see the first tangible evidence that an idea of two years ago was beginning to take form and that soon in Subathu—the home of the Regiment—there would be a hostel to ensure continuous schooling for orphans and other needy children.

To reminisce for a moment: the idea had formed in outline after the reunion of 1977, and after a number of exploratory letters and various overtures to organisations here and in India, a plan was drawn (with unofficial Trustees—largely self-appointed!)—to provide and equip for residential education a hostel for thirty Gurkha children so that they might be able to pursue an uninterrupted education. The partners in the enterprise were Highfields School, Wolverhampton; the Rotary Club of Wolverhampton and Solan, India, and of course 14 GTC Subathu. The initial aim was to raise five thousand pounds and the launch of the UK side of the project was assisted by 1/2nd GR—then stationed at Church Crookham—and by the Band of the Brigade of Gurkhas—who created quite a stir at the School.

Right from the start the progress was nothing short of spectacular: Highfields School alone raised in excess of four thousand pounds in three weeks; the Wolverhampton Rotary Club quickly hit its target figure of £1,500 and the small Solan Club in India did sterling work with bazaars and fairs: at which point application was made to Rotary International for a Special Grant of £1,500 and to our great delight this was successful.

Subsequently all ranks of 1 GR and 4 GR were asked to donate a day's pay and in January 1982 or thereabouts, the Indian Government promulgated a scheme to assist dependent children of those who had died in service: by dovetailing all this provision together it was now possible to contemplate a greatly enlarged scheme in the knowledge that future maintenance would be assured.

The building will be constructed in local stone and timber, cut into the hillside, verandah style with magnificent views to the Simla Ridge. When completed—at a cost of some forty thousand pounds—it will house not thirty children (the original target) but ninety-six, after a three phase building project now under way. The children will be accommodated in small dormitories, each with bed, table, chair and locker: there will be communal washing facilities and a dual purpose dining hall.

At the same time other people, Gurkha, Indian and British have been encouraged by this project to endow scholarships and bursaries to support needy pupils of the School: the sixth formers of Highfields School, for instance, have "adopted" six Gurkha children and send to each child a grant of twenty-five punds a year: there is also a Malhotra Memorial and a Sen Scholarship along the lines of the Hamish Mackay Merit Award. This is a most encouraging development and a valuable extension of the original scheme.

It was as coordinator and I dare say gadfly on this project that in April '82 I flew out East to witness, as I thought, the laying of the foundation stone; and after an initial four days in the Kathmandu area (to recover from the rigours of a Spring Term in the UK!), I arrived in New Delhi to be greeted personally by the Colonel of the Regiment—quite a moment for an ECO and in stark contrast to my first arrival in 4 GR on the back of the Pathankot milk truck in the misty light of a Punjab dawn! This time I was greatly honoured and deeply appreciative of the gesture by General Brijendra and was delighted that he was accompanied by Lieut Colonel P. K. Ghosh who had recently been commanding 4/4th GR.

It was only then that I discovered that far from being a witness I was in fact being invited as guest of honour to perform the foundation ceremony and I felt overwhelmed.

My next stop was—inevitably you may think, for such is their legendary hospitality—at the Sodhi house and thence after some delightful days with this charming family—with Brigadier Harinder up the hill to Subathu. Here I was to see great changes and improvements since 1977: the Museum in particular has been set up with great pride and affection and is a worthy home for the visible history of the two Regiments: all of the exhibits have been set out with professional expertise and there is plenty of room for expansion.

April 16th, the day set aside as auspicious by the priest, was sunny and warm; we first visited the little School where flowers were presented and I was introduced to the teachers: then a variety show of singing, recitation and dance by youngsters—beautifully turned out as one would expect: and then a presentation from me—in the first instance—to the School itself of a gift of one hundred pounds from Wolverhampton Rotary Club and then to each of the six children adopted by my sixth formers a package containing casual wear, a silver Royal Wedding crown and a Rubik Cube: knowing the extent of Gurkha exasperation when confronted with a seemingly insoluble problem, these could well end in small kukri-dissected pieces; and I could achieve a similar notoriety in the foothills to the man who introduced rabbits to Australia.

Now came the moment for the ceremony: accordingly in that magnificent setting of green hills and pines, of wooded ridges and distant snows and in the presence of smiling and neatly-uniformed little children and their parents, hundreds of Gurkha riflemen, senior officers of the Regiments and members of Solan Rotary Club, together with Brigadier Dharam Panesar—the Commandant—his Deputy, Colonel K. K. Prodhan and the Subedar Major, I was escorted down steps cut into the hillside to the beflagged site of the hostel where a low wall with a curtained stone awaited the ceremonial in bright sunshine. Throughout I was accorded precedence and found it both surprising and overwhelming.

The priest gave me marigolds and flowers which I placed on top of the wall and then he offered me a coconut—clearly an invitation rather than a comment—and I should have known, though I had to ask—that the spilling of the milk was the Hindu equivalent of champagne: fortunately for the future, I split the coconut with the first blow and this was greeted as in the old days with bursts of machine gun fire from the hillsides. The curtain fell apart with a tug on the strings and there for all to see was the name which the Regiment had chosen to grace the hostel—"STOKE POGES

HOUSE". I felt very emotional when I saw this inscribed in stone—and I understand that the choice of name was unanimous—and more than anything else it underlined for me personally the true and remarkable bond which exists between the past and present members of this Regiment—British, Indian and Gurkha.

Later there were more celebrations: an invitation to officiate at the GB Football Tournament match between 5/4th and 1/11th GR. I could not forbear to mutter "Jitnu paryo" to the 4 GR captain at the end of the line and received an odd look from the 11th GR team as I turned to them: fortunately the right result ensued and I was not called upon to disallow a goal on a technicality: I only wish that I had been playing myself—it was a great temptation. Eheu fugaces!

Then a tea party to meet all the officers and men of 4/4th GR then in station—and this pleasure I shared with Brigadier Harinder himself, a former CO of the fourth Battalion. There were presentations of ceremonial kukris on inscribed stands and a 14GR flag inscribed "with gratitude to Highfields School"—and the same evening after a most spectacular storm with the fiercest lightning which I have ever seen—there was a barakhana and singing and dancing into the small hours. Some of the tunes are new—but Naini Tala is ageless and I dredged up a few from the past—"Mero Koililo Joban" and "Oh, oh-ni Kati ramro" which 4/4th burhos will remember with affection.

The visit was soon over—and I was sad to leave, for not only had I been treated most royally by Brigadier Dharam, Colonel K. K. Prodhan and all ranks of the Centre, but I had been made to feel a friend and very much still a member of the Regiment: and I know that all who have visited Subathu in recent years have felt the same—and it is both truly remarkable and widely accepted in the Indian Army: numbers of officers serving and retired from other Regiments whom I met in one place or another during my stay in India made the same point with a certain envy.

On the way down from the hills, I addressed the Rotary Club of Chandigarh on the project and they gave a standing ovation in support of what was being done: and on return to the UK I heard from the Colonel of the Regiment that site work on the hostel is under way with the shifting of water pipes and that the necessary wood, stone and cement is being procured so that construction may start as soon as the rains finish. I look forward very much to the first children taking up residence in Stoke Poges House.

The Coronation of His Majesty the King of Nepal

By G. C. Nagra

It was, I think, in the last week of March that I read in the newspapers that the Coronation of the King of Nepal would take place in the first week of May and that an Indian Army contingent was to take part. I remember wishing that I could have the good luck to be there, but I saw no chance of it because at that time we were terribly busy at the Centre getting things ready for the COs' conference and the Amalgamation Day Celebration scheduled to start on the 12th May. Also I was PMC and very heavily involved because the Mess building was undergoing extensive repairs and we had planned to rearrange the lay-out of the Mess, and the display of trophies. Even if I was considered worthy of selection, it seemed unlikely that I could be spared for a week in Nepal.

After reading the news we daily awaited orders on the subject from Army Headquarters. These finally arrived on 5th April when we learnt that an Army Contingent led by General Sant Singh, GOC-in-C Eastern Command, would attend the Coronation Ceremonies in Nepal from 29th April to 6th May, 1956. It was to consist of two officers personally selected by the General; one officer, one JCO and two Other Ranks from each of the Gorkha Regiments; and the brass bands of the Rajput and 58th Gorkha Training Centres.

On receipt of these instructions our Commandant asked battalions of the First and Fourth to forward recommendations of the composition of their contingents, and I had the luck of being selected to lead our contingent of which the other members were Hon Capt Moti Lal Gurung, MC, IDSM (2nd Battalion), C. H. M. Preetam Singh Rana, IDSM (1st Battalion), and Naik Puran Bahadur Thapa, MM (3rd Battalion).

I was overjoyed at the prospect of going to Nepal, the land of our men (of course at that time I did not realize that old Freddy Harrison would rope me in to describe the visit!). I felt that I was certain to meet some of the old *Buros* of the Regiment but unfortunately I did not meet any, not even Nar Bahadur, the Bara Hakim at Pokhra. I also hoped that some of our Regiment's old British Officers would come with the HMG Contingent from Malaya. But, alas! I was again disappointed though I did get some first-hand news of R. N. D. Williams and Bill Tee, whom I knew when they were in the 4th Battalion in Burma in the same Brigade as myself, from officers who came with the HMG Contingent. We also looked forward to meeting those of the Regiment who were serving with the Military Mission at Kathmandu.

We had been warned on 5th April that our contingent should be prepared to move at short notice, and it was not until the 24th that firm dates for the move were received. We were to leave Palam on the morning of the 28th April in a Dakota which would touch down at Lucknow to pick up the General's party; other contingents were also to travel in a Dakota on 30th April, and the Bands were to go all the way by road.

At 12 noon on the 28th we landed at the recently modernized Goucher airfield and were met by many senior Officers of the Nepalese Army and by Major General Sarda Nand Singh, Commander Indian Military Mission, and his principal staff officers. During our 4-mile drive from the airfield, we saw feverish activity to improve the roads and the general appearance of the city which were nowhere near what they should be for the historic occasion. The main road (Nai Sarak) from the Palace to the Tundi Khel Maidan had been widened by shifting back the compound walls of the Royal Palace and the old Prime Minister's Palace, and was looking most untidy with debris lying all over the place. There were only three days left, and some doubt crept into my mind as I wondered whether all would be tidied up by D-Day.

We were accommodated as State guests in Shital Nivas, the palace presented to the Nepalese Government by General Krishna Shamsher Jung Bahadur Rana. The catering was arranged by the proprietor of the Royal Hotel and I learnt from most reliable sources that the Government was paying him at Rs 90 per guest per day for catering alone! New crockery bearing the Royal Crest (manufactured by Bengal Potteries) was provided by the Government, which also supplied the proprietor with drinks for the guests in abundance and without calling for any accounting of the amount consumed. All the servants were flown in, mainly from Calcutta. And on top of this a large fleet of cars for the use of the guests was brought in on hire from Delhi and Calcutta. All these arrangements must have cost the Nepalese Government a packet.

Being the first arrivals we had quite a lot of problems to solve because the arrangements for looking after the guests had not really got going as yet. In fact the catering staff for the Palace where we were staying had only arrived the same morning from Calcutta by air. However, they produced a good lunch for us in record time.

The Nepalese Government was determined to make the occasion the greatest show of the year in Asia and had drawn up an elaborate programme for the six days of the celebrations which opened on 1st May with "Purvanga" at 9 am followed in the afternoon and evening by the Opening of the National Exhibition, Royal Reception and National Drama. The Coronation on the following morning was to be followed by the Royal Procession from Hanuman Dhoka to Tundikhel where the Royal Durbar was to take place, the great day ending with a display of fireworks and a State Banquet. The programme for the next four days included a Tattoo and the National Sports Finals at the Stadium; folk songs and dances; a Garden Party at the Royal Palace; a Buffet Dinner in the Gallery Hall of Singha Durbar ; and, on the final day, the Royal Review at the Stadium in the morning and the Kathmandu Tennis Finals in the afternoon. I, being a junior officer, was able to attend only some of the functions.

On the morning of 29th April, the day following our arrival, General Sant Singh presented to the King a sword on behalf of the Indian Army to mark the conferment on His Majesty of the Honorary Rank of General in the Indian Army. The ceremony was held in Durbar Hall of the Royal Palace and was attended by some high dignitaries. Of our party only the two Lieut-Colonels accompanying the General were able to witness the presentation. I heard that the ceremony of the presentation was more or less the same as described by Brigadier B.-K. on pages 72 & 73 of Volume II of our Regimental History, when he presented the Regimental Sword of Honour to HH Maharaja Sir Bhim Shamsher Jang Bahadur Rana in 1931 to mark his appointment as the new Honorary Colonel of our Regiment in succession to HH Maharaja Sir Chandra Shamsher Jang Bahadur Rana.

That evening I was delighted to meet Richard Proud at a cocktail party given by General and Mrs Sarda Nand Singh. I had last met him in December 1944 at Kohat when he was commanding the 1st Battalion. We talked at length about the Regiment and the 1st Battalion in particular. I was also very pleased to learn from him that Moke Murray was expected to arrive the next day as ADC to Lord Scarborough, the leader of the British Delegation.

Next day we spent sightseeing and enjoyed visiting places of historical and architectural importance like Pattan and Pashu Patti Temple. I noticed that my doubts as we had driven from the airport had been unnecessary; Kathmandu already wore a festive look—even the temples were being repainted and their wood work polished.

By the evening of 30th April all the visitors, including delegations from 14 nations, had arrived. The delegations included high dignitaries from the United Nations; India, the UK, the USA, France, Burma, Switzerland, Japan, Laos, Cambodia, Indonesia, Ceylon, Thailand, Pakistan and Afghanistan, and the city was humming with foreign visitors, photographers, pressmen and official guests.

With the arrival of guests completed all was set for the long and almost continuous chain of events which were to start on the following day. The General was the only member of the Indian Army Contingent to be invited to the Opening of the Exhibition and the Reception at the Royal Palace. This was just as well because it was not until the afternoon of 1st May that we were told that our Contingent would be participating in the Coronation Procession next day. We had not expected this honour, and were faced by the problem of getting our one set of summer uniform (which had been all that it was possible to include in our 40-lb baggage allowance) fit for a Ceremonial Parade. Arrangements for *dhobying* were very sketchy; however, despite the short notice, we managed to get everything ready and to put our uniforms into good 4th Gorkha ceremonial shape.

In the evening we heard the good news that the officers of both the Indian and HMG Contingents would be able to attend the actual Coronation Ceremony. Owing to the limited number of seats being available, we had not originally been invited, but our Liaison Officer from the Nepalese Army, Colonel Ghana Shamsher Rana, was extremely kind and managed to get passes for us. The JCOs and men, however, were unfortunately unable to attend.

The Coronation Ceremony on 2nd May, in the Courtyard of the King's ancestral Palace of Hanuman Dhoka, started at 9 am. The streets were so filled with enthusiastic crowds that we had a lot of difficulty in getting through them; almost every Nepali who could possibly make the trip to Kathmandu was in the Capital. The streets and the Palace were richly and colourfully decorated with bunting and miniature national flags of all the nations represented by their delegations, and hundreds of ceremonial arches had also sprung up during the night with inscriptions wishing King Mahendra a long and successful reign. We were told that two shifts of 5,000 labourers had worked day and night to get things ready. It really was a gigantic task but they managed it well and, I should say, in record time.

The Courtyard of the Palace was also well-decorated with carpets and floral bunting. In one corner a thatched miniature pavilion, where the actual ceremony was performed, had been constructed. Seats were arranged all round the courtyard and were occupied by the official representatives of foreign countries, members of the Royal Family, and high civil and military officials including the Cabinet Ministers in their picturesque and dignified ceremonial dress. The courtyard itself was packed with amateur photographers and camera crews, from India and Hollywood, with the latest equipment to record the colourful event in Cinemascope and even for televising.

At 9 o'clock the King entered the Hanuman Dhoka at the head of a procession of Ministers and Officers and was taken inside for the Anointing Ceremony according to the traditional Vedic rites. At 10.30 am exactly—the auspicious moment appointed by the astrologers—the Royal Priest placed on the Monarch's head the gold and silver domed Crown set with jewels. Priests chanted Vedic hymns and blew conch shells, the bands struck up the National Anthem and guns fired the Royal Salute to announce the Enthronement of His Majesty King Mahendra. After this ritual, the paying of homage started. One by one people came and bowed; they laid their tributes at the foot-rests of the Throne, bowed again and retired. While the King was receiving this homage from his people, we left for Shital Nivas to get ready for the Procession which was to start from Hanuman Dhoka at 2 pm.

The 3-mile long Procession, which accompanied Their Majesties the King and Queen, who were borne on a richly caparisoned elephant, to the Tundi Khel Maidan, included marching columns and people mounted on horses and elephants or riding in cars.

Before it started all of us were issued with the Coronation Medal which we proudly displayed along with our other medals. It was a spectacular parade in which diplomats, dignitaries, detachments of the Nepalese Army and Police, and the Contingents of the Indian and HMG Gorkha Regiments with their bands all participated. The whole route was lined on both sides by thousands of Nepalese who cheered their ruler till he reached the specially constructed 40-foot high pavilion in the huge Maidan. As the King ascended the pavilion, the guns fired a 31-gun Royal Salute. He then made a

Royal Proclamation laying stress on the democratic aspirations of his country.

This Royal Durbar was followed in the evening by an impressive display of fireworks and the State Banquet to which invitations were issued only up to Lieut-Colonels.

The next four days were fully occupied. We were invited to all the functions, and on the last morning of 6th May we witnessed the Royal Review, at which the Nepalese Army looked very smart and impressive in their scarlet ceremonial uniforms.

With the National Drama at Singha Durbar that evening, the week-long ceremonies connected with the Coronation came to an end. They had indeed been a big event for Nepal and its people—something they will long remember. This Coronation, with its cosmopolitan concentration of foreign representatives who had arrived in such large numbers, was in great contrast to the Coronation of King Tribhuvan, the present ruler's father, which was witnessed by no foreigners other than the British Resident and members of his staff.

Our short visit to Nepal was even more pleasant than we had anticipated. The kindness and hospitality we received everywhere had to be experienced to be believed, and we are all so very grateful to the Government of Nepal for looking after us so well, and in particular to Colonel Ghana Shamsher who performed his duties magnificently and was always willing to do anything possible for us.

One part of our visit to Nepal which we specially enjoyed was our meeting of the HMG Contingent who lived next door to us in the same Palace. It was the first proper meeting of people from the two Gorkha Brigades since they parted company in 1947. The *Milap* between the two Contingents was terrific and we were able to learn a great deal about each other. It was also nice meeting Moke Murray who was thrilled to meet Moti Lal and to get news about his old battalion and regiment.

On the morning of 7th May we left Kathmandu, again by air, with heavy hearts, and returned to Chakrata just in time to complete the formalities for the Amalgamation Day Celebrations and the Commanding Officers' conference.

What a wonderful trip it had been!

The Valley of Nepal

By R. A. N. Davidson

In May last year I was in luck. I was asked to accompany my Brigadier (from our HQ at Barrackpore) and his wife to Katmandu on an official visit.

This was indeed a treat in store. Nineteen years had passed since that memorable occasion when I had been there as a member of our Regimental Deputation which presented the Sword of Honour to our Honorary Colonel, Maharajah Sir Bhim Shamsher. Moreover; I would meet Richard Proud (now First Secretary to our Ambassador in Nepal); I had not seen Richard for ten years, during which he had commanded the First Battalion in Burma and Kohat, so we would have plenty to talk about. Finally, there was the pleasing prospect of a few days' respite from the heat of the UP.

After a night at Raxaul in the Rest House, outside which a Gold Mohur tree flowered in full and perfect bloom, we were off at sparrow-twitter on the 14th May, armed with our "rahdaris" (road passes) to board the little train which chugs its way via Birganj across the plains and through the jungle of the Terai to Amlekhganj.

At railhead we were welcomed by a Mukhia and, after a 30-mile drive in a station waggon, arrived at Bhimphedi by 1 pm. Well-remembered landmarks were the tunnel at Churia, where Ochterlony by-passed the Gurkha position in 1814, and the moving silhouettes of the loads on the ropeway from Dhursing. (A pleasantly contrived combined operation, David, but weren't those loads *sky*-marks?—Ed).

At Bhimphedi we transferred our baggage to coolie transport and ourselves to the sturdy ponies sent for us from the Maharajah's stables. We spent the night in the pleasant and clean Rest House, which is just above the old fort at Sisagarhi, at the bracing height of 6,000 feet. A cool night was doubly ensured by a large line in thunderstorms which fairly lashed the building just before we dossed down.

Next morning we were again off to an early start of 5 am to cross the 6,400-foot pass at Chisapani Garhi—a hazy day, alas! so we could not see the snow-capped hills. Dismounting we walked down to the valley of Kulikhani, past Markhu with its suspension bridge and dharmsala, and through Chitlang. (On reaching this point in the narrative my red-haired secretary has started humming "Far away places with strange-sounding names."—Ed).

Throughout this trek it seemed that every inch of the rich soil was cultivated. Again and again, as we passed through their villages, we were struck by the thrifty and ordered industry of the inhabitants. Each house had its neat stack of wood and potato store, and every household its quota of chickens and ducks.

At this season, about a month before the monsoon is due, every man, woman and child, seemed to be in the fields—reaping, or carrying, or winnowing—and they sang and smiled as they worked in the small terraced fields of golden wheat and waving barley which stretched around us everywhere. The terraces, interspersed with the brilliant green of nursery rice-beds and the darker green of strong and healthy maize in varying growth, formed a gay patchwork.

The well-built houses, most of them double-storeyed, added to the beauty of the scene with many of their stout timber uprights and cross-beams handsomely carved ... with their well-thatched or red-tiled roofs, the walls colour-washed half white and half burnt-sienna, and the wooden windows gay with window boxes or pots of brightly-flowering geraniums.

And everywhere there was singing and smiling and cheerfulness.

After a picnic lunch a short way beyond Chitlang, we remounted our sure-footed ponies for the climb to the Chandragiri Pass (7,700 feet). Yet again our hopes of a view of the distant snows were dashed—this time by thick clouds. As we began the descent, distant rumbles warned us of an approaching storm, which broke fifteen minutes before we reached the road-head at Thankot where a station waggon from the Embassy was awaiting the arrival of a rather moist party.

By five o'clock we had arrived at the Embassy, where Richard Proud took me over and off to his house which, in olden days, was occupied by the Residency Surgeon. Again, as in 1931, I was struck by the number of rare trees, the variety of the birds, and the profusion of flowers. (At this point David's narrative closely resembles a horticultural catalogue. Just take our word for it that it must have been very lovely, and we will pass on.—Ed).

It was all peaceful and quiet and cool.

And so to the social round and daily sight-seeing. (Be patient, dear reader, Baedeker has nothing on David!—Ed).

There was sociability in plenty. Richard himself was the soul of hospitality; we paid a formal call on His Highness, and were invited to dinner or for drinks by everyone of the small European community and by the First Secretary at the Indian Embassy.

And there is so much to see ... the temples of Boddnath and Swayambunath, with their enormous eyes of Buddha following you with unceasing gaze wherever you move within their sight; of Machendranath, Mahabuddha and Pashupatinath; and the five-storeyed Nyatpola, its ten guardians paired off to flank the steps ... Katmandu's Durbar square, which contains Hanuman Dhoka, Kal Bhairab, the Royal Durbar Hall and also the lowlier old wooden building which yet has given the city its name ... Patan with its five stupas set up by Asoka ... Bhatgaon with the golden door in its Durbar square ... Balaji with its statue of Narayan recumbent in water, and its gaily-painted and carved water spouts ... the Maharajah's Palace Singha Durbar and the new Gallery, built after the earthquake in 1934, its well-planned gardens ablaze with colour.

The old Swiss Chalet of the Residency (also a casualty of the earthquake) has been replaced by a large modern house. Another modern development is the aerodrome at Gaucher which has encroached on the golf course laid out by Charles Boucher and Roy Kilburne, the electrical engineer. Roy is still in Katmandu where he has been for twenty-five years; I think that he will be retiring in two years' time.

Needless to say Richard and I reminisced regimentally to no mean tune. One evening, as we were yarning on his upstairs verandah, the clouds cleared and we had a perfect view of the distant snow-clad amphitheatre of Daurishankar, Lam Tung, and other noble peaks standing in their full splendour beyond the chestnuts at the bottom of the garden.

Came the 20th May and the start of our return journey, which (by a different route) took us over four suspension bridges erected by Maharajah Chandra in 1928. The ropeway was not in action as it had been on our way out; the motionless loads hung forlorn and stark against the sky. That night at Sisagarhi was the last of the coolth; the evening light-and-shade was very lovely; there was a new moon and, later, the stars shone crystal clear ... .

I enjoyed that trip.

Return to Burma

By Alan Wiltshire

On the first Sunday in February '86 my wife and I flew to Bangkok having obtained a seven day visa for onward travel to Burma: after a short stopover and a forty-five minute flight, our Thai Airways plane was landing at Mingaladon—seemingly unchanged over the years.

At the terminal, reception was chaotic as arrivals and departures are all dealt with in the same room and all baggage—outgoing and incoming—is pitched indiscriminately into a single heap on the tarmac. Eventually we were met by a Burman and a Karen in the teak trade—our first two days being on business with the State Timber Board: they had a taxi waiting and had booked a room for us at The Strand Hotel on the Rangoon River waterfront.

At The Strand I found not much alteration to when I had last seen it in 1947: a bit run down and slow service—bedrooms much the same and the large fans were still working: the temperature was 91 °F but it was a pleasant dry heat with plenty of sun. After settling in—we went for prawns and lobster in the dining-room—absolutely superb and very cheap—and a beer from the People's Brewery at Mandalay which was as good as ever: and so to bed at 9 pm, when everything closes down.

Next morning I was soon out on the balcony to watch the sunrise and view the activity on the Rangoon river just the other side of the road. Soon the buses—overloaded as usual with people clinging to the back and sides—were running to work: quite a lot of traffic but nothing like the amount in other cities in the East. I noticed that most men and women still wore the traditional longyi and not westernised dress. Rangoon itself had not changed much but most of the city urgently needed a coat of paint, the pavements had subsided and the kerb stones were at all angles. The Sule Pagoda is as beautiful as ever but now sits in the middle of a huge traffic island.

I visited the nearby Tourism Burma Office where all internal air and long distance rail fares must be booked and my Burmese friend helped me to book two seats for the next day to Heho in the Southern Shan States: I was told to come back that evening to collect the tickets—a typical bureaucratic delay. For the rest of the day I went to Ahlone on the western outskirts—the terminal for all the rafts of teak which float down the Irrawaddy from Upper Burma: all teak is in the hands of the state monopoly Timber Corporation and Incidentally the Deputy Director of Sawing and Marketing was a very charming and efficient Burmese lady.

Next morning the Tourism Burma bus collected us from The Strand but near Inya Lake we broke down and had to wait thirty minutes for a replacement: we had been advised to leave our case behind in safe custody and to travel with just a rucksack—which was much easier. We flew in a Fokker Friendship, which took about thirty passengers, and were soon over the desiccated paddy fields of Lower Burma with just an occasional river and pond visible. The Pegu Yomas appeared on the port side and shortly afterwards we were over the foothills of the Shan States—most of them jungle clad but a fair amount of soil erosion was clearly visible. It felt almost like coming home after many years away, as I had been stationed at Kalaw with the 4/4th and later at the Burma Army Weapon Training School—oddly enough in our old lines.

Heho Airport is nothing more than a tarmac strip in a field with a shed about the size of a village hall and is on the undulating Shan plateau twenty five miles west of Taunggyi, the administrative capital. The main road from Thazi via Kalaw to Kengtung was a mile to the South and the oxcarts were now returning from the countryside to the villages: everywhere was very dry but the fields were well tilled and just waiting for the rains in three months time.

Taunggyi market was in full swing which was very lucky for us as it takes place every five days and we had a wonderful opportunity to see representatives of the many different hill tribes who live in this region. Our destination was the Taunggyi Hotel which lies about a mile from the town centre on the Kengtung road: incidentally the Government's writ runs out some four miles east of the town and the area is controlled by Shan rebel troops.

I managed to hire a pick-up and when it turned up next morning the driver had put a deckchair in the back for me whilst my wife sat in the cab: halfway to Lake Inle I saw a flash of blue on a tree stump in the front of a small garden: I stopped the pick-up and realised that we had found a perfect specimen of an orchid called Vanda Coerulea. I was so pleased because some years ago I enquired at Kew and was told that this orchid did not always flower even in their ideal conditions. As we neared the lake, the surrounding country gradually became swampy with many water buffaloes wallowing.

Yaunghwe at the northern end is a fair sized village with many houses constructed on poles over the swamp and silt, and all around the lake edge water hyacinth is growing. After some fifty years this plant and the silt makes a layer of humus three feet thick and the Government sells this to the local Inthas in strips three hundred feet long and six feet wide: these are then towed across the lake to the villages where they are anchored and cultivated for tomatoes, cucumbers, cabbages and flowers.

When we stopped in the village we were immediately approached by three young English girls and an American who asked us to share a longboat: these have two crew and use an outboard motor—providing the only means of getting to Gwama some eight miles away where there is a daily floating market. We set off down a side canal through the swamp to the lake proper and passed waterways running at right angles: we met several longboats coming towards us full of produce for sale at Yaunghwe and also overtook others filled with goods which they had traded. All of a sudden the vista of the lake opened before us and was one of the most memorable sights that we have ever seen. Its beauty defies description with the high hills on either side, the water flat and calm with a hint of overlying mist and dotted with patches of hyacinth and isolated fishing boats: these are propelled by the famous leg rowers who wear a conical bamboo hat and stand on one leg on the stern of the boat and wrap their other leg around the oar. Every now and again we would pass a stationary boat with the fisherman holding a tall trap with a net inside: when he sees movement in the clear water he thrusts the trap to the lake bottom—nowhere deeper than ten feet—and the net drops down catching any fish within range. These Intha fishermen originally came from Tenasserim in the far South and on migration to Lake Inle re-created their own original form of agriculture and fishing.

As we neared Gwama we passed many of the long strips all fully cultivated and with narrow canals between each of them: the streets are all chaungs and business is carried out from boats which acted as floating market stalls, selling many types of fruit, vegetables and even antiques, carvings, opium weights, Shan shoulder bags and longyis. After half an hour in the market we circulated round the canals until we approached the Phaungdan Pagoda, which contains gold images of the Buddha which in September are taken round the lake in a royal barge with a large golden Karaweik bird on the prow: during this festival the leg rowers have races against each other. We disembarked near the Pagoda for a restaurant meal and watched weavers making longyis and shoulder bags; many of the houses had bamboo pots of orchids hanging outside.

Now it was time for the return journey and all this time we had enjoyed warm sunshine and wonderful views across the lake. We met up with our driver again and set off for the Pindaya cave where there are countless statues of Buddha. We headed west towards Kalaw and passed through a most fertile area with countless bullock carts turning from the fields as the afternoon was drawing in. Pindaya village itself lies behind a small lake with a high ridge running behind it: the cave is halfway up this ridge and a steep staircase runs up from the lake. The cave was absolutely crammed with Buddhas from floor to very high roof and there were many side galleries as well. When we came out there was only about half an hour of daylight left and we made haste to return to Aungban and thence to Kalaw, where we arrived in darkness.

Here we put up at the Kalaw Hotel—better known to many in 1946 as 98 Brigade HQ—and had a fine dinner before an early drive around the town next morning. The pine woods are still there and an occasional house and bungalow. After about a mile and a half we were stopped by a barrier manned by military police: the spokesman turned out to be a Pathan born in Lashio where his father had been in the army and he spoke reasonable English. He was curious that I should want to have a look round these side roads which are still army lines after forty years: he was most interested in the fact that we had started the camps in 1946 and sent a note to his CO to see if we could proceed further. When the runner returned we were allowed to go up to the HQ which was a house just the town side of where the old 4/4th Mess had been. The CO was Burmese and had no English but the 2IC understood what I was saying: they were very interested that I had been there both in 1946 with 4/4th and in 1947 with the Burma Army: however, this was now considered a high security area and it was in any case time to proceed to the plains.

And so we set off down the escarpment—many hairpin bends with dense jungle and teak forest interspersed with small paddy fields sustaining small villages: every now and then a grossly over-laden lorry or bus with people on sides, back and roof laboured its way uphill to the Shan States. The first large village was Hlaingdet, where the trade seemed to be the making of earthenware containers for water and rice: they were stacked everywhere, sometimes acting as a wall to the road; and as we ran out of the foothills the railway to Thazi ran parallel until it met the main Rangoon-Mandalay line. Thazi is a busy place with much traffic being an important rail junction—quite recovered now from the pounding it took during the War. We pressed on into Meiktila where we paused for a drink at a half-completed new hotel and then turned north on the road to Mandalay, very wide but almost entirely devoid of traffic. Sometime later we pulled up in a village for petrol—no pumps but brought out in open cans. Here it was very dry and flat though at one point we passed a large irrigation project where they were still cutting canals with bulldozers. As we neared Mandalay itself, now was the time to say goodbye to our driver and mate, who had no love for Burma proper and were glad to be returning to Taunggyi.

Our hotel faced onto the south-east corner of Mandalay Fort (the Royal Palace) with a wide moat between the road and the very thick walls: today the fort serves as Burma Army HQ. I went to the Tourist Office to book reservations on the Rangoon train.

Next morning we hired a tonga whose driver was at university and wanted to try out his English: our first stop was the Shwe Nandaw Kyaung—a very old teak building which was originally part of the Palace but was re-erected by King Thibaw on its present site as a monastery in the 1880's. All the walls inside and out are fully carved and it gives a good insight into how the Royal Palace must have looked before the flames of war destroyed it. From here it was but a short ride to the foot of the stairway to Mandalay Hill where we were asked to remove our sandals: at the bottom are two large Chinthes and the stairs are roofed from top to bottom which keeps them tolerably cool. There are in fact 1729 steps to the top but with plenty of stone seats the climb is very enjoyable.

At the three quarter mark my wife decided that as the climb was becoming steeper she would wait there for me: considering she had a hip replacement some two or three years ago, I thought that she had done extremely well. On two of the smaller temple areas there were craftsmen making teak and sandalwood beads and stringing them into necklaces: these were turned on a simple lathe operated by a bow held in the left hand whilst the man turned, bored and cut the beads with his right.

I then started up the last flight and a Burmese girl selling soft drinks from a stall acted as guide and showed me two pillars on the topmost shrine: on the left was the memorial tablet to the men of the 4/4th who lost their lives in the night attack on Mandalay Hill on 8/9th March 1945: the right hand tablet recorded that the Battalion had donated 2,500 rupees to the Abbot for restoration of the shrines. These tablets were certainly in an honoured position just near the temple bell. From this eminence there are magnificent views and looking down on either side of the hill with its rocky out-crops covered in scrub, I had a feeling of great pride in the dogged determination that must have gone into the capture of the hill: given that it had taken place at night you would have thought it impossible. After some reflection, I bought a drink from my guide and some of the wooden bead necklaces for my daughters and went down to the landing where I had left my wife—to find her surrounded by Burmese boys and girls, correcting their homework and giving them the finer points of pronunciation.

Once at the foot of the hill we set off in the tonga for a look at the Irrawaddy along a laterite road full of potholes and running through a very poor quarter. Soon we were on the banks of a large backwater with many oxen bringing logs out of the water from the remains of a raft which had come down from Upper Burma. My wife thought that this wide creek was the main river but when we came to the real thing we marvelled at its width so far from the sea. I must say that I was taken aback, my 1946 memory of it had narrowed considerably.

The following morning we took a tonga in the darkness to catch the 6 am train to Rangoon: few people were about, save for the Buddhist monks and even a file of nuns with their bowls, and there were no lights save for an occasional food stall being set up for the day's trade. Even the station lights were on a war basis, the carriages were completely unlit and there was no glass in the windows, only wooden slats. The train was soon packed—with many standing—

but this did not deter vendors of nuts, fried locusts and bottled drinks from carrying on a roaring trade, both on the train itself and through the windows. However, we left on time, still in darkness and dawn was beginning to break as we drew into Kyaukse twenty-five miles down the line, the Shan plateau making a lovely silhouette against the sun. Thazi was a very busy station and then the old familiar names—Yamethin, Pyinmana and eventually crossing the Sittang at Toungoo, this time on a proper bridge instead of the old pontoon of 1946: here the river was very low and people were washing their clothes right underneath the bridge. We were held up for some twenty minutes between Toungoo and Nyaunglebin—a few villagers walked along the track including a boy monk in his saffron robes holding aloft a lacquer sunshade; another boy with a giant shrimping net was heading for nearby ponds. Soon it was dark and we drew into Rangoon at 7.30 pm having to fight our way out of the station and thence by taxi back to the Strand Hotel, where we just managed to secure the last room for the night.

Next morning we spent in wandering round Rangoon visiting Bogyoke Aung San Market—better known in our day as Scott's Market—where you can pick up some beautiful wood carving. We bought a painting in a small shop on Sule Pagoda Road, owned by Burmese Christians who advised over a cup of tea that if ever we returned to Burma to bring Windsor and Newton paints, especially the rarer ones, and they were very willing to swap pictures for them. Similarly, my wife was asked for any spare make-up and the tip is to carry things which are easily packed and for the most part which we take for granted.

Eventually the time came to head for Mingaladon, and on boarding our Thai Airways plane all the ladies were given a spray of orchids. Looking out of the window we both felt a tremendous sadness at leaving Burma: the people are so natural and up to now untainted with the all-pervading influence of the West. We would both love to be going back.

The Winds of Change—
1947 to 1949

By Bill Tee

Bill Tee has, at long last, been persuaded to contribute to the Newsletter, and has produced the article which follows. It must be one of the most interesting accounts of the period of transition ever written—a splendid piece.

D. S. D.

In outline my story is that eight British Officers from 1st Bn 4th PWO Gurkha Rifles moved to 1st Bn 10th Gurkha Rifles; from one Regiment to another, from one Army to another, from allegiance to an Emperor to allegiance to a King, from India to Malaya (as it then was), from Amritsar in the Punjab to Kuala Lumpur in the State of Selangor.

It happened a long time ago and much that I write is possibly, even probably, inaccurate—for memory is a deceiver. But all that I now write is for me the truth, the whole truth and nothing but the truth, so help me God. The period was as climactic for multi-million peoples as for individuals. The Wind of Change, identified later, blew its hurricane track over the Indian continent with dire and historic results. As an aside the greatest soldier/statesman produced by any nation during Hitler's war declined to oversee the transition of the Indian Empire to the Republics of India and Pakistan. Archie Wavell—he will forgive my familiarity after all these years—had an unequalled depth of understanding of the peoples of the Indian continent, and it persuaded him that the time for an end of Imperial India and its independence was not yet. Rather than preside over the charnel house that he foresaw, he resigned the high office of Viceroy. Clement Attlee, the British Prime Minister of the time, brought in his playboy Prince to fill the vacancy with a brief to achieve the impossible. Well, Dickie Mountbatten did achieve the impossible but at a cost which the Lancet Magazine estimated at between seven and eight million lives lost as a consequence. Against such an awesome background, personal loyalties and heartbreak are as nothing. Yet, believe me, they were real and hurtful at the time; and still are.

In Amritsar, the Boy, Stevenson-Hamilton (also irreverently known as Huff-Puff, his initials were VEO and I am sad to admit that I do not to this day know what his given names were!) was the Commanding Officer of 1/4GR. From a base in Amritsar not too far from the Golden Temple of the Sikhs, we patrolled the countryside among the temples, the peacocks and the standing corn. We were unwilling and saddened spectators of horrible and nauseating events. My memory recalls the time as hurtful, traumatic and poignantly sad. Trains left Amritsar Station in India moving Muslims to Lahore in Pakistan and returned to Amritsar jam-packed with Hindus. Only those who have seen Indian trains packed and with coaches covered with passengers will appreciate the numbers involved; and yet some of these trains arrived in Amritsar without a living soul among the multitude that had set out from Lahore. Men, women and children were massacred and left to complete their journeys as corpses. In the countryside itself smaller numbers were done to death in the paddy and corn fields and the villages. Families who had lived in amity with their neighbours and whose ancestors had tilled adjacent fields for centuries were obliterated in the name of religion, while great men wrangled at their conference tables in London, Delhi and Karachi. What makes men great? Is it position, power, riches, or is it that the hopes and aspirations of people, when placed in the hands of leaders, give those leaders the cloak of greatness? I believe it is the latter and the souls of India's multi-millions cry out in my dreams that they were ill-represented by less than great men.

Throughout this time the Gurkhas moved among the chaos and slaughter quietly helping those in trouble; repelling savage raiders, offering practical assistance where they could. They were then, as they had been in the past, and have been ever since, magnificent servants of the Governments who employ them.

Before the first two Indian officers joined 1/4GR, Stevenson-Hamilton, for his own personal reasons, left us. Two Indian officers, Pandit and Amerkhoj, arrived to take over the Battalion and it was I who was the last British Commanding Officer of 1/4GR. Our Regimental History does not show this. Pandit and I had all of 30 hours together for the handover! I was also present at that nautch in Amritsar when 1 and 2/4GR met for the first time since the start of Hitler's war. It was some party! Quite a lot of raksi was shifted one way and another!

Notwithstanding the heartbreak that I and others knew and the multi-million dead, in the broadest sense (can anything be broader, than all those dead?) independence was probably inevitable even if the timing and method adopted for the change could have been better devised. In the aftermath of the War and of Japanese co-prosperity, of the INA, of Ghandi and the impact of the inter-war years, the spread of radio and the new impact of television, the trend of history—all these led to the events that took place around us. We were powerless to influence their torrid course. I was born in Ranikhet in the hills above Dehra Dun and I wish so much that I had had no part in monitoring those fearful years in the Punjab.

While the thunder and lightning of religious discord flashed about us we handed over 1/4 GR and, taking what farewells we could, we left by road for Bakloh. Our party consisted of James Castle, Henry Burroughs, Derek Royals, David Cotton, Tom Gibson, Ken Saxton, Mike Smith and myself—the last British officers to serve with 1/4GR. A page in the history of our Regiment turned and a new chapter began.

We left Amritsar and climbed to the cool, peace and tranquility of Bakloh. What a lovely place that was—and surely still is. I shall never forget it; I always experienced a feeling of wellbeing and homecoming as I reached the top of the slope at the edge of the 1st Battalion's parade ground with the stone wall on the right that rose above the short range in the gulley below. As I remember, No 4 Bungalow stood above the tiered steps on the other side of the parade ground. It was in that bungalow that I lived most of the time I was in Bakloh. Bakloh has a special place in my heart. It was the place where I got my first military rocket; it was delivered by Freddie Harrison, my first CO. I have never received a softer nor more devastating rocket in all the years I spent in the Armies of the King or Queen. I recall the palms on the edge of the 2nd Battalion parade ground that are the descendants of date stones abandoned there by the Hoplites of Alexander's army so many centuries ago. The panorama of the five rivers of the Punjab, seen from the Mess verandah, is with me still. A truly magnificent view. And I recall the splendid mess Library—too few of whose books I had the opportunity to read; and the rogues gallery of past Commanding Officers—where are those splendid photographs now? Do you remember the ceremony of the Quaich? Does it still persist in 4GR's Mess? I remember the Arsenal and the Quarter Guard—John Masters initiated me in the arcane ceremony of turning out the guard. Do you remember Banikhet on the road to Dalhousie and its dangerous little golf course? Every hole seemed to share the same fairway. And over the hill from Dalhousie on into the wilderness of foothills into the State of Chamba. The hand of God seemed and still seems, to have been laid on that magic and beautiful part of India.

Hamish and Mischa Mackay greeted us in Bakloh; calm oases of serenity in the shifting sands of change. Rumours of murder and mayhem came in from the villages but they seemed unlikely in the stillness and peace that prevailed in Bakloh. We were involved in the evacuation of nuns and pupils from the Roman Catholic Convent in Dalhousie; it went off without any hitch other than the unashamed tears of the nuns as they left their beloved sanctuary for ever. I remember that the resident priest had his ears syringed by our medical officer before he left—what an untidy detail to recall from that time so very many long years ago!

Finally we came to leave Bakloh—all eight of us—on our way to join 1/10GR in Rangoon. So many final and absolute farewells numbed the mind. I still feel that the soldiers thought that, come the morrow, we would all be back! We left on a bright sunny day with fleecy clouds chasing each other in the blue depths of the sky against the background of the high hills, in a variety of vehicles including two jeeps, one of which was a non-runner to be delivered to a motor pool in Pathankote. James Castle steered the non-runner on a tow rope ahead of the runner that I drove, down the hill to Dhankuta and on until the country flattened out. We then changed places and the journey was completed in a more usual towing order. This method of downhill progress is not to be recommended. It requires steady nerves in the leader—no trouble there with James of course.

From Pathankote we moved on by rail to Delhi and were accommodated at military expense in Maiden's Hotel in Old Delhi. How and when we were to move on to Rangoon was to be made known to us by GHQ. There by happy coincidence, we found Jack Masters who was on the Auch's staff at that time. He seemed a focus of sanity in the general state of flux and uncertainty that prevailed. I remember that while I waited in his office, Jack demonstrated his ability to catnap in his chair for a few minutes; an ability shared with Napoleon!

While we were staying at Maiden's, the first of a series of elaborate hoaxes on Henry Burroughs was played out. At a formal Orders Group, Henry was detailed to return to Bakloh to collect some papers that were not to fall into Indian hands. An unlikely story—but the times were unlikely! Henry fell for it hook, line and sinker! He hurried away to order a taxi and repack his kit. He was to be met by a Bakloh vehicle in Pathankote. He would then return and subsequently fly to Madras to rejoin us on our journey to Rangoon. All the detail was laid out in a movement order in the approved format. With the taxi ticking over outside, Henry bustled back and handed his heavy kit over to Tom Gibson; he saluted and asked if there was anything else as he had better leave if he was to catch his train. We had the greatest difficulty persuading dear Henry that the whole thing was a leg pull! Henry was rightly livid and I doubt that he has forgiven me even to this day. These boyish pranks continued over the years culminating in Henry being ordered over the radio by the then CO of 1/10GR, George Bolton, to move his patrolling company in the Malayan jungle to, in Henry's humble opinion, a ludicrous place; he came to the mistaken conclusion that this was another spoof set up by James Castle; Henry did not move. George Bolton was not celebrated for his sense of fun and required a lot of placating when he found that dear Henry had disobeyed his orders!

In due course we moved off by train on the long journey to Madras. There we stayed in the Connemara Hotel and met Maurice and Cynthia McCready for the first time. Maurice had been posted to 1/10GR as CO and I sadly removed the 4GR half colonel's badges that I had worn so proudly since Stevenson-Hamilton had left us from Amritsar. I still have those epaulettes in this house! From Madras I 'phoned Liz in England to tell her where I was and where I was going. The line was so very bad that she did not know what was happening, nor where I was going until my letters reached her some weeks later.

So we sailed to Rangoon from Madras arriving there among the Limbus and the Rais and a few, pitifully few, 10GR British officers. Maurice McCready took over from A. J. Stringer (funny how initials stick in the mind when much else of greater importance is totally forgotten!), 1/10GR were housed in bashas and considerable discomfort. At the "opt" only 300 ranks of 1/10GR chose to transfer to the British Army in Malaya. No "line boys" joined us and so we had no drivers or signallers when we moved but we did have the nucleus of a new battalion.

(Thinking back I find it strange that 1/10GR had not trained "hillmen" as specialists—we certainly had had many in 4GR.) I do not know why those 300 Gurkhas volunteered in the face of INA inspired difficulties and conflicting loyalties—but they did. Better pay perhaps; loyalty to their officers—they knew few of those present; loyalty to the British Crown; a sense of adventure and opting for the unknown. Service in Malaya was known to be no great shakes and we all knew that we would not have the equivalent of Bakloh or of Shillong as a home.

Those were dynamic and historic times and the small potatoes of personal involvement were nothing in the tumultuous sweep of change around us. We were blown along by the Hurricane of Change.

Leaving Rangoon was sad; too many armies had used its roads and public utilities over the war years and the city was a shambles; as indeed it still seemed to be in 1988 if the television pictures that we saw were anything to go by. We sailed to Penang in North Malaya and moved by train from there to Kuala Lumpur where we were again housed in those horrid bashas—this time on the outskirts of the town. Under Maurice McCready's direction we set out to create a fighting unit.

To start with each Regiment had its own training company; 10GR's was in Kluang in the eastern part of Johore State; 6GR were located in Ipoh, 7GR in Seremban and 2GR in the backwoods of Singapore Island. Except for 2GR housing was again in those ubiquitous bashas; a far cry from the comforts of Abbotabad and Shillong and of Dehra Dun. Our Riflemen stayed Riflemen but Naiks became Corporals, Havildars became Sergeants and Jemadars and Subedars became King's Gurkha Officers. After some time an economy of scale persuaded the powers that were, to concentrate training companies in one place; Sungei Patani in Kedah State in North Malaya was chosen. More bashas. The whole ethos of the place lacked any feeling of permanence or commitment; the place had no distinction. I spent two years there as 2IC to Freddie Shaw of 6GR. I wonder why officers of 6GR seemed to lack any sense of fun in those years. Every visit by a visiting fireman was preceded by "dry runs"! Sungeipatani was—still is probably—flat and humid and enervating—a boring place with the Training Depot located partly in a rubber estate and partly round the edge of a dusty and sultry airstrip. But I do recall the recruit who had travelled variously from the scenic splendour of his home in the foothills of the Himalayas by foot to the recruiting Depot; by strange train to Calcutta; by stranger ship over the Kalu Pani to Penang; and finally by train again on to Sungei Patani; and when at long last he set foot on terra firma he looked around and said, "Trees in straight lines— now I've seen it all!" (or Khaskura words to that effect). Sungei Patani was no sort of place to build Brigade morale and I felt then and feel now that our senior officers failed us. In Malaya any one of the hill towns of Cameron Highlands, Fraser's Hill or Maxwell

Hill above Ipoh would have been far better places—of course, they would have cost money to develop!

Six months after our arrival in Malaya, the Communist Terrorists (shortened to CTs) under the direction of Chin Peng, started their shenanigans. Their timing was awry for they gave us just that breathing space to create fighting units from the truncated rumps which had arrived in Malaya in December 1947.

As always the soldiers were magnificent but I admit now in a 4GR Newsletter that I never gave my heart to 10GR. My willingness to change my commitment finally foundered in 1957 on the 10GR's History that was published that year. It was written by one Mullaly and covered the period up to and including the Queen's Coronation in 1953. It covered the difficult years in Malaya from 1947 to 1953 after our arrival there and the fascinating difficulties and successes of welding units into cohesive fighting formations; battalions had too high a proportion of young, very young soldiers; NCOs and Gurkha officers promoted before they were ready; a hotch potch of British officers from other Gurkha Regiments. In that History no ex 4GR British officer is mentioned anywhere in the text nor in any appendix or annex! I could hardly believe my eyes when I read my mandatory copy. I have again checked this surprising fact and it is so. It's a peculiar volume of history; Archie Wavell is mentioned once; Bill Slim twice and Dickie Mountbatten, thrice. 1/4GR is mentioned eight times and Mullaly or his relatives, eighteen times. I was appalled by the affront to those officers who came with me from 4GR (and to myself!), but doubtless the author has a plausible explanation.

My allegiance remained and remains with 4GR and Bakloh and the cool places in the eternal hills up there. We lived through tremendous times and saw changes the like of which had not occurred since Ghenghis Khan troubled the peace of Asia or since Alexander's Hoplites left their date stones on the edge of the 2nd Battalion's Bakloh parade ground.

Among my treasured memories is joining 4GR in Bakloh and finding Budhe Gurung, the then Subadar-Major, in total control—most of all, of himself. He was a rock of granite, a splendid man—I have met none finer. Were he with us still the Wind of Change would still have blown away the accidents of history but he would have remained in control of all about him. For me he has remained the standard by which other soldiers were judged and it is he who to me epitomises 4GR; and it is to 4GR that my loyalty is still given.

Tales from the Malayan Woods

By Bill Tee

I suffered the misfortune of soldiering in Malaya during the excruciatingly boring years from 1948 to the end of what became known as The Emergency. This personal account which is centred on a few days and many years is written to amuse rather than to record history, although I find difficulty in dredging even a flicker of humour from our moronic military existence.

Most of us were mentally, if not physically, exhausted by our efforts in Hitler's War. Our best commanders and many of our best soldiers had long since left to enjoy the retirement that they had earned. Few names of commanders persist in my mind although Gerald Templer stands out as an exception. Others were so lacking in personality that they were not even spoken of by their Christian names. We turned in upon our regimental traditions, our routines, our sport and forgot the world.

The situation I describe is broadly epitomised by the expression "jungle bashing". No commander came up with a better method of getting to the enemy. For the uninitiated, jungle bashing was the too often repeated patrolling of jungle for no worthwhile military reason. We patrolled because we were there and commanders did not (or could not) imagine any other activity that might bring us face to face with the terrorists.

Jungle bashing meant that every one on patrol carried 70 to 80 lbs on their backs through terrain more hostile than the enemy. Patrols varied from about four or five men to about 100, and from three or four up to 40 or more days. When necessary we were re-supplied by air drop. For every 10 days on patrol we "enjoyed" about three in barracks. The expression "Jungle Bashing" was forbidden us by one of our commanders, possibly General Walker! He at least recognised that "jungle bashing" did not sound a bugle call to arms for those involved in it!

We criss-crossed the jungles, cultivations and plantations of Malaya randomly and endlessly, year in, year out, working routinely; sometimes more, much more, by luck than by judgement, we met the enemy—the CTs (Communist Terrorists). We routinely killed or wounded some of them and sometimes we lost men ourselves.

Whenever we met the enemy we were encouraged to make use of massive RAF or RAAF bomber aircraft. We had massive fire power available and were told that we might as well use it! We were told that one of the more effective ways of cracking nuts is with a sledge hammer! A truism—if only the ruddy nut would stay put! Our difficulty was to know the location of CTs long enough to hit them with bombs. Air strikes could be laid on at about three to four hours notice.

Intelligence about the enemy, the CTs, was minimal. Oh, yes! We knew names, his order of battle and his organisation, his weaponry and his political leanings but we did not know where he was or what he was doing or planning to do. We knew the names of his leaders; Chin Peng and Manup Japun come to mind even after all these years; (Manup Japun, a Malay, put it about that he led a charmed life which could only be ended by a silver bullet. He was actually killed by a very ordinary bullet fired by a patrol of 1/10 GR!). But tactical intelligence was noticeable by its absence or, if we had any at all, by its vagueness and inaccuracy.

It was a soldiers' war (Was it a war? Police action maybe?) directed too closely by remote commanders and staff who seemed to live in the lap of luxury a long way away. Routine patrolling, patrolling for the sake of being active, was the order of long and exhausting days and sleepless nights over a period of years. Gurkha battalions served in Malaya for years and years continuously with an occasional break of a year in Hong Kong. British battalions came and went more frequently.

The enormous area over which the so called emergency was conducted, consisted of rubber and palm oil plantations set in a frame of jungle (or woods!). A few tarmacadam roads and a few more dust tracks threaded through plantations. Our maps were more or less accurate (or inaccurate!) in populated areas but the jungle was shown as green without much contouring or definition. Generally rivers were marked and the high points of hills. We were often "lost"; except that we knew Malaya to be a country where, if you head east (or west) with sufficient energy, you are bound to hit the coast! We always knew more or less where we were but would often have been hard pressed to give an accurate fix to our position. As a guide "lost" patrols were advised to head downstream as they would inevitably reach civilization after a time!

The jungle varied from dense to open; from swamp to bamboo to teak. Occasional clearings were big enough for helicopters to land. Most of the jungle was flat; but some was hilly, a little, even mountainous. The thickest and most unpleasant jungle grew where trees growing in swamps had been cut down and left to grow back with mixed undergrowth; and there was plenty of that.

Temperatures at night varied from cool to warm; but by day it was never less than warm and often unpleasantly hot; but day and night, except in the hills, it was always muggy and humid. Rain fell most afternoons and we sweated—how we sweated! Fortunately drinking water was plentiful even if it had to be chlorinated and have salt added to it.

The area that concerns the nub of this story is that part of South Johore not too far from Singapore, between Kulai, Rengam and Mersing. It was important to the enemy because it gave covered access to Singapore. Generally the enemy was quiescent there as they wanted their lines of communication to be tranquil.

Because the area was important to the enemy we patrolled it often and sometimes in large numbers. On the occasion of which

I write I was sent out with about 35 men to bash the jungle in the hope that we might find something worthwhile.

We struck lucky.

On about the sixth or seventh day a recce patrol of a few Gurkhas reported that they had found a trail made by about 60 men two days ago. We moved off and followed the trail. We were not more than five miles from the jungle's edge.

Gurkhas are incredible trackers and I had learned over the long years to accept their jungle lore without doubt. We followed on and the next day the Gurkhas said we were catching the enemy. Our habit was to bivouac an hour or so before last light; send out a few local patrols; erect radio aerials and report progress; cook and eat; post sentries and sleep; move on shortly after first light. Moving in primary jungle by night is strictly for the birds. As an aside I still remember the benediction of rum in sweet tea to get me moving in the mornings after picking up my 75 lb pack! I also drank a large rum every night to relax exhausted muscle and mind so as to be able to catnap for short periods.

We were not excited as this sort of thing had happened often before without us bringing the enemy to battle. In this context "battle" sounds rather pompous but I am too lazy to find other words that would better describe the situation. On this particular evening while I waited for the radio to get through, a patrol came back quite quickly with exciting news. They had found an occupied CT camp for over 100; they had not been seen; the patrol commander, Sgt Dambarbahadur, had a map reference for the CT camp. At that time a young officer, Ivor Ramsden, was attached to my Company and, for experience, I had sent him out with Dambarbahadur. Ivor had been seconded from the Welsh Guards to my Gurkha Battalion; an unusual posting, as Guards officers do not normally soldier much further afield than Caterham. Ivor was, and is, six feet three inches tall; a splendid officer and still one of my dearest friends. I later proudly became godfather to his eldest son, David.

When Dambarbahadur had left after making his report, Ivor sat with me in the fading light while I worked out what to do. Ivor murmured that he thought the map reference which I had been given by Dambarbahadur was wrong. We discussed the why and the wherefore of Ivor's thinking.

After some thought I decided that Dambarbahadur, a splendid and hardened product of the long war years in Burma and in Malaya (where he had won the DCM) was more likely to be right than Ivor; even if Ivor had been educated at Hoppers in Wiltshire.

Anyway I made my decision and got onto our commanding officer, George Bolton, by radio. We arranged a massive air strike on Dambarbahadur's map reference; it was to be timed at first light the following morning. In all probability the CTs would not leave their camp until they had eaten their morning meal. Such was their routine.

The night passed slowly, quietly, without incident.

At the appointed hour next morning we heard the hum of 14 Lincoln bombers, dimly at first but gradually growing massively louder until they were overhead. They each released $14 \times 1,000$ lb HE bombs into the jungle about 1,000 yards from where we waited. The ground beneath us shook; and leaves cascaded from the high trees as the thunder of the bombs and the splintering of crashing trees reverberated round us.

While the thunder of the bombs was at its height the leading CT from their camp ran panic stricken into a sentry post on the outskirts of our position. He was fired on and, leaving a blood trail, escaped into the surrounding jungle.

The noise of the last bombs stopped; then the aircraft noise receded. We had not seen any of them through the high trees. The familiar sounds of jungle life started up again. We moved forward cautiously to see what the bombs had done.

The jungle was devastated, flattened; huge ancient trees had been torn from the ground and flung like match sticks against each other, what had been thick jungle was now a clearing almost impossible to walk through. The acrid smell of HE (was it cordite?) pervaded the area; but no CTs at all.

The bombs had hit Dambarbahadur's map reference precisely. Five hundred yards away at Ivor's map reference the huts, cook houses and sentry posts of the CT camp were unoccupied and untouched. Cooking pots still simmered on their fires! Abandoned equipment and clothes littered the place.

I owe an abject and humble apology to Hoppers! How could I, with any logic, accept the map reading of an untutored Gurkha NCO in preference to that of one of their past pupils? And I again tender my regrets to Ivor for doubting him! I think he may have forgiven me.

A few days after the failure of my airstrike, Stalin died; but I doubt that the impact of the military action outlined here is in any way connected to that event!

Waiting in the Jungle

By John Cross

During the retreat down the Malayan peninsula in January 1942 Naik (Corporal) Nakam Gurung of 2nd/1st Gurkha Rifles, suffered from a debilitating attack of malaria. His company commander, Captain Charles Wylie, later to look after the sherpas on the first conquest of Everest in 1953, told him to wait and that someone would come back for him. He was left by himself with a few days' rations.

Days turned into weeks, into months. When he was stronger he made traps for catching pig and fish. After some six months he gave up hope. Sitting in the cleft of branches of a big tree where he had made himself a temporary shelter he realised it was the end. Black despair and the loss of the will to live forced him to plait a vine rope, make a noose and put it round his neck. He tied the other end round a branch and jumped off. The vine snapped and he hurt his leg as he hit the ground. He then took his rifle and tried to shoot himself, but it misfired. "I am ordained to live", he thought with the deliberation of a peasant's wariness of the unusual and the unknown.

He was periodically visited by Chinese guerrillas and slowly the years passed. Peace was declared but he knew nothing about it. The Malayan Emergency started in June 1948 and he continued farming his cleared patch of jungle. The aircraft he heard, RAF fighter-bombers attacking the Communist Terrorists, were, according to the Chinese guerrillas who visited him from time to time, theirs, firing against the Japanese. And one day in 1949, some seven years after he had been told to wait and he would be fetched, a patrol of 1st/10th Gurkha Rifles came across him as he was working on his patch. Talking among themselves one said, "What a scruffy-looking man, not worth capturing is he?".

The lone man suddenly realised with a surge of hope flooding all other emotions that they were speaking his own language and he was alone no longer. The patrol's suspicions had to be allayed. They had taken him for a guerrilla and the fact that he spoke Nepali meant that he might be a spy. "We ought to kill you", they said.

Nakam Gurung tried to explain how it was he was in the jungle. "Told to wait and someone would come and fetch you?" The patrol commander was scornful. "Who is your officer, then? If you can't tell me that then we will shoot you as a spy."

And now the magic of coincidence—the adjutant of the 1st/10th a different battalion in a different army, fighting a different war, was the same Captain Wylie who had given the order to wait so many years before. And when they met, the soldier in utter sincerity and simplicity, said to his one-time company commander, "I knew you wouldn't forget to send for me". Both men broke down and wept—the soldiers never knowing that the patrol was, in fact, on the wrong compass bearing in the first place.

The tailpiece occurred when Wylie, now a major, in 1953 returning from the conquest of Mount Everest, paid a visit to the 2nd/1st Gurkhas in India. He met Nakam Gurung, now the Provost Havildar (Sergeant). Why was he still serving? Yes, he had received his back pay but, as it did not count towards his pension, he was not going to waste all those years waiting in the jungle!

Obituaries

Lieut General Moti Sagar PVSM

By Dicky Day

General Moti Saga has died in his house in New Delhi. With his passing was lost one of the small band of Indian Army Officers, who linked the past, present and future of the greatest volunteer Army the world has ever known. As the years pass, it is so easily forgotten that, in the Second World War, irrespective of race, caste or creed, 910,000 volunteers from India and Nepal joined the fight against tyranny and evil, suffered 25,000 killed, and won 4,800 decorations, including 31 Victoria Crosses.

Moti Sagar was commissioned in 1934 from the Indian Military Academy, and, after the obligatory year's service with a British Regiment, joined the 1st battalion (Queen Victoria's Own) 7th Rajput Regiment. The Army List shows, amongst other officers in the battalion, Major Cariappa and Lt Raj Bir Chopra. They, together with Moti Sagar, were three officers who, after distinguished war records, guided the Indian Army through all the problems which arose from the division of the army by the Partition of India, and ensured that it maintained its greatness and long traditions, traditions that were never inimical to the dignity of India but added to its pride. Major Carriapa became a Field Marshal, Lt Raj Bir Chopra the first Indian Commandant of the Regimental Centre of the 4th Prince of Wales's Own Gurkha Rifles, whilst the third member of this illustrious trio was the first Indian Commandant of the 2nd battalion, and became Colonel of the Regiment in June 1955, an appointment which he held until July 1969. (The Regiment had been re-titled 4th Gorkha Rifles.)

Clear headed and far seeing, he was referred to recently by a very senior serving Officer as "simply the best General I ever knew". His juniors remember him with particular affection for his guidance through each stage of their careers.

Moti epitomised the story book professional officer. First and foremost he was a gentleman every moment of his life—his standards never changed. A leader of men, and a powerful commander, yet gently spoken. His gentleness and consideration showed so clearly to all who met him. A deep thinker and scholar, his love of the Indian Army and his loyalty to it transcended all else.

After commanding the 2nd battalion of 4th Gorkha Rifles, his career progressed both as a Staff Officer and a Commander. Deputy Director of Organisation at GHQ, commanding a Brigade in the first conflict with Pakistan, Brigadier General Staff, Southern Army, then a Divisional Commander. He then moved to GHQ again as Director of Military Training, before becoming Military Secretary. Before his final appointment as Commander-in-Chief, Southern Army, he was Chief of General Staff at Army Head Quarters.

He returned to New Delhi, where his hospitality was legendary. In his house, with his devoted wife Kimmie and his beloved family, the fun loving side of his character shone through. He maintained close contact with all Officers, past and present, of the 4th Gorkha Rifles, and all Regimental affairs, and conducted a regular correspondence with retired British Officers, who never failed to meet him if they were visiting India.

A truly remarkable Officer—and to know Moti was to love him. Jai Gorakh!

By Brig Chandra S. Khanduri FICHR 1GR (Ret'd)

It was in 1960 in Solan, when acting as Liaison Officer to General Moti Sagar, that I had an opportunity to meet him. At the end of three days of my duty I became an ardent admirer of Moti Sagar and remained vocally so until his death on 31 January 1994, in his eighty first year.

It was only in 1987 that I again got close to him. The mission at that time was the biography of Field Marshal K. M. Cariappa. Despite his serious handicap of audibility he was correcting my drafts and guiding me in this work. No one has taken such pains to contribute effectively to my effort as he has. How I wish he were alive so the book could be released by him.

During the sessions on Cariappa he would often turn emotional about the values Cariappa had imbibed and which he personally emulated. To me it looked as if Cariappa was his hero, who could never deviate from the traditional moral code of an ideal Indian, and still less breach it. It also seemed that he found in me a painter who could portray his profile.

Brigadier Inder Sethi, who worked under him when he was Chief of the General Staff (CGS) in 1962, recalls that Moti Sagar worked as a Principal Staff Officer at Army Headquarters in those most difficult days with total equanimity and balance throughout the period of our reorganisation, raising and equipping the formations, moving them into new operational areas and organising their training for high altitude warfare. It was here, Inder again recalls, that the clarity of his strategic vision for the Indian Army of the future contributed greatly to its overall growth.

Born on 8th July 1913, virtually a year before the First World War, in a prestigious Kayasth family of UP, Moti Sagar completed his early education and then joined the second course at the new Indian Military Academy in 1932, from where he passed out in February 1934 fairly high in order of merit. IC-25, he used to chuckle, was as prestigious to him as Bhagwati Singh's IC-1. Moulded into Spartan discipline, a self-imposed vow of abstinence and frugality in life, he began his military career in the famous 1/7 Rajputs (Cariappa's battalion) in 1935. Before that, as the practice then was, he did an attachment to the Black Watch Regiment. He left a mark on this British regiment, who continued to keep in touch with him all his life.

How did he find life with the British, I asked him recently. He said that he thought two things added lustre to their Regimental soldiering—stoicism and a sense of humour. And what of the often repeated discrimination against Indians, I asked him further.

His answer showed the man he was, generous, pragmatic and understanding. He said, "That happened when people shied away from the British; but I never let a communication gap trouble me."

Into his Rajputs, and he was soon on the ball. Adjutant, Quartermaster, and in less than five years, posted as Instructor at Mhow. By his tenth year (1943) he had been to Staff College, Quetta, and was appointed Brigade Major of the Bannu Brigade in the NWFP. By February 1947, as Independence drew closer, he was one of the few who picked up their Acting Lieutenant Colonelcy. Those who served alongside him will remember him turning out a real Moti—the pearl gem—through his assimilation of character qualities and professionalism. He was setting standards for himself to be emulated by others.

Independence, Partition and Indianisation brought Moti to the Brigade of Gorkhas and in command of the Second battalion of the Fourth Gorkha Rifles (2/4GR). Ten months was not much of a command, especially of the Gorkhas, in whose case not only was their language different but so were their drills, procedures, customs and traditions. An intensive course in Gorkhali helped him. Even outside the Regiment, later on, he continued to study and learn the language and all about the Gorkhas, who were to become his true regimental love. "We are not only known by the Regiments in which we were commissioned but equally by the battalions we command," he would say; and he would add, "Make your command a memorable contribution, a new experience."

In 1947 the Gorkha Brigade, now officered by Indian officers, needed reorganisation and they (the officers) had to prove their true worthiness to the men and their regiments, whose chivalry and gallantry were already legendary. Fortunately for the Gorkha Brigade, officers like L. P. Sen, Prem Chand, Korla, Pathania, Palit etc, had filled the gap admirably and they all began to provide the essential leadership. The British, too, continued to oversee this function with fatherly affection. Bill Slim, Joe Lentaigne, and so on, remained as Colonels of the Regiments and thus helped the Indians settle down.

When he took over as Colonel 4 GR, one of the important tasks that lay before Moti (and, indeed, Sen) was to find a new and permanent home for the combined Centre of 1 and 4 GR. It had moved from Dharamsala to Chakrata, and was then made to move to Dehra Dun; but that, too, served no useful purpose. In arranging a permanent shift to Subathu most credit, I think should go to Moti. Equal credit should also go to him for fostering an esprit de corps in the Gorkha Brigade there. That spirit he continued to espouse whenever he had an opportunity. His last clarion call was at the Gorkha Brigade Dinner in November 1993. "Keep the flag flying and spirits alive," he had said on that night.

Moti's rise in the Army had been enviable, even meteoric. On completion of his command of 2/4GR he did a useful stint as Deputy Director of Organisation and, by the end of 1948, he took over command of 5 Infantry Brigade. He attended the JSSC in UK in 1951, and on return he came to Southern Command as its BGS. By 1956 he was asked to be the Commandant of the Infantry School, Mhow. His rise continued, as it should have done. By 1957 he was commanding 26 Infantry Division in J & K. The post of Director of Military Training followed in 1958; and by 1960 he was planning officers' careers as Military Secretary. His appointment as CGS (later redesignated Deputy Chief of the Army Staff) taxed him to the core, but it was during his tenure that the Indian Army rose from 300,000 to 1,000,000.

By early 1965 Moti was GOC-in-C Southern Command, deeply involved in keeping the Pakistani incursions into the Kutch in check, and later controlling a limited offensive against it, while the main battles raged in the Punjab and J & K. By the time he retired in 1969, he had had one of the longest tenures of an Army Commander and he had served the country for three and a half decades. He added to its history and he was a history in himself.

Moti was a quiet and a simple man, who made no ostentatious show of the virtues he believed in, nor did he display openly his long row of medals showing meritorious service. Even when the Government awarded him a PVSM he gracefully accepted it as an honour. His letter heading, in fact, never showed it. He wanted to be known and remembered just as "Moti".

But if Moti was a gem in his personal qualities and attributes he was equally a gem-cutter, who moulded people, especially the officers he commanded or those who came in contact with him. While knowledge, sincerity, loyalty and hard work (to quote his brother), were his great virtues, he was also a trainer, a persuader, a preacher and a crusader for these qualities among the officers. In 1964, I recall, he addressed a gathering of officers where he spoke on "Leadership", and he said, "The nation has done us great honour by commissioning us as officers, it is now our moral duty to repay the Government by trust and dedication." It meant a lot to us. His own standards of leadership and personal conduct epitomised what he valued.

Another strong point of his leadership and individuality was his human approach to all problems. He did not hesitate to correct an erring person, but he cared to do it without causing grievous affront or wound to his human dignity. In the words of Mrs Moti Sagar (married for 53 years) he never hurt or let anyone down. I could see that personal success repaid by the way the Army planned a ceremonial funeral for his last journey; by the thousands of callers who thronged the house for condolence; and by the rare feeling that Harish Dutta conveyed, when he said at the Nigam Bodh Ghat that day, "I have never heard anyone speak ill of Moti." A great tribute, I would say.

In conclusion, I would not hesitate to mention his command of the English language. If I ever read good English, I say, it was by Moti. He wrote much after Francis Bacon's style of precise, comprehensive and measured language. There are few who could write so faultlessly and charmingly.

My meetings with General Moti Sagar filled me with joy and always made me enthusiastic to meet him again. The reason was simple. Moti was a true gem of a man and an officer and a gentleman of yester-year, from whose glory the Indian Army of today draws its sustenance.

Sweet Memories

By Brig Rajbir Chopra

Although I was posted to the Regiment in January 1948, in a sense the story begins earlier. At the time of the partition of India in August 1947, I was an instructor at the Staff College in Quetta. Although it had been decided that the Staff College would go on "undisturbed" until November 1947, Army Headquarters issued orders towards the end of September that I was to move as soon as possible to Dinapore in Bihar as GSO 1 at the Area Headquarters there. The aftermath of partition was at its height and Bihar was the scene of much communal barbarity. Major General H. H. (Hugh) Stable was in command there.

Rail and other communications between Indian Army Headquarters and establishments located in the newly formed Dominion of Pakistan were extremely ropy. In fact I first heard my posting orders over All India Radio! The next leg of the exercise was the physical business of moving out of Quetta and crossing the sub-continent to far off Dinapore. With the virtual breakdown of the administrative machinery and mob rule rampant across most of the Northern and Eastern parts of the land, there were strict orders that not less than a company of troops would carry out any move. This meant that even individual posting orders could only be carried out when an opportunity to travel with a Company could be found.

My family "contingent" at the time consisted of seven individuals; Kamal, our daughter Veena, our son, Ranvir, who was on his summer holidays from the Welham Preparatory School in Dehradun, plus myself and in addition, Kamal's sister and her two children who had come to us in July to "spend the summer"! In truth nobody repeat nobody had ever imagined the extent and intensity of the violence which broke out soon after the 15th August 1947 right across the land and particularly in the North Western and Eastern parts of India and Pakistan.

Mercifully, the Royal Air Force was still flying between the two Dominions on special missions and, once again, we (Lt Col Leslie Sawhny, who had been posted as GSO 1 to East Punjab Area, and I) received instructions over All India Radio that we should hold ourselves in instant readiness to fly out of Quetta in any Service aircraft which might happen to be going in the direction of the Dominion of India.

The Chopra family and guests, therefore, had not only kept their "accompanying baggage" in immediate readiness—the heavy baggage was to come out with the main Staff College party in November but we used to pack our beddings every morning, only to unpack them again at bed time. On the 4th October we received another message over All India Radio that the new Agent to the Governor for Baluchistan was flying to Quetta in a VIP Dakota of the Governor General's flight and we were to fly out of Quetta and into Delhi in that aircraft. The "Chopra family" left for Quetta airfield in the afternoon on the 5th October, escorted by a number of brother officers, including Moke Murray (Col E. D. Murray DSO OBE) of the Regiment (he was attending the course as a student and became an extremely close friend of ours) who had ostensibly accompanied us to say goodbye but were in fact armed with loaded revolvers, such were the conditions in the countryside even immediately outside the Cantonment area.

We landed in Delhi the same afternoon and a dispatch rider from Army Headquarters met me at the airfield with an envelope which, I thought, must contain our rail tickets for Dinapore. On opening it I found instructions that we were being put up at the Khyber Pass Mess at the furthest end of old Delhi and that I was not to proceed to Dinapore but, instead, to report to the Director of Staff Duties at Army Headquarters the following morning!

The DSD, Brig S. P. P. Thorat, DSO, who was to become CGS and finally to retire as an Army Commander, apologised for the change in my orders and added that he had specially asked for me to be posted as GSO 1 in SD4, which was the Section responsible for co-ordinating all troop movements within India and between India and Pakistan. I then said my piece, which I had duly rehearsed and had intended to say to General Hugh Stable immediately on arrival at Dinapore. I had been away from troops since the end of 1944 and, whilst I would naturally carry out whatever assignment was given to me, I would be grateful if I could return to regimental duty at the earliest. Brig Thorat responded by promising that he would not ask me to stay for one day longer than three months.

Those were truly hectic and unusual days. Although there was serious trouble between the two countries, telephone communications between the two Army Headquarters had somehow been kept going. I used to speak to my opposite number in Pakistan Army Headquarters, John Young, at least once a day and we would exchange information about the moves of units from one Dominion to the other. John was a most extraordinary and highly decorated Medical Officer and must have been one of the few doctors ever to have held the appointment of GSO 1; he had been a student at Quetta during my time as an instructor and we knew each other well.

After a fortnight of a fourteen hour a day schedule I decided that I would take one Sunday afternoon off and spend it peacefully with the family in Lodhi Gardens. We used to leave in the Office, daily, complete details of our movements during non-working hours, so that we could be contacted in an "emergency with the emergency". Precisely that happened on this Sunday at about lunch time, when a dispatch rider tracked me down with a message that the "General Sahibs" wanted me in the Office. On arrival I was ushered straight into the room of the then Chief of Staff, Lt Gen Sir Roy Bucher, where I found myself in the company of all the PSOs at Army Headquarters plus the DSD. The first information of the Kashmir trouble had been received at Army Headquarters that day.

By the following morning an infantry battalion had already been flown into Kashmir and that was the beginning of perhaps the busiest couple of months in my entire working life. After a week I remember taking to the DSD a tabulated statement of about 300 unit moves which were pending, all of them "operational immediate"— moves between India and Pakistan, moves into Kashmir, moves to strengthen the forces on the Punjab border and moves out of the princely State of Hyderabad as the Nizam evidently did not want our troops there! My simple question was "which of these are more operational immediate than the others?" The DSD and I went into the Chief of Staff's room with this pretty picture and, thankfully, between the two of them they worked out an order of priority, which made life relatively orderly thereafter.

On the day that my 90 days' stint was complete, I found that my boss was in the Military Hospital in Delhi Cantonment with a boil on his posterior (through long hours in the chair, I suspect) and I was told that he would most likely be kept there for a few days. I decided to take the risk of seeing him in his sick bed and reminding him of his promise on the day of my arrival at Army Headquarters.

I was relieved to find Brig Thorat in a most equable mood despite being in pain—in fact he was one of the most calm and unflappable officers under whom I have ever worked. He said that he had not forgotten his promise and had in fact requested the Military Secretary to post me in command of his own old Battalion, the 2/2nd Punjab Regiment (I belonged to the 7th Rajput Regiment at that time). Here was a completely unforeseen situation and I had to do some pretty swift thinking. I told Brig Thorat how deeply honoured I felt that he had considered an outsider like me to be fit enough to take over command of his own beloved Battalion. However, I was a Punjabi and the troops in that Battalion would not be new to me. On the other hand, just at that time there were Gurkha units with virtually no officers—most of the British Officers having left already—and I wondered whether I would be considered good enough to be posted to one of those. To his eternal credit, Brig Thorat took this virtual turning down of his own Battalion by me in a most wonderful manner. Instead of blowing off his top, as I thought he might do despite his phlegmatic disposition, he said he entirely understood my request. He went further and immediately telephoned the Military Secretary and asked him whether it was possible to meet my desire.

Before we reach Bakloh, let me narrate another incident which, in fact, constituted my first contact with the Regiment. Sometime in November 1947 I received an SOS from my family that a great aunt of mine was still in one of the ancestral houses in Lahore, having refused to move out when that particular branch of the clan left Lahore in a hurry in August. I took two days off for this errand and remember being given a three ton lorry together with an escort from our 2nd Battalion, which was then in Amritsar, for my trip to Lahore and back. We left early one morning and returned the same evening, complete with the great aunt and every possible piece of baggage which could go into the three-tonner, with the escort perched on top of the mound, keeping a look out in all directions.

Kamal, our two children and I arrived in Bakloh late one afternoon and the date must have been the 18th of January since all other accounts say so. That would mean that I started taking over command on the following day—my birthday. Very appropriate, for a new birth it undoubtedly was. We were given a most cordial welcome by David Davidson, who had taken over command of the Centre a few days earlier after handing over the 2nd Battalion to Moti Sagar. We were put up temporarily in one of the bungalows below the road leading to Leslie Lines and I think it was the one next to the bungalow which gained fame later in Jack Masters' "Bugles and a Tiger". It was almost dark when we got into the house and I then realised that we would soon be getting used to living in a peace station without electric lights.

It had been arranged that we should dine with an officer who lived in the adjacent bungalow and in due course we trooped out in single file, led by my orderly carrying a hurricane lamp. The footpath to the next door house went through some fairly tall grass and mercifully nobody else in this little party saw what I saw; a sizeable feline tail disappearing into the undergrowth and away from us. It was too large and too far above ground level to be that of a common-or-garden cat and there is no reason why it should have been created by my imagination; Jack Masters' book was written many years later. We arrived at our host's bungalow without further let or hindrance and I did not mention the incident to anyone, least of all to the family, until many weeks later.

Taking over from a gentleman such as David was the smoothest of operations. Much more important was the friendship which sprang up immediately between the two of us, with never a ripple or even an awkward moment. Everything was fully accounted for, except for some mess silver in Bombay and one important piece which was missing. More about this part of the story later.

With the handing over completed, I asked David what his next posting was. He replied that he had received no instructions from Army Headquarters or any other Headquarters. I thereupon asked David whether he would like to stay on at the Regimental Centre until the end of his contract, which was due to give over in about two months, on the 31st March. Such was the depth of our relationship within even that short period of three days that I felt absolutely certain that David would never be in my way. In fact, I would welcome such an arrangement because his presence would give the other officers and myself the only possible opportunity which we would ever get of learning about the Regiment from someone who knew it well and was utterly devoted to it.

The conditions were so fluid in those exciting times that one thought nothing of sending a signal directly to Army Headquarters. I signalled the Military Secretary that Col Davidson had handed over command of the Centre to me and, unless MS Branch had some plans for him, David and I would be equally happy if he were to remain attached to the Centre until the end of his service with the Indian Army on 31st March. Overwhelmed by problems as they were at that time, I think MS Branch were grateful that this particular problem had not merely been put to them but a solution had also been suggested in the same breath. A reply came back in record time accepting the suggestion, which made us one of the most fortunate Gurkha Regiments in the Army, because I do not think that any of the others were blessed with this kind of continuity.

I am trying to recall my feelings after a gap of 40 years and the main thing that comes back to me is just one distinct conclusion which I evidently arrived at in the manner that most of us do in human affairs, without necessarily going through the formal step-by-step thought-processes of "appreciating a situation". Here was a unit which I had taken over in splendid working order and, whilst it is natural for one to wish to run things one's own way, in order to make improvements in line with one's own experience and judgment, it was clear to me that my main task was to establish a strong bond between the new set of officers on the one hand and the JCOs and men on the other. I could sense that, whilst everything was running smoothly, there was a latent question which one could almost see in the eyes of the JCOs and men and this could be summed up in the two words "ko ho?" The JCOs and men wanted to feel sure that their new officers would take care of them in at least something approximating the same way in which generations of dedicated officers had done in the 90 years since the Regiment was first raised.

The first priority, therefore, was to ensure that my officers were of the right type and "clicked" with the men. Just at that time came a very welcome letter signed by the Military Secretary himself and addressed personally to each officer who had been placed in command of a Gurkha Unit. Its gist was something like this. "I have been directed by the Commander-in-Chief to tell you that you have been hand-picked to take over your present command, because he considers it of the highest importance that the change-over in the officer ranks of these units should be such that there is no lowering of the morale of Gurkha troops. You will, therefore receive every possible assistance from the Military Secretary's Branch in your task. You will be left undisturbed even when your turn for promotion comes so that continuity may not suffer. Being passed over in this fashion will not affect your career adversely but, on the other hand, successful command of a Gurkha unit will be considered a special feather in your cap".

The assurance of "every possible assistance" from the Military Secretary was particularly welcome because it very soon became clear to me that two of the officers posted to me needed to be changed. Fortunately, a conference of all Gurkha Unit Commanders was called at Army Headquarters at the end of January and I was able to shed these officers without much loss of time. However, the manner in which the wheels of authority grind is familiar to all of us and I should be surprised if this were very different in the years before 1948 or at the time of this writing. The day after I had ben assured that these two officers would be posted away from the Centre, I was once again passing by the Office of the individual in MS Branch who had given me that assurance when the Commandant of another Gurkha Regimental Centre came out of that Office beaming, with a freshly signed letter in his hand. As I knew him well, I took the liberty of asking him what could make anyone so happy in a corridor at Army Headquarters. I knew that he was desperately short of officers but when he showed me the letter, I had my work cut out controlling my first reaction. I found that my two discards had been off-loaded on to him!

Almost immediately after taking over command, I naturally established communication with General Sir Arthur Mills, who was then our Colonel. I like to think that, despite distance and lack of personal contact, rapport was very soon established between us as a result of this exchange of letters. Both of us spoke from the start of "past and present officers" as distinct from "British and Indian Officers" and I shall always remain grateful to Uncle Arthur for his tremendous understanding and his patience with someone so much younger in both age and experience. It was soon agreed that the boxes containing Regimental silver, which were lying in Bombay and waiting to be shipped to Malaya, should return to Bakloh and I immediately sent Major Uzgare, the senior Company Commander who, incidentally, hailed from Maharashtra, on "temporary duty" to Bombay. With him went an escort of a NCO and three riflemen and in due course the boxes returned to Bakloh. I had them opened post haste because, unknown to anyone else, what I was looking for most of all was the missing hunting knife. Unfortunately, it was not there.

Within a fortnight of taking over command, I felt sufficiently confident to be able to tell the Acting Subedar Major that henceforth everyone was to speak to me in Khaskura and if I did not understand, I would seek a translation in Hindi. I was fortunate, having studied Hindi and Sanskrit in School; the base for Gurkhali is, of course, Sanskrit. I had already started learning the language formally under the excellent guidance of Honorary Lieutenant Babar Singh Thapa and within three months I was able to pass the elementary examinations, both written and oral. I was then in a strong position to "persuade" the other officers, because I felt that if I could find the time for this very necessary first step in the command of our men, there was no reason why they should not be able to do the same.

My task was made a great deal easier by the presence of the four Gurkha JCO's who had recently been granted Officer Commissions, Agam, Gaggan Singh, Manbir and Bhagwan Singh. Agam in particular was a veritable pillar of strength; he had extra-ordinary vision for a JCO and his love of the Regiment was unbounded. His advice, always given fearlessly and, if necessary, even without being sought, was without question or exception in the best interest of all concerned in the new circumstances.

Having been given the honour of taking over such a fine command, I did not feel the need to make any major changes and this greatly helped in achieving the primary aim of creating a comforting feeling amongst all ranks that "business went on as usual". Almost the only change that I did make was to decide that I would not live in the traditional "Colonel's Bungalow" atop the hill adjacent to Leslie Lines. The bulk of the Regimental Centre with all the training companies was located in Tytler Lines and, therefore, I chose Bungalow No 19, next to the Church. From there I could hear the "madals" playing in the lines in the evenings and when I could hear that lovely sound I knew that all was well.

Unfortunately, a Subedar Major for the Centre had not been appointed before my arrival. This was not surprising, with the number of changes that had taken place in the hectic months between August '47 and January '48. Besides, David had hardly taken over command of the Centre when I arrived on the scene. A somewhat ticklish situation, therefore, arose because I was told that Subedar Lal Krishan Gurung had been specially brought over from the 2nd Battalion for promotion to Subedar Major. However, he was not the senior-most and, whilst I could also see even in the short time that I had been there that he was more suitable than the senior-most Subedar, I felt that I could not supersede the other man since my acquaintance with the Centre and, indeed, Gurkhas was only a few days old.

I did not like making this decision but I felt and still feel that in the circumstances it was the best one. Both David and Agam saw my view-point, I think. When Subedar Lal Krishan came up in Orderly Room and submitted that he wished to proceed on retirement, I was able to persuade him that he should not do so because I felt sure that, in the end, he would be the winner. I am glad that subsequent events turned out as I thought they would and Lal Krishan finally retired as an Honorary Captain after many more years of devoted service and therefore with additional honour and recognition.

I think it is as well to record now the story of the missing piece of silver. This was the hunting knife presented by Edward VII when he visited India as Prince of Wales in the last century. The family of the recipient had given it in the safe keeping of the Regiment and, although David and I searched high and low, there was no sign of it anywhere. Meantime, I was receiving letters from the current head of the family, asking that the hunting knife be returned to him. Not the prettiest of situations to find one's self in! I dared not disclose the truth to him or, indeed, to anyone else except David, who of course knew the correct situation. I, therefore, wrote off in reply that although times were difficult and disturbed, there was no reason to think that the Regiment would not go on as before and therefore, the most suitable place for the hunting knife was the Regimental Centre Mess.

David returned from Malaya to spend the Dushera of 1948 with the Regiment. Kamal and the children were away and I was, therefore, having all meals in the Mess at the time. One morning, whilst we were having breakfast together in that delightful glazed verandah at the back of the Mess, the conversation turned once again to this missing article and I thought aloud "Surely such a present could not have been made by any old back-yard silversmith". The name of Wilkinson suggested itself to both of us simultaneously and, as a result, I wrote off to Wilkinson's in London the same morning, providing them with the full description of the hunting knife as given in one of the Appendices to our Regimental History, with complete details of the size, shape and the inscriptions on the obverse and reverse. Back came a reply by the next airmail, confirming that they had indeed made that piece of silver for His Royal Highness. I immediately placed an order for an exact replica to be made and requested our Military Adviser in the High Commission in London, who was an old friend, to collect it personally and send it by the hand of the next officer returning to India. This is the piece which now adorns the Regimental Centre Mess and I hope the telling of this story will not in any way diminish the value of the gift either for the Regiment or for the recipient's family.

Soon after I had taken over, there was an incident involving the family of one of the other ranks. I was relieved to learn that such cases were traditionally dealt with by a "Panchayat" of Gurkha Officers, their recommendation being subject to ratification by the Commanding Officer. What a sensible arrangement and how well it has worked over the years.

A few weeks later, however, along came a more serious matter where the wife of one of the senior-most Gurkha Officers from our 2nd Battalion charged the Subedar-in-charge of that Battalion's rear party with trying to break into her quarter in the middle of the night! A highly ticklish situation in every sense of that word, but the "Panchayat" was more than equal in its task. I went over the evidence most carefully, before coming to the same conclusion as the Panchayat; it was clearly a trumped-up charge. I decided that this particular wife would have to go back to Nepal as an exemplary case. Luckily for me, Moti Sagar was commanding our 2nd Battalion; Moti and I had been together in the 1st Rajputs before the war and knew each other extremely well. Although we could not meet and had to write to each other about this incident, Moti supported me to the hilt and the errant wife's good man came up from Amritsar, where the Battalion was stationed, to collect her. The entire matter was handled in low key and in the strictest confidence with only a handful of people knowing the real reason for the lady's departure. The husband took the decision in absolutely the right spirit and all went smoothly except, I heard later, that after reaching Amritsar where they halted for the night enroute to Nepal, the lady had a swipe at her husband with a khukri—for "taking it lying down" I suspect. Luckily the khukri got stuck in the canvas of the tent on its upward stroke!

Brigadier Raj Bir Chopra

By Dicky Day

One of the best known Officers of the Indian Army, and a friend of many very senior Officers of the British Armed Forces, died peacefully in his New Delhi home on the 20th August 2003 at the age of 87 years.

Raj Bir was one of the first Indian Officers to be commissioned into the old Imperial Indian Army in 1936—when the relative Army List shows as his classmates two future Field Marshals!

Before the Second World War it was the custom that cadets from the Indian Military Academy, Debra Dun, on being commissioned, would spend the first year of service in a British Infantry battalion.

2nd Lieutenant Raj Bir Cbopra reported for duty with the 1st Battalion of the 22nd (Cheshire) Regiment at Kasauli in the Shimla Hills in July 1936. Thus began an association which lasted well beyond the year Raj Bir Chopra spent with the Cheshires, culminating in June 1997 in an invitation to become an Honorary Member of the 22nd (Cheshire) Regiment Officers' Association.

The time Raj Bir spent with the Cheshires may have been short but the friendships forged continued after both had gone their separate ways; through correspondence and the hospitality he showed to Cheshire Officers passing through or posted to India over many decades.

Amongst his contemporaries in the Cheshires, many of whom are sadly no longer with us, Raj Bir Chopra is remembered for his sense of humour, his determination to excel at all aspects of soldiering, his sporting prowess, especially on the cricket field, and his enjoyment of life.

In 1948 just after Indian Independence, and the division and handover of the Indian Army, Raj Bir became the first Indian Commandant of the 4th Prince of Wales's Own Gurkha Rifles

Regimental Centre. He came with a very special arrangement he had made whereby he had direct access to the Commander-in-Chief—a privilege he used rarely, but to great good effect. All Officers posted to the 4th were of very high quality, and led by Raj Bir rapidly assimilated Regimental tradition and pride, and in next to no time were speaking Gurkhali relatively fluently.

A tremendous liaison between the past and present was established—a close friendship which exists to this day. Visits are made regularly to the Regiment in India by old British Officers, and in turn Indian Officers, some very senior indeed, have been welcomed at our annual Remembrance Day at Stoke Poges, where the Fourth have what is probably the only dedicated Indian Army Regimental Memorial in the UK.

Serious illness forced Raj Bir's early retirement, as otherwise he would surely have reached the highest rank. He continued to exercise great influence over his successors. With his passing an era has ended.

He was truly the rock on which the Regiment of today is founded—a very special unit steeped in history, traditions and valour.

Raj Bir, we salute you. You will never be forgotten.

Frankie Redl

By Robert Williams

Not long ago Martin Fuller told me that David Redl, the son of Frankie Redl, had approached him, to see if he could discover more about his father's life. Frankie had died in 1992, but had apparently seldom discussed his experiences. I therefore sent David a copy of my book "Ambush in the Shahur Tangi", in which Frankie is mentioned several times.

I knew Frankie in Gardai in 1946/7, but I had also known him in Bakloh in 1941, and it so happened that his wife Joan's, 28th birthday was on the 13th April 1941, the day after my 21st. It was therefore agreed that we should hold a joint party. I know that Tom Hughes was also one of the hosts, but I cannot remember why.

Someone, presumably Frankie, decided to hold a "Shipwreck Party" in their bungalow, to which nearly all BOs and wives in Bakloh would be invited, and I have been able to send David a copy of the original invitation, which I have in my scrapbook, and which was:

Radio Bakloh

"The following Admiralty Communique has just been received:

> *We regret to announce the loss of HMS Carnegie, on the Goddam Islands, in the vicinity of Bakloh Harbour, at 4.0 pm on the 7th of April, through the incompetence of the joint mastership of Messrs Redl, Hughes and Williams. Reconnaissance aircraft of the Bakloh command report that all survivors presented a most peculiar and ill-clad appearance. It is hoped that all survivors—**however unsuitably clad**—will have contrived to battle their way to these barren (but otherwise hospitable shores) by 7:30 pm on the 12th April"*

Everyone except the Berkeleys having answered this was sent to them:

> *"This is Bakloh calling. One raft of HMS Carnegie is still missing, with a crew of two survivors. It is believed to be battling a storm off Cape Restous. Observers please report any further news of this craft."*

In the event, the Redls' cleared all furnishings from their sitting room, and strewed sand on the floor, placed greenery all round the room, and lit it by candles placed in jam jars. Frankie then stole the show by appearing in one of his wife's nighties. Following this, a good time was had by all 21 people there.

In his reply, David said: "Some party that must have been, because I can remember my Mother telling me, many years later, that at some stage of the party, ink was thrown over everything and it took weeks to get remotely removed." He goes onto say: "Whose idea was it to have a 'Shipwreck Party' anyway? If it was my father's idea he was, though little did he know it at the time, bringing a curse upon my mother and me, and that happened just over a year later. On the 6th November 1942 the ship SS City of Cairo on its way from India to Recife in Brazil, was sunk in the middle of the South Atlantic by a German U-Boat. My mother and I, two years old, were on board. After the sinking we spent two weeks in a lifeboat (one of only six) before we were picked up by another British ship and dumped on the island of St Helena. There we spent six months, before being transferred to another ship, which joined a convoy, again under U-Boat attacks, and got us back to the UK. Because of the fate of some of the other lifeboats from the City of Cairo, a journalist by the name of Ralph Barker decided to write a book about this story, published in 1984. The title is: "Good Night; Sorry for Sinking You".

These were the last words of the U-Boat Captain before he left the scene where the Cairo had gone down, but where some of the lifeboats had managed to get away. The best bit of the story for me personally was actually meeting the U-Boat Captain, Karl Friedrick Merten, on HMS Belfast in the middle of the River Thames back in 1984. What he was not reckoning with was, first, having to meet some of the survivors that he knew nothing about, some 42 years later, and, secondly being spoken to in fluent German. My German is reasonable, having lived and worked in that country, on and off, for 17 years!

The meeting was arranged by the Ellerman Line, which had owned the ship, to commemorate the publication of the book. Ten out of the original 200 survivors (out of 300 on the ship) attended.

Kapitan zur See K. F. Merten, commander of U-68, made the special journey from his home in Waldshut, near the Swiss German border. He had sunk 29 allied ships, totalling 186,064 tons, between September 1941 and November 1942. The City of Cairo, being the last. He was highly decorated and was used by the German propaganda machine to boost naval morale.

The City of Cairo's cargo included, it is rumoured, silver bullion now valued at £20 million. It was on its way to America in payment of just a little bit of Churchill's shopping list.

As an annex to my story about the Redl family, a friend of ours, who lives a few miles away, was at the High Commission of India in London recently, to obtain visas for him and his wife to go to Goa in January. He found himself sitting next to a man he did not know, but who was also waiting for visas for India. In the course of conversation it transpired that this man had had connections with Gurkhas and had recently been in correspondence with me.

Our friend saw me in this village a few days later and told me the story, although he could only remember that the man was called David. I remained in the dark about his identity until I received a Christmas card from David Redl, telling the tale from his point of view. It is a small world!

Hon Secretary's note:
David Redl joined the 2nd Battalion 2nd KEO Goorkhas in July 1960 on a Regular Army Short Service Commission. He was the Intelligence Officer for most of his time in the Battalion.

Re-union 1998

By Harinder Sodhi

An ex-British Officer and a Gorkha, then Rifleman, now Subadar, met recently after having fought together in the same battalion during the Burma campaign of the World War II. The occasion was the reunion of the 4th Gorkha Rifles at Subathu, and the two had served together in its 3rd battalion, which had also taken part in the Chindit operations. Subathu, the home of 14 Gorkha Training Centre, has just hosted the reunion of the 4th Gorkha Rifles.

Reunions are an occasion for nostalgia when old comrades meet after long gaps—a bonding between the old and the new, remembering that the serviceman of today is the ex-serviceman of tomorrow; a means of passing on Regimental values and traditions. Continuing the very strong ties that make regiments into an extended family. These facets are unique to the Army service and bonding that transcends all time, language, culture and religion.

The battle of Malaun, fought in 1815 between the British and the Gorkhas, was the start of a long and very fruitful association between the Gorkhas and the Indian authorities. The very first Gorkha unit raised was at Subathu and now, after changing a number of designations, is the 1st Gorkha Rifles. The last Gorkha Regiment to be raised by the East India Company was the 4th Gorkha Rifles in 1857 at Pithoragarh. Under the British the two Regiments found their permanent homes in Dharamsala and Bakloh, respectively, but these had to be given up after Independence due to the perceived danger from across the new border. Considering the traditional close association between the two regiments, it was decided to merge the two regimental centres, first at Dharamsala, then shifted to Chakrata and finally at Subathu, which now houses the only Regimental Centre in north India, west of Lucknow.

This was abundantly evident during the reunions. Opportunity for Officers, serving and retired, and the jawans of the same categories, to mix and recall past events, hardships and achievements, brought a glow of recognition and pride on all faces, obscuring, for a while at least, the current problems, whatever they might be. It was so easy to slide back into the old associations and attitudes, irrespective of the vintage dividing them. The participants ranged from pre-Independence British Officers who had come specifically for the occasion, to jawans of the same vintage, through the post-Independence to the current serving ones. Old associations do not die. There were cases of the grown up children of past officers attending and becoming very much part of the ambient atmosphere.

The dedication and sentiments of those taking the trouble to attend has to be admired and emulated. Such close feelings can only exist where the brotherhood is knitted; by living, eating, fighting and dying together.

The Regimental Centre was the personification, like all cantonments, of neatness and cleanliness. A lot of development has taken place for the welfare of the jawans, including cheap shopping facilities, which also provides employment to the families of the jawans. The sight of so many cheerful and ever-smiling Gorkhas of both sexes, and exchange of "Jai Gorakh" greetings between officers and jawans every time they meet, is indeed very stimulating and infectious.

The 4th Gorkhas had a contingent of 21 from Britain. Among the oldest ones attending were retired Brigadier B. C. Pande, a sprightly 85 years, and the only Padama Shree of the armed forces. After the reunion some of the British officers went to Bakloh where they had served with the Regiment.

In all among those attending, there were 10 Lieutenant Generals and Major Generals, 5 Brigadiers and 75 other officers. The number of JCOs and jawans attending were 680. The oldest among them was of 1935 vintage, having retired in 1950.

The 4th Gorkhas was known as the most travelled Regiment during the British times, having seen action in Europe, China, the Middle East, Gallipoli, the Caspian area, the Far East, apart, of course, from service in all parts of India. Right now its 2nd Battalion is doing UN duties in the Lebanon.

The Regiment has produced a large number of senior officers, including the Vice-Chief of the Army Staff. Its officers have been the first two Commandants of the Indian Military Academy, Dehra Dun, and the first Commandant of the Staff College, Wellington. For its strength of just five battalions, it has perhaps, the maximum number of Staff College qualified officers. Its 3rd Battalion earned many decorations in the Siachen area in 1989. Its 1st Battalion took part in the link-up with Poonch in 1948 (the 50th anniversary being celebrated now) and again defended it during the 1965 war. The Regiment has earned 42 Battle Honours. A book giving details of each gallantry award earned, along with the photo and citation, has been written by Lieutenant General (Retd) Y. M. Bammi and was released during the reunion.

The reunion programme included the release of a special first day postal cover and other activities that gave officers and jawans plenty of opportunity to mix together. A highlight of this was the *Bara Khana* when they all mixed together, ate together and indulged in vigorous dancing together, with every such song/dance ending with the resounding, full throated shout of *Ho Ki Hoina! Honu Hi Parcha.* (Is 4th Gorkha the tops or not? Has to be!)

The rapport between the officers and men, among Gorkha units especially, is always very good and it is particularly so with this Regiment, thanks to it having been located in small stations where the officers and men are thrown together for recreation. Subathu is a delightful station from all points of view. It is very close to Malaun fort that is visited by the officers. Subathu, before the advent of the railway line to Shimla, was on the route, for people going to the hill station. For this purpose the Vice-Regal Lodge had been built here. Only the shell of the building now remains, used as offices for the time being but to be eventually used as a holiday home for visiting officers and men of the regiments. The present Officers' Mess of the Centre was originally the home of the second Commanding Officer of 1st Gorkhas after the 1815 war. The Mess has some historic trophies dating from the very inception and also containing a shield captured in the Bangladesh war from a Punjab battalion of the Pakistan Army, which had been presented by the late Field Marshal Sir Claude Auchinleck. A fine museum is maintained containing artefacts of both the regiments, demonstrating their achievements.

The reunion was also marked by the arrival of a contingent of cyclists from each battalion. Leaving their respective locations independently, joining other contingents enroute, until they all arrived together at Subathu, covering a combined distance of 3,500 kms. Each battalion contingent was led by an officer.

A Sainik Sammelan was held and addressed by Brigadier Bhasin, the Commandant, Major General (Retd) B. D. Kale, ex Colonel of the Regiment, Major (Retd) Dicky Day, President of the

British Association of the Regiment, Subadar (Retd) Puran Singh and finally Lieutenant General Chandra Shekhar VCOAS. They all spoke in Gorkhali. They extolled the deeds of The Regiment, gave an account of the ongoing welfare measures and the importance of such gatherings. Subadar Puran Singh aptly mentioned that the Regiment was like a green tree and the retired ones are like the leaves that fall in the fullness of time to be replaced by younger and greener ones.

The impulse of those attending was well personified by Lieutenant Colonel (Retd) Birender Mehra. Originally of Amritsar, now in Geneva, who makes it a point to attend all reunions on the plea that who knows how many more times this would be possible and which old friends would still be around. It is time of memories coming alive in the form of old comrades, now wrinkled, maybe fatter and with some teeth missing, but still full of old tales and anecdotes, reliving past associations on. What a glorious way to fade away. Old soldiers never die. They just fade away.

Soldiering at High Altitude

By H. S. Sodhi

Serving in a "High Altitude Area", which means at heights of not less than 10,000 feet, is no new experience for the Indian Army and there are many who, like me, have done two such tours of duty. My own have been separated by a time gap of twelve years and a distance of over a thousand miles; but, although conditions have remained unchanged, our adaptability and preparedness have been greatly improved.

The problems peculiar to such conditions are derived from the rarefied atmosphere, the terrain, and the climate which combine to introduce hazards to health, to make living conditions exceptionally hard, to complicate training and administration and to induce a sense of isolation.

The physical effects of the "thin air" vary according to the height. The most common of these are breathlessness, which for the first few nights causes sleeplessness owing to a feeling of suffocation, headache, stomach-ache, nausea and loss of appetite. When these symptoms are prolonged they cause a disease with the awe inspiring name of Pulmonary Oedema, and the victims are evacuated and are seldom sent back to areas of high altitude.

This disease was unheard of until 1957. Prior to this our Third Battalion once travelled from the plains to 13,500 feet in the space of six days; the feeling of "something heavy on the chest" was, of course, experienced, but no one gave it a second thought and there were no casualties. Perhaps some of these troubles today are psychological and result from knowledge of the risk of contracting this disease.

One lesson which has been learnt is the importance of progressive acclimatization. As a first step we now spend eight nights at 9,000 feet and, during this period, the troops carry out training by day up to 12,000 feet. The process of living at lower and working at higher levels is stepped up at short intervals for troops who are destined to live at heights of or above 12,000 feet. Even so the first few days at the ultimate height are likely to be uncomfortable.

The terrain is rugged with steep and often precipitous rocky slopes, the tree-line varying from 9,000 to as high as 12,000 feet. The hazards to movement are considerable. A slight misjudgment due to fatigue or a lapse of concentration when climbing on snow or slush-covered ice can result in a tumbling slide (or worse) of a few hundred feet. The really dangerous stretches have to be railed off.

Climbing uphill is a back-breaking business and frequent halts are necessary to avoid over-exertion, and sweating. Descent is knee-breaking (and a second ascent heart-breaking) with one most enjoyable (and, for the spectator, hair raising) exception for our boys; when the snow is lying it is a common sight to see them swishing downhill, sitting on an empty jerrican with broad grins on their faces and not worrying about what path their improvised toboggan decides to take. Fortunately we had no casualties.

In the winter two to six feet of snow cover the ground. This lasts several months; during our first winter the pass was closed to vehicles for six months and also to mules for short periods, and everything had to be man-handled by the troops with the help of porters. With the construction of unmetalled roads for one-ton vehicles the situation has been much improved. The picquets on the hill-tops are served by mule tracks. During bad weather there are heavy demands on manpower for snow clearance to keep roads and tracks open, and also for carrying parties.

The bitter cold is intensified by the strong winds which normally prevail and often reach gale force. The winter clothing which is now issued is warm and, as such things go, light; but the problem of providing warm gloves and boots which are not unwieldy, has not yet been solved. The natural tendency is to overdress and this causes sweating at the slightest exertion; this in turn leads to the catching of common colds which are difficult to shake off. Other health hazards are wounds which take a long time to heal, and skin-diseases and foot troubles which can be avoided by regular washing and bathing and meticulous care of the feet. Each man has at least two baths every week. The risk of frostbite is avoided by guarding against exposure and carrying out warming-up exercises during inactive periods of training.

Every exposed portion of the body takes on a dark tan. For healthy skin our doctor's persistent advocacy of Lacto-Calamine lotion led to a sharp rise in the sale of this medicament, unfortunately without any corresponding improvement of the complexion. Moustaches are another hazard and those who sport them, mainly officers, continually wipe off the condensed moisture to prevent its turning into ice; despite this, ice does form and necessitates a long and dripping stand on return to the nearest stove which may be hours away. If the growth is luxuriant it has then to be combed, and hair on being combed crackles with minute sparks throughout the year.

Another trouble is that the intense cold greatly shortens the life of wireless batteries, and this decline is accelerated when the set is in use. Frequent heating of the battery helps.

To offset the abnormal expenditure of calories special rations are issued in addition to the basic ration. These consist of eggs, chicken, fish and various types of beverage, including rum which is a daily issue. These rations are good and plentiful and are quite an attraction for service in what might otherwise be unpopular conditions. Companies specialize in their choice of beverages; during our last tour of duty "A" Company went in for coffee, "B" for chocolate powder, "C" for Bournvita and "D" for tea. Snacks and hot drinks invariably materialized as soon as a visitor arrived, and a round-robin visit to them all was quite an ordeal. Another problem which faced us was the difficulty of cooking rice and dal adequately; normal methods resulted in these being undercooked. This has been satisfactorily solved by the use of pressure cookers.

The onset of thaw does not end the toughness of conditions. The Spring brings rain, accompanied by sudden short spells of thunder and lightning which have frightening effects. It is dangerous to touch any metal; telephones have to be disconnected (miles of cable are liable to be burnt by one flash). As far as possible everyone remains under cover during these thunder-storms. Although fatal casualties are not numerous, cases of shock and near misses are frequent. One of our Riflemen had his clothes ripped open and his body hair burnt from his chest down to his navel; then, luckily the flash ripped down the front of his right leg and earthed after splitting his boot open. (The Brigade Ordnance Officer was most sceptical when we insisted that this damage was due to fair wear and tear.)

This stormy season is followed by a brief period of clear weather before the heavy rains come and give us a prolonged soaking. Flat areas become boggy and mule tracks are transformed into tumbling fast-flowing and ever-widening streams. This is also the season of landslides and avalanches, the frequency of which is increased by the constant blasting of the mountain sides to make roads and tracks, and we are again back to the winter's routine of road clearance and the transhipment of stores at odd places.

Accommodation varies from bunkers on hill-tops to huts in

rear areas. Bunkers are normally fitted with wooden slats on earth platforms for sleeping, furnished with a *bukhari* and decorated with a pin-up calendar. The original double-walled huts have been replaced by pre-fabricated huts of CGI sheets with an inner lining of thermocole and fitted with double-decker bunks. The cold-resisting lining makes the huts very warm with only one *bukhari* burning.

A *bukhari* is a round iron stove about two feet high which burns wood or kerosene, the latter being the type of fuel normally issued. A flue which requires daily cleaning extends outside the bunker or hut. Kerosene is poured into a separate container with a tap to regulate the flow through a pipe which connects it to the *bukhari*. Although this is a fire hazard, it is a most effective heating appliance.

Administration is a big problem and is complicated by the disruption of communications by landslides, avalanches, and snow. There are times when roads and tracks cannot be negotiated by the GS mule which has to hand over its duties to its puny local counterpart. These small local pack mules, despite their appearance, can carry a full load and are incredibly sure-footed. When conditions are beyond even their scope our boys take over with their *namlos*. Water has to be brought up for all purposes and, before the rains break, we follow the downward progress of water-points with increasing anxiety.

Our daily routine of stand-to, patrols and guards, normal maintenance, a certain amount of training, and interior economy and administration, keeps everyone busy for fairly long hours. And to this there is added the heavy demands on man-power during bad weather. "Holidays" are unknown, each day is like every other day.

Training, owing to the conditions, is mainly confined to individual and section training. This is supplemented by centralized training and promotion cadres. One of the advantages of serving in a high altitude area is that it affords excellent opportunity for education, map-reading and the training of specialists. Weapon training is no problem because natural ranges abound; it is often possible to fire weapons, using natural features as targets, from battle positions though the range seldom exceeds 200 yards. Application practices are, of course, not normally possible. The biggest problem is psychological. It arises from the mental reaction to living too long continuously in these hard conditions which prevail in high altitude areas. Life is hard and lonely. The absence of those amenities which have come to be considered basic to civilian life induces a sense of boredom, and the best way of curing this—a visit to civilization—is a distant dream. Lack of mail from home is equivalent to a national disaster and, during winter when it is brought up by dak runners, it can be delayed by the vagaries of weather for up to three weeks and even then may contain no letter for some of us. The effect of this is that any one's view of all events is exaggerated. Small incidents become magnified, tempers tend to grow short, a feeling of isolation and neglect prevails.

But problems are there to be overcome, using our own resources. Keeping the boys busy, minimum changes of orders and proper administration all help. In place of games, which are not allowed owing to the danger of over-exertion, snowball fights and toboggan races, and "Bingo" and variety shows are organized. The festivities of Dushera, Regimental Day and Holi help a lot. With the traditionally excellent spirit which exists between Officers, JCOs and men, impromptu parties often take place and enable everybody to *dance* off steam.

And there is always the scenic beauty which in clear weather, often with a sea of cloud below you, is sharply etched owing to the rarefied atmosphere. At such times Kanchenjunga dominates the beauty and, as the morning sun tinges its topmost snow-clad peaks softly pink across a white ocean of cloud, we seem to be separated from it by only a narrow gap. During the brief spring and autumn mountain flowers and vividly coloured bushes abound and give the effect of a painting with great splashes of colour.

"Soldiering at high altitude" ... life is certainly hard; but our boys remain remarkably fit. Nothing can damp *their* spirit. In fact, with the extra allowances and special rations and with "bull" reduced to a minimum, they like it.

The evening stand-to is over, and those who are not still on watchful duty can relax. They sit chattering over their tots of rum in their huts and from the bunkers we hear the beat of muted *madals* and snatches of Gorkhali songs. There is not enough room to dance.

The *madal*-beats and singing fade out. In the huts the kero flame starts flickering. It is 2000 hours.

All is silence ... Our boys are asleep.

Battle of Bilafond La September 1987

By Major Copal Chatterjee, MVC 3/4 GR

General

Bilafond La was the scene of one of the fiercest engagements in the ongoing struggle for the control of the Siachen Glacier. Men of my Battalion, whose predecessors were the veterans of the Chindit operations, covered themselves with glory while fighting at dizzy heights on the highest battle field in the World. This defensive battle fought from 23 to 25 September '87 will remain an example of personal courage, valour, determination and sacrifice of our brave troops.

The Terrain

Perhaps some of you are generally quite familiar with the terrain in Northern Jammu and Kashmir but a brief description of the Siachen Area may be useful. Siachen in the local language means "a rose garden". Paradoxically, it is the name given to the glacial wastelands nestling between the Saltore Ridge line to the West, the main Karakoram range to the North and the Apsara peaks to the East. The area, a mountaineer's dream, is the largest glacial region outside the polar regions. Siachen Glacier is surrounded by the largest group of first magnitude peaks in the World. The area is glaciated heavily and it is appropriately called the "Third Pole". The area remains snow bound throughout the year with extreme subzero temperatures. Winter temperatures fall down to minus 55 degrees centigrade and below. In summer, night temperatures are around minus 15 degrees centigrade.

High velocity blizzards regularly sweep the area adding to the wind chill factor. These blizzards can lift a man and propel him down ravines and into deep crevasses. Living shelters are frequently blown off, leaving troops in the open facing the extreme subzero temperature. Movement is possible only on foot or by helicopters. While foot movement is extremely hazardous, due to frequent avalanches and omni-present crevasses, helicopter movement is restricted to fair weather conditions.

In addition to the treacherous terrain and inhospitable climate, the rarified atmosphere (lack of oxygen) on the towering heights has adverse physical and mental effects on men. A man inducted to these heights without acclimatisation is sure to lose his life within hours. Even well acclimatised troops have succumbed to high altitude pulmonary oedema, wherein the lungs are filled with water and cardiac arrest results. The only way these casualties can have a ray of hope is by immediate evacuation by helicopter to lower heights for expert medical attention.

The cumulative effect of terrain, climate and high altitude makes survival and fighting extremely difficult. If one touches metal with bare hands, it is sure to result in the hand being frozen on to the metal and resulting in a cold injury. On an average every second man who is inducted is destined to become a casualty. The rate of casualties is higher than in any war.

Cause of Conflict

The root cause of the problem is the non-demarcation of the Line of Control (LC). After the Karachi Agreement in 1949, the Cease

Fire Line (CFL) was demarcated only up to a map point NJ 9842. Thereafter it was designated to run Northwards to the Glaciers. Again in the 1972 Shimla Agreement the LC was demarcated up to the same NJ 9842. The Indian understanding of the LC is based on terrain configuration, which runs along the Saltoro Ridge Line up to Sia Kangri. This also happens to be the northward alignment. Pakistan claims the LC to be the line joining NJ 9842 to Karakoram Pass north of the Indian "Daulat Bag Oldi" outpost. The Karakoram Pass is, however, accepted by Pakistan to be part of India. The Pak claim is illegal and illogical as it does not relate to the naturally accepted principles of demarcation of frontiers. This claim line cuts across the river valleys of Bubra; (this is the Valley where "D" Company of our Second Battalion under late Honorary Captain Moti Lal Gurung, MC IDSM, operated immediately after partition of the Country, against Pakistani raiders) and the Shyok region of Ladakh claiming 10,000 sq km of Indian territory.

In 1974, Pakistan opened up Karakorams to foreign expeditions. The accounts of the expeditions, published in mountaineering journals abroad, provided Pakistan the much needed publicity, resulting in all American atlasses and official maps showing the LC extending from point NJ 9842 to the Karakoram Pass. Consequently India planned and conducted several mountaineering expeditions to establish its claim over the area. This generated a Pak reaction including exchange of protest notes between the two countries.

In 1983 India had intelligence of Pak preparations to occupy the Siachen area. This move was forestalled by Indian troops, who in April 1984 swiftly occupied the dominating heights and important passes on the Saltoro Ridge Line. This was a military operation par excellence, in which the Indian Army proved its superiority over the adversary. Since then there have been consistent attempts by Pakistan to dislodge Indian troops from the Saltoro heights, west of Siachen. These attempts have been foiled with heavy casualties to the adversary.

In 1987, 8 Jammu and Kashmir Light Infantry (8 JAK LI) captured a Pak post called "Quaid" at the height of 21,153 feet in a daring operation. This operation deserves a special mention. The

Jammu and Kashmir Light Infantry was formed out of the erstwhile Jammu and Kashmir Militia. The Militia was raised by the emergency Government of Sheikh Mohamad Abdullah who formed an adhoc administration after the collapse of the Maharajah's Government in the wake of the invasion by Pakistani and tribal raiders in October 1947, just after partition. The militia was an entirely volunteer force raised for internal security duties and to fight the raiders. Over the years this force acquitted itself so well that in the 1962 operations against the Chinese a few battalions were made into a regular regiment—The Ladakh Scouts. Later after the excellent showing of the militia in 1965 and 1971 wars against Pakistan it was formed into a new Indian Army Regiment, the Jammu and Kashmir Light Infantry. The capture of the Quaid Post by Subedar Banna Singh and his men of 8 JAK LI will go down as one of the finest feats of military operations at a sub unit level. Following an earlier attack by his Battalion which the Pakistanis had beaten back with casualties, Subedar Banna Singh and his men resumed the attack and in a display of sheer physical courage and mountaineering virtuosity killed all the Pakistanis and captured the post. Sub Banna Singh was awarded the "Param Vir Chakra"—The Nation's highest award for gallantry. 8 JAK LI's actions will long remain unparalleled. The loss of "Quaid" post eliminated the only Pak toe-hold on the Saltoro Ridge. In an attempt to regain prestige, Pakistan attempted a brigade-size operation to capture Indian posts in the vicinity of Bilafond La in September 1987.

The Battle

It was at this stage that my Battalion arrived on the Siachen to relieve 8 JAK LI. During the process of this relief, Pakistan launched its misadventure at Bilafond Pass or La.

Indian Army posts named "Ashok" and "U Cut" are the Northern shoulder of the Bilafond La and dominate the pass. The Pak post named "HMG Ridge" leads on to these posts from the Bilafond glacier and is about 1.5 km long. On 18 September, the enemy started shelling all our posts along the front. On 21 September this pattern changed and he concentrated on "Ashok", "U Cut" and the neighbouring localities. On 22 and 23 September the shelling intensified and the enemy also fired TOW missiles at our positions. Under cover of this fire the enemy managed to move forward and position themselves in a defiladed position behind a feature named "Tota" on HMG Ridge. We called for artillery and mortar fire and were able to inflict a number of casualties on the enemy. During this period we too suffered our initial casualties.

While I and my boys were at Bilafond La and in the process of taking over from 8 JAK LI, my Commanding Officer, Colonel Puran Gurung rang me up to find out the latest position. I explained the situation to him. He ordered me to defend the posts at all costs. I immediately instructed the boys to move to Sohrab Top. On reaching there, I ordered 5343213 Lnk Hira Bahadur Thapa and one boy of 8 JAK LI (who were already at Sohrab Top) to rush to the highest point and pass information of the enemy to me. As they were moving up, the rifleman of 8 JAK LI (unfortunately I never got to know his name) was shot enroute. Despite the firing, Lnk Hira Bahadur continued, undeterred alone to the top and started passing information. With accurate information provided by him, I called for effective artillery and mortar fire on the enemy. Meanwhile, I, therefore, ordered 2/Lt Ashok Sharma to rush with five boys to "Ashok". I later learnt that Subedar Lekh Raj's head had been blown off by a TOW missile. Sub Tol Bahadur Ale was also at Ashok post and had subsequently moved forward to the Ashok Listening Post (LP) and was engaging the enemy though he was under intense artillery bombardment. At about 1100 hours, when the enemy had closed in, he ran with the LMG to Ashok Post. While he was rushing to the post, he was hit by a splinter. His stomach was torn open but he came back to the post with the LMG and refused to be evacuated. I ordered his evacuation but he did not survive and succumbed to his wounds later.

Subsequently, I moved to the highest point on Sohrab TOP where Hira Bahadur was passing valuable information to me. With the help of Hira Bahadur I managed to reach the trench from where he was passing accurate information. Hira Bahadur had been noticed by the enemy and therefore we were getting heavy pounding by artillery and mortar fire besides bullets. Despite the enemy fire, we effectively engaged the enemy and caused heavy casualties. I was in the trench with Hira when he suddenly yelled "Sahib". The next thing I heard was a whizzing sound and Hira was blown to pieces by an enemy TOW missile. With my face splattered with Hira's blood, I realised that he had shouted "Sahib" to caution me and perhaps saved my life in the process.

From the highest point of Sohrab Top. I noticed that enemy continued climbing, with approximately one company each, towards "Ashok" and "Sohrab" posts with one company each following. Despite our medium machine gun (MMG), Light Machine Gun (LMG), artillery and mortars fire the enemy kept advancing. Enemy suffered heavily and the attack was finally beaten back by about 1600 hours. Enemy was thereafter seen withdrawing towards "HMG Ridge". I was then ordered by the CO to move to "Ashok" post. Rifleman Chet Bahadur Thapa and two more jawans crossed over to "Ashok" picquet under intense shelling. Enroute Rfn Chet Bahadur was hit in the stomach by splinter of a shell and was profusely bleeding. I tried to help him but he said "Ma theek bhai hal chhu, Sahib, tapai janus" (I will be alright Sahib, you carry on). Since my presence at Ashok Post was important, I left him there. Immediately on reaching the post I sent back some boys to evacuate him. Fortunately, Chet Bahadur survived.

Night Attack of 23/24 September

On night 23/24 September, enemy launched yet another attack on "Ashok" post. This attempt however appeared half hearted as the enemy did not even manage to come up to the Ashok LP. This was also possibly due to accurate artillery and air defence (AD) gun fire; AD guns were used against the advancing Pakistanis in the ground role. These guns perhaps played a key role in dispersing the advancing Pakistanis and the attack petered out by 0200 hours the next morning.

Rifleman Jai Kumar Gurung was at the Ashok LP. Despite the

snow and bad visibility, instead of trying to get under shelter, he showed an uncanny sense and smelt the enemy! He spotted the enemy through a peep-hole in the clouds and came panting to me "Sahib, civilian manchi haru hamro picquet mathi charhi rakhe ko chha" (some civilians are climbing towards our picquet). Having informed me, he ran back to his position and started engaging the enemy with the MMG located there (Jai Kumar was injured later due to enemy shelling and was evacuated—fortunately he survived).

I placed Nb Sub Bhim Bahadur Thapa on the left approach and Nb Sub Ram Kumar Thapa on the right approach to Ashok Post; alongwith some boys I was guarding Ashok Top. I was woefully short of weapons. The one HMG that was with us had been rendered ineffective by the enemy. During the second attack i.e. night 23/24 September, the HMG was very effectively engaging the enemy. The Pakistanis thus resorted to firing TOW missiles to silence this weapon. The missile pilot was good. He achieved a direct hit resulting in killing all the four boys in the HMG bunker and damaging the gun. The boys had been blown to smithereens; it was difficult to identify the bodies. I placed one LMG each with Naib Subedars Bhim Bahadur and Ram Kumar on each of the approaches and balance weapons on Ashok Top. I asked for artillery and mortar fire ahead of Ashok Post and asked the AD guns to fire at enemy trying to climb Ashok Post. Since we had some time before the enemy would close up, we filled all the LMG magazines and tested our weapons by firing a few rounds so that they do not jam at the crucial moment.

While all this was happening, I intercepted a message on my radio set "Janab, I am Major Rasheed. I have established a base on 'Ranbir' and am waiting for the troops to fetch up for the past one hour. Despatch the troops fast, it is becoming dark, visibility is also poor". This confirmed that the Pakistani attack was building up and perhaps some special troops were being used (Climbing Ashok Post from this direction was very difficult as there was a 300 feet sheer cliff on one side). The Pakistani Company Commander was definitely a mountaineer.

The first attack came around 2100 hours on both the approaches. On the right approach Sub Bhim Bahadur Thapa kept the boys together and controlled their fire as we had very limited ammunition. He was cool throughout and by effectively controlling the fire and actions of the boys managed to thwart the Pakistanis on this approach. He was temporarily blinded by an air-burst shell but refused to be evacuated and stuck to his task. He was later to be decorated with the Vir Chakra. With effective artillery and small arms fire we beat back the first attack.

Enemy managed to cut off Ashok Post from Sohrab Top by firing artillery, HMGs and TOW missiles. L/Hav Nar Bahadur Ale was the MMG detachment commander at Ashok Post. He had been performing tasks efficiently and coolly all through the previous three days battle. He suddenly jumped out of his post and shouted "Saheb, Ab ma ini haru lai agaari anu dinna (Sir, I will not let them come ahead now). He rested the MMG on his hip and started mowing down the enemy! This was indeed an unusual display of courage but he had to pay with life for violating the rules—he was shot in the forehead. He was posthumously awarded MVC. Sacrificing himself, he managed to beat back the Pakistanis attack. There was a lull thereafter.

At about 0100 hours on 25 September, I could see enemy concentrating ahead of LP in front of Ashok shouting "Allah-o Akabar". As the enemy was only 50 metres away from my post, I asked for the Defensive fire (SOS). I told the boys who were all around me "I shall fight till death". The boys were all geared up to take on the enemy.

The attack finally came in at 0140 hours. We opened fire with all weapons including artillery and mortar fire. 5342711 Naik Prem Bahadur Gurung was performing the duties of MMG Detachment Number 2. He noticed two Pakistani soldiers stealthily climbing the post. He jumped out of his trench, unsheathed his kukri and hit the first soldier on the head, thus killing him. The second soldier fired with AK 47 rifle at Prem Bahadur's chest. However, Prem Bahadur lunged at him and hung on to him. Another of our boys then shot the Pakistani. However, Prem Bahadur was fatally wounded and was awarded the MVC posthumously. After this, there was once again a lull in the battle. The Pakistani attack was once again beaten back. I also learnt from a radio intercept that Major Rasheed, the Pakistani Company Commander who was leading the attack had also been killed. Shortly thereafter the few boys that were with me informed that they could observe the enemy retreating. However, since it was dark, I ordered them to stay put and be prepared to face the Pakistanis again.

After some time, I was greatly relieved to see more of my boys who came up and reported "Sahib, reinforcements ayi pugyo" (Sahib, the reinforcements have come). They also brought three boxes of belted ammunition for the MMG. I thanked the Almighty as I was now sure of beating back any further Pakistani attacks—I now knew, we had won the day!

As dawn was breaking, I went ahead with some of the kanchas and collected about 11 weapons including AK 47 rifles, a Chinese LMG and a RPG launcher. I also collected a radio set which was being used by the Pakistani Company Commander. We counted approximately 42 dead on Ashok Post itself. We learnt later that attacks on Ashok Post were launched by three battalions of Pakistanis—the 39 PUNJAB, 4 SINDH and one Battalion of the SSG. Pakistanis reportedly suffered 150 officers and men killed in the three days battle.

On 27 September within two days of the battle, our Army Commander visited our post at Bilafond La. I gave him the report in our formal military manner—he however, took me in his arms and said "Son, you have created history". This was indeed the most wonderful moment of my life—I was proud to be an Indian Army and a Fourth Gorkha Rifles Officer.

Subsequently, our Colonel of the Regiment, Lt Gen Vijay Madan, VSM, who is Commanding a Corps in the Eastern Sector paid a visit to the post at Bilafond La. Despite, lack of acclimatization and the hazards of high altitude he visited us on 5 November. He went around the entire area and spoke to the boys. He was pleased to see as to how bravely the boys had fought despite all odds. He gave a "Thulo Shabash" to the boys and said that we must give the enemy a befitting reply again if the occasion arises. The boys were indeed thrilled to see the Colonel at this God forsaken place and vowed to do even better, if and when the opportunity presented itself.

My narration of the battle will be incomplete, if I do not mention the deed of 2 Lieutenant Ashok Sharma, an Army Ordnance Corps Officer, who was on infantry attachment training with us. This youngster, having donned uniform barely two months earlier was everywhere, all the time. On 23 September when we were surprised by the Pakistanis he was the first one to move up to Sohrab Top despite intense enemy shelling. I thereafter ordered him to move to Ashok Post with six boys. He immediately moved off through heavy enemy shelling and HMG fire and that too in broad day light!! On night 24/25 September, he tried to rush up to Sohrab Top from Bilafond La, where he was resting on my orders after two days of battle. While leading the reinforcements on to the ladder (to scale the sheer cliff) he was injured and had to be evacuated (he had nine splinters in his body—some I am told still remain lodged). His acts of courage inspired the boys to carry on undeterred for which he was awarded the Vir Chakra.

In the fierce battle which raged for three days and nights, 17 of our boys gave the supreme sacrifice and almost all of us were wounded. I dedicate this article to the memory of those who are no more and to those who silently carried out their tasks in defeating the Pakistani designs but have not been named in this narration. These battle scarred veterans of Bilafond La "live to fight yet another day".

IV

Journey to India—travelling in a Gurkha family's footsteps March/April 2000

By Julie Draper

As a child, I was always enthralled by stories told by my mother, aunt and grandfather of their time in India. My grandfather, Allan Maxwell Arnott was a major in the 4th PWO Gurkha Rifles and was commissioned in 1908. Although my aunt (Elspeth Gardner) was born in Burma, my mother (Audrey Pearson) in Lansdowne, and an uncle (Michael Arnott) in Kasauli: it was always to Bakloh that my mother came back to when she was telling us stories. Because that was where she and her siblings spent most of their short childhood when in India, before being sent home to Scotland for good. The church, the bungalow, the hills, the flowers, ayah and what my grandfather loved to talk about most the Regiment were lovingly remembered. My grandmother kept a "Baby Book" a faithful record of all her children's lives, in India and Scotland. It was read and reread by all my five brothers and sisters, and two cousins. From the book it was possible to piece together some parts of this little family's life together; where they lived and travelled to in India, where my grandfather was stationed and fought in the first world war, and when my aunt Alison died from gastro-enteritis aged 19 days in Bakloh.

In 1957, my grandfather took my mother back to India for the centenary celebrations of the Regiment. I remember her letters to me, and the photos they took, including a cine film of their trip. As well as going to Bakloh they visited Kaphurtala, Agra, Delhi, Dalhousie and the Kulu valley. So when after many years I persuaded my husband Peter an art historian, that we might at last go to India, he was enthusiastic. My younger sister Jessica and first cousin

(Elspeth's daughter) were very keen to come along too. Elspeth had always kept in touch with the regiment and is an Associate Member. I had been to one or two reunions at Stoke Poges over the years, and as a student had attended the local Cambridge reunion instigated by my grandfather in the early 60's, and met such splendid people as Freddie Harrison, and Frank and Sidney Money. So in 1997, Elspeth and I went to the June reunion at Stoke Poges, and there my wonderful connection with the Regiment began again. It was quite a special reunion as I'm sure you all remember. I met for the first time, Geoffrey Lloyd, Bill Tee and Anne-Marie, Martin Fuller, and of course Veena Nath, Raj Bir Chopra's daughter. We struck up an immediate friendship, Geoffrey bringing her over to tea at our house near Cambridge the day after!

The next two and a half years were spent feverishly planning with the help of Raj Bir and Veena, Geoffrey and Martin Fuller, and our agent in Dharamsala, Mr Gupta of Ways Tours. Bill and Anne Marie's trip in 1994 (written up in the newsletter of the next year) was an invaluable start. Many happy hours were spent on the phone and writing letters and emails. Raj Bir and Geoffrey were splendid in helping us to visit Bakloh and Subathu. Smoothing the path of the military!

We arrived in Delhi on March 13th and spent the first two weeks travelling around Rajasthan. It was thrilling for us all to see the sights of the capital. Agra, the Taj Mahal, the Red Fort and Fatipur Sikri. Our Hindi came in useful. We travelled by train, "air-conditioned taxi" (auto rickshaw), cycle rickshaw, bus taxi and our own two feet. The visit to Gwalior coincided with the festival of Holi. We were "painted" with wondrous colours by the local population. Udaipur proved to be the most beautiful of all the cities we visited. Peter was in raptures over the Jain architecture at Ranakpur and Mount Abu.

I was impatient to get to the second half of our trip up north. The beginning of March found us on the sleeper to Pathankot. We woke early to see the sun rise lighting up the Himalayas in the background as we rattled along the edge of the plain in a lush countryside. Mr Gupta had laid on "P. J." to be our driver and guide for the next 10 days. He was there to meet us. All smiles and as excited as we were. We telephoned Lieut Colonel K. S. Gurung just to make sure that we were expected and then we were off climbing steeply out of the plain. The drive to Bakloh was just as I expected, beautiful with spectacular scenery. The foothills terraced for wheat growing and deep ravines everywhere. After two and a half hours we could see Bakloh, high on the hill ahead. Our driver was a little nervous of entering a military area, but we were soon there and welcomed with such generous and warm hospitality. Lieut Colonel Gurung, Capt Gagar Singh Gurung, Ex-Lt Nathuram Banal and Subadar Roop Singh Gurung took us round the village. They showed us the church where my mother was christened, Number 5 bungalow, the officers' mess, parade ground and many other sights, interspersed with lots of stops for drinks, lunch, tea and biscuits, served beautifully by Nathuram's wife. It was so moving to hear the stories of the Regiment, and of course the one about Jack Masters who killed the tiger (which we later saw in the officers' mess at Subathu). My mother and grandfather had travelled out with him to the centenary celebrations at Bakloh in 1957. I had brought the photos of their trip with me and we had a most interesting time trying to identify places and people, sometimes with great success. Some of the soldiers were still living and it was an honour to be able to hand over the prints. Jessica got on particularly well with Nathuram—a school friend's father who had been his commanding officer in the 60s. We were especially thrilled to see the centenary plaque inscribed "Time passes, friendship remains". Given to the Regiment by the British members of the 4th PWO Gurkha Rifles Officers Association. My grandfather had unveiled it in 1957. We were able to raise our glasses to the toast "Jai Gorakh, Jai Chautha Gorkha" (*which we had been practising all week*)!

We heard later that there is a plan to restore Bakloh to a working base again. I think for another Gurkha Regiment. Our hosts were sad to see how it had run down over the years and were most apologetic. When I asked to see the cemetery where my aunt had been buried "taken by gastro-enteritis at the age of 19 days" I was told that unfortunately it had not been kept up.

We would have loved to stay longer in the place where my grandmother wrote in September 1927. *"Here we are in the little place where the children spent most of their Indian life only there are no babies now and the house feels quiet and empty and everything reminds me of them"*. But with promises to return we set off in the late afternoon on one of the most beautiful and precipitous drives on the back road to Dalhousie. I especially wanted to see this hill station that Geoffrey Lloyd had said we must on no account miss. I had a wonderful photo of the Himalyas, taken from the Grand View Hotel, which I was determined to see! Our stay in this hotel was a superb experience. It was cold at night and we were supplied with hot water bottles. There was an electric fire on in our rooms, which was a warming sight. The next morning we woke to a spectacular view of the Himalayas (the same view as my photo) and into the Chamba Valley. Despite the cold, we had breakfast outside so that we could feast our eyes on the mountains. Our only disappointment was not to have enough time to do the walk to Kalatope and Kajjiar, which Geoffrey and Bill had suggested.

The next five days were spent going down the Kangra Valley to Dharamsala, where we spent a very happy time. We met a young American who was training to be a Buddhist monk at Sherabling monastery. Thence to Mandi and then up the Kulu valley to Manali, with many adventures on the way! One disappointment was not meeting the present Raja of Mandi whose father had been a friend of my grandfather. Because his mother had died 10 days before our visit there. However, I will now write to him to introduce my brother Rev Henry Pearson who will be making a trip similar to ours in March 2001. He will then be able to hand over the photograph.

On April 5th we drove from Shimla to Subathu, which we were able to visit thanks to great efforts by Raj Bir. It turned out to be one of the highlights of our trip. Our driver was very nervous of going through the gates, expecting to be apprehended at every turn. However, we had a truly royal welcome first from the charming adjutant Major Kuldeep Singh and then Capt S. B. Gurung. We were then entertained by Brigadier K. Sood, who generously spent half an hour talking with us. Again the photos were brought out and discussed in great detail. We had lunch in the officers' mess with, Colonel and Mrs Gopal Chattergee and Major Prem Kumar Baru. Their hospitality was truly heart warming and it was fascinating to hear about the Regiment and its present duties. My most moving moment was to find the familiar caricature of my grandfather hanging in the billiard room along side many others. Although Veena had told me it was there, I had forgotten; a replica had hung on the wall of my grandfather's drawing room when I was a child and I had loved it.

It was hard to wrench ourselves away but we still had Kasauli to visit, (my Uncle Mike had been born here), and what a beautiful place it was. We walked to the top of Monkey point and watched the setting sun over the plains to the south and west. That night was spent on the sleeper to Delhi, and so our trip was nearly at an end. My sister and cousin then flew home. Peter and I took the plane to Kajuraho, where we had a fascinating time seeing the Hindu temples. April 10th was our last day in India. Having lunch with Raj Bir and Veena in the Delhi Golf Club lightened the sadness of leaving. We were royally entertained and had such fun relating our adventures to them.

So nearly a year later, I am writing this up, and still having such fun sticking all the photos in the album. What a trip it was! Made so magical by having connections with the 4th GR, and so much help from so many people. It made our visit so memorable. I only wish that we could have talked it all over endlessly with my grandparents, and my mother and uncle, but my Aunt Elspeth Gardner has been a wonderful listener and enthusiast. I am so proud to join her as an Associate Member of the 4th Gurkha Officers' Association.

Like our forefathers we have fallen in love with India. My brother Henry will follow our footsteps in March. He and I and another cousin are going to South India to trace other "Indian connections" this spring. My husband and I hope to go to Ladakh in August 2001, and will have time to stop off in Delhi to see Raj Bir and Veena. So, our heartfelt thanks to the 4GR for welcoming us into its family, and

"Jai Gorakh, Jai Chautha Gorkha"

Could this be Shangri-La?

By Peter C. Read

J. Hilton's well known novel "Lost Horizon" tells the story of a plane crash somewhere in the Himalayan mountains, and the rescue of the survivors by unknown inhabitants of a mysterious and beautiful city called Shangri-La. No one knows where Shangri-La is or even if it exists, but I like to think I may have been there.

I had joined my parents in India in the autumn of 1940. The next summer I travelled with my mother and younger brother to the hill station of Dalhousie that is located at approximately 7,000 feet above sea level in the foothills of northern Punjab, bordering on the independent state of Chamba. It was customary for the families of British military and civil service personnel to move to hill stations to avoid the extreme heat of the plains, which would be subject to temperatures of 110° Fahrenheit and above.

Not long after I arrived in Dalhousie I was introduced to Prince Lakshman Singh, the heir apparent to Chamba State. He lived with his mother, the Rajmata (Queen Mother), in a house on the outskirts of Dalhousie called Jandrighat, and was being educated by a private English tutor. We were both around sixteen years old and soon became friends. He was about the same height as myself, good looking with dark wavy hair, fair complexion and fine aquiline features. We were both physically fit and frequently played tennis and went horse riding on the local trails. Occasionally we tried our hand at shooting game birds without success.

In the autumn of 1941, I enrolled as a cadet at The Prince of Wales's Royal Indian Military College in Dehra Dun. This city was hundreds of miles south of Dalhousie, so with the beginning of my military career, for a while I lost touch with Lakshman Singh. When I graduated from the RIMC in the summer of 1942 I went to OTS Bangalore. This involved a four-day journey by train to southern India.

In January 1943 at age eighteen and a half I was commissioned into the 4th Prince of Wales's Own Gurkha Rifles and returned to northern India and their training centre at Bakloh. Fortuitously Bakloh was approximately 30 miles by road from Dalhousie at the 4,500 foot level. I was therefore able to see my mother occasionally and renew my friendship with Lakshman Singh. In 1944 he came to Bakloh for a few months for some basic military training prior to his investiture as Raja of Chamba. He had his own state army comprising infantry and cavalry and he felt he should have some military knowledge even though an ex Gurkha officer efficiently commanded the army. He was attached to my training company and trained under my guidance. His accommodation was in a suite of rooms in the same bungalow in which I lived, so we were able to keep touch both on and off the parade ground. His beautiful wife Devendra, Rani of Chamba, also stayed with us briefly. She was a most charming, well-educated young lady. She had grown up with an English nanny who nicknamed her "Tummy" because she was a very chubby baby. She was in no way chubby when she married Lakshman Singh. I believe the affable Lakshman Singh benefited from his brief stay with the 4th Gurkhas and learned the basics of weapons and drill. His only problem lay in marching in step with any group of men. As someone said, he appeared to have two left feet!

In the following year on the 4th April 1945, I received a formal invitation that read as follows:

> "*His Highness Raja Lakshman Singh, Raja of Chamba, requests the pleasure of the company of Captain Read, at Chamba on the 4th May 1945, and following days on the occasion of his investiture. RSVP Secretary Chamba*"

In addition there was a separate note that read:

> "*It is also requested that the following information may kindly be enclosed along with the reply:*

Time and date of arrival in Dalhousie

Transport required-
  Riding horse,
  Mules, or coolies for luggage.

Meals-
  European style:
  Indian style.

This led to the once in a lifetime adventure of travelling as an honoured guest to the Investiture of the Raja of an independent Indian State nestling somewhere in the foothills of the Himalayas. Could this be Shangri-La?

The journey to Chamba starts with a drive on a tortuous single lane mountain road to Dalhousie. There are no roads into Chamba State or in Chamba City itself which accommodate vehicles of any sort. Just imagine a city with no traffic problems! It was necessary to stay overnight in Dalhousie because the next stage of the journey was 25 miles on a mountain trail. Your options were to walk or ride a small horse. This meant a full day of travelling. There were two other guests from our regiment, the Commandant, Colonel T. D. C. Owens MC and Lieutenant F. Brassington. We all requested horses for the journey, which started around six am. From Dalhousie, at 7,000 feet, the trail climbed to around 9,000 feet before dropping into the valley where Chamba City was built circa 930 AD. This trail wound between tall conifers including Deodar (Himalayan Cedar) and fir and followed the contours of the mountains. It was only about 10 feet wide. On one side of you was a rock face and trees and on the other side there was a sheer drop of 1,000 to 1,500 feet covered in part by tall conifers somehow clinging to the steep slopes which swept down to the valleys below. Through these trees there were occasional glimpses of terraced "Paddy" (rice) fields on the lower slopes of the valleys.

The number of travellers was minimal and comprised mostly of citizens of Chamba City, villagers from the valleys and merchants.

They were dressed simply. The men wore Jodhpur type pants, long shirts and loosely tied turbans. Some wore vests and some carried blankets over their shoulders. The women wore white baggy pants and long shirts some with embroidered necklines; others wore brightly coloured "gypsy" style skirts and coloured bodices. All wore coloured headscarves or shawls. On their feet they wore Chamba chapplis (sandals) or other slip on sandals. Many were barefoot and probably did not possess any form of footwear. The majority of the travellers were on foot, some carried their few possessions in bundles, while heavier loads were carried in rope slings on the backs of coolies or on donkeys and major loads, were carried by mules.

Being one of the privileged guests I was on horseback. However, my particular horse had a very unnerving habit. Every time another horse, mule or donkey came from the opposite direction it would turn across the trail with its head hanging over the sheer drop and lash out with its hind legs at the oncoming animal. Being in the saddle, as its hind quarters rose, so did I and momentarily I had a hair raising view of the sheer drop. After going through this exercise a few times, and being unable to discourage my trusty mount from it's antics, I decided that "discretion was the better part of valour" and dismounted and walked most of the way to Chamba!

However, about half way on the journey there was an oasis in the form of the village of Khajiar, and a traveller's rest house. Khajiar must be one of the most beautiful places in the world. As you emerge from a trail surrounded by trees you suddenly come upon an emerald green bowl nestling between the mountains with a small lake in its centre. Local folklore says that there is no bottom to the lake, and this could well be true because I believe it is the crater of an extinct volcano. To one side of this mountain meadow are a few small wooden houses which comprise the village of Khajiar and close by is the guest house where one can rest, have a meal or even stay overnight.

We were welcomed to this haven by gracious members of the palace staff and invited to freshen up while they prepared the most delicious meal for us. We were only too happy to relax for a while as we had been walking or riding for five hours or so. It is very hard to find superlatives to describe Khajiar. It was so quiet, peaceful and totally absorbing, we almost wished we could stay there forever. However, that was not to be, as we still had another four or five hours of walking ahead of us before we reached the city of Chamba.

As we continued our journey there were still glimpses of paddy fields and cultivated areas as well as isolated flat topped dwellings. At one point we could see two lower trails winding their way around the foothills. Eventually we reached Biskit Point as we emerged from the high mountain trail and from there had the first breathtaking view of Chamba City, with a backdrop of the Himalayas. It is built on a small plateau adjacent to a wide ravine through which flows the river Ravi. With the sun shining on it, the city reminded me of childhood fairy tales where everything in a town or city was dwarfed by the palace where the Prince and Princess lived happily ever after. The city of Chamba completely covers the plateau and there in the middle of it is a huge building, the Raja's Palace.

From Biskit Point the trail begins to slope down into the valley below. One passes through paddy fields and pastures and there are deciduous trees growing round the flat-topped dwellings on what we would call smallholdings. The dwellings are built with clay bricks and have roofs of mixed straw and clay supported on wooden beams. There is no electricity, heating or plumbing in them. The occupants depend on heat from their clay cooking area and glowing charcoal in "Fire pots". Water is collected from streams and a few wells. Many of the inhabitants of the valley and hill areas outside the city are shepherds or Gaddis. Because of their outdoor life, they wear homespun woollen garments, Jodhpur style pants and smock like shirts and a small roughly tied turban. The most noticeable thing about the men is that they wear a great length of rope made from goat hair and wrapped around their stomachs outside their smocks. This serves as a colic belt, or as a rescue rope if anyone falls over a cliff, or for tying up goats or sheep and many other uses.

The trail continues up to the edge of the Ravi River ravine where there is a suspension bridge that is the only access to the city plateau. After crossing the bridge you pass through the lower bazaar and climb a steep path to the Chaugan. The Chaughan is a long grassed area that stretches the entire length of the City of Chamba between the bazaar buildings and the precipitous drop from the plateau to the river. It is used by the population for walking, playing, resting, riding and any festivals or parades that take place from time to time. When you walk along it you are conscious of the palace towering above everything. It is called the Khanchandi Palace and compared with many other oriental palaces with domes and minarets it is of simple design with gabled roofing and arched windows rather like an English mansion and painted white all over. It contains a Durbar Hall for formal ceremonies, a banquet room and many offices and bedrooms all encompassing a number of inner courtyards and gardens. Houses of different sizes and standards together with small bazaar stores surround the palace, not in an orderly manner but packed together in unplanned confusion as they developed over the centuries. The shops in the bazaar areas cater to the basic needs of the population and open directly on to the streets. There are no shop fronts, so in effect they are open cubicles, which are closed with shutters at night.

Merchants and artisans work in close proximity to each other and as a result, side by side will be found silks and other fabrics, rice, flour, spices and cooking oil, shoe makers, tailors, silversmiths, blacksmiths, brass and copper utensils, jewellers, carpets, fruit and vegetables, cook while you wait food products and so on. This is but a small sampling of what you will find in the bazaar, which is entertaining as well as colourful. In a mountain area, subject to heavy rain and snow with no drainage system, both merchandise and merchants must be above the street level to allow the natural flow of water down the street. So the merchants sit at the front of their stores on platforms above the street, and as a customer you stand at street level to bargain for your purchase.

There are a number of temples in the city which have been built over the centuries since 930 AD the tops of most of them can be seen from the Chaugan, paradoxically at the western end is a small

Scottish Presbyterian Church. Regretfully I know nothing about its date of construction or whether there was still any missionary activity in the city. The majority of the population is Hindu. Other buildings adjacent to the Chaugan were Ravi View (the guesthouse) where guests of the state were accommodated, the hospital, the post office and the museum. The post office received and dispatched mail and sold stamps. I still have in my possession some rare postage stamps. They are standard Indian stamps with an overprint "Chamba State" on them bearing the images of King George V and King George VI.

It is appropriate at this point to mention that the mail was carried from Dalhousie to Chamba in a mailbag slung over the shoulder of a mailman. He travelled on foot and carried a short handled spear with bells on it to scare off wild animals or to defend himself against them. There were Himalayan black bears and panther in the forests of this region.

The most intriguing building was the Bhuri Singh Museum. Named after the founder Raja Sir Bhuri Singh when it was opened on September 14th 1908. It contained objects relating to the history of Chamba State, products of local art and industry and natural history specimens found locally. Of particular interest to me were grants of land recorded on large copper plates engraved in the Hindi script. The earliest dated back to AD950 and others were dated AD1067, AD1080, AD1330, and AD1396 and so on up to AD1734. These must be some of the earliest land transactions recorded anywhere.

With the large number of guests attending the investiture, the guesthouse could not accommodate everyone, so we were in tents. That may sound a little alarming and out of keeping for a guest of the Raja, but these were tents with a difference. They were luxurious, straight out of the "Arabian Nights". About 20 feet square, with 4-foot high walls and two tent poles. The walls were covered with colourful tapestries and there were Indian carpets on the floor. The furniture included a bed, dressing table, some comfortable chairs and a coffee table. There was electric lighting. The bathroom was in a small tent attached at one side and had a tin tub, washbasin and commode. A water carrier brought hot water for the tub, or washbasin, on demand. Under the circumstances this was pretty luxurious.

On the morning of 4th May 1945 at 10 o'clock in the morning at an investiture ceremony held in the palace Durbar Hall, Lakshman Singh was proclaimed Raja. Dignitaries of the state attended the ceremony, dignitaries from outside the state, including the Honourable Mr Thompson, British Resident of the Punjab states, and distinguished guests. It involved a certain amount of pomp and circumstance, but to me the many coloured costumes and turbans provided the pageantry that made it such a memorable occasion. During the rest of the day there were a number of events and entertainment for the citizens of Chamba. I thought the most notable was the Gaddi Dance which was performed by some thirty or so Gaddis (Shepherds) in their traditional costumes with additional colourful scarves, decorated turbans and beaded pouches on their belts. They performed to drum rhythms and as they turned and whirled with their rope belts over their smocks it gave the impression of kilts and slow moving Highland dancing. A most fascinating performance.

I also received a formal written invitation from "His Highness Raja Lakshman Singh to a banquet at the Khanchandi Palace" at 9 pm that evening. Dress-dinner jacket, uniform or Indian dress, and of course I accepted. I had no option but to wear uniform. It was a unique experience to attend a banquet in a palace. I was duly seated with other guests at a very long dining table, with the Raja seated at the head. Apart from the numerous courses served, the most impressive thing was that there was a servant behind each and every guest.

The Grand Finale to the investiture celebration on the morning of 5th May was a ceremonial parade. The most colourful part was a parade of citizens accompanied by many coloured flags and pennants and an amazing assortment of brass and copper trumpets and horns. Some were straight and others curled in unbelievable shapes and sizes. The cacophony issuing from these instruments was a discordant mixture of sound that could hardly be described as music, but it somehow conveyed an uninhibited expression of exuberant feelings which were so appropriate for the occasion.

Following his subjects was the Raja riding on the state elephant. He was seated on a very ornate silver open howdah with two scarlet-coated minions standing behind him wielding horse tail fly whisks. In front of him on the elephant's neck was the mahout (the elephant's driver). Under the howdah the elephant was covered with colourful trappings of red and gold. The elephant also had a head decoration of fabric, a necklace of large gold and silver medallions around his neck and a ring of bells around each of its front ankles. Truly decorated in a manner fit for a king. At the saluting base the elephant was made to assume a dismount position with its front legs stretched in front and its back legs stretched out behind. A small ladder was placed up to the howdah and the Raja was able to dismount. Once on the ground he was greeted by the Honourable Mr Thompson. This was followed by three Gurkha Subedars each with no less than 20 years of service, who presented the Raja with a silver mounted Kukri on behalf of the Officers of the 4th Prince of Wales's Own Gurkha Rifles. To end the ceremonies the Raja took the salute from a march past of his army. First the cavalry, followed by a band leading the infantry company.

The rest of the day was filled with a variety of competitive events for the entertainment of the citizens. It included, tug of war, recovering bags of coins from the top of a greasy pole, a football match, a chatty race (running with a clay pot balanced on your head) and finally torch drill with flaming torches. For guests there was a movie show in the evening. I regret I have no recollection as to what it was.

So once more after a good night's rest we returned by the same trail to Dalhousie. I was provided with a different horse for the return journey, and happily it responded to my control so I did not walk very much. On reflection I still wonder if I really visited Shangri-La, which has been described as "an imaginary paradise on earth". Paradise is defined as "a place or state of complete happiness". Chamba in general terms, in many ways is a place of complete happiness to a visiting occidental traveller. Its surroundings are very beautiful, vehicles and the air pollution they create do not plague it. There is no television, no telephones and, except for the sound of the Ravi River in the gorge below, there is no noise. The population lives a simple but rewarding life resulting from their own efforts and achievements, and they are not subject to the stress that we experience in the modern world. In a sense, Chamba is out of this world, living a simple and tranquil existence. When I reflected on what I had to face on my return to the outside world in the way of population, noise, conflict and stress, I could only conclude that I had indeed visited Shangri-La.

The Haunted Simla Road

By Khushwant Singh

Seven years ago (1947) the bells of St Crispin's woke up the people of Mashobra on Sunday mornings. We threw open our windows and let the chimes flood into the room along with the sunlight. We watched the English folk coming from the hotels and houses for service. It was the only day in the week that they were up before the local inhabitants. All morning visitors continued to pour in from Simla in rickshaws, on horseback and on foot. At evensong when the religious were at prayer, once more the road to Simla echoed with songs and laughter of people returning to the city. The bells of St Crispin's do not toll any more. The lych gate is padlocked and there is mildew on the golden letters of the notice board. The haunts of the English holidaymakers—Wild Flower Hall and Gables, have not had their shutters down since they were put up in the autumn of 1947. The only white people about are a couple of elderly missionary ladies who walk about briskly shopping occasionally to inspect a wild flower and inhale the crisp mountain air with their arms stiff at their sides and beatific expressions on their upturned faces. Sometimes, Italian priests from the monastery of San Damiano stray into the bazaar to buy provisions.

Little else has changed. There is the deckle edged snowline beyond the peaks of Shali in the north and the plains of Hindustan to the south; one can see the Sutlej winding its course through the orange haze. All day long the Lammergeyers circle in the deep blue of the sky. There are things that make you pause and wonder whether the British have really left. Houses, which still look like English country homes, are unoccupied and give the impression that they await their departed masters. Local inhabitants never tire of gossiping about memsahibs who did shopping in the bazaar. Even now the "Bania" will slip into quoting prices for the pound instead of the seer. Then there is the cuckoo—the English cuckoo with its two distinct notes which people say was imported by an Englishman in a fit of nostalgia.

In the evening when the mules are tethered and the muleteers sip tea or smoke their hookahs, they tell of the many foreigners who had lived in or around Mashobra. The eccentric American missionary who converted all the inhabitants of the apple growing valley of Kotgarh to Christianity and then converted them back to Hinduism.

It is a long walk back from Mashobra to Simla. The road is deserted after sunset and only the lights of the city scattered in profusion on Jacko Hill keep your spirits up. On the right is the Koti Valley with its stream glistening like quicksilver and the soft glow of oil lamps that come on unnoticed in distant farmsteads. There is something that makes you keep looking back over your shoulder. You hear the stamp of the rickshaw pullers feet, and get the whiffs of cigar and perfume—smell steals mysteriously across the moon flecked road—and your heart is too full for words.

IV

HMS Gurkha

By R. A. N. Davidson

Despite the prevailing arctic winter, the commissioning of *HMS Gurkha*, the fifth of her line, at Southampton on Wednesday, 13th February 1963, was well favoured by a sunny afternoon. Lt Col Strickland, Maj and Mrs Biggs, Maj and Mrs Hayes and I made up our party. I had the honour to represent our President.

Punctually at 3 pm, the Ship's Company marched on, headed by the Guard of Honour from its own Royal Marine Detachment, with the Royal Marines Band of Portsmouth Command and Pipers of the 6th QEO Gurkha Rifles.

The Captain, Commander J. D'O. C. Lewis, RN, then read the Commissioning Warrant and performed the Acts of Dedication, one of which asked for God's blessing on the ship by using the ancient Gaelic Blessing of 1589; the Colours were hoisted and the Commissioning Pennant broken at the masthead, and there was enough breeze in the cool crisp air to keep them stirring in the sunshine. This was followed by a Service which ended with Drake's Prayer: "O Lord God, when Thou givest to Thy servants to endeavour any great matter, grant us also to know it is not the beginning, but the continuing of the same unto the end, until it be thoroughly finished, which yieldeth the true glory". After this there were two very fine addresses to the Ship's Company, the first by the Captain who was followed by the President of the Gurkha Brigade Association, Field-Marshal Viscount Slim, who then presented the trophies on behalf of the Brigade of Gurkhas and the Association.

The Captain then left the parade and was piped on board, shortly afterwards receiving Lady Carrington, wife of the First Lord of the Admiralty (who had launched *HMS Gurkha* on 11th July 1960, and during the reception cut the Commissioning Cake), and Field-Marshal and Lady Slim.

After the Guard of Honour, Band and Pipes had marched off, the Ship's Company were dismissed, and the guests went on board for the reception. For this VIPs were entertained in the Captain's cabin, and the rest of us in the Wardroom, where traditional Naval hospitality was dispensed by the officers. There were conducted tours of inspection all over the ship.

HMS Gurkha has a displacement of 2,500 tons and combines the functions of Anti-Submarine, Anti-Aircraft and Aircraft Direction frigates. Her Ship's Company musters 16 Officers and 240 Ratings, and her armament includes two 4.5 inch guns, two 40 mm guns and anti-submarine mortars; a small Wasp helicopter extends her anti-submarine capabilities even further. She was built by John I. Thornycroft and Co. She will be joining the Middle East Station as a unit of the 9th Frigate Squadron.

Amongst the presentations and trophies were four paintings of Gurkhas by our Lt Col C. G. Borrowman, two of which were originally presented to the third *HMS Gurkha*. Another water colour of the fourth *HMS Gurkha* fighting off an air attack was presented by Captain C. N. Lentaigne, DSO, RN, who commanded her throughout her life: he is Lieut-General W. D. A. Lentaigne's younger brother.

In addition to the "Captain's Cup", and eighty pewter tankards from the Gurkha Brigade Association and a Presentation Kukri from the Brigade of Gurkhas, *HMS Gurkha* has inherited the bronze replica of the Gurkha War Memorial at Kunraghat and the letter box originally presented by the Gurkha Brigade to the third and fourth *HMS Gurkha*.

It had all been a wonderful occasion. To meet her officers and see the Ship's Company of those fortunate enough to serve in "our warship" at the start of her life was indeed a privilege and an unforgettable experience. In Field-Marshal Slim's apt phrasing: "In the past all ranks of the Gurkha Brigade have felt themselves linked to the ships of the Royal Navy which have borne an added lustre to the name of Gurkha .... That feeling of personal pride in the *HMS Gurkha* of the time and her achievements has remained always with them. Now once again we have "our warship" and once again every

Gurkha soldier will feel comradeship with her Ship's Company and follow her career with the warmest of good wishes"

"God Speed you Well".

Historical Note

The First *HMS Gurkha*, built in 1888, was sold for breaking up in 1920.

The Second, built in 1907, was sunk by mines in February 1917 off Folkestone. She won the Battle Honour "Belgian Coast—1914–1916".

The Third, built in 1938, was sunk by German bombers off Norway in 1940. She won the Battle Honours "Norway—1940" and "North Sea—1940".

The Fourth, built in 1941, was hit by a torpedoe and had to be scuttled off Sidi Barrani on 17 January 1942. She won the Battle Honours "Atlantic—1941", "Mediterranean—1941" and "Malta Convoys 1941–1942".

The crest of *HMS Gurkha* carries crossed Kukris and the Ship's Motto "Ayo Gurkhali"

Full Circle

By Sharwan Kumar

I have chosen the above title for this account of "the old regimental home" because it was at Bakloh that I began and ended my service with our Chindit battalion. It was there that I joined it as a newly commissioned Second Lieutenant in January 1954; and it was to Bakloh that I returned as CO of the battalion seventeen years later. And it was there that I left it in June 1971 when I was posted to the Staff College.

To refresh memories of 1954 I referred to News Letter No 8 in which the opening paragraph of the 3rd Battalion's news contained these words:—"Fortunately one thing has not changed and that is the home of the Regiment". Indeed at that time Bakloh had hardly changed at all from the description recorded in our Regimental History. But now ...?

The battalion returned to Bakloh in January 1971 after $3\frac{1}{2}$ years in the high snowclad mountains of the north-east. After that long experience of the tough conditions "On Top of the World" it was pleasant to find oneself back on the road from Pathankot. We noticed many changes on our way and on our arrival, yet there were also many familiar sights to remind us of past associations including the welcome of our families and the pensioners, and the backdrop of the Dalhousie hills and Dhayenkund. But over the years of my "Full Circle" vast changes had taken place.

Bakloh is no longer an island of the Punjab State, nor for that matter is Dalhousie. They now form part of Himachal Pradesh (HP), whose boundary extends to Katori Ridge. In fact, travellers—in and out—are required to pay toll to HP at a barrier erected on the road outside the Katori Rest House.

Travelling from Pathankot it is difficult to recognise the old road to Chakki as it runs through a built-up area for most of the way. The Chakki Rest Camp still exists but only as a clearing in a forest of buildings. However the training area for our drivers is still the same as it was shortly after the outbreak of the Second World War, but Dhangu is a mass of new buildings.

From Chakki the road winds its old way up to Bakloh and Dalhousie, but it has been widened and the hairpin and other bends are no longer as hair-raising as they were. However, like it or not, gate timings are still the rule of the road for all motor traffic. En route we noticed a new road branching off to the west under the shadow of Dhar Rest House; as we drove on I spotted the old bridle path to Bakloh which still connects the same villages.

At Dunera we paused for the usual cup of "chha" at the Dak Bungalow, but we missed the smiling welcome of the old Chowkidar who passed on some time ago; his successor is a smiling pensioner of the 3rd Battalion. Dunera itself and the Training Camp site are unchanged, but new metalled cross-roads have been constructed running east and west towards the Chakki and Ravi rivers respectively. Further on, the roads to Kakira and Ghatasani are also metalled.

There has also been considerable road development around Dalhousie. A wide motorable road connects Banikhet with Chamba. Another runs from Dalhousie to Chamba roughly following the alignment of the old bridle path through Khajiar. Before I left the battalion I did a trip along it with Ashok; it had not been completed but was expected to be fit for all types of traffic by 1972. Khajiar is the same old green meadow, ringed by tall pines and with the lake set in its centre like a gem. It is a popular resort for golfers in the summer, and a number of tourist huts have been built.

Dalhousie Club still flourishes in the season, but the old hands like Mr Waugh (Club Secretary), Sub Parsram Gurung (Office) Das (Tennis Marker) and Singhoo (Barman) are no more. The old favourite picnic spots, Dhundiara and Nainikhud remain unspoilt.

Bakloh is also better known than it used to be, and no traveller on the road to Dalhousie would look up as he (or she) passed it and enquire: "Who lives there?" and, on being informed, ask: "Why? What have they done?"!

Since 1954 Bakloh has undergone many changes, some of which had inevitably resulted from no battalion of the Regiment having been stationed there since the brief sojourn of the then newly raised 5th Battalion in 1963. This particularly applies to the Officers' Mess which was denuded to furnish our Training Centre's Mess at Subathu and looks very bare. It would be beyond the means of any battalion to furnish it. Moreover they have been "birds of passage" whose residence in Bakloh has lasted for only a year or two.

The romantic Tree, immortalised by John Masters in *Bugles and A Tiger*, on which the Mess Mali's young daughter sat, is no more, and the generator hut lies vacant because the whole station is now electrified. Bijli Lines above the road bend near Chankhe's house are now an Electricity Colony. The tennis courts have been so seldom used that they have been neglected, and only one of the two

"Anda Ghars" (Squash Courts) is in use, but the glazed verandah is still there with its familiar view—the Chakki and Ravi linked by the Katori and Dhar ranges; Basohli and Taragarh; and the Beas down south.

On reaching the Tytler parade ground, the first thing to strike me was the growth of its surrounding hedge, originally planted by our battalion during J. C. Kapur's day in 1953. Another scenic change was the new buildings which have replaced many of the trees and undergrowth. I doubt whether another tiger will be able to take cover near No 8 Bungalow—the place where John Masters shot his tiger in 1938. No leopard has been seen for about two decades, and it is most unlikely that anyone will be able to emulate George Frost who shot one from his bathroom window in No 2 Bungalow in 1918. It is also now rare to hear the call of a pheasant or chikor, though one can encounter some kakar and ghoral in the Taragarh Fort area.

All over Bakloh there is a tremendous lot of building activity. All available flat, or near-flat, space has been utilised, and now they have started demolishing old buildings to give place for new ones. New family accommodation for JCOs and Other Ranks is under construction along the upper slopes of the Bhomdara–Ghatasani road. Most of the footpaths in this area have been cemented.

The old bungalows No 6 (Travers) and 13 have been demolished and replaced by new single officers' quarters, which have also been built opposite No 8 bungalow. New Flats have also been built near No 2 which is likely to be demolished—a fate which has befallen "Hutch's Bungalow" whose site is now a MT park; this is likely to be extended by the demolition of the bungalow next door which was badly damaged by a storm; an additional MT park already exists on the JCOs' Club old tennis courts, and the club building itself is being demolished. Another new bungalow is coming up between Nos 1 (Buck House) and 23. No 12 is the Officers' Mess of the unit occupying Lentaigne (the old Leslie) lines.

The other undisturbed officers' bungalows are Nos 4, 5 (named "Shangrila" by our battalion in 1953), 8, 9 (now occupied by Mrs Agam), 11, 12 (built by Maj General Sir Philip Carnegy), 16, 19

(Brodhurst and Freddy Harrison), 20 (Scott) and the MES Inspection Bungalow next door to St Oswald's Church. Motorable drives lead up to all the old officers' bungalows except Nos 8, 16 and 20, but one can still stroll along Lovers' Lane.

One thing which has vanished is the swimming pool constructed as long ago as 1882; I recall seeing it in 1954 so it had a long life. It cannot have "died of thirst" because the old shortage of water has been rectified by an additional 6-inch pipe-line laid to the same catchment area. But one can no longer enjoy the "Chiso Pani" of Bhomdara which is now an MES storage tank.

I was glad to find the three Temples (the Lokeshwar Mandir in Tytler lines, the 2nd Battalion's Gorakh Baba Mandir, and the Kali Mandir on Sealy Hill) in a satisfactory state. Our battalion has also completed the Sansari Mai Mandir, the foundations of which were laid by us when we were stationed at Bakloh in 1954. St Oswald's Church, built in 1894 with the money collected by Mrs F. M. Rundall, is also well cared for, though services in it are held only once a year; the five memorial tablets are still there. There have been no additions to the fifteen graves in the cemetery.

Of the old ranges Ghatasani is not in use and the short range below the Mess has vanished, but the others are all there, including the one below Sealy Hill. Chilama is completely changed. The old hockey ground is now a Helipad. Chesty Jennings, with his memories of the Blackpool airstrip which he chose and operated during the Chindit operations in 1944, would surely be pleased to see this helipad in its picturesque setting flanked by the date palms planted by Alexander's army.

Bakloh is well-provided with schools in and around it. There are a Higher Secondary School at Kakira, two Middle schools located at Ghatasani and near the site of the old Mess kitchen garden, and a Primary initiated by Sita Ram and run by the Cantonment Board in the Tytler Lines bazaar.

The two bazaars have not changed much. Babar Singh's house still stands with its snow-white camellias (the only ones in Bakloh). The Mess garden is as attractive as ever with Jacaranda, Chestnut, Silver Oak, Medlar, Eucalyptus and other ornamental trees planted over past years thanks to the efforts of old officers like Brigadier Kingsley and Geoff Lowsley.

There are two Cantonment Board fruit orchards, next to St Oswald's Church and in place of the old Mess kitchen garden. Strawberry plants have also been introduced (or possibly re-introduced?) by our battalion from Srinagar.

No account of Bakloh would be complete without mention of the Gorkha Sabha which, under the leadership of Subedar Major and Hon Lieutenant Amar Jang Thapa (son of Subedar Chandrabir of the 1st Battalion and whose father-in-law was Subedar and Hon Lieutenant Babar Singh), continues its welfare work for the Gorkha Ex-Servicemen and widows living in and around the cantonment. Its office and library have been in the old NCOs' Club in Tytler Lines ever since it leased Sealy Hill bungalow at a rent of Rs 40 per month some years ago, and the Centenary Memorial Plaque hangs in the library. The 2nd Battalion's Golden Jubilee Commemorative Block has been retouched to restore the look which it had on 10th October 1936.

Most of the widows live in their own houses; there are only six of them in the old 1st Battalion Widow Lines and three in those of the 2nd Battalion.

One misses old staunch "Burhos" like Chankhe, Babar, Agam and Dalip, but it is heartening to find that their devoted service is being carried on by worthy successors.